WIRELESS NATION

WIRELESS
NATION

*The Frenzied Launch of the
Cellular Revolution in America*

JAMES B. MURRAY, JR.

PERSEUS PUBLISHING

A Member of the Perseus Books Group

Cataloging-in-Publication Data is available from the Library of Congress

ISBN 0–7382–0688–1

Published by Perseus Publishing
Perseus Publishing is a member of the Perseus Books Group.

Find us on the World Wide Web at http://www.perseuspublishing.com

Perseus Publishing books are available at special discounts for bulk purchases in the U.S. by corporations, institutions, and other organizations. For more information, please contact the Special Markets Department at the Perseus Books Group, 11 Cambridge Center, Cambridge, MA 02142, or call 617-252-5298.

Text design by Jeffrey P. Williams
Set in 9.5-point Stone Serif by the Perseus Books Group

First paperback printing, June 2002
1 2 3 4 5 6 7 8 9 10—04 03 02

CONTENTS

FOREWORD

Where were you in 1985? For most of us, it's not difficult to remember; a mere fifteen years have passed since then. Now, think of it another way: What was your life like before wireless telephones, computers and the Internet changed the way you communicate? Though these products have become widely available only in the past fifteen years, it's already difficult to remember what life was like without them.

The sheer scope of the unfolding communications revolution is astonishing, but one factor in particular makes it truly incredible: No one saw it coming. The two industries that have most affected American society and the economy in the last decade—wireless and the Internet—sprang seemingly out of nowhere. And now they affect nearly every aspect of our lives, from work to play. At a most basic level, they have changed the way we interact with others.

In *Wireless Nation*, Jim Murray tells the story of how the U.S. wireless industry evolved from fledgling to powerhouse. It's a bizarre story, a Wild West–style tale replete with larger-than-life characters and unexpected twists. No one could have predicted the path the industry would take. Similarly, it's difficult to predict where exactly it's going from here. But one thing is certain: Wireless—and especially the coming convergence of wireless and the Internet—will only grow in importance, utility and popularity in the coming decades.

It's no exaggeration, in fact, to say that wireless—as widespread as it is already—is only in its infancy. Though the number of users continues to climb steadily worldwide, there are still huge pockets of populations where wireless has yet to make a dent. And perhaps more important, the technology itself is still in a relatively primitive stage. In ten years, the kinds of wireless devices we'll be using will look completely different from the telephones of today; within our lifetimes, we'll see wireless technology seamlessly embedded in our lives. Though the wireless explosion up to now has been remarkable, it's nothing compared to what's coming.

In the first three decades of the twentieth century, motorization was one of the biggest influences on American life. A transportation revolution swept the nation: Cars replaced horses and buggies, new railroad tracks spider-webbed across the country and airplanes took to the skies in increasing numbers. Dozens of new companies arose to take advantage of this new development; most of them went bust, unable to keep up with the pace of change, but the ones that survived became pillars of the American economy: companies such as Boeing, McDonnell Douglas and General Motors. We'll see the same thing happen with the communications revolution. Who will thrive? Will Verizon, VoiceStream and Sprint PCS still be around in twenty years? Will Amazon.com, Yahoo and eBay? Or will a raft of new names have captured the market?

Wireless Nation is fascinating for two reasons: First, it tells the human stories behind the revolution—and what stories they are, tales of good guys and bad guys, people with vision and people without a clue. We've lived through a genuine modern gold rush, a frantic stampede by latter-day pioneers seeking to lay claim to a priceless commodity: wireless spectrum. And second, it shows how remarkable that stampede was, because, by and large, no one among the pioneers had any real idea how important the industry would become.

The fact that the wireless and Internet industries emerged so suddenly tells us something: The same thing could happen again, at any time. For that reason, *Wireless Nation* is not just a history, it is a foreshadowing of things to come. With the help of this book, we can examine how a brand-new industry evolved, better understand the forces that shaped it and hopefully learn from our mistakes.

—JOHN SIDGMORE,
Vice Chairman, WorldCom, Inc.
January 2001

PROLOGUE

Looking down at the bulky, molded-plastic box in my hand, I was momentarily confused. It looked like a big portable calculator, but why did it have that rubber stick poking out of one end? My brother-in-law Graham Randolph, who had just handed me the odd-looking instrument, grinned knowingly and said, "Why don't you call home?" When I glanced again at the box in my hand, I recognized the stick as an antenna and the numbered buttons as a telephone keypad.

It was March 5, 1981, and Graham and I were standing on a Baltimore sidewalk outside his office in the bright, late-winter sun. I punched in my home phone number as Graham sauntered off in the direction of our luncheon engagement, and after a ring or two I was doing something I'd never done before: talking on a phone as I walked down a city street.

Like many other businesspeople, I'd seen mobile phones before, but in 1981, "mobile phone" meant pretty much one thing: a big suitcase full of electronic equipment, wired and bolted into a millionaire's Cadillac limousine, with a three-foot steel antenna drilled through the trunk lid. Mobile phones were car phones, and not very good ones at that—but this was something different: a phone you could carry anywhere.

Twenty years later, with handheld cellular phones now nearly as ubiquitous as wristwatches, the novelty of that scene is difficult to fathom. But on that day, the heavy handmade device I used was one of only a dozen that had ever been made; because of the amount of money Motorola had spent developing the technology, it was nicknamed the "million-dollar phone." The handheld cell phone I used that day was part of an experimental system, and it was something almost no one in America had ever heard of—much less seen or used.

When we got to the restaurant I placed a second call, this one to my office. As we waited for the waiter to bring menus, I had a chance to get a little business done, and I had a sudden revelation—car phones were cool, but this handheld thing could change your life.

There was, I sensed, a lucrative business in these new phones, but I felt sure it would be a game for the biggest of the big boys. At that time, as a young lawyer-turning-struggling-entrepreneur, I couldn't in my most optimistic daydreams have imagined that I could get in on it. But the upcoming new industry would offer, it turned out, opportunities for some unlikely new businesspeople, including me.

A few months after my Baltimore revelation, in the late spring of 1982, I learned something else. It happened when I went to Alexandria, Virginia, to help Graham negotiate an employment contract with his new employer, Metrocall.

Metrocall was, I knew, one of the East Coast's largest paging operations. But when I drove up to Alexandria armed with the company's street address, I was in for a surprise: Instead of a marble-and-brass corporate headquarters, I found myself in an industrial district, facing a small, three-bay brick garage at the far end of a potholed asphalt lot. The faded blue sign over the door read "Metrocall," but I couldn't believe this was the place.

Inside the little office sat two secretaries toiling away at army-surplus-style metal desks. Harry Brock, Metrocall's CEO, was a boyish, sandy-haired young man seated behind another metal desk. As I looked around at the bare plaster, the vinyl-tiled floor and the well-worn file cabinets, I realized I had a wildly overinflated image of the size of this company.

After a quarter-hour of pleasantries, Brock asked if I'd like to see the company's "technical operations." Relieved, and holding out hope that perhaps we were headed to another, more impressive building nearby, I hastily agreed. Instead, he led me to what looked like a broom closet. What I saw there changed my impression of business forever.

Lining the walls of the tiny room were metal racks of what looked like stereo components. Bundles of black wire snaked through a jagged hole in the cinder block rear wall, and looking out the hole I could just see the gray steel legs of a large radio tower. As Brock proudly prattled away about the function of each component, it quickly became apparent that this hardware—not fancy buildings or furniture—was all he cared about.

Brock's business was simple: A commissioned salesman would rent some-one a Metrocall digital pager for anywhere from $18.50 to $28 per month. The salesman would get a one-time $20–$25 commission, leaving Metrocall with little or no margin on the first month's income—but no sales expense by the second month. A secretary would enter the new pager's number into the transmitter, and the equipment in the broom closet took care of the rest. Any time someone telephoned to page a customer, a black box would auto-matically send out a signal to two dozen other towers, broadcasting the page across Washington, D.C., Baltimore and northern Virginia.

And that was all there was to it, save for one thing. Once a month, a Metrocall employee would go to the data-processing firm down the street to drop off the magnetic tape that had recorded each page. There, the little cas-sette was promptly converted into boxes of bills headed to the post office. "Three days later," Brock said smugly, "we start getting checks in the mail."

With more than 10,000 pagers clipped to the belts of doctors, contrac-tors, repairmen and salesmen from Wilmington, Delaware, to Virginia Beach, Virginia, Brock had more than $3 million a year in revenue coming in. Every one of those $100 pagers was bank-financed, and Metrocall's ex-isting equipment would handle tens of thousands of new customers before more capital would be needed—meaning Metrocall had sinfully minimal expenses. The operating margins had to be huge—and, furthermore, it ap-peared that the business was growing at 30 or 40 percent per year and com-pounding. If Harry Brock wasn't clearing $450,000 a year, I reasoned, he should be well on his way.

Why was it that Brock could make these kinds of profits without a smart and well-financed competitor taking the business away from him?

It didn't take long to figure out the mystery. Brock's competitive edge lay in the special licenses he held that allowed him to transmit pager signals in certain bands of radio spectrum in certain geographic areas. Those licenses gave him exclusive use of a particular slice, or "frequency," of spectrum in his markets: No competitor could use those same crucial slices of the public airwaves, so there was no one to drive his pricing down. It wasn't surpris-ing, then, that his profit margins were north of 50 percent.

Spectrum is like the interstate highway system of the atmosphere: Who-ever gets the right to use it can put up a tollbooth and charge the public to reuse it. As you'll see in this book, the story of the cell phone industry is in many ways the story of the spectrum on which it runs—how it was doled out, who received it and how they made money on it.

The Federal Communications Commission is the government agency tasked with deciding how spectrum is used in the United States, and who gets the right to use it. As I learned on my visit to Harry Brock's paging business, an FCC decision to grant a spectrum license can mean huge profits for the lucky company receiving it. That spring of 1982 I learned something else even more astounding: When the FCC awarded these invaluable licenses, it asked for virtually nothing in return. It simply doled them out for free to whoever, like Harry Brock, had been smart enough or lucky enough to ask for them.

Spectrum giveaways had been standard public policy for nearly fifty years, but the policy would be turned on its head when the FCC began offering spectrum licenses for the new industry called cellular. As the industry got under way in 1982, the combination of free spectrum licenses and the prospect of making millions of dollars on a revolutionary new technology fueled a competitive rush.

Two years later, the FCC made a decision that would throw the industry into a complete frenzy: It would henceforth award these spectrum licenses—irreplaceable, invaluable permits to run lucrative cell phone systems—based on a lottery system. Anyone could enter, and anyone could win. Across America, application mills arose and pumped out FCC applications until the photocopiers ran ink-dry, and ordinary citizens—"pig farmers and hairdressers," in the words of one executive—joined in a mad dash to win spectrum licenses. This was the spectrum rush.

The spectrum rush turned ordinary business on its head. A lot of novice businesspeople suddenly became millionaires, and a lot of big, cocky companies got outmaneuvered by smaller, gutsier players. Hustlers, hucksters and entrepreneurs found every possible way to manipulate the rules of the great federal giveaway to their advantage. But despite the chaos that marked the first decade of the cell phone industry, a workable, competitive wireless industry developed—and it has transformed the way Americans communicate.

Following my introduction to the value of spectrum in Brock's garage office, I began applying for spectrum licenses myself. After winning a few paging licenses in 1982 and then a minority stake in a handful of cellular licenses, I went on to become a broker of cellular licenses. Eventually, in the late 1980s, I helped found a small investment-banking firm that did billions of dollars in deals with most of the cellular-industry legends. Though I was only a bit player in the development of the industry, I met and brokered deals with players up and down the food chain, from the big companies that dominated the industry to the simple folk who claimed their small piece of it in the lotteries. And I was lucky enough to make more money than I could have ever dreamed of as a country lawyer.

But I consider myself even luckier to have had a front-row seat in the wild and unpredictable business drama that played out in the last two decades. The birth of America's cellular telephone industry is a story filled with more geniuses, charlatans, heroes and goats than any novel or play. On these pages, for the first time, you can read the story of how it happened.

1

YOU COULD BE A WINNER!

BOB PELISSIER COULDN'T SLEEP.

It was 1 A.M., and the velvet-black night pressed against the windows of Pelissier's ranch-style home in Redwood City, California. He'd been feeling ill all day—nothing serious, just a slight fever and a cough—and as he lay in bed he slowly gave into the realization that sleep was unlikely to come.

He got up and made his way into the living room, pausing to flip on the TV before sinking into his favorite chair. As he settled his six-foot-two-inch frame into his recliner, a familiar face materialized on the screen: Talk show host Mike Douglas, an icon of '70s television, was midpitch in a late-night infomercial.

"Cellular technology, an unprecedented breakthrough in telecommunications, can and will change the lifestyles of millions," Douglas announced. "Some prominent financial experts have heralded it as one of the greatest business opportunities, not only in your lifetime, but of the century!"

It was the fall of 1985, and Pelissier, a fifty-six-year-old truck driver with more than thirty-five years behind the wheel, had never heard of a cellular telephone before. Mildly intrigued, he watched as Douglas continued his pitch. "There are estimates indicating that in the future, 40 percent of all telephone communications will involve cellular mobile telephones," Douglas declared, "and cellular may even substantially replace the wire telephone system we now use. According to a recent AT&T report, higher profits are projected for cellular than any other communications technology in history."

But the real pitch was yet to come: "You and I," Douglas announced, "have an equal opportunity to compete with the corporate giants for a piece of the multibillion-dollar pie!" The U.S. government, a voice-over went on to explain, was holding a lottery to give away licenses to run cell phone systems—licenses that were worth a whole lot of money, perhaps millions of dollars. Anyone could send money in, buy a chance in the lottery, and possibly win big.

"What a bunch of bull," thought Pelissier, and changed the channel.

A few nights later, Pelissier again couldn't sleep. He made his way to the living room and switched on the TV, and as the screen flickered to life, he once again saw Mike Douglas making his pitch. This time, Pelissier watched a bit longer, and he found his curiosity rising. Was there anything to this? Was it true that anyone in America could enter and win this lottery, and be handed these licenses for free? If they were so valuable, why would the government just give them away? There had to be a catch, he thought. Now as intrigued as he was skeptical, Pelissier pondered Douglas's words before drifting off to sleep.

A week passed before Pelissier again found himself wandering into the living room late at night. This time he didn't stumble upon the Mike Douglas ad—this time, he flipped around the channels until he found it. Pelissier suddenly got an inexplicable gut feeling. He picked up a pen and jotted down the number shown on the screen.

━━━━━━━━

A FEW PHONE CALLS LATER, PELISSIER—a man with a high-school education and no business experience—found himself facing a young sales associate on the sixth floor of a nondescript building in San Mateo, California. It couldn't be easier, the salesman told him, to take a chance in the big cellular giveaway. There were no requirements other than willingness to take a risk, and the ability to pay for it.

For $100,000, the young man explained, Pelissier could have what amounted to a handful of lottery tickets: applications to win the cellular license for one of fifteen markets the Federal Communications Commission planned to lottery off in April 1986. These were licenses to run cellular systems for cities like Pensacola, Florida; Atlantic City, New Jersey; and Santa Barbara, California—the licenses for bigger cities had been given out earlier, and those for even smaller cities were yet to come.

If a lottery number assigned to one of Pelissier's applications got chosen, he'd own the majority share of a city's license—50.01 percent. The other 49.99 percent would be owned by a vast alliance comprised of dozens, even hundreds of other applicants solicited by the salesman and his company, part of a convoluted scheme to make sure everyone could win at least a small fraction of a license.

For his $100,000 fee, Pelissier would be part of that alliance too, meaning he'd share in that 49.99 percent if another member of his alliance pool won a market. The pitch sounded compelling: Even if Pelissier didn't end up winning the majority piece of a license himself, he still had a good chance of winning at least a small fraction—and the payoff, the salesman assured him, would be worth many times the investment. Cell phones were the wave of the future, and these cellular licenses were as good as gold—even if you only owned a tiny percentage of one.

Was it all a scam? Pelissier was intrigued by talk of million-dollar payoffs, but he was wary of laying out so much money. These guys could just be quick-buck artists, ready to make money off gullible investors like himself. On the other hand, how could this be a scam if Mike Douglas—a trusted TV personality, a man Americans had welcomed into their living rooms every day for twenty years—was lending his name to it? It couldn't be, Pelissier decided. There must really be something to it.

But the $100,000 price tag was too much. After thinking it over, Pelissier asked a few friends to join him in a partnership and split the cost, but no one was willing to take the risk—a risk they told Pelissier he was crazy to take. This was serious money, after all, and what in the world did Pelissier—a man who'd driven a truck his whole life—know about cellular phones? What would he do if he didn't win? And, even more worrisome, what would he do if he did?

"Something keeps telling me to do this," he told his wife, Lorraine. At age fifty-four, Lorraine worked as hard as her husband did—she owned her own little catering truck, a specially rigged vehicle out of which she sold sandwiches, sodas, potato chips, candy bars and other snacks. She was on the road each morning by 5 A.M., driving her truck—Bob called it her "roach coach"—to a construction site or across the street from a school, where she'd sell her snacks for twelve solid hours before heading home in the evenings.

Though he'd never gambled on anything bigger than charity raffle tickets, Pelissier made a decision: He wanted in on the cellular lottery. He and Lorraine didn't have that kind of money in their bank account, though, so the couple would be forced to borrow it. With the applications' filing date fast approaching, they had to hurry: They quickly arranged a home-equity loan, and Pelissier presented the salesman with a check for $37,500. That amount would buy him one-quarter of a partnership ($25,000), with the remaining $12,500 tacked on to cover something called "associated filing costs," related to the bigger alliance Pelissier would be part of.

The salesman set him up with the two other men who were to be his partners—a wealthy octogenarian and an Iranian-born structural engineer, neither of whom Pelissier had met before. His two partners didn't want to be burdened with any paperwork or phone calls, so Pelissier agreed to be the point man for the little partnership.

A few weeks earlier, Bob Pelissier had heard the words "cellular telephone" for the first time. Now, based on a late-night infomercial, he had bet tens of thousands of dollars, entered a partnership with people he didn't know, and declared himself able to finance, build and run a highly technical, multimillion-dollar telephone company. The lottery drawing was to be held in two and a half months, on April 21, 1986. More than 8,000 applications had been filed for the fifteen markets up for grabs; these were expensive lottery tickets, and with the flood of applications, the chances of winning a license outright weren't good. Now all Pelissier could do was wait.

The day of the lottery drawing, Pelissier stayed home in California, tending his roses and puttering around the house. He figured he'd end up with a modest windfall from the small fractions of license ownership he'd get when someone else in the massive alliance won something. It might not be a huge payoff, but hopefully he'd at least break even.

The phone rang. When Pelissier picked it up, a woman on the other end of the line told him, "You've won." Pelissier and his partners had won the license for the market covering Manchester and Nashua, New Hampshire, a quiet New England metropolitan area with a combined population of 277,000. More than 500 applications had been filed for Manchester-Nashua and, remarkably, Pelissier's little three-man partnership was the one whose lucky Ping-Pong balls were drawn from the lottery drum.

"Thanks," said Pelissier, with only marginal enthusiasm. He had misunderstood. He thought the nice young woman meant that the big alliance had won, and so he figured his share would be, as the salesman had explained, a little less than 1 percent. He thought that perhaps, with luck, that tiny percentage might be worth the $37,500 he'd invested. Or it might not. He thanked the woman for calling and hung up.

A moment later, she called again. "I don't think you understand what I meant," she told Pelissier, who thought her voice sounded like she was suppressing a smile. He and his partners had won the license, she told him. They needed to have a cell phone company up and running in six months.

As blood began to pound excitedly in Pelissier's veins, he heard the woman say one more thing: "You should get an FCC attorney."

Just like that, the unlikely California trio of a middle-aged trucker, an elderly gambler and a highway engineer became the new owners of a cellular license for the towns of Manchester and Nashua, New Hampshire. Now they had a cellular telephone company to build—a company that would be competing for customers with an established telephone company.

"Oh boy," thought Bob Pelissier, "What do we do now?"

2

AT THE STARTING GATE

Bob Pelissier's unlikely conversion from truck driver to cell phone entrepreneur took place in the spring of 1986, nearly four years after the FCC began distributing cellular spectrum licenses. By that time, cell phone systems were up and running in many of America's larger cities, the FCC's rules governing the giveaway had been rejiggered numerous times, and ordinary Americans like Pelissier were clamoring to get in on the gold rush–style dash for licenses—the "spectrum rush."

It didn't start out that way. To understand the unique mania of the spectrum rush, we've got to go back a few years, back to the beginning of the license distribution. At that time, it didn't seem like it would be too hard to distribute the spectrum fairly and quickly. But for the FCC, that seemingly simple goal would prove an unattainable dream: Over the next two decades, the commission would bend, tweak and, in desperation, completely overhaul its rules in an effort to fix a hopelessly broken process.

When the FCC announced its initial rules for doling out the nascent cellular industry's allotment of radio spectrum—the unique, invaluable commodity that carries energy through the atmosphere and underlies all manner of wireless communication—there was no mention of a lottery. The FCC declared it would award spectrum licenses for each U.S. city based on merit: Any company wanting to compete for a city's license could submit a detailed application, and if more than one applied in a city, FCC judges would determine which applicant was best qualified to run the system.

It was spring of 1982, and almost no one in America had heard of cellular telephones, much less about the upcoming spectrum giveaway. Of those few who had heard about the giveaway, most dismissed it as too risky to invest in. But a brave handful—mostly telephone companies, paging companies, and a few stout-hearted and experienced entrepreneurs—decided they wanted a piece of the action. So when the FCC announced it would accept applications on June 7, 1982, for spectrum licenses to run the cell phone systems in America's thirty largest cities, they scrambled for ways to get in on it.

ONE AFTERNOON IN APRIL 1982, Robert Edwards took a short, enigmatic phone call from his friend and fellow paging-industry executive Graham Randolph.

"Come to the Waldorf Towers for a meeting," Randolph bade his friend. "I think it's something you'll be interested in. It'll be well worth your while." Beyond that, Randolph couldn't or wouldn't offer any other explanation; he simply gave Edwards a suite number and a time to be there. Edwards thanked him, hung up and immediately made a quick couple of calls to try to deduce who was calling this meeting, and why.

When Edwards, the president of the publicly traded New York–based paging company Radiofone, later strode through the ornate lobbies of the historic Waldorf-Astoria, he already had an idea why he was there. With its soaring spires and stately limestone façade, this sprawling Art Deco skyscraper on Park Avenue was a paean to elegance, luxury and the whisper of old money. As Edwards's phone calls had confirmed, an invitation to meet in one of the residential suites in the Waldorf Towers was bound to come from someone with impressively deep pockets.

Edwards, a shortish, heavyset man with a crown of white hair, stood patiently as the elevator swiftly ferried him skyward. Upon being let into suite 37-H, he found himself in an exquisite entry hall with marble floors, mirrors and a built-in bar to one side. A massive living room stretched across the apartment, which was decorated with upwards of $10 million worth of oil paintings, sculptures and other objets d'art. But Edwards was not here to admire the suite and its decor: His destination was a small conference room down the hallway. He entered, shook hands in restrained greetings with a small group of acquaintances and took a seat at the table. No one said much; the atmosphere in the room, which was lined with books, was chilly and museumlike, not conducive to idle conversation.

Soon all heard the *clomp-clomp-clomp* of heavy, resolute footsteps. Into the room strode a short, stocky, balding man in his late sixties: John

Kluge. A legendary entrepreneur and the CEO of Metromedia, a public company he ran like his own private fiefdom, Kluge had scratched his way up from a modest childhood as a German immigrant in Detroit to become a widely respected and wealthy baron of industry. This was his apartment and his meeting, and he was ready to get down to business. He immediately turned his attention to Edwards and offered up some affable chitchat. In spite of himself, Edwards was charmed: Even though this was a business meeting—perhaps one of the most important of his life—he found himself taken in by this friendly gentleman with the elfin smile and slight trace of a German accent. After a few minutes of light talk, Kluge got to the point.

"Mr. Edwards," said Kluge, "I know you're very busy, and I am too, so I won't beat around the bush. I want to buy your company, and I would like to offer you $24 a share."

It was a generous offer. Though Radiofone was one of the largest paging companies in America—a sprawling operation, it stretched from Connecticut down to Delaware and Eastern Pennsylvania and covered more than 20,000 square miles of East Coast megalopolis—its stock was trading that afternoon at only $18.75 per share. Edwards had come expecting an offer, though, and he didn't flinch. "It'll take $26 to buy it," he replied.

"Well, then," said Kluge pleasantly, "it's a done deal. Thank you very much." He rose and shook hands with Edwards to seal the bargain. Having committed Metromedia to a $56 million purchase in about twenty seconds, he then left the room.

A casual observer of this scene might have deduced that John Kluge had an intense interest in the paging industry. He'd just bought Radiofone for a price that amounted to eight times the company's projected sales—forty-three times the prior year's earnings. And he hadn't even bothered to negotiate.

In fact, paging had virtually nothing to do with Kluge's decision to purchase Radiofone—or any of the seven paging businesses he spent $300 million on in a hectic five-month whirlwind of acquisitions in 1982. His interest lay in the cell phone industry—and he believed buying these paging companies would help him get an early foothold there. Though Kluge was nearing seventy and already possessed a greater fortune than he could spend in his lifetime, he saw a promising opportunity in the new industry. And he was willing to risk his company in a series of daring wagers to get in on it.

THAT SAME SPRING, another pivotal business meeting took place on the other side of the country, this one among complete unknowns in a far less impressive venue than Kluge's lavish Waldorf suite.

It happened on a gray March afternoon in Bellevue, Washington. As misty rain floated gently earthward, a tall young man walked up to the door of a small cable-TV company and prepared to enter, perhaps for the last time. For months the young man, a consultant with the national accounting firm Ernst & Whinney, had been trying to land a consulting contract with the company. But each time he went knocking on their door, he was met with a kind of bemused indifference. Now he was almost ready to give up.

This spring day marked John Stanton's fourth visit to McCaw Communications, and he had decided that, if the company still wouldn't hire him, this visit would be his last. At twenty-six, Stanton was handsome and intense, a hyperkinetic man with perpetually tousled sandy-brown hair and blue eyes. With his good looks, his Harvard Business School pedigree, and his robust young ego, he did not like to be told "no." But neither was he the type to give up easily; despite the persistent indifference he'd faced at McCaw, he arrived that day with a new tool to attract the company's notice: a customized set of financial projections for the brand-new cellular telephone business.

At the time, McCaw was a smallish, essentially unremarkable cable and paging company, little known outside the Pacific Northwest. Led by an eccentric, ambitious young CEO named Craig McCaw, the company was a loosely organized, fly-by-the-seat-of-its-pants affair populated by a cadre of smart, aggressive young executives. Though it had enjoyed healthy growth and steady (if modest) success throughout the '70s, there was no reason to suspect that this small company would play anything more than an exceedingly marginal role in American business history.

The potential promise of cell phones had attracted McCaw's notice—Craig McCaw, in fact, already had one of those early, clunky noncellular mobile phones installed in his Pinto—but the company's executives were wary of the cost and the risk involved in trying to get into the yet-unformed industry. Though there had been lab tests and a few small experimental systems, cellular technology was untested on a large scale; customer interest seemed largely speculative, and investing a lot of money in it at this early stage threatened to be like throwing money down a deep black hole.

And it wouldn't be cheap to enter the fray: First, each complex application for each city would cost hundreds of thousands of dollars to research and produce. Second, it would take tens of thousands more to hire lawyers to shepherd each application through the comparative hearing process, in which an FCC judge would weigh competing applications for the same city and decide who should receive the license. Win or lose, simply applying was an expensive proposition.

If a company applied for a city's license and lost, it was just money down the drain. And if they won, they would suddenly face the hugely expensive proposition of building a city's cell phone system from scratch—purchasing potentially buggy equipment; building a complex, multimillion-dollar network of towers; and trying to attract customers in direct competition with the telephone company. The big question was: Would enough customers then sign up and spend enough time on their cell phones so that the system could ultimately make money? No one knew for sure, but John Stanton thought he had a pretty good idea.

A long row of three-ring binders lined the bookshelves at Stanton's office in nearby Tacoma: FCC reports filed on two experimental cellular systems that had been built in Chicago and the Baltimore-Washington, D.C. metropolitan area in the late '70s. In an unregulated industry, the marketing data contained in these reports would have been jealously protected as priceless trade secrets—but thanks to the FCC's rules governing experimental systems, all the data were part of the public record, available to any researcher willing to dig for it.

Stanton had spent hours poring over the reports, and comparing them to little-noticed data from an early Canadian cellular system. After dissecting the available information every way he could, he decided to try an experiment: He plugged the fruits of his research into an Ernst & Whinney financial model originally designed for cable TV.

The results were startling. Stanton had created a blueprint of how a typical city's cellular system could make money—and what was shocking was *how much* money it could apparently make. No matter which way he massaged the data on his archaic, no-memory PC, Stanton saw a phenomenal business: Huge demand, fat prices, impressive usage and a tremendous return on investment. Across America, a few dozen cellular hopefuls were generating estimates, but Stanton's calculations were different in two ways. First, they were based on real marketing data rather than speculation. And second, they would ultimately prove to be far higher than anyone else's— so high, in fact, that they seemed almost absurd.

Armed with these numbers, Stanton finally got in McCaw's door. That overcast spring day, he was invited to meet Ed Hopper, a seasoned cable executive who had been hired with the encouragement of McCaw's bankers to keep an eye on the cash-poor company's spending. As the designated financial watchdog, Hopper was vetting Craig McCaw's proposed foray into the nascent cellular industry. He was prepared to nix the effort if it looked too risky—McCaw was a cable company, after all; why should it burn badly needed capital in an unproven, uncertain new industry? But when Hopper met Stanton, there was immediate chemistry between the two men, and it took Hopper only a moment to decide what to do. After months of being shunted aside like a traveling salesman, Stanton finally heard the words he'd waited for.

"You're hired," said Hopper. "Start tomorrow."

With that encounter, McCaw's future—and by extension, the future of the cellular telephone industry—was forever altered. Thanks largely to Stanton's early insights into cellular values, McCaw would spend the next few years racing to purchase licenses and cellular properties at prices that were regularly deemed astronomical by competitors—including John Kluge—who dropped out one by one in awe of what they considered McCaw's overinflated optimism. And as each competitor dropped out, McCaw would buy up more and more properties, each time being proven increasingly prescient as cellular usage skyrocketed beyond everyone's projections and spectrum values continued to spiral upward.

But all that lay ahead. For now, McCaw was just another of the few dozen hopefuls preparing for the government's great giveaway of real estate in the sky. And though its tiny cellular budget was miniscule compared to the $300 million Kluge's Metromedia spent to get its applications, McCaw was still not the smallest applicant to line up at the starting gate.

━━━━━━

A FEW MILES NORTH OF WASHINGTON, D.C.'S BELTWAY, in the quiet bedroom community of Columbia, Maryland, the lights of a certain townhouse basement could be found burning at all hours of the night. Peter Lewis had set up a makeshift office in his home, and it was there that the former army captain spent late nights with a few army buddies figuring out how to fulfill his lifelong dream.

In the late 1960s, Lewis, then a high-school junior, had read a science magazine article about a new cellular technology under development at Bell Labs. For most high-school students, the article might have proved a bit too dense for study, much less for enjoyment, but Peter Lewis was not your average teenager. From very early on, communications enthralled him.

As a nine-year-old in 1961, he had awakened Christmas morning to find a brand new pair of Sears & Roebuck "Jaguar" model walkie-talkies under the tree. With that first set of two-way radios, young Peter embarked on a lifelong obsession with communications. He spent much of his youth scrambling onto friends' rooftops to position antennae and trying out any new equipment that came along—including CB radios, which he began using a full decade before the "Convoy" craze of the late '70s. By the time Lewis was in high school, he was a budding communications expert, and he even had his own car phone—a then-unheard-of accessory, especially for a high-schooler.

Lewis's late-sixties-model car phone was nothing like the cell phones of today—each channel could carry only one conversation at a time, so even though there were very few users in Lewis's hometown of Washington, D.C., there often was system gridlock. Lewis frequently found himself waiting in interminable queues for airtime, a difficulty he remedied by taking flowers and boxes of chocolates downtown to the system operators in an effort to woo them into letting him cut in line.

As a young man, Lewis began visiting the FCC's headquarters in downtown Washington, trying to find out when the commission might make spectrum available for cell phone systems in America's cities. He was an unlikely sight wandering around the commission's hallways—a tall, thin, African American with a perpetually serious expression on his face, cornering FCC staffers to inquire earnestly about rulemaking procedures and technical specifications. Always impeccably dressed and courteous, Lewis soon made friends of the FCC's Mobile Services Division staff, who were impressed at the breadth of his knowledge and curiosity.

For his part, Lewis understood that it was the FCC that could enable cellular technology to make the jump from experimental to commercial, whenever it made decisions about the radio spectrum on which the new phone systems would run. His friends at the FCC assured him it was only a matter of time until that happened, and he wanted to get in on it from ground zero.

He was so determined, in fact, that after joining the army he made a vow to himself: Whenever the FCC issued its rules for cellular, he would immediately resign his commission and try to get a piece of it. In April 1981, when the FCC at last announced its tentative rules for the cellular spectrum giveaway, Lewis was ready. He sold his furniture, ran up his credit cards and, together with an army friend, formed a little firm called Metropolitan Radio Telephone Systems, Inc. (MRTS). Though he had virtually no business experience, little money and only a skeletal framework of a company, Lewis, naive but determined, was ready to shoot for the big time: He aimed for MRTS to win the license to construct and operate the cell phone company for his hometown of Washington, D.C.

It didn't take long for Lewis to learn the first of many bitter business lessons. The cost of paper, supplies, maps and other material he needed to assemble a cellular application was daunting; though his army buddies pitched in and worked for free, he needed someone with deeper pockets than his to get his fledgling venture off the ground. With the June 7, 1982, filing deadline approaching, Lewis wasn't sure where to turn. Unlike Kluge or McCaw—or any of the other initial applicants, in fact—Lewis had almost no business connections. But he was sure he knew the technology as well as anyone, and he had waited a long time for a shot at running it.

A "long time" is, of course, relative. In one sense, Peter Lewis had been waiting his whole life for the opportunity now unfolding. More prosaically, he had been forced to wait more than a decade for the FCC to announce its cellular rules—a wait that had seemed practically interminable. The technology existed back when Lewis read about it in the '60s, after all—why couldn't the government get its act together and get the industry going?

Considering the history of wireless development, Lewis shouldn't have been surprised. Though simple wireless communication had existed since the turn of the century, it was a long, tortuous path to the modern-day cellular revolution.

3

THE LONG AND WIRELESS ROAD

On a bone-cold December day in 1901, a young Italian man sat in a barracks building on the rugged coast of Newfoundland, a box of electronic gear on a table in front of him and a listening device pressed to his ear.

As the wind raged outside, a kite the man had rigged up whipped violently hundreds of feet above the coastline. He had already lost a kite to brutal winds the day before; today, December 12, he had sent up another, in an attempt to prove a theory that many of the smartest men of the age thought was pure folly. At age twenty-seven, Guglielmo Marconi was convinced he knew something his skeptics didn't, and he was determined to prove them wrong. He sat listening as intently as he could, and after a time he heard a sound: three short clicks.

The clicks—Morse code for the letter "S"—were emanating from thousands of miles across the Atlantic Ocean. An assistant of Marconi's was tapping them out on a transmitter in Cornwall, England, and Marconi received them by an aerial wire attached to the kite whipping around in the Newfoundland wind. The fact that Marconi could hear the taps proved what had been derided as an audacious theory: Radio waves travel around the curve of the earth.

Until that moment, virtually everyone in the scientific community believed that radio waves traveled only in a straight line and would simply shoot out into space upon passing the horizon of the curving earth, making it impossible to utilize wireless communications over large distances. So entrenched was this thinking, in fact, that Alexander Graham Bell reportedly still insisted that was the case, even after Marconi's successful experiment.

("I doubt Marconi did that," he is supposed to have said. "It's an impossibility.")

It was this ability to challenge the expected scientific order of things that led Marconi to some of the most exciting discoveries in communications. Several years before his transatlantic transmission, Marconi was the first person to successfully transmit Morse code via invisible waves in the air. He also was the first to demonstrate that wireless communication could take place at greater distances if the receiving elements were elevated—the thinking behind the modern-day radio tower. Marconi made these discoveries while still in his twenties; his combination of remarkable scientific acumen and a driving desire for commercial success led the young Italian to precociously pry open the secrets of wireless telegraphy.

Modern cell phone technology, like so many scientific innovations, grew out of numerous interconnected roots, Marconi's among them. Bell's introduction of the telephone in 1876 showed that the human voice could be transmitted over distances. German scientist Heinrich Hertz deduced the existence of wireless waves in 1887, though he was dismissive of the idea that his discovery would have any practical applications. Marconi proved Hertz's pessimism wrong by harnessing the power of the "Hertzian waves" to transmit Morse code communications without wires. And, at the turn of the century, an American professor named Reginald Fessenden figured out how to transmit the human voice across radio waves, bringing together the two technologies—wireless and telephony—that would be the earliest seeds of the modern cell phone industry.

Though the conception of cellular technology was a half-century away, simple wireless communication was put immediately to use. The earliest— and perhaps most obvious—application was in ship-to-shore communications. Long-distance communication was already possible on land thanks to Bell's wired telephone, but at the end of the nineteenth century, there was no effective means of communicating with ships.

Marconi was a gifted scientist, but he was no bloodless academician. From his earliest experimentation, he intended to put his discoveries to commercial use. In 1896 he patented the world's first wireless telegraph, and soon afterward Marconi's Wireless Telegraph Company was in business, installing so-called Marconi rooms with wireless equipment in ships.

Despite a few early instances in which Marconi operators helped avoid or mitigate maritime accidents, the technology was initially viewed not as a safety tool, but as a profit source. Passengers on liners were encouraged to send and receive their personal news and greetings via "Marconigrams," just as they would via telegrams. In fact, it wasn't until the Titanic sank in 1912 that the role of wireless as a safety tool was thrust to the fore. As the gargantuan vessel sank, the Marconi operator's insistent pleas for help were answered by the *Carpathia*, which steamed more than fifty miles through the frigid North Atlantic to rescue hundreds of frightened, freezing passengers who would otherwise have been swallowed by the sea.

Use of wireless expanded, especially as other technologies were developed. Though air travel was unknown when Marconi developed his wireless telegraph, the Wright brothers completed the world's first powered flight less than a decade later, in 1903. As airplanes began taking to the skies, wireless would evolve into an ideal way to maintain communications with the ground—a fact illustrated on the White House grounds one November morning in 1918, when President Woodrow Wilson gamely chatted with a pilot circling overhead in a product demonstration.

The 1920s saw the advent of wireless communications in automobiles, though in the beginning the technology was very primitive. In 1921, for example, the Detroit Police Department began using mobile radios in its cars—but only one-way transmission was possible, from dispatcher to car, so policemen still had to pull over and find a telephone if they wanted to communicate back to headquarters. Two-way communication appeared in 1933, when the Bayonne, New Jersey, police department first employed a two-way push-to-talk system. Though it required filling the squad cars' trunks with a jumble of heavy equipment, the system's public safety benefits were obvious, and other police departments quickly followed Bayonne's lead.

All these early applications of mobile wireless technology had a common requirement: a cumbersome source of plentiful energy. Users of these first car radios quickly realized that they should leave their cars running whenever their radios were on; otherwise the car's battery quickly drained. The radios were "mobile" in the sense that they worked in moving vehicles—but still, they were huge, hot and heavy, with the user tethered to the vehicle's power source. True "portability" was, in the '30s, the stuff of science fiction.

That changed in the early days of World War II. In 1940, Motorola (the name was a hybrid of "motor" and "Victrola," coined in 1930 with the release of the company's first car radio) introduced the first truly portable two-way communicator, dubbed the "Handie-Talkie." Before this hefty, foot-long, battery-operated instrument was introduced, soldiers had been forced to rely on wired field telephones for communicating in battle. Those telephones worked reasonably well, but they came with one hazardous drawback: The lines had to be strung over the battlefield, and any break in a line would knock out communications entirely. Whenever a shell, grenade or other explosive device broke a line, some unlucky soldier had to race out under fire to repair it. The wireless Handie-Talkie eliminated that particularly unsavory duty—provided the operator could keep its batteries charged.

Because the Handie-Talkie was a short-range radio with a relatively small battery, it was only really useful for communication between troops in the same battle area. For longer-range communications, Motorola developed the walkie-talkie, which came in a big backpack filled with a heavy battery, hand-wired circuits and hot, orange-glowing glass vacuum tubes. These were the precursors to the portable phones of today.

Handie-Talkies and walkie-talkies were the stuff of American legend, futuristic tools that helped "our boys" triumph over the enemy in the century's greatest cataclysm. Not surprisingly, these relatively primitive communicators fired the imagination of adults and children alike—what a concept, to be able to walk around and communicate over distances at the same time! But the popular imagination really took flight on January 13, 1946, when an even more futuristic device captured Americans' attention.

On that date, square-jawed superdetective Dick Tracy introduced his "2-Way Wrist Radio." A no-nonsense, unflappable private eye wearing a trademark fedora, Dick Tracy was already an icon of the funny papers when he first strapped the miraculous radio to his wrist. And for the times, it truly was miraculous—in reality, a two-way communicator with that kind of power would require a dozen bulky glass vacuum tubes and a cannonball-heavy battery. But Dick Tracy's 2-Way Wrist Radio was small enough to fit on a watchband and powerful enough to send and receive messages over distances; not surprisingly, it instantly took its place in the top ranks of fantasy accessories. Across America, children begged mothers for toy replicas (or simply barked commands into their wristwatches), and adults giddily contemplated the age of superscience unfolding before them.

The country was on the brink of a new era. The horror and promise of atomic energy had been unleashed. Televisions were taking over more and more American living rooms. The United States had emerged victorious from a bloody war, establishing its dominant spot in a world that would come to seem even more starkly divided in peace than it had in conflict. America had survived the depression years and seen its economy thrive in wartime. Now modern science and the beginnings of American affluence were converging in a way that would change how Americans lived.

Mobile communications would be a part of that change. In 1946, the Bell System, using radio spectrum newly licensed by the FCC, began offering mobile phone service for automobiles in twenty-five U.S. cities, starting in St. Louis. The phones used push-to-talk technology, like the police mobile-radios of the 1920s and '30s; users were connected to a local operator, who, in turn, dialed a telephone to connect the call.

Unfortunately the systems, which could accommodate very few users to begin with, were soon too crowded to work efficiently: Each conversation tied up one whole channel of radio spectrum for seventy-five miles or more in every direction, depending on the terrain. The spectrum was quickly overcrowded, and adjacent radio channels that might have been used to accommodate the overflow were assigned by the FCC to other users—such as taxi dispatchers, fire departments and the military—deemed more critical to the public interest than casual mobile-phone conversations.

The dilemma was clear: More Americans desired mobile communications than there was available spectrum to throw at the problem. Spectrum is a finite commodity, after all, and once a certain frequency band (like a station on the radio dial) is assigned for a certain use, it's not available for any other use. The solution was equally clear: Someone needed to figure out how to utilize the available spectrum more efficiently—to subdivide it into smaller slices. At Bell Laboratories, the research arm of AT&T, a team of scientists and engineers set about figuring how that could be done.

The legions of Ph.D.'s working at Bell Labs were widely regarded as America's most brilliant inventors. (They still are today, in fact, having won a phenomenal eleven Nobel Prizes and receiving an average of four new patents every workday.) The wizards behind numerous technological advances, Bell scientists had devised ways to use previously fallow higher-frequency radio waves, had shrunk batteries to more portable sizes and had boldly experimented with a new class of machines—the "electronic brain," or computer. When computers evolved from academic theory to their first practical demonstration in 1945, the Bell scientists promptly set about programming them to switch telephone calls, turn radios on and off, change radio frequencies and automatically connect radios to the telephone system. These applications were the building blocks for what would ultimately become a network of mobile telephones. But another science fiction–style invention had to emerge first: the transistor.

In 1947, Bell Labs scientists found a way to replace the large, fragile, power-sucking, heat-generating vacuum tubes that formed the core of every computer and radio with something more compact: little beads, each having microscopic layers of chemicals encased in plastic with three tiny wires poking out. Soldered together onto a circuit board, these new transistors enabled electronics that were small, light, virtually indestructible, and required the power of a flashlight-size battery to operate. With this miraculous invention, true portability was now possible: The electronic revolution could begin.

Also in 1947, Bell Labs first offered the world a peek into the future of communications by showing how these diverse inventions could be combined into a radical solution to the mobile telephones problem: a revolutionary new concept called "cellular" communications. Cellular promised a quantum leap in quality over the old mobile-phone systems, which relied on a single transmitter blasting away at maximum power from the highest point that engineers could find or build. This system design dated back to Marconi, and it was proving hopelessly inadequate—it was invariably marked by interference, poor sound quality and limited capacity, with very few people able to use their mobile phones in a given area at the same time.

How limited was that capacity? As late as 1981, just a couple of years before commercial cell phone systems made their debut, only twenty-four people in all of New York City could be on their mobile phones at once, and system limitations meant that New York mobile-phone operators could sign up only 700 total customers. Not surprisingly, that small group of carphone users took on the aura of an elite club, as thousands of less lucky New Yorkers languished jealously on waiting lists.

Cellular technology would solve the spectrum shortage, with a design that was simple but ingenious: Instead of using a single powerful transmitter for a large area, coverage would be split up into smaller areas, each served by a smaller, less powerful transmitter. When a caller crossed the boundary from one area to another, a specialized switching computer would recognize the move and automatically "hand off" the call from one transmitter to another, selecting a new radio channel; the user would never notice any interruption in sound. The honeycomb of smaller coverage areas resembled biological cells—hence the name "cellular."

In a sense, Bell's new design turned Marconi's principles upside down. The Italian inventor figured out that signals could travel farther and be better heard if more electric power was applied and the resulting "louder" signal was emitted from a great height: For years, "loud and high" had been the rule for radio systems. The problem was, these powerful signals drowned out the possibility of having more than one conversation on each channel for seventy-five miles or more in every direction—so total capacity was severely limited. The Bell Labs scientists took a counterintuitive tack: They developed transmitters that worked at lower heights and less volume. With this "low and soft" design, each radio channel in a given area could be used multiple times, reusing scarce radio spectrum and dramatically increasing capacity. Thanks to the newfound power of computers, callers and radio channels could be switched from channel to channel at nearly the speed of light, making this cellular system feasible.

Throughout the 1950s and '60s, and into the early '70s, scientists at Bell and elsewhere around the world labored away at the cellular dream, refining the elements and incorporating bits of technology into other mobile devices. By the 1970s, they had hit on ways to improve existing (noncellular) mobile phones: They "trunked" together separate blocks of radio channels and developed simple little computer circuits that would automatically find an open channel or connect callers to the phone company. There was a wholesale overhaul of the way telephone systems—both wired and wireless—worked. For wired telephone systems, the new computer switches replaced the old switchboard operators who had spent their days connecting calls by hand, with clumsy wired plugs laced into a wall of sockets in front of them. And for mobile phones, the new circuits meant that callers no longer had to painstakingly try each channel separately in an effort to find an open one—the phone automatically found the open channel.

But these improvements in existing systems were incremental; mobile-phone systems were still plagued by the problem of too little spectrum and too many users, resulting in long lines of frustrated users and would-be customers. Until cellular service was introduced commercially, the problems would remain.

By the early 1970s, AT&T was telling the FCC, Congress, the trade press and anyone else who would listen that their technology was basically ready. Now there was just one more puzzle piece that had to be fit in its slot: Who would be granted use of the spectrum needed to run the new cell phone systems? This was potentially a multimillion-dollar decision, and it lay in the hands of the FCC, the government agency responsible for distributing spectrum licenses of all flavors and stripes.

To a physicist, the term "spectrum" refers to a means of measuring and defining energy as it moves through time and space in any of its many forms—light, sound, X rays, or television and radio waves. In a colloquial sense, spectrum is the commodity on which every kind of wireless communications runs, from garage door openers to pagers to satellite dishes and beyond. Any particular frequency of spectrum is geographically exclusive:

Only one user at a time can broadcast or otherwise put energy into that particular segment of the public airways.

You can't touch it, you can't see it, you can't box it up, but spectrum has value, like real estate in the sky. It is licensed, rented by the minute, bought, sold and even subdivided. And because it is essential to every wireless business and closely regulated, the right to use it is very valuable indeed. Unfortunately, the agency tasked with controlling its use—the FCC—is historically one of the more dysfunctional bureaucracies in Washington.

In classic bureaucratic fashion, it would take the commission years to make its cellular spectrum licensing decision—thanks in part to pressure from hundreds of lobbyists, from equipment manufacturers (such as Motorola and GE) to competing operators (such as paging companies and independent telephone companies), all of whom had their own agendas in the still-unformed industry. Everyone wanted a seat on the gravy train, and they would stalk the FCC hallways for the next decade trying to ensure they got one.

As the 1980s approached, the FCC had two paramount considerations. First, the spectrum licenses needed to be distributed soon, as consumers, equipment makers and others were anxious to get the new cellular industry going. And second, the spectrum should be distributed fairly and sensibly, in a way that would ensure it went to someone who was actually capable of building and growing a cell phone business.

Within these two general guidelines, the FCC had to decide on the specifics: How many cell phone systems should be designated for each city? Who should run them? Should the whole block of spectrum just be given to AT&T, which had, after all, invented the technology and spent $200 million over the years attempting to perfect it?

These were difficult questions, and the FCC took its time answering them while the cacophony of lobbying roared around it. Initially, the FCC intended to grant the whole block of spectrum to AT&T, a move that was firmly opposed by the U.S. Department of Justice (thanks in part to vigorous encouragement from the giant's would-be competitors). Why, the Justice Department argued, should the FCC create a cell phone monopoly when it would be so easy to divide up all that radio spectrum and create several competing systems per city? Wouldn't multiple systems be better for consumers?

The department wanted the spectrum divided into thin slices, as many as five or six per city, so there would be plenty of competition. AT&T executives, on the other hand, felt that they deserved to run the new systems—

after all, cellular was an AT&T invention, and besides, no other company had the financial clout to promise unequivocally that it could get service up and running quickly.

AT&T was adamant, but it was an inauspicious time for the company to be seeking permission for a new monopoly: In November 1974, the Justice Department filed an antitrust suit against the company based on its monopoly of America's wired phone systems. This was the opening salvo in a battle that would end a decade later with the breakup of the telephone behemoth. Given the political climate, it's perhaps not surprising that in 1975 the FCC changed its draft rules to eliminate the proposed cell phone monopoly, declaring that nontelephone companies could compete with AT&T for the licenses. Slowly the bureaucratic machine was inching forward, but there would be much more lobbying and internal debate before the FCC would announce its final rules seven long years later.

In the meantime, cellular technology was at last making its first forays from the laboratory to the street. In 1973, Motorola executive Martin Cooper made the world's first call on a portable, handheld cell phone—a blocky chunk of plastic officially named the Dynatac and quickly nicknamed "the Brick."

At nearly two and a half pounds and the size of a Kleenex box, the phone was technically portable, if not conveniently so. Still, it was a breakthrough, and as the new star of telecommunications, the Brick was accorded the peak achievement of scientific celebrity: Its photo appeared on the cover of the July 1973 issue of *Popular Science* magazine. "New Take-Along Telephones Give You Pushbutton Calling to Any Phone Number" trumpeted the headline on the cover, which also boasted articles like "Detroit Hot Line—What's Coming in the '74 Cars" and "You Can Make Your Own 25-Foot Inflatable Dome."

A photo inside the magazine purported to show the future of communications. A contented fisherman floated lazily on a one-man rubber raft with a coffee mug in one hand, a portable phone in the other, and a smug grin on his face. "Fishing offshore, driving home from work, or riding horseback—this phone user could place and receive calls anywhere with new system planned by Motorola," bragged the caption. In the body of the text, writer John R. Free declared that "With Federal Communications Commission approval, the first Dynatac system may be operating in New York by 1976."

Unfortunately, Mr. Free's estimation was overly optimistic. New York wouldn't get a commercial cell phone system until 1984—and most other

U.S. cities would get theirs even later. But in the interim, another kind of communications craze would sweep America.

━━━━━

"TEN-FOUR, GOOD BUDDY!" became the hippest phrase in the United States for a few years in the '70s, as millions of Americans installed citizens' band—or CB—radios in their Pacers, Volkswagen Beetles, and yes—trucks. Simple push-to-talk radios that allowed users to talk on a kind of party line system (no private conversations and no telephone connections were possible), CBs soared to popularity thanks to a few factors: They were relatively cheap to buy and easy to use; they had no per-minute charges; they came with their own catchy jargon; and they were embraced by Hollywood and the music industry.

Even those who didn't own CBs got swept up in the craze. Burt Reynolds became a rebel icon as he sped recklessly across the country in *Smokey and the Bandit*. C. W. McCall's anthem, "Convoy," with its simulated CB conversation crackling between verses, reached the number-one spot on *Billboard*'s country and pop music charts in January 1976. And when "Convoy" was adapted into a movie—starring Ernest Borgnine, Ali McGraw and Kris Kristofferson as the "Rubber Duck"—nearly everyone in America could tell you what "bears in the air" were or how to put your "pedal to the metal."

At the peak of CB popularity, as many as 50 million Americans used the radios. The technology behind CB radio was not new—it was simply old-fashioned AM radio, equivalent to a kind of wireless Model T. It was a free-for-all, a low-and-loud system with no central control switch and no connection to the telephone system.

Though CB radios didn't represent state-of-the-art technology, they did incorporate another technological innovation that was second only to the transistor in its critical contribution to mobile communications: "integrated circuits," which were invented in 1958. Now transistors smaller than pinpoints could be laid by the hundreds on a silicon semiconductor chip the size of an infant's thumbnail. Not only were the chips tiny, they also made possible mass-production manufacturing of electronic equipment—an art soon mastered in Japan, where automated assembly lines began spewing off a new class of commodities: "consumer electronics." This new wave of microtechnology included smaller transistor radios, clocks, calculators and, eventually, two-way radios.

With mass production of cheap CB radios, Americans went wild for mobile communications—as many as one in seven U.S. cars carried CBs in the late '70s. Still, the FCC and most communications executives saw it as no more than a blue-collar fad; no one really recognized it as a clear indicator that Americans were clamoring to drive and talk on the phone.

In the midst of the CB craze, the FCC took another step toward bringing cellular to the public. In 1977, seven years after AT&T first requested it, the FCC finally authorized construction of two experimental cell-phone systems—the first one in Chicago and then seven months later another in the Washington, D.C.-Baltimore metropolitan area—to test whether cellular technology could actually stand up to large-scale usage. AT&T was granted the right to build the Chicago experiment through its Advanced Mobile Phone Service (AMPS) subsidiary, while its biggest potential competitor in equipment manufacturing, Motorola, teamed with a local paging and mobile operator called American Radio Telephone Services Inc. (ARTS) to build the Washington-Baltimore system. Though these systems would be smaller than the commercial systems that were expected to start in a few years' time, the FCC wanted to find out how the equipment held up, and how the test users reacted to the service.

Then-FCC chairman Charles Ferris was one of the enthusiastic users: In 1982, he told a *Time* magazine reporter, "I had a mobile phone in my car when I was a commissioner, and the quality was so poor I couldn't really use it. But the cellular phones I've tried from the Chicago test are so good I became a convert." (So much of a convert, in fact, that immediately following his tenure as FCC chairman, he joined a company that vied for cellular spectrum licenses.) And AMPS executive William Newport enthused to another reporter, "Even we were surprised by the enthusiasm in the Chicago test market. We had to turn down all sorts of people who saw it and wanted to try it out."

With the experimental systems running to great acclaim, pressure grew for the FCC to make a move and at last permanently grant the spectrum licenses the new industry required. But true to form, the commission would dally several more years before finally settling on the rules for the giveaway. In the meantime, a few countries that had less red tape to struggle through (generally those with government-owned telephone systems) got cell phone systems up and running—Saudi Arabia, Sweden and Japan were among the first.

———

AT LAST, ON MAY 4, 1981, the FCC announced its decision: It would divide the 40 MHz of spectrum it had designated for cellular into two equal blocks, so there would be two cell-phone systems in each market. With that amount of spectrum, there would now be 666 channels designated for U.S. mobile communications in each market nationwide—a phenomenal leap from the 44 channels that had served since 1946. And not only that, but thanks to cellular technology those 666 channels could, unlike the earlier 44 channels, be reused up to a half-dozen times each, increasing capacity a thousand fold.

One block would be awarded to a local telephone company (the "wireline" side in FCC parlance), and the other would be up for grabs among any non-telephone ("nonwireline") companies who wanted to try to win it. This was, some commissioners felt, a perfect compromise: Having two systems in each market protected consumers from a monopoly. And designating one of the two specifically for telephone companies served two purposes: First, it would help get the industry going faster, as the phone companies would presumably be both financially and technologically able to get a system running more quickly. Second, it protected the FCC from potential embarrassment of further delay or failure in getting the long-awaited cell phone systems running.

The FCC would accept applications for certain cities at dates to be announced. If more than one company applied for either block in any given city (a prospect that was uncertain, considering the great financial risk involved), the FCC staff would turn the competing applications over to an administrative law judge, who would then conduct a "comparative hearing" to decide who was best qualified to receive the license.

The judges, the FCC went on to explain in its published rules, would make their decisions based on certain criteria—such as financial plans for the systems, information on expected usage and pricing, an engineering plan for frequency reuse, intended geographic coverage and number of cell sites. In addition, applicants would be judged on more esoteric qualities, such as "knowledge of and ability to serve the local community" and "public service attributes"—criteria the applicants were free to interpret in any way they liked. On the surface, the rules seemed straightforward. But as the FCC would soon discover, they were vague enough to be open to some fairly wide interpretations, which would cause plenty of headaches for the applicants—and for the FCC itself.

But as amorphous as they were, at least there were now some rules. After years of inaction, bureaucratic entanglements, lobbying, arguing and ineptitude, the FCC had finally made a decision. All that remained now was taking care of a few administrative details (which would ultimately take nearly a year) and the giveaway—and, by extension, the cell phone industry—could begin.

━━━━━━━

AS IT TURNED OUT, there was yet one more drama to be played out before that could happen.

Ever since the Justice Department filed suit against AT&T back in 1974, the question of what might happen to the telephone juggernaut loomed large. On January 8, 1982—after the FCC's cellular decision, but before it set a date for accepting the first applications—U.S. District Court Judge Harold Greene issued the long-awaited consent decree that would break up AT&T's telephone monopoly. AT&T agreed to split itself up by January 1984, divesting itself of its local telephone service, which would fall into the hands of seven "Baby Bells," or independent Regional Bell Operating Companies (RBOCs), set up for that purpose. The parent company would continue to exist as a long-distance telephone company, and it would retain control of its lucrative equipment manufacturing subsidiary, Western Electric (now Lucent Technologies).

The breakup would be a mammoth undertaking—AT&T was the largest corporation in the world at the time—and a radical change for Americans, who for more than 100 years had gotten all their telephone-related service from "Ma Bell." Though it was a monopoly, many Americans felt secure having the venerable old company in charge of their phones. Now many feared that after the January 1984 breakup, the cost of telephone service would rise and service would suffer.

With all the plots and subplots revolving around the breakup, the question of cellular's future at AT&T was a relatively insignificant one. With the huge money at stake in wired telephony, long distance, equipment sales, and even phone books, the executives had plenty of other things to worry about. As former AT&T executive Sam Ginn later put it, the company was "more interested in the Yellow Pages at the time than wireless."

One reason the suits seemed untroubled by the fate of cellular was that they didn't expect it to be much of a business. One widely quoted—and later, widely ridiculed—study commissioned by AT&T in 1980 gives evidence of how drastically the company underestimated the future demand for cellular.

The study claimed that by the year 2000 there would be only 900,000 U.S. cell phone users—a number that dramatically underestimated the snowballing effect of falling prices and the desire of Americans to talk while moving. One could hardly blame AT&T for exhibiting only passing interest in cellular if it believed that figure—what kind of profits could possibly come out of an industry that would cost hundreds of millions of dollars to build, but attract fewer than a million users in twenty years? If these numbers proved true, the cellular industry would hardly be worth the trouble. Unfortunately for AT&T, the numbers were spectacularly wrong: By mid-2000 there were more than 100 million U.S. cell phone users—more than 100 times the number AT&T predicted. Had AT&T realized how lucrative the cell phone industry would become, perhaps it would have paid more attention to this seemingly unimportant side business.

Throughout the long-negotiated settlement, a handful of executives—such as the ones in charge of AT&T's experimental Chicago system—had pressed their superiors for an answer: What would happen to cellular when the company broke up? Some argued that it was an obvious "local" service and should therefore fall to the RBOCs. Others pointed to its great cost and technical complexity, and argued that it should remain with AT&T. When January 8 came and the settlement was announced, no answer was forthcoming from the AT&T hierarchy.

The first indication of where cellular would fall came when AT&T chairman Charles Brown was in the hot seat on a popular TV news show. In an appearance on the *MacNeil/Lehrer Report* on January 11, 1982, Brown got into a discussion with Democratic Representative Tim Wirth of Colorado, who was pressing him to distinguish between which services would fall to AT&T and which to the new RBOCs. When asked about cellular, Brown glibly offered that AT&T wouldn't interfere in "the local companies' business. . . all we'll do is make the technology available."

To the shock of many of his junior executives, Charles Brown had effectively given away AT&T's claim to cellular with an apparently offhand remark: The wireline licenses set aside for telephone companies would fall into the laps of the RBOCs following divestiture in January 1984. The company that invented cellular technology would have no part in the industry it spawned. No part, that is, until it would buy its way back into the industry a decade later, at a staggering price.

In March 1982, the FCC finally wrapped up its administrative details and issued its final rules for the cellular giveaway. Because there were potentially hundreds of licenses to distribute—two each for all the cities, towns and rural areas in the U.S.—it would divide up the distribution of cellular licenses into "rounds." Many believed there would be no interest in licenses for any areas less populous than the largest cities, so initially the FCC only made plans to distribute those. First up were the thirty largest cities in the United States—so-called Round I of the giveaway. June 7, 1982, would be the deadline for submitting applications to win licenses for these cities—the only cities, some believed, in which cellular systems had any chance of turning a profit. Application rules and deadlines for smaller cities would be announced later. (Round II would be the thirty-first to the sixtieth largest cities, Round III would be the sixty-first to the ninetieth largest, and so on through the 305 Metropolitan Statistical Areas, or MSAs.)

The debate and delay were over for the moment; now it was time for anyone who wanted to take a chance on this new industry to step up. On the wireline side, things were relatively staid: Most of the local telephone companies fell under the aegis of either AT&T or General Telephone and Electronics (GTE), so it was obvious to all who the competition would be for the wireline spectrum block.

But the nonwireline side was a free-for-all. From colossal pillars of U.S. business such as Western Union to scrappy, underfunded entrepreneurs such as Peter Lewis, a colorful and varied cast of characters lined up to try and claim a part of the new industry.

THE PLAYERS

ONE OF THE BEST THINGS ABOUT WORKING AT MCI, thought Herman "Whitey" Bluestein during his first few weeks with the company in April 1982, was that they sprang for a platter of cold cuts each afternoon to feed the employees. He'd never worked in a place where the employer fed the troops, and the free lunches were a pleasant surprise.

It wasn't long before Bluestein, who'd joined the Corporate Development division to work on the company's cellular effort, began working later and later each day. The Round I filing deadline was just two months away, and Bluestein had landed right in the middle of the frantic effort to get the applications ready. More and more often, when the sky grew dark outside the windows of MCI's Washington, D.C., offices two blocks east of the FCC, Bluestein found himself still stuck inside, his six-foot frame hunched over his desk. To his surprise and delight, MCI soon started having dinners delivered to the office as well.

It wasn't until he started getting free breakfasts after all-night stints at the office that he began to think, "Maybe this isn't such a great deal after all." His workdays grew longer and longer, until finally, just before the filing deadline, Bluestein, his boss Gerald H. Taylor and a few colleagues spent a couple of days on twenty-four-hour duty, taking turns grabbing catnaps on an office couch. When June 7 arrived, Bluestein and the rest of the exhausted team had succeeded in preparing massive, complex applications for twelve of the top thirty markets.

Cellular was a perfect play for MCI Communications Corporation, a company that had spent the fourteen years of its existence making itself into

America's first alternative long-distance telephone operator—and bashing AT&T at every turn in the process. Led by an exuberant, cigar-smoking, workaholic CEO named William McGowan, MCI (which originally stood for Microwave Communications, Inc.) was running long-distance service in sixty U.S. cities by the early '80s, and its revenues were nearing a billion dollars per year.

MCI's bold incursion into an industry formerly monopolized by AT&T was one strike in a new phenomenon that emerged toward the end of the twentieth century. Voice communications in the United States had always been dominated by AT&T, but now MCI and a handful of other carriers had begun exploiting loopholes and sidestepping regulators in an effort to get into the telephone industry. The communications monoliths of yore— AT&T, Western Union and ITT—were bloated, slow-moving megacorporations that were used to getting everything handed to them by federal regulators. But now, young and hungry new companies such as MCI were determined to wrest away a piece of their lucrative business however they could.

Then a brand-new telecom opportunity appeared—the cellular phone industry—and it was completely up for grabs, for anyone who wanted in on it. MCI wasted no time lining up for the landgrab.

In Round I, MCI would apply in twelve cities: Los Angeles, Cleveland, Dallas/Fort Worth, Denver, Houston, Kansas City, Miami, Minneapolis, Philadelphia, Pittsburgh, Portland and Tampa. Though MCI was in one sense a telephone company, it ran only long-distance rather than local services, so it wasn't eligible to apply for the wireline block of spectrum—a fact that rankled AT&T hater McGowan, who bitterly opposed any kind of competitive concessions to the phone giant.

Though McGowan's company wasn't qualified for the wireline handout, MCI's twelve cellular applications in Round I qualified it as a major presence on the nonwireline side. Aggressive and dynamic, MCI seemed poised to dominate the fledgling industry. In a 1983 book called *High Tech: How to Find and Profit from Today's New Super Stocks*, authors Albert Toney and Thomas Tilling sounded a warning for possible competitors when they wrote of MCI, "Yes, the terrible telephone upstarts are moving into cellular mobile radio! Watch out, everybody."

Never one to hide his blustery optimism (he was renowned for having famously crowed, "MCI—that stands for 'Money Coming In!'" at one shareholders meeting), McGowan was absolutely certain MCI would win the FCC's comparative hearings and become a cellular powerhouse. His cocky self-assurance seeped through the ranks, metamorphosing into a kind of entrenched corporate arrogance that ultimately would cost the company at least one valuable license, and arguably its entire cell phone business.

―――――

IT WASN'T UNTIL THE WEEK BEFORE THE FILING DEADLINE that Graphic Scanning CFO William S. Wheatley, Jr., got scared. For months, dozens of employees on the company's cellular team had been preparing Round I applications—assembling the paperwork, proofreading, checking and rechecking the engineering plans for proposed cellular coverage, counting copies, collating and binding. In the week before the deadline, the printer Graphic had contracted was furiously churning out duplicates by the ream. It had to: Graphic Scanning, unlike any of the other Round I applicants, was planning to file in every single one of the top thirty markets—a total of one and a half million pages of applications.

This was a flagrant poke at the FCC's filing rules, which required any applicant in any city to demonstrate financial ability to construct that city's expensive cell phone system. How could Graphic, a fourteen-year-old communications company with less than $100 million in revenues in 1982, even suggest it had enough financial power to build thirty systems? Surely, feared Wheatley, the FCC would never allow this kind of maneuvering— and the rest of the applicants were bound to be furious at having to compete with this upstart company no matter which market they were in.

One evening a few days before the June 7 filing, Wheatley approached Graphic founder and president Barry E. Yampol, who was the architect and prime proponent of the idea of filing in all markets. After months of work and millions of dollars spent, all thirty applications were nearly ready. Wheatley, as Yampol recalls it, was so scared he was shaking. Afraid of backlash from the FCC and the other applicants, as well as the financial implications if Graphic went ahead with its plan, Wheatley made a timid suggestion to his boss: "Would you be willing to file in only three markets?"

Yampol stared incredulously at his CFO. He knew that some employees had been concerned about how it looked for the company to stretch the rules, and he had tried in the past few weeks to assuage their fears. "It's okay," he had told them. "If you're concerned about making enemies, you shouldn't go into the communications business. The business is all about attacking your competitors and slowing people down." But those were employees, not high-ranking executives like Wheatley—the CFO should be helping lead the company in its charge, not whimpering about the bruised feelings Graphic's daring strategy might cause. Without a second thought, Yampol turned Wheatley down flat.

Those concerned about how others perceived them couldn't have found a less sympathetic listener than Barry Yampol. Mercurial, intuitive, arrogant and combative, Yampol was the most controversial figure in the telecommunications industry—"a rising star that lives dangerously," as a *Business Week* reporter put it.

The son of a middle-class New York garment manufacturer, Yampol had gotten into telecommunications fresh after his graduation from the City College of New York in 1961, when he began leasing telecommunications equipment. At twenty-nine, Yampol founded Graphic Scanning, and the young entrepreneur soon developed an uncanny knack for exploiting the latest technology to grab business from the telecom giants.

One of his first feats of giant-slaying was luring clients away from Western Union by developing a faster and more reliable financial data communications network. Though Western Union had had Wall Street's business sewn up for decades, Yampol convinced the New York Stock Exchange and most of its blue chip members—firms like Morgan Stanley and Goldman Sachs—to sign up for his network, dealing an embarrassing blow to the staid old telegraph behemoth.

Under Yampol's guidance, Graphic grew and expanded into other telecom areas. By 1983, Graphic's 160,000 paging customers made it the nation's largest paging company, and it extended its reach into a host of other telecom businesses as well, including direct broadcast satellites, mobile phones, low-power television, electronic funds transfers and nationwide paging.

It was an impressive array of high-tech endeavors. But most remarkable of all—and most indicative of Yampol's superlative ability to see over the horizon—was Graphic's "Graphnet" business, which linked together disparate computer networks, telex machines, early facsimile machines and new microcomputers to create a data network for New York City's banking industry. Between 1975 and 1982, Graphic invested a risky $34 million, turning Graphnet into the United States' first commercial nationwide packet-switched data communications network. When it was finally up and running, there were only a few specialized networks comparable to it, most notably Telenet and its government- and university-run sibling, Arpanet, the predecessors of the commercial Internet.

It is no stretch to call Yampol a genius. But his brilliance was offset by his damaging personal foibles: greed, unchecked ego and an overarching distrust for his fellow man. He was extremely secretive, and his interests extended into esoterica far removed from the business of Graphic Scanning. A collector of rare gems, Yampol invested in a Brazilian gem-mining operation in 1981, and by 1983, he had amassed a jewel-and-mineral hoard that the *Washington Post* called "one of the finest private collections in the nation." He loved sports cars and racing boats, and spent what little free time he had working on how to improve the power of marine racing engines. On his secluded estate adjoining President Theodore Roosevelt's Sagamore Hill on Long Island's Oyster Bay, Yampol lived the life style of the eccentric multimillionaire that he was.

Yampol was, in the words of Ed Taptich, a Washington, D.C.–based attorney who worked with Graphic for years, an "ectomorphic genius. An extraordinarily bright guy. Extremely demanding of others. And the worst I can say for him, he's terribly impatient with others who would not grasp things and pursue matters as insightfully and as tenaciously as he did. And that encompassed about 96.8 percent of the population."

Despite Yampol's many successes, he'd never had a chance to milk the real cash cow: voice telephone service. "The real business was the telephone business," Yampol recalled later, "but there was no way to get in due to regulation and lack of money." But when he read about cellular in the *Bell Labs Journal*, he, like MCI's Bill McGowan, recognized it as his back door into the telephone business. Cellular, he was convinced, would be huge. And even if it wasn't, he wanted to win the spectrum licenses anyway: In Yampol's eyes, spectrum of any kind was valuable. He had made a career of going after as many licenses as possible—in paging, satellites, whatever he could get his hands on—no matter what the spectrum was designated for.

So when Bill Wheatley approached Yampol the day after his first timid entreaty and asked again if he would consider filing only a few Round I applications, Yampol couldn't hide his disgust. "We are going to file thirty, then thirty, then thirty," he snapped, referring to all the markets in rounds I, II and III of the giveaway. And that was the final answer. Wheatley had been slapped down twice; now he had no choice but to send the applications off to the FCC. It took two semitrailers to hold the 240 cardboard boxes into which Graphic's mountain of applications was stuffed.

Wheatley was right about one thing—when the other Round I applicants learned what Graphic had done, the reaction was swift and unanimous: This was an outrage! Graphic was obviously and knowingly flouting the rules! No one could quite believe Yampol's chutzpah and blatant disregard for convention—and their fury was further stoked by the fact that they hadn't thought of it first. As much as its competitors hated Graphic Scanning, they envied the company too, for having—at least temporarily—claimed the best position in the new industry.

———

ONE PERSON WHO CONTINUED TO HOLD A GRUDGE against Graphic, even years later, was former Western Union CEO Robert M. Flanagan. Even fifteen years after the Round I filing, he couldn't hide his disdain for the company: "I feel very bitter that Graphic Scanning paid no attention to the [financial] requirement," he said. "Graphic Scanning simply got away with thumbing their noses at the regulations and were blessed for it." Considering what happened to Western Union in the course of the cellular boom, Flanagan had a lot more to be bitter about than just Graphic Scanning's antics.

An apocryphal story holds that, in 1876, Western Union president William Orton dismissed an opportunity to purchase Alexander Graham Bell's fledgling telephone company with the remark, "What use could this company make of an electric toy?" If true, the story is a remarkable tribute to shortsightedness—a trait that, unfortunately, Western Union executives would exhibit in abundance during the cellular era.

By the time the June 1982 Round I filing deadline rolled around, Western Union had been in business 131 years. Founded in 1851, the company became a household name for generations of Americans as a reliable source of major news events as well as personal announcements such as distant family births and deaths. In the first half of the twentieth century, Americans of every age and class could recite the Western Union jingle: "Miles away we can laugh, our hearts entwined by telegraph." By the early 1980s, Western Union had built itself into a telex and telegram behemoth, a Dow Jones Industrial cornerstone, and a trusted, proven name in telecommunications.

The flip side of the company's steady, staid modus operandi was its complete lack of entrepreneurial zeal. Western Union might have been great at telexes and telegrams, but these were the communications tools of the past, and the fact that they were regulated industries meant the company was burdened with expensive union contracts and a bloated bureaucracy. Like an ostentatious leather executive's chair, everything about the company exuded an overstuffed, creaky old-world air. The board still held luxurious meetings at the Waldorf-Astoria in New York City, and a fleet of limousines was at the ready to ferry around executives, who dined out at expensive restaurants and puffed hand-rolled cigars bought with open expense accounts.

By the time the cellular-licensing process began, Western Union was still powerful, but precariously so. Years of union featherbedding and technological neglect were catching up—the company carried a $155-million unfunded pension liability and its ratio of current liabilities to current assets was nearly five to one. Revenues were flat or falling. Debt was rising. CEO Bob Flanagan's efforts to expand the company presented a challenge that left no room for bad luck, as he acknowledged when he later commented to *Business Week*, "We had the problem of turning an elephant around in a bathtub without spilling any water. The trick was to keep the investors and workers with us while growing at an acceptable rate and making some profits."

The Harvard-educated Flanagan was the latest in a long line of conservative Western Union executives who had played hospice while the company needed hellraisers. Though he did have an appreciation for technology and kept abreast of news on the upcoming cellular giveaway, he waited until it was almost too late to explore getting in on it. Only a few months before the Round I filing deadline, he pulled James T. Ragan, a former marine who had fought in the Korean conflict, off the company's satellite division and gave him ten days to report back on whether the company should commit to cellular.

Ragan was a great choice for the job; unlike the swarms of Western Union career drones that populated the company's New Jersey headquarters, he was bright, ambitious and technologically savvy, as well as being a creative, likable deal-maker. It took Ragan barely a week of research to reach his verdict: Cellular, he told Flanagan (in his odd pronunciation, the word always came out "cell-a-lar"), was a "no-brainer." That was all Flanagan needed to hear: He ordered Ragan to get on it. It was time for big, slow-moving Western Union to make an uncharacteristically bold move in a new direction.

But where to start? Like John Kluge's Metromedia, Western Union had decided late to get into the game—there wasn't enough time for the company to prepare its own complex applications for Round I. Twenty-five miles from Western Union's New Jersey headquarters, Kluge was at the same time making the decision to purchase paging companies to get into the cellular race. But Western Union was short on cash, and decisionmaking at the massive company was glacially slow. Ragan needed to get in on some applications cheaply and quickly; in an inventive stroke, he did it by creating joint ventures with those ahead of him in the race.

Ragan began at square one. Using the *Wall Street Journal* and word-of-mouth as his guides, he set out to learn who was already geared up to apply. Then he picked up the phone to call them and inquire about doing deals.

Over the next few months, Ragan jetted back and forth across the country, meeting company executives and arranging joint ventures in as many markets as he could. He was able to convince many of the small companies to give him a percentage for no money up front, in return for two things: the clout that Western Union's name and balance sheet would add to their applications, and the promise of technical engineering and management help when it came time to operate systems.

The more he learned, the more Ragan became convinced that Western Union should apply on its own in a few markets. So at the company's Upper Saddle River, New Jersey, headquarters, he assembled a small team that hurriedly set about putting together applications for Buffalo, Kansas City and New Orleans.

As the June 7 deadline approached, Ragan had managed to negotiate and sign joint ventures with a varied array of partners, including the *Providence Journal* newspaper chain, Palmer Communications of Omaha, FMI Financial Corp. and Ram Broadcasting Corp., among others. Back at company headquarters, his cellular team was racing to finish up its own applications. But time was running so short that Ragan decided he would take no chances: He arranged for two sets of cars, a light plane and a helicopter to be on standby in case the applications had to be rushed to Washington at the last moment.

Despite the late start, Ragan and his team had done an impressive job. By June 7, Western Union had stakes in fifteen of the top thirty markets—a position second only to Graphic Scanning on the nonwireline side. The creaky old mammoth of a company was poised to jump into a brave new world of wireless communications. Unless, of course, it somehow lost heart and squandered its chance, as William Orton had so foolishly done more than 100 years before.

ALL ACROSS THE COUNTRY, ASPIRING CELLULAR OPERATORS who rushed to complete their Round I applications were mostly unaware of who their competitors might be; apart from rumors and the odd press report, there was no way to know who might suddenly appear on the scene for the June 7 filing. As Metromedia, Graphic Scanning and Western Union teams toiled within a few dozen miles of each other, two other companies that would claim a major stake in the industry kept the lights in their New York City headquarters on all night as well: Metro Mobile CTS and LIN Broadcasting Corp.

A New York City–based startup formed specifically to file cellular applications, Metro Mobile was led by an ambitious, martini-drinking, cigar-smoking, socially competitive multimillionaire named George Lindemann. A stocky, swarthy man with thick black hair and a ruddy complexion (attributable in part, perhaps, to the copious amounts of alcohol that routinely coursed through his veins), Lindemann had a forceful, acerbic personality. Everything about him was outsized, from his bushy black eyebrows to his luxury homes to his opinion of himself and the influence his company should wield.

Having made a fortune in cable with his New Jersey–based Vision Cable Communications (which he sold in 1981 for $220 million), he entered 1981 determined to get in on what he saw as the next big thing. "I couldn't believe," he said later, "that anybody who had a phone and was sitting in a car for half an hour isn't going to use that phone." Led by Lindemann, Metro Mobile applied in nine Round I markets: Cincinnati, Denver, Houston, Kansas City, Miami, Tampa, San Diego, Minneapolis and Phoenix.

Like many Round I applicants, Lindemann tried to apply in markets where he thought there would be less competition. As a result, his applications were all in midtier markets, which conventional wisdom held to be less valuable in terms of how many customers were likely to sign up. LIN Broadcasting's Donald Pels, on the other hand, directed the LIN cellular team to file in fewer markets—but they were, like Kluge's, all top-tier markets: New York City, Los Angeles, Houston, Philadelphia and Dallas–Fort Worth.

Pels, an unassuming, penny-pinching CEO, believed cellular would prove profitable—but not nearly to the level that others, like John Stanton, did. The LIN team's assumptions were modest: By the year 1990, they believed, cellular penetration might reach 2.5 percent of the market, split evenly between wireline and nonwireline carriers. The average subscriber would use the phone only fifteen minutes a day, bringing in an average revenue of about $30 a month. By the end of the decade, the LIN number crunchers reckoned, the company would have fewer than 200,000 subscribers—in all a very respectable $70 million business, comparable to that of a couple of LIN's television stations.

As it turned out, these estimates were off by a factor of four. LIN would close the decade with some 340,000 subscribers and revenue of $75 per subscriber—a mammoth business with more than $300 million in revenue. And unlike many of the early license holders, LIN would actually have the patience it needed to fully capitalize on the meteoric rise in cellular values. For Donald Pels, slow and steady would ultimately win the race.

As June 7 approached, the company that would ultimately trigger the explosive rush in spectrum prices, McCaw Communications, was still edging toward its own epiphany about cellular. Though Ed Hopper had hired John Stanton on a consulting basis and the tiny cellular team was now racing to put together Round I applications, the cash-strapped company still shied away from putting too much of its scarce resources into this unproven new field. Too cautious to apply on its own, McCaw planned to share the risk, applying jointly with other paging companies, even in its hometown of Seattle. As Hopper recalls: "[CEO] Craig [McCaw] said, 'Go ye forth and build a cellular company—but you can't have any money.'"

In the previous decade, Craig McCaw had gotten plenty of experience in building businesses with no money. He hadn't been left with much choice following the family tragedy that changed the course of his and his brothers' lives.

Craig and his three brothers, Bruce, John and Keith, grew up in an atmosphere of privilege, in the tony Highlands neighborhood of Seattle. Their father, Elroy McCaw, was a pure entrepreneur, involved in a sprawling cornucopia of enterprises: He owned radio and television stations, a few small paging businesses, cable television systems and investments in more than fifty companies. His success in this panoply of businesses allowed him to indulge in the trappings of wealth—the McCaw boys grew up in a massive mansion with a personal staff, and went on trips with their father in his boats and airplanes.

But the McCaw patriarch's wealth, as the family would soon learn, was far from free and clear. Like many entrepreneurs, Elroy McCaw had built a pyramid of businesses on a foundation of borrowed money. The fragility of his precariously balanced empire became apparent soon after the tragic day in August 1969 when nineteen-year-old Craig, then a sophomore at Stanford University, walked into a bedroom to discover the lifeless body of his father, killed by a stroke at fifty-seven.

Calls from creditors and lawyers soon began pouring into the McCaw mansion, and the family quickly realized that the burden of debt, taxes and lawsuits left in the wake of Elroy's death threatened to crush them. Elroy's widow, Marion, a trained accountant, set about fixing the situation in the only way she knew how: by liquidating everything. Businesses were dealt off and bank accounts emptied, and before the creditor vultures stopped circling, most of the McCaws' property was gone. Though the family would be comfortably sustained by payments from a $2 million life insurance policy, Elroy McCaw's eclectic domain was reduced to a mere handful of assets.

There was one business, however, that Marion soon discovered she didn't have the legal right to sell: Twin Cities, a small cable television system in Centralia, Washington, where Craig and his brothers had spent their youthful summers stringing cable and selling subscriptions door-to-door. Unbeknownst to Marion, Elroy had engineered the transfer of the company to his sons a few years prior to his death.

This miniscule company would be the seed of eventual powerhouse McCaw Communications. At the time, it was nothing more than a tiny cable business in a tiny town: the company had fewer than 4,000 subscribers among a population of 12,000, and in 1970 its monthly gross income was only $8,000. Still in college at Stanford, Craig began running the company from his dorm room—his older brother, Bruce, wasn't interested, and his younger brothers Keith and John were still in high school. The boys could have sold the company—they received an offer in 1970 from the *Seattle Times*—but Craig McCaw would hear none of it. It was the last remnant of his beloved father's business empire, and Craig was determined to make it a success.

Shy, awkward Craig McCaw was not someone likely to be picked out of a crowd as a business mogul in the making. A slightly built, clean-cut young man with short brown hair, a blocky mustache, wide-set brown eyes and an oddly intense stare, Craig made up for a near-total lack of charisma with an unwavering singularity of purpose. In childhood, the dyslexia he suffers did little to impede his performance in school; in adulthood, his ability to focus only grew. Even in his early twenties, Craig McCaw went about the business of running his company with a surprising fearlessness and near-manic intensity.

From the start—while still running the company from college—Craig began learning and refining the strategy that would eventually make him a telecommunications mogul: Almost immediately, he began trying to acquire other cable systems. No matter how little there was in the company's bank account, the mandate never wavered: Sign a deal for whatever anyone would sell, and worry about the details later. And when the fledgling young businessman learned from an investment banker how he could leverage his business using cash flow rather than hard assets to secure debt, it was as though he'd been given the keys to the magic kingdom. The more McCaw built cash flow, the faster it expanded its borrowing capacity. More borrowed money meant more systems purchased, which meant more cash flow, which meant still more money borrowed. The cycle fed itself, in ever-widening circles.

Craig and his small band of employees set out on the road with messianic zeal. They traveled across the western states by car and company plane, calling on every mom-and-pop cable system they could find. Craig soon honed a unique hands-off management style that befitted his marginal communications skills: hire the brightest minds, give them ambitious goals and broad authority, and then turn them loose. Any employee who was sent out to do an acquisition was given the authority to close the deal himself, on the spot. No ego-fueled hierarchy would slow the drive: the main thing was to get the deals done before someone else made an offer, and then to get on to the next deal.

Throughout the '70s, McCaw's deal-makers played a daring game of chance: First, they would contract to buy a cable system that they couldn't afford, promise to take over management immediately and rely on regulatory delays to defer closing. Then, in the words of one McCaw veteran, "We'd paint the trucks, answer the phones, and jack the rates." The combined impetus of improved management and rate increases allowed McCaw, in many cases, to boost system cash flows to the point that the entire purchase price could be bank financed by the time the deferred closing date arrived.

Craig McCaw was building a formidable cable empire without spending cash—an empire built on an increasing mountain of debt, leavened occasionally with shared joint ventures and sales of minority equity stakes, but without a single penny of McCaw family cash.

No one knew it at the time, but McCaw's cable acquisition frenzy in the '70s was creating a culture tailor-made for a similar blitzkrieg in the as-yet-unheard-of cellular telephone industry. The storied McCaw organization was taking shape.

Although the company had dabbled in spectrum when it branched into paging in the late 1970s, cable was still the McCaw's mainstay in 1982 when John Stanton and his team set about preparing the Round I cellular filings. As Stanton's little team prepared applications for six markets—Denver, Kansas City, San Francisco, San Jose, Portland and Seattle—it seemed unlikely that cellular would, within a few years, entirely replace cable as the company's core business.

METROMEDIA'S ACQUISITION OF BOB EDWARDS'S RADIOFONE in April 1982 was only one purchase in a spring and summer buying spree. Advised by his behind-the-scenes team—right-hand man Stuart Subotnick, a slightly built, nattily dressed tax lawyer who orchestrated Metromedia's cellular strategy; and genial, outgoing George Duncan—John Kluge was so certain of cellular's eventual worth that he willingly overpaid by 50 percent or more for the paging operations he purchased.

No one could have blamed any Metromedia stockholders who questioned why Kluge was suddenly wagering tens of millions in overpayments on what appeared to be a wild speculation, but as Kluge and Subotnick saw it, the cellular applications alone were worth the prices they were paying. The paging businesses—solid, fast-growing, moneymaking enterprises in their own right—were just a bonus in the bargain.

This mammoth wager on cellular was no surprise to those who knew John Kluge. A lifelong card player, Kluge (whose surname means "clever" in German) supported himself in college by winning countless poker games; he still engages friends in half-day-long gin rummy matches at his sprawling estates in Virginia, Palm Beach, Scotland and Germany. In business, too, Kluge has always been willing to bet on a chance at big returns, often finding industries early, riding their accelerated adolescent growth curve and then adroitly selling out as values multiply.

Initially, there was nothing to suggest Kluge would become an American entrepreneurial baron of the late twentieth century: He emigrated from Germany with his parents in 1922, at age eight, and passed a relatively unremarkable childhood in a Detroit tenement. It was after he received a scholarship and enrolled at Columbia University in the depth of the depression years that he first began showing signs of an unusual knack for making money; not only did he routinely thrash his friends at poker, but he also started a handful of small businesses to supplement his scholarship.

Following graduation, Kluge joined a small paper company and immediately put his competitive drive to use as he hustled about trying to increase sales. With a friendly, relaxed manner and warm smile that regularly lit up his round face, Kluge proved a natural salesman: Within four years, he had single-handedly doubled the company's sales, earning himself one-third ownership of the firm in the bargain. But his burgeoning business career was interrupted by events in his former homeland: When World War II broke out in Europe, Kluge put his business aspirations on hold to serve in U.S. Army Intelligence.

After the war Kluge, now in his early thirties, went into business for himself. At a cost of $15,000, he started AM radio station WGAY in Silver Spring, Maryland; this was the first in the long series of entrepreneurial endeavors that would culminate in his being recognized as the richest man in America in 1989. The way he got there was, in Kluge's eyes, simple. As *Forbes Magazine* related in 1996, Kluge has two basic operating principles: Buy cheap, and buy things that can be improved. He proved to have an uncanny eye for simple businesses with dependable cash flows that allowed for high leverage and outsized returns.

Kluge was an equal-opportunity entrepreneur: The commodities he bought and sold could be the sexiest, most talked-about businesses around, or they could be utterly mundane. After founding a small food-brokerage firm, Kluge and Company, in 1951, he spent the next four decades building an eventual $11 billion fortune on a motley array of businesses, from Fritos and Cheetos to billboards to the Harlem Globetrotters and the Ice Capades. He was convinced of the moneymaking potential of radio and television, and, defying conventional wisdom of the time, he assembled a stable of independent TV stations across the country. Because they lacked a network affiliation and mainstream programming, these stations were all cheap and largely ignored, but Kluge turned them into cash cows by featuring reruns and low-budget programming.

Kluge renamed his company Metromedia in 1961, reflecting its increasing presence in broadcasting. Under his guidance, and utilizing the uncanny financial insight of CFO Subotnick, who joined the company in 1967, Metromedia saw its stock price rise from $4.25 in 1974 to $175 a share in 1982—the fastest rise of any issue on the New York Stock Exchange during that time.

By then, Kluge seemed to have it all: He was in his late sixties; recently married to a stunning British socialite (and former nude model) forty years his junior; building a forty-five-room mansion in the rolling hills outside Charlottesville, Virginia; and possessed of greater wealth than he could reasonably be expected to spend in his lifetime. No one could have blamed him had he decided to close up shop and enjoy a well-deserved retirement.

But then cellular came along. In Kluge's estimation, the new cellular industry offered the kind of huge moneymaking opportunity that he craved—but only, he believed, in America's largest cities. It was difficult to imagine that very many people would be willing to shell out thousands of dollars for a fancy car phone in Kansas City or Milwaukee, so Kluge shied away from those markets. But he charged after the bigger markets with a vengeance—

waving Metromedia's fat wallet—and by the time June 7, 1982 rolled around, he was well in the game. Metromedia had bought seven paging companies and their cellular applications, giving it stakes in applications for eight of America's largest cities, including New York, Los Angeles, Chicago, Boston and Washington, D.C.

FORTUNATELY FOR PETER LEWIS, just about the time he recognized his need for a deeper-pocketed investor, he was introduced to a former corporate lawyer named Bernard J. Cravath.

A friendly, freckle-faced attorney with a knack for business, Bernie Cravath was initially unconvinced of the promise of cell phones. In fact, he viewed any kind of mobile phone—and the people who used one—as worthy of suspicion. His years as the general counsel at a finance company had provided him with a wealth of experience in dealing with commercial loans and collecting from deadbeats, and from that experience he had developed one rule of thumb: If a prospective borrower had a car phone, he was, in Cravath's estimation, a show-off and potential deadbeat.

"Nearly everybody that I had ever known in business that had a car phone turned out to be dishonest," he later recalled. "If you had a car phone, you were probably dishonest, or were going to become dishonest eventually. . . I had this impression in my mind that if I got a car phone, I would go to jail." Clearly, Cravath was not the most natural choice to get involved in the new cell phone industry.

But after meeting Peter Lewis, Cravath was impressed. Cravath knew as little about cellular technology as Lewis knew about business, but after talking for a couple of hours at Lewis's townhouse office, Cravath decided to help the young entrepreneur find some investors. He invited Lewis and his army buddies to set up shop in his Kensington, Maryland, law offices, and an unlikely partnership was born.

Ever the technophile, Lewis had introduced himself to the Motorola technicians who were in Washington, D.C., overseeing the construction and operation of the Washington-Baltimore experimental cellular system. The Motorola specialists took a liking to the eager young ex-army officer with the neat haircut, endless curiosity and no-nonsense demeanor, and when Lewis needed their help to get his little business going, they were happy to oblige.

Together, Lewis and Cravath planned a demonstration intended to lure investors to Lewis's company, MRTS. Lewis would set up a presentation about cellular technology, and Cravath would invite some of his more well-to-do business friends. Then, the *piece de resistance*: Lewis's new friends at Motorola agreed to lend him one of their "million-dollar phones" to use in a product demonstration. This was a true coup: Hardly anyone in America had seen these handheld phones before; if ever there were a way to entice a reluctant investor, it was by showing off this futuristic portable phone.

Lewis reserved a conference room in the Washington Hilton (which had assumed the unfortunate nickname "Hinckley Hilton" following John Hinckley's assassination attempt on President Ronald Reagan there just a few months earlier—an event that drew plenty of remarks from those at the presentation). Lewis stationed a car just outside the hotel, so potential investors could place a cell phone call from a car phone (using the experimental cellular system then running in Washington), and inside the building, he proudly showed the awed money-men how to call home on the "Brick."

But as Cravath tried to close on an investment commitment from his attendees, he was dismayed to find that the wealthiest among them showed the least interest in investing—he was woefully short of MRTS's modest cash goal. But Lewis's infectious enthusiasm had succeeded in making one thorough convert: In the end, Cravath himself and a friend of his named Bill Welch put up the cash to keep Lewis's dream alive. With Cravath's funding and encouragement, little MRTS could now expand its reach beyond Washington to new markets. And under Cravath's tutelage, Lewis began marketing his expertise to others, making MRTS into the nation's first cellular application services firm—a new concept that would soon be plagiarized in big and unexpected ways by a host of copycats.

Flush with Cravath's capital, Lewis and his team of army buddies redoubled their efforts to get the applications finished in time. By the time the June 7 deadline rolled around, MRTS had stakes in applications for Miami and Tampa (traded for applications services) to go along with its own applications in Washington-Baltimore. Lewis's long-held dream of running a cell phone system was now one step closer to reality.

At last, the months of preparation came to an end. Across the country, teams of engineers, lawyers, printers, clerical workers and executives breathed a collective sigh of relief as their applications were trucked, flown, driven or otherwise delivered to Washington. The filing meant an ever-so-slight reprieve from the schedule of racing to prepare applications—at least until the Round II deadline was announced.

But for the FCC, the hectic days were only just beginning.

THE VOICE COMING THROUGH TOM GUTIERREZ'S phone was frantic. It was the Office of the Secretary of the FCC calling, and there was a problem on the second floor of the FCC's headquarters on the afternoon of June 7, 1982. Where, the caller wanted to know, were they supposed to put all the boxes of documents that people were carting into the office?

All afternoon, delivery couriers and law clerks had pulled up to the blocky edifice at Nineteenth and M Streets, in the heart of Washington's business district, to deliver heavy boxes crammed full of three-ring binders. At first the staff stacked them along the wall, but as the number grew the pile spread to the middle of the floor and then to any available surface in the Secretary's office. By late afternoon there was no room even to wiggle— and still the boxes kept coming.

"Take them up to the sixth floor," responded Gutierrez, an affable young staff attorney with a smart, closely trimmed beard and wire-rimmed glasses. At thirty-one, Gutierrez was a well-liked, capable lawyer, an amiable red-head whose quiet manner lent an air of calm and competency to the office. He knew this day marked the beginning of what would be a hectic time for the FCC's Mobile Services Division staff, so in the days leading up to the fil-ing deadline he'd put together a little office pool to lighten the mood: Who-ever guessed closest to the number of applications filed in Round I would get to take a day off work. And not just any day off—the winner would spend a day with Gutierrez on his 16-foot fishing boat, angling for croakers and sea trout on nearby Chesapeake Bay.

As it happened, some of the staffers' guesses weren't too far off. By the close of business, 190 applications had been filed for the first thirty markets, and the winning guess in Gutierrez's pool was 194. Some had guessed even higher, expecting 300 applications or more: These were licenses for Amer-ica's thirty largest cities, after all, and markets such as Chicago, L.A. and New York City were much more likely to yield large numbers of cell phone customers—and therefore bigger profits—than the smaller cities and towns. One unnamed FCC official told Communications Daily the staff had "heard rumors that as many as seventy-five would apply for Los Angeles."

But if they weren't surprised by the number of applications, Gutierrez and the rest of the staff were flabbergasted at how voluminous those appli-cations were. There were attachments and addenda of all sorts—maps and charts and graphs and reams of appendices, all carefully indexed into cus-tom color-printed binders. In an effort to get any kind of advantage in the upcoming comparative hearings, the applicants had done whatever they could to try and differentiate their applications. "We looked at them and thought, 'This is overkill,'" remembers Gutierrez.

One could hardly blame the applicants for that—the FCC's rules governing the applications were, in one FCC official's understated judgment, "a little vaguer than perhaps they should have been," so no one wanted to risk leaving something out. Having taken more than a decade to settle on the rules for the cellular spectrum giveaway, the FCC never did come up with specific guidelines for how exactly it planned to choose a winning application.

Not knowing what was expected of them, applicants threw everything at the wall in the hopes that something would stick. Longer, more detailed analyses were considered better than shorter, more concise ones. Colored maps were preferable to black and white. When everything was put together, a single copy of a single application, with all the related addenda, could fill three or more three-inch binders—more than a half-foot stack of paper. And the FCC had requested five copies of each application.

The applications were essentially carefully prepared works of speculative fiction. Applicants had no way of knowing how many people might sign up for cell phone service, what kind of prices the market would bear, or how many cell towers they'd need to serve as-yet-unknown demand. The dirty little secret was that everyone was guessing about almost everything—and frequently guessing very badly.

Though it wasn't clear at the time whether the cell phone industry would prove to be anything but a fancy technological bust, some of these early applicants had spent upwards of $300,000 per application. And now the boxed-up results were clogging the FCC's rooms and hallways.

When the FCC's doors closed at 5:30 P.M., staffers took stock of what they'd received. A total of eighty-five companies had filed 190 applications in Round I: Fifty-five applications for the wireline block of spectrum and 135 for the nonwireline block.

Some of the markets had only one wireline applicant (usually AT&T or GTE), but every market had multiple nonwireline applicants—and surprisingly, the smaller, less valuable markets tended to have more of them. Tampa, for example, had eleven nonwireline applicants, while the blue-chip Boston and Chicago markets each had only two. This was odd—no one expected Tampa to be a more valuable market than Boston; why would there be so much more competition for it?

"If you had told me that Boston would have two filings," George Lindemann remarked later, "I would have laughed at you. . . But everyone was just saying, 'Where *aren't* people?'" In trying to avoid competition, the nonwirelines had applied in what they thought were the *least* attractive markets—but the trouble was, everyone had had the same idea.

Meanwhile, on the wireline side, the fate of each license was, for all practical purposes, already decided. The rules stated that only local phone companies operating within the geographic area designated for a particular market could apply; in some markets, only one company met the qualification, so it would receive the wireline license outright. In other markets, several phone companies' coverage areas overlapped, so these applicants were expected to go to comparative hearings, just like the nonwirelines. But here the phone companies wrote their own rules.

These companies were brethren of a sort—they were all in the same business, they were acquainted with each other, and none had ever suffered the indignity of having to compete for business, because they were all government-protected monopolies. Their mossback executives shared one other common value—awe at the power of AT&T and, to a lesser degree, GTE. So, few observers were surprised when the telephone companies decided to join ranks, agreeing simply to share the licenses.

On June 8, the day following the Round I filings, AT&T and GTE announced that they and the rest of the wireline applicants had agreed to split ownership of the top thirty markets. The two wireline heavyweights had successfully intimidated scores of smaller independent telephone companies, convincing them that they could never assemble the capital or expertise needed to launch these new cell phone businesses. If the small companies would just stand aside, AT&T and GTE declared, they would graciously condescend to share minority interests in the contested markets. But AT&T and GTE would, of course, be in charge—and they would bill their minority partners for the service.

The June 8 press release announced that AT&T would run twenty-three of the thirty wireline cellular systems, and GTE would run seven (AT&T would, of course, run its systems only temporarily; following the January 1984 divestiture, its systems would be handed over to the independent RBOCs). It was clear that the wirelines—who had been quietly meeting and negotiating for months—had applied with the expectation of settling: Though AT&T applied in twenty-nine of the top thirty markets—only one fewer than Graphic Scanning—it submitted a mere 57,600 pages in its applications. By contrast, Graphic, which expected to face fierce competition in the comparative hearings, had submitted 1.5 million pages.

By agreeing to these partnerships, the wireline applicants would avoid the time-consuming comparative hearings, allow the FCC to award their licenses more quickly, and get a head start in marketing—by as much as a year or more—on the nonwireline side, which would be mired in competition for the licenses.

The value of this "wireline headstart" couldn't be overstated. When new technologies are launched, it often happens that the first customers—the early adopters—are generally the heaviest users. They are also the easiest—and therefore cheapest—customers to entice. The first system to get on the air in any particular cellular market could expect to snag 70 percent or more of the early adopter prospects. Settling was a perfect end-around maneuver by the telephone companies, and one that soon had the nonwirelines shrieking in objection.

MCI, with its long and well-documented antipathy toward AT&T, led the charge. "They may think the Federal Communications Commission has given them immunity from the antitrust laws, but they're going to find out differently," spluttered Bill McGowan to the *New York Times*. "This is so clearly preemptive of the market that no court will stand for it." The irony of handing AT&T's local phone companies a huge competitive advantage was not lost on the FCC commissioners either, some of whom were reported to be deeply embarrassed at their part in the process. Others were ecstatic that the wirelines were settling: They were doing the FCC's work for it, deciding among themselves who would get the license in each city. Settling, in their minds, saved time and money; instead of protesting the wirelines' action, they encouraged the nonwireline applicants to do the same.

In the coming six months, the telephone companies would complete their settlements of all thirty top markets, clearing the way for the FCC to grant the construction permits needed to get their systems up and running. On the nonwireline side, that same six months would see the launching of a vicious paper war, as each applicant tried to convince the FCC that every other applicant was for some reason not qualified to hold a cellular license. The worst-case scenario was set to come true: Instead of getting cell phone systems going as soon as possible, the nonwirelines would be stuck in an ever-intensifying gridlock for months, if not years, to come.

Meanwhile, did anyone besides the applicants and the equipment makers care? The short answer in 1982 was: not really. Though the cellular battle was just beginning to rage in the hallways of the FCC, it elicited little more than snores from the rest of the country.

5

THE ROUNDS AND THE FURY

IN A NONDESCRIPT, MIDDLE-AMERICAN LIVING ROOM, a woman surrounded by family members shouts into a telephone. "Hello, Uncle Ralph! Uncle Ralph, long distance from California! We'll talk fast; this call is expensive. . . !"

The scene is taking place on television: It's a commercial for AT&T. Seated on a couch, watching intently, is a spindly limbed, leathery creature with a heart-shaped head. E.T., the Extraterrestrial, turns his attention slowly from the TV commercial to the telephone in the living room, gradually understanding that it's a device that can be used to communicate over long distances. This scene, in Steven Spielberg's blockbuster 1982 film, is the precursor to one of the most famous lines in movie history. A few moments later, the alien points his finger skyward and utters the immortal phrase, "E.T. phone home."

Soon enough, E.T. begins to construct his own "phone"—out of odds and ends such as bobby pins, a folding umbrella, a record player and a coat hanger. In 1982, the year *E.T.* was released, most Americans were more familiar with this ersatz intergalactic transmitter than they were with the almost completely unknown communicators known as cellular phones. There might have been great excitement among applicants, equipment manufacturers and communications lawyers (who stood to make a bundle in the upcoming comparative hearings)—but the rest of the country didn't know, or didn't much care, about the new technology.

America in the early 1980s was a relative technological backwater compared to the tech-savvy nation of today. IBM introduced its first PC in 1981, a development noted by almost no one except technogeeks. Fax machines, printing fitfully on unwieldy rolls of thermal paper, were just finding their way into offices. Basic telephone-answering machines were still considered a luxury rather than a necessity. There was no voice mail, no commercial Internet, no e-mail. Many American homes still had rotary phones, and most of those were rented from AT&T.

Thanks to the technology-fueled boom in the U.S. economy throughout the 1990s, it's difficult to remember now that in the beginning of the '80s, America was struggling to break out of a long period of recession. Ronald Reagan's election as president in 1980 was a direct response to the malaise—economic and otherwise—that befell the country during Gerald Ford's and Jimmy Carter's terms in office. By 1982, Americans had spent years enduring inflation, high unemployment and a waning of American power and influence abroad.

In this atmosphere, a car phone seemed frivolous, a pretentious waste of money. Who in their right mind couldn't wait until they got to the office or home to make a call? In fact, when the FCC had earlier debated its first cellular plans, Commissioner Robert E. Lee had opposed a large allocation of radio spectrum, calling it a "frivolous use" of the public airwaves to provide "each automobile owner another status symbol—a telephone for the family car." Was it really so desperately important to be in touch that someone needed to have a phone at their side all the time? "It's not going to be something you and I put in the car to call home and say we're on the way home for dinner," commented one FCC official to the *Washington Post* at the time. The only potential users, it seemed, were people whose jobs kept them in their cars much of the day—contractors, for example, or repairmen. And even for them, the phones and rates were exorbitant—could these phones possibly be useful enough to justify their cost?

Around the time of the Round I filing, AT&T offered its estimate of what cellular service would cost: $2,000 to purchase a car phone, plus about $100 a month for the service. Some industry analysts predicted monthly costs of up to $150 a month—a princely sum in an era when the average annual household income was slightly less than $19,000. It seemed likely that the cell phone industry would face a common emerging-industry conundrum: Costs wouldn't go down significantly until there was a critical mass of users—but people would be reluctant to sign up for service until the cost went down.

How long would it take for cellular to catch on—assuming it would at all? One marketing survey commissioned by a Cleveland applicant offered a pessimistic outlook on that question.

Researchers polled 400 business respondents chosen randomly within the Cleveland area, posing a variety of questions on potential cell phone usage. To the question of how interested they were in mobile-phone service "at a reasonable price," 60 percent of respondents said they were "not interested at all," easily overwhelming the second-place answer, 23 percent for "somewhat interested." Those who were "very interested" and "not too interested" were split evenly, at a mere 8 percent each.

More interesting were the reasons why that 60 percent was "not interested at all" in having a mobile phone: In a follow-up question, 92 percent of those respondents said they had "no need for one." By contrast, only 14 percent of respondents said they believed "it would be too expensive." (The total exceeds 100 percent because respondents were allowed to choose more than one reason.)

Shades of William Orton! When he uttered his immortally obtuse phrase, "What use could this company make of an electric toy?" about the telephone, he betrayed his own lack of imagination about convenience and human nature. Yes, it was true that people lived just fine without telephones for most of human history. Technically speaking, no one really needed one. But once people started using them, no one wanted to be without one—and what Orton dubbed a "toy" quickly became a tool. The same would happen with cell phones, but almost nobody understood that yet.

The gamblers in Round I were betting millions that cell phones would follow the same pattern. Yes, they would be expensive in the beginning, but cell phones—especially the handheld kind that Motorola was demonstrating—still offered something completely new: Dialing a telephone number now meant connecting with a *person* rather than a *place*.

Craig McCaw, who would ultimately gain almost as much fame for his odd, oblique way of looking at things as he would for the success of his company, expanded on this view in an interview with the American Academy of Achievement. Wireline-telephone technology, he said, "makes absolutely no sense. It is machines dominating human beings. The idea that people went to a small cubicle, a six-by-ten office, and sat there all day at the end of a six-foot cord, was anathema to me." With regular telephones, McCaw believed, "[P]eople were being subjugated needlessly to 1890's technology."

John Stanton's projections (which, unlike most applicants' projections, were based on real-world usage of mobile phones in the largely ignored experimental systems) made a good mathematical argument for the ultimate success of cellular, but Craig McCaw's holistic, intuitive view captured the technology's simple appeal: People are nomadic and want to be free, and this tool would help free them.

WHAT WAS DECIDEDLY *NOT* SIMPLE, though, was getting these wonderfully liberating tools to the masses—especially for the nonwirelines. Now that the Round I applications had been filed, they were, theoretically, a step closer to getting the systems up and running. In reality, the filing day marked the beginning of thorny legal entanglements that threatened to hold the non-wirelines up indefinitely.

One avalanche of paper had already buried the FCC; now another was on the way. When the Round I applications were filed, they were placed on "public notice," allowing each applicant to look at their competitors' filings. And this was not merely for the sake of politeness: The FCC then gave applicants forty-five days to file "petitions to deny"—legal arguments explaining why a certain competitor should be denied the license in question.

If the FCC thought the Round I combatants would approach this in a gentlemanly way, it was wrong. Soon inch-thick files of petitions to deny were flying like "so much confetti" (in the words of one applicant). Everybody tried to get everybody else booted out of the running. And why shouldn't they? There was no penalty for filing a petition to deny that failed, and the upside to filing a successful one was knocking out a competitor for a market.

Not surprisingly, Graphic Scanning was a magnet for petitions: By Labor Day, other applicants had filed nearly 100 petitions to deny against the company. But it was all part of the game, and true to Barry Yampol's indifference to public opinion, the company blithely accepted the challenges and fired back petitions of its own.

Ed Taptich, one of Graphic's lawyers, later described the frenzy of filings that followed: "You had a reply round of exhibits which said, 'Not only are we right because we told you all this stuff, but these guys are out of their minds for the following foot of reasons: Their engineering is bad, their economics faulty, their management structure isn't effective.' You name it. 'Their sister owns ten thousand shares of Whitewater.' Whatever was thought might be pertinent." What was meant to be a serious process quickly devolved into a war of minutiae.

Larry Movshin, Taptich's fellow attorney at McKenna, Wilkinson and Kittner, joined the Graphic team the day after the Round I filings. He and Taptich quickly assembled a team of associates to work on the petitions and comparative hearings. "We set up the entire fourth floor as our cellular war room," remembers Movshin, a diligent young lawyer who would watch his weight balloon as he spent more and more hours fighting Graphic's wars at the office. "And from June through the end of that summer, we had a team of lawyers who were either filing petitions to deny. . . preparing our own amendments, responding to petitions to deny, opposing other people's responses to ours, replying. It was just an incredible mess. . . . I billed three thousand hours in that span of twelve months," Movshin says—a figure that dwarfs the standard 1,800 annual billable hours for an average attorney. "We were all working that kind of crazy hours. Seventy-hour weeks were the norm."

Graphic was an obvious target for petitions to deny—and not only because of its having applied in all thirty markets. "Our bank financing was somewhat unique," admits Movshin, "in that it was based on internal financing with guarantees as opposed to specific bank loans. . . We were attacked on our engineering, which turned out was somewhat shaky." Graphic utilized a different number of cells in its plan than other applicants did, which "immediately made us subject to petitions to deny on the basis of 'the system wouldn't work.'"

But the biggest objection other applicants had to Graphic Scanning was that it was suspected of having cheated in an earlier spectrum giveaway. In 1981, when the FCC took applications to win spectrum licenses for low-band paging CEO Barry Yampol stacked the deck in Graphic's favor by creating four straw man companies to apply for the licenses. Though they were theoretically independent companies, each had a series of one-sided construction and management contracts that would ensure Graphic played a substantial or controlling role in any paging systems they set up. And Graphic would, of course, collect the majority of any revenue generated. This was clearly in violation of the FCC's "one company, one application" rule—and though the commission didn't realize it, it foreshadowed similar violations that would come to plague the cellular spectrum giveaway.

In the clubby world of paging operators, which historically had been a cozy collection of mom-and-pop local operators and family fiefdoms, Yampol's cutthroat tactics were viewed as a threat not only to businesses but to a way of life. So when an enterprising young paging entrepreneur named George Perrin discovered Yampol's chicanery, it took him no time to amass an industry-wide coalition against Graphic.

Alerted by Perrin, the FCC initiated an investigation (the so-called ASD investigation, named after one of the four companies). If it found that

Graphic was in fact the real party-in-interest behind the companies, it could strip Graphic of all its spectrum licenses, and all its applications for licenses—a move that would destroy the company. Yampol's telecom empire was balanced on a huge pile of debt, and Graphic's bondholders and institutional stockholders looked to the company's spectrum licenses as the safety net that ultimately secured their investments. Equally important was the fact that if those licenses were suddenly stripped from the company, there would be little left to support the empire—radio-based services accounted for 57 percent of Graphic's revenues and an even larger share of its profits in 1982. Without the lifeblood of cash flow from paging, Graphic would stumble into default and certain bankruptcy within a matter of months.

Driven by greed, Yampol had wagered his empire for a relatively unimportant slice of spectrum—low-band paging licenses that might end up worth a mere few hundred thousand dollars. On the other hand, once Graphic applied for every one of the top ninety cellular markets, as it planned to do, Yampol would be sitting on hundreds of millions of dollars worth of potential cellular assets—and it could all be taken from him with the stroke of the FCC's pen. One McCaw executive summed it up neatly: "He had done a very, very, very stupid thing and really had been quite deceptive to the FCC, over something that turned out to be piss-poor worthless: narrow-band paging." There was something supremely ironic in the fact that Yampol, who valued spectrum above all else, had been so cavalier about putting his ownership of it in jeopardy.

But it was not only Graphic Scanning (soon nicknamed "Graphic Scamming" by angry competitors) who would suffer the consequences of the ASD scandal. The entire nonwireline side of the new cell phone industry would suffer as well, for reasons that were not immediately apparent.

In the fall of 1982, the FCC was just getting around to reviewing the mass of applications and petitions that had been filed; the comparative hearings wouldn't come until that was finished, and depending on how many applicants there were in each market, the hearings could take months. To top if off, an FCC judge's decision to award a license could be—and in most cases, almost certainly would be—appealed, drawing out the process even more.

Adding to the confusion was the fact that Graphic's permission to hold FCC licenses was now in doubt. If Graphic were to win a comparative hearing, it could only be awarded the license if it were exonerated in the ASD investigation, which could go on for years. During that time the wireline systems would be free to rake in customers and revenues, while the non-wirelines sat stymied on the sidelines.

There was another option for the nonwireline applicants, but it was only marginally less attractive than fighting long, expensive battles: They could follow the wirelines' lead and agree to share ownership of licenses. There were two ways of doing this: On the one hand, two or more applicants could enter into a "partial settlement" of a particular market, agreeing to join forces against other applicants in hopes that their shared expertise and magnified financial strength would give them the upper hand in the comparative hearing. Or, on the other hand, all the applicants of a given market could settle, as the wireline companies had done, and simply agree to share the license in a "full settlement," thereby sidestepping the FCC's lengthy, expensive comparative hearings altogether.

Settling was problematic on several levels. First, most applicants believed they somehow had the upper hand and were destined to win in comparative hearings, either outright or by successfully petitioning to deny their competitors the licenses. "When you're in comparative hearings, everybody thinks they've got the winning applications, right?" remembers MCI's Bluestein. "You can't tell somebody they've got an ugly baby."

Second, these applicants were businesspeople, combative capitalists and instinctive competitors for whom conceding an equal share to an adversary is heresy. Proud, fiercely independent entrepreneurs like George Lindemann and John Kluge had built their own empires; they had no interest in any partnership they couldn't control.

And third, while a one- or two-party partial settlement might enhance an applicant's odds, it did little to accelerate the lengthy litigation process: Only a "full market settlement" could do that. But a full settlement in any market could only be accomplished by cutting a deal with industry pariah "Graphic Scamming." No one wanted to do a deal with Graphic, because no one knew what would happen if Graphic were subsequently declared ineligible to hold licenses.

It was ironic: Graphic was the only applicant with an FCC threat hanging over its head, and it was also the only one to apply in all thirty markets. The one man no one wanted to sit down and negotiate with was the one man they couldn't avoid: Barry Yampol.

A clash in Dallas perfectly illustrated how the rampant animus toward Yampol could hold the industry up for everyone. George Perrin had come to the meeting to negotiate on behalf of a company called CellNet. Perrin arrived early and greeted each person who walked through the door, proffering his hand and making polite small talk while simultaneously sizing them up.

Then Graphic's Bill Wheatley walked in. Perrin all but ignored Wheatley, choosing to wait until everyone had taken their seats before making any fuss. With the meeting ready to begin, Perrin stood, announced he would not participate in any settlement involving Graphic Scanning, and then walked out the door, leaving a shocked silence in his wake. Without Perrin's participation, there was no chance of reaching a full settlement; the rest of the discouraged executives soon left the meeting, resigned to suffering through the lengthy comparative hearing process.

The curious thing about the industry-wide disdain for Graphic was that it wasn't aimed solely at the company; it was aimed equally at Yampol himself. "[Yampol] was so terribly assertive and intolerant," remembers Ed Taptich, "that it was very easy for other people to bristle and to react negatively." So Yampol enlisted the help of junior Graphic executive Richard J. Sherwin to be his envoy in the industry.

Sherwin, an electrical engineer and ex-IBM account manager, was a Brooklyn native with a taste for gold jewelry, dirty jokes and stiff drinks. With his dark, slicked-back hair and his ebulliently profane eruptions, he had the air of an oddly jocular gangster.

In nearly every way, he was the antithesis of Yampol. Yampol was introverted and secretive; Sherwin was disarmingly candid and embarrassingly public. Yampol had a slithery air of perpetual disingenuousness; Sherwin was scrupulously honest. "Dick says everything he thinks," says Larry Movshin. "He doesn't have a dishonest bone in his body. At times, you just wanted to tell him to stop talking, because he was so nice he would give the store away if you didn't finally say, 'No, no, Dick. We don't need to. We already won that point.' His exact opposite was Barry Yampol, who wouldn't give anything away."

Sherwin's style was crude and abrasive; he loved to shout and his utterances were more often than not peppered with profanity. But even in this he found ways to endear himself to others: He was always happy to see himself as the butt of his own locker-room humor. "Everyone would call him an asshole, and it's almost a term of endearment for Sherwin," remembers Bluestein. "He was almost lovable for being such a jerk."

Even the indignant Perrin was swayed. "Had it not been for the fact that we all liked Dick, we'd have pissed all over the Graphic guys all day long," he remembers. "You can't take much of him, but I like him."

With Sherwin in the role of peacemaker, and with the clock ticking away as the wirelines built out their systems and prepared their marketing materials, the nonwireline applicants got down to the business of settling. Though they understood it was the expedient thing to do, most participants still approached the idea cautiously, circling each other like wary fighting cocks.

The break in the anti-Graphic dam came from an unexpected source: Western Union. An outsider (even, in some ways, at his own company), Jim Ragan felt no loyalty to the paging brethren that made up much of the Round I applicants' pool. He had no pent-up animosity toward Yampol and no problem doing business with him; a pragmatic, no-nonsense capitalist, Ragan just wanted to get on with the business.

Indianapolis was the first market settled, followed closely by Buffalo. Under Ragan's guidance, lawyers and executives from the three applicants—Western Union, Graphic Scanning and Associated Communications—sat down together over a two-week period and hammered out the business equivalent of a Mexican standoff. The negotiations were tense, lengthy, and at times heated, but in the end it was clear to all that there was only one way to structure the settlement: by creating a general partnership. "The whole notion of settling," remembers Movshin, who wrote the agreement, "was that three equal partners had so much distrust for each other that you would figure out a way that nothing bad could ever be done to any one of them." Each partner would have an equal vote, and "no one could do anything without the other two agreeing. You couldn't go to the bathroom without everyone saying okay," says Movshin.

The agreement, less than fifty pages long, would become the blueprint for dozens of nonwireline settlements that would take place across the United States. While each iteration would contain its own subtle permutations, all traced their evolutionary roots, like strands of DNA, to Movshin's Indianapolis document. For the first time—but by far not the last—Graphic Scanning was welcomed into a partnership.

But the initial response to the Indianapolis and Buffalo settlements was hardly one of acclimation. Industry reaction, according to Western Union's Michael Sullivan, was swift and negative: "'Why are you going to bed with this dirty fellow?'" But the other two partners had covered their bases: The agreement contained an "ASD contingency" clause stipulating that Graphic's participation in the partnership was contingent on the FCC's allowing it to hold FCC licenses.

Now that Graphic had been included in a settlement, it was as though a spell had been broken. Similar settlements quickly followed, and slowly the nonwireline side tried to catch up to the wirelines, which would soon begin receiving their FCC construction permits, the next step in getting systems up and running. But unlike the wireline side, which had arranged quick mass settlements for all markets, the nonwirelines were forced to approach settling piecemeal, market by agonizing market.

The agony was compounded by the fact that many of the settlements went far less smoothly than Indianapolis had. In Cleveland, for example, MCI opened the bargaining with the kind of shortsighted bullying that would draw scorn from fellow applicants and ultimately derail the company's cellular push. Rather than agreeing to split the license into equal parts, MCI sought to claim the upper hand: MCI's cellular chief, Jerry Taylor, proposed that his company build the system, run it, and collect 25 percent of the revenue as a management fee. Dick Sherwin was appalled. "What, are you out of your mind?" he recalls asking Taylor.

"MCI had this thing," recalls Sherwin with a laugh, "They were it: 'Nobody is smarter than MCI.' So Jerry Taylor is sitting there with his cigar. He always had a cigar in his mouth, and he said, 'I'm from MCI, man, I know how to do this.'" Sherwin and CCI's George Blumenthal refused to agree to MCI's plan, and negotiations for the market dragged on, frustrating all sides, until MCI finally gave in months later.

Meanwhile, there was another pressing matter to attend to: The Round II filing date, which had been set for November 8, was fast approaching.

―――――――――――

IN A CAVERNOUS WAREHOUSE IN THE NEW JERSEY SUBURBS, Dick Sherwin was indulging in one of his favorite activities: shouting. Sherwin had rented the warehouse in downtown Englewood, down the street from Graphic's offices and just across the Hudson River from New York City, and had filled it with Graphic Scanning employees, at whom he now was bellowing.

"Page forty-seven ends with the word 'adjacent'; page forty-eight begins with the word 'market.' Flip!" As Sherwin roared, the forty-five or so employees gathered in the warehouse dutifully flipped their pages.

Sherwin had devised this applications assembly line just a few days before the Round II filing. Once again, Graphic was applying in all thirty available markets, and Sherwin wanted to avoid the rush and mess of the first round. Then, there had been such a hurry to get everything finished the applications came out sloppy, with missing and misplaced pages; Sherwin was determined that this round of applications would look sharper. Also, thanks to new FCC rules, Graphic had to make a huge number of copies—forty or so—of each application, to present to the FCC and any competing applicants.

Seated at one of the rows of tables was Movshin. Graphic needed every available body to help put together these thousands of pages, so Movshin had made the trek up from Washington, leaving Ed Taptich there to handle the ongoing Round I paper war at the FCC. "We did thirty markets in, like, three days in the warehouse, with every available body working twelve hours going through that process," remembers Movshin, "then we'd go out and get drunk and then we'd wake up the next day [and do it again]." The Graphic applications machine was in full gear.

—————

ON THE OTHER SIDE OF THE COUNTRY, McCaw was preparing applications as well. McCaw Cellular—a newly incorporated company with John Stanton as employee number one (he'd accepted a full-time position and quit Ernst & Whinney)—was in the process of making a rare strategic mistake. The smarter companies were now emulating Graphic, spending money on quantity rather than quality—filing as many applications as they could without worrying too much about how competitive they would be. Meanwhile, the McCaw team stubbornly plowed ahead with complex, detailed, finely tuned applications designed to win at comparative hearings.

There was a growing belief in the fledgling industry that applications in the later rounds would never go to comparative hearing, for one of two reasons. Either the nonwireline side would agree to settle their markets, or the FCC would give up on comparative hearings and decide to lottery off cellular licenses. Either way, the quality of the applications would be a moot point.

The idea of using a lottery to assign cellular licenses was hugely controversial from the moment rumors starting floating that the FCC was considering it. To some, it made perfect sense: All the applicants so far were essentially qualified to run cellular systems; why spend all this time and money duking it out in comparative hearings? Why not just leave it to the luck of the draw? But others saw the lottery as a travesty, a flippant way to make critical decisions on a valuable new public utility.

As early as September 1982, the FCC commissioners weighed in on the issue. At a public debate on September 23, Commissioner Joseph Fogarty declared, "Cellular radio isn't a prime candidate—it's not a candidate at all, for lottery. I totally oppose applying lottery to this telephone service." Commissioner Abbott Washburn chimed in, "It would be so much easier. . . to leave it to the turn of the wheel. But it isn't fair to change the ground rules at this point." The FCC had spent fourteen years debating its cellular rules, after all; could it really just turn around and change them so drastically after a mere three months in action?

Two weeks later, the extent of disagreement among the commissioners became clear when one of them lashed out on a panel discussion. After Commissioner Anne Jones declared her support for a cellular lottery, Commissioner Fogarty responded angrily, "She is just wrong on this. This is a valuable service needed by the public and it shouldn't be decided on a roll of the dice." It wasn't the first time Fogarty and Jones had clashed—he had supported the wireline set-aside in all markets, which she opposed—and it was indicative of deep rifts in the FCC.

The buzz about possible lotteries was still just a whisper at this point, but it was becoming clear to just about everyone that the current system would have to be changed.

———

STUPIDLY, THE FCC THOUGHT the worst might be over.

When the mountains of Round I applications had arrived at FCC headquarters on June 7, most staffers believed they were seeing the most applications likely to be submitted for any round. On the surface, this made sense: Big markets meant more customers and less risk, so there would naturally be more competition for their licenses. "My understanding and the understanding of the people in the commission," remembers former staffer Tom Gutierrez, "was that [cellular] would be a niche issue. We all missed the boat big-time. And 99 percent of the people on the outside missed it too. We didn't think there'd be much demand for licenses in markets beyond the top thirty." Who would want to spend the money to build a cell phone system for Allentown, Pennsylvania, after all?

But when the Round II filing date rolled around, the FCC was in for another surprise. If staffers had been shocked at the two semitrailers Graphic had rented for the Round I filing, they were amazed to look out their windows on November 8 and see a line of trucks on the street below. All day long, boxes and boxes of three-ring binders were once again trucked up the elevators on dollies and stacked shoulder-high in the Secretary's office, the hallways and anywhere else they could go.

Round II brought in nearly twice as many applications as Round I: three hundred fifty-three of them, virtually all from nonwireline applicants. Two days later, *Communications Daily* reported that it still couldn't print the full list of applicants, because the FCC staffers who were spending marathon hours checking in the applications had become so exhausted that their writing was illegible.

With an average of twelve applications per market, the paper war was now about to increase geometrically. More applications, more petitions to deny, more responses to petitions—the FCC's carefully planned-out process was threatening to degenerate into a farce.

6

THE WHEELING AND DEALING BEGINS

THROUGH THE WINTER OF 1984–85, companies across the country reluctantly engaged in an odd tango: They tried to form settlement partnerships while simultaneously fighting each other in comparative hearings. As the wirelines steadily built out their systems, the nonwirelines watched with frustration and fatigue as their resources drained away.

And that wasn't all. On March 8, 1985, Round III applications—for the sixty-first to the ninetieth-largest cities—would be due. For most of those already in the race, that meant devoting ever-scarcer resources to working up yet more applications.

Thanks to Graphic's much-disparaged (and envied) decision to file in all sixty markets in rounds I and II, many companies increased the number of markets they applied in. Why not get as many chances as possible? If Graphic was right, the FCC might well ignore whether an applicant really had the financial means to construct multiple systems. And dozens of new companies decided to join in the race as well, encouraged by reports in the business press that nontelecommunications companies (such as the Washington Post Company) and small-time entrepreneurs (such as Peter Lewis) were filing for the licenses.

The result: A bruising 567 applications were trucked into the FCC's headquarters on March 8, 1983. Officials locked the door at exactly 5:30 P.M., ignoring the pleas of the few panicked latecomers. This was now getting ridiculous: Shelves at the FCC creaked under the weight of the boxes, and rooms were literally crammed so full that no one could get into them. And these were just the applications—what would happen when all these applicants filed petitions against each other? Who in the world would have time to sort through this mountain of paper, much less make intelligent decisions about which applications were superior to the others? Clearly, things were not working out as the FCC had planned. Even assuming the FCC had enough staff to wade through all these applications quickly (which it didn't), there was still no good way for the administrative law judges to decide which applicant should receive each license.

"Everybody filed essentially the same thing," remembers then-FCC staff attorney Michael D. Sullivan (no relation to the Michael Sullivan of Western Union). "'Well, we'll do exactly what our customers want, and we'll have low rates. We will have orderly expansion in response to demand.'" Why shouldn't they say that, after all—nobody had done this before, and nobody could prove them wrong.

Tension mounted among the applicants as the handful of FCC judges slogged their way through the morass of pleadings, counterpleadings, expert testimony and mind-numbingly complex exhibits. Adding to the difficulty was the fact that the judges were essentially long-lived federal staff attorneys, most of whom knew little or nothing about cellular technology or the new, faster-paced world of competitive telecommunications.

When initial comparative hearing decisions started coming in, a pattern slowly emerged. Faced with a host of complex, vaguely defined criteria, the FCC and its judges began opting for expediency, awarding licenses based more or less on a single metric: initial coverage area. Who had the biggest system? That's who would get the license.

There's something vaguely absurd but also quintessentially American in this decision: Size matters. And in many cases, it was just about the only thing that mattered—not the marketing studies, rate plans, expansion plans or the "public service attributes." "It's kind of stupid to grant one over another because the guy's got a square mile larger coverage," acknowledged Sullivan. "But, on the other hand, if you've got to pick one over another, what are you going to do it on?"

As the word of the judges' early decisions spread from the Washington lawyers to their clients across America, some applicants rushed to amend their pending applications and modify the new ones still on the assembly line. "Some people said, 'If the Commission wants big, we'll give them big, god damn it!'" remembers Tom Gutierrez. "Other people said, 'Clearly, they want genuine big, not big for bigness' sake; surely the Commission must understand the goal of this exercise is not to have the most circles on a map.'"

Most applicants on the nonwireline side were caught blindsided by the FCC's single-criterion trend. Many—including McCaw—were still struggling to put together the most impressive applications they could; providing elaborate "local presence" credentials and gold-plated financial qualifications; and anxiously following the letter of the comparative hearings rules. These people, not to put too fine a point on it, missed the boat entirely.

When the FCC shut its doors at the close of business on March 8, 1983, would-be cellular companies had locked in their chances to run America's ninety largest cities, from New York down to Charleston, South Carolina. These markets covered some 132 million people—over 60 percent of the 1980 U.S. population, and an even greater portion of the affluent consumers. As it had done with the top thirty markets, the wireline side settled its markets quickly and set about pressing the FCC for permits to construct systems. Among the nonwirelines, the contours of the battle were becoming clearer.

Graphic Scanning had applied in all ninety markets. George Lindemann's Metromobile had applied in sixty-four, MCI had applied in fifty-one, and Western Union—that slow-moving paragon of yesterday's technology—had applied (with partners) in an astonishing seventy-two. McCaw, on the other hand, was still reluctant to commit scarce cash to the yet-unproven business and played it safe, applying in only twenty-six of the ninety markets. In the spring of 1983, it looked for all the world like Graphic Scanning and Western Union were positioned to dominate the new cellular industry, going head-to-head with the remnants of AT&T's empire.

But when the wheeling and dealing heated up, all bets were off.

As some applicants would soon discover, filing in a particular market didn't necessarily mean you had as good a chance as everyone else to win it. As in any business environment, the cleverest negotiator or the coolest bluffer could end up with a better hand than he was initially dealt. Graphic Scanning's experience with poker expert John Kluge and his equally artful executives made that plain.

Thanks to fear of competition, only two nonwireline companies had applied for two of the biggest, most valuable Round I markets: Chicago and Boston. The ubiquitous Graphic was one, and the other was Metromedia.

The two companies couldn't have been more different. Metromedia was the exquisitely appointed Waldorf Towers suite; Graphic was the crumbling warehouse on the Jersey side of the Hudson River. Metromedia was affable, charming John Kluge; Graphic was arrogant, abrasive Barry Yampol. Metromedia was smooth-talking, impeccably tailored Stuart Subotnick; Graphic was crude, boisterous, flashy Dick Sherwin. And in their negotiations, Metromedia was shrewd; Graphic was clumsy.

Subotnick and Sherwin (who, coincidentally, had grown up in the same Brooklyn neighborhood, though they didn't know each other as kids) were in charge of their respective companies' negotiations. Settling seemed the prudent thing to do—with only Graphic and Metromedia as applicants in the two cities, they could reach an agreement reasonably quickly and start competing with the wireline cell phone companies. Two cities, two applicants in each—why not split them both fifty-fifty?

Subotnick took the lead, offering Graphic an equal share of the Boston license in return for a prompt settlement. "We'll get to Chicago next," he told Sherwin. "Maybe we'll use the same pattern." This looked like a good deal to Sherwin, not only in terms of sidestepping long comparative hearing battles, but also because it promised a crucial public relations boost at a time when Graphic desperately needed it. A willingness on the part of Kluge and Metromedia to partner with them would help strengthen Graphic's standing as someone other applicants could do business with.

The deal was announced on March 14, 1983: Boston was now the fourth complete nonwireline settlement (Indianapolis, Milwaukee and Buffalo were first), and the first for a top-tier market. With the settlement signed, Graphic and Metromedia could soon receive a construction permit and start building what would hopefully become a lucrative system.

Pleased to have a major market taken care of, Sherwin then turned his attention to Chicago. "Okay," he told Subotnick, "let's do it the same way." But here the diminutive tax lawyer turned the tables on Sherwin.

"Oh no," Subotnick blithely responded. "I think we're going to fight you in Chicago."

Metromedia's lawyers and engineers had offered Subotnick some valuable advice on the Boston and Chicago applications. The Boston application, they told him, was flawed—better to settle that market than risk losing in the comparative hearing. "Had they fought us in Boston," Subotnick said later, "they probably would have gotten the whole thing." But in Chicago, the experts advised, Metromedia had a superior application.

If Subotnick believed Metromedia had a better chance to win Chicago based solely on the applications, he was doubly heartened to see who the administrative law judge for Chicago was: Judge Thomas B. Fitzpatrick, who also at this time was presiding over Graphic's potentially crippling ASD case. After a relatively quick comparative hearing, Fitzpatrick ruled on August 13, 1983, that the Chicago license should go to Metromedia, based on his some-what odd reasoning that Graphic's system was overdesigned and too ex-pensive.

Judge Fitzpatrick's ruling was a two-fold travesty. First, it flew in the face of precedent: Graphic's system was much larger than Metromedia's, and yet it lost. Second, it failed to recognize the foresight of Yampol. Graphic had proposed more cell sites—four times as many as Metromedia, according to Yampol—because he, ahead of anyone else, anticipated that Motorola's handheld phones (which, due to their low power, required more cell sites than car phones) would become ubiquitous consumer products. But Judge Fiztpatrick was unconvinced by Yampol's visionary argument.

Enraged by Fitzpatrick's decision, Yampol filed an immediate appeal. Metromedia, anxious to get the license and to begin constructing the sys-tem, offered Graphic 15 percent of the system if Yampol would drop the ap-peal. Stubborn, angry and righteously indignant, Yampol refused; when the appeal was later dismissed, Graphic ended up with nothing in Chicago.

Two markets, two companies—and Metromedia ends up with all of one market and half of the other. Yampol was irate—but his ire was misdirected: Metromedia had simply outplayed Graphic, in a textbook example of supe-rior business savvy. Sherwin later acknowledged as much: "We got screwed on that. We screwed ourselves. . . Nobody was paying attention."

―――――――――

THOUGH MORE AND MORE COMPANIES with Round I applications were agree-ing to settle with Graphic, antipathy mounted in the industry, in the FCC and on Wall Street toward the firm's volatile president.

The FCC, for its part, was stuck in an untenable position. If it ruled against Graphic in the ASD matter and stripped the company's right to hold spectrum licenses, Graphic would certainly file appeals that could take years to sort out—leaving in doubt the ownership of every nonwireline cellular li-cense across America. But it was becoming apparent that the four paging companies in the ASD affair were indeed shell companies created by Yam-pol for Graphic's benefit—a maneuver so blatant and unethical that it would be impossible to overlook.

There was no way out of the conundrum—or was there? The ASD imbroglio and the galling scheme of filing in all cellular markets were widely seen to be the handiwork of Yampol alone, who ran the company without regard to the opinions of his executive team, board, public stockholders, analysts or anyone else. No one really had any problems with Dick Sherwin, Bill Wheatley or the company per se; it was Yampol—who had recently provoked yet another lawsuit when he single-handedly arranged a patently avaricious compensation plan for himself—who was the target of industry bile.

The fact that many colleagues and competitors didn't like him had never had much of an effect on Yampol. But there were a couple of other constituencies whose opinions mattered more—whether Yampol wanted to acknowledge it or not.

Because Graphic's stock was considered a high-tech stock—risky but capable of soaring returns—it attracted a number of growth-oriented investment managers. These managers were looking for big returns; these were not patient people, and they were growing increasingly nervous over Yampol's brinkmanship and the resulting risk to Graphic's stock price. In addition, much of Graphic's debt was funded by bondholders who were clients of the most powerful firm—and the most powerful man—in the American economic landscape: Drexel Burnham Lambert's Michael Milken.

In the go-go "greed is good" decade of the 1980s, Michael Milken reigned supreme. With his high-flying junk bond empire, Milken influenced the U.S. economy more pervasively than anyone since John D. Rockefeller. Many of Graphic's bondholders were Drexel clients, and Yampol's litany of high-profile embarrassments caused them no little dismay. With the ASD imbroglio, it looked as though Graphic might lose its spectrum and default, leaving the Drexel bondholders empty-handed; Milken couldn't afford to let that happen.

By early 1983, as the ASD prosecution piled up evidence of Yampol's perfidy, the stockholders and bondholders began to panic about Graphic's apparent impending implosion. With the FCC afraid of rendering justice in the ASD case, there was only one answer to the problem: Rather than killing the company that broke the rules, banish the man who devised the scheme. In the late winter of 1983, the phone calls flew fast and furious between Wall Street lawyers, the FCC, Drexel and Graphic. Yampol, came the consensus, would have to take the fall.

On March 16, 1983—just two days after the Boston settlement—Yampol resigned as CEO, and his handpicked board promptly named Bill Wheatley to take his place. Soon after, Yampol moved to Florida—a state, not coincidentally, with no income tax and plenty of opportunity to race motorboats.

Wheatley, the former CFO who had begged Yampol to apply for only a handful of markets back in Round I, was a taciturn, aloof executive. Neither brilliant like Yampol nor likeable like Sherwin and not a particularly strong leader, Wheatley was, by Yampol's warped logic, a perfect successor: someone he could manipulate without trouble or resistance from his remote perch in Florida.

Forgettable in appearance and possessed of a bland demeanor, Wheatley's most striking trait was his unaccountably inflated ego. Yampol had his critics, but even they had to acknowledge his uncommonly sharp business acumen. Wheatley, on the other hand, made his biggest impression on fellow industry executives in a slightly different way. At a meeting of the Boston cellular partnership, Graphic's partners and management executives sat astounded as Wheatley casually chewed tobacco and spit into a trash can during a crucial business presentation by a senior executive of a major advertising agency. With Wheatley's elevation to president, Graphic added a serious leadership vacuum to the list of its woes.

In the meantime, the debate about lotteries intensified. For Graphic, Yampol knew, lotteries would provide a huge advantage: By virtue of its ninety applications in the ninety top markets, Graphic would have an equal chance in every twirl of the lottery drum—or a seat at every bargaining table, if markets were to be settled.

Though FCC commissioner Joseph Fogarty had declared definitively that cellular was not a candidate for lottery, the idea had actually been under discussion at the FCC since the first avalanche of filings. "I think that after the very first filings, the FCC staff realized they had a problem," recalled Larry Movshin. "They didn't have a processing staff to do the petitions to deny, much less the litigation staff to actually litigate thirty markets. I mean, we [at Graphic] were understaffed with eleven people. They probably didn't have eleven people in their entire litigation department."

Commissioner Anne Jones, who clashed repeatedly with Fogarty over cellular issues, spouted the party line when she declared at an April 1983 trade show in Chicago that "[C]ellular is not being considered for possible licensing by lottery." But the crush of paperwork, the quagmire of comparative hearings and the increasing pressure to get the licenses out finally proved to be too much. In October 1983, the Commission issued a Notice of Proposed Rulemaking asking for public comment on a plan to distribute cellular licenses via lottery.

JERRY TAYLOR WAS PLEASED, but not thrilled, when he called Brian Thompson on July 29, 1983. "I've got some good news and some bad news," the head of MCI's cellular team told his colleague. "The good news is, we won. The bad news is, it's Pittsburgh."

At last, the administrative law judges had begun handing down their comparative hearing decisions. Now, in addition to the growing numbers of full market settlements, there was another way for the nonwirelines to start getting construction permits for their markets. Taylor was happy to have won Pittsburgh, though his happiness was tempered by the fact that the city of three rivers is extremely hilly, necessitating a large number of expensive cell sites in order to spread radio signals deep down to the valley roads. The terrain was so challenging, figured MCI's Whitey Bluestein, that building out Pittsburgh's system, which would serve 2.3 million potential customers, would be just as expensive as building out all of the Los Angeles system, which would serve 7.5 million.

It wasn't only MCI executives who reacted to winning licenses with such ambivalence. Though they'd spent thousands, if not millions, of dollars in the race to win licenses, the nonwireline competitors knew that constructing their systems would be expensive, time-consuming and terribly draining on their little cellular teams. They were anxious to get into the competition for customers against the well-funded wirelines, of course, but the operations part of cellular was very different from the license competition, and it could potentially end up being far less satisfying, especially if customers didn't materialize.

John Stanton remembers the call he got when McCaw won its first comparative hearing, for the Kansas City license, in the fall of 1983. "It was," he recalled, "like the end of the Robert Redford movie *The Candidate*: 'We won. What do we do now?' Because we were entirely geared toward this litigation process which, however much you talk about operations. . . it's not operating." It was time to start building the systems, but the race for licenses was still far from over.

———

THROUGH THE SUMMER AND FALL OF 1983, the public buzz over cell phones slowly built.

In October, the first commercial system went on-line in Chicago (with the first historic call going to Alexander Graham Bell's grandson in Germany), ushering in the cellular age in the United States. Early adopters— those on waiting lists for car phones, and the tech-savvy gadget lovers who are always in line for the latest new gizmo—couldn't wait to start using the new technology. Many, in fact, had bought their cell phones even before Ameritech had turned on its radio towers. In Chicago, Motorola had started marketing its phones in May, months before the system would be turned on; by midfall it had sold 3,000 units.

Before a single system was turned on, car rental companies and General Motors Corp. latched on to the new phones' appeal as high-end automobile accessories. Hertz, Budget and National all announced they would offer phones in some of their rental cars in the Chicago market.

GM was sufficiently convinced of the demand for car phones that it declared it would offer them as options in some of its 1984 models—the first automaker to do so. For $28,000—a $3,000 premium over the regular price—consumers could buy GM's ultimate status car: a Buick Riviera Coupe with a built-in cell phone. For a monthly fee of $45 plus per-minute charges, drivers could chat nonstop as they cruised along.

The moment of truth was finally approaching: Commercial systems were at last starting up, and soon it would be clear whether customers would come in a flood or a trickle.

———

THAT SAME FALL, a frustrated group in a crowded conference room coined the name that would come to define the industry for many Americans.

The group, representatives of the multiple partners in the recently settled Baltimore-Washington, D.C., nonwireline system, had gathered in a massive conference room at the venerable D.C. law firm of Covington & Burling to hear presentations suggesting possible trade names for their new cellular service. With companies as diverse as Metromedia, Graphic Scanning, the Washington Post Company, Harry Brock's Metrocall and Peter Lewis's little MRTS making up the partnership, it would be no easy task deciding on a name that suited everyone.

In the front of the room, well-dressed advertising reps made pitch after pitch for possible names—none of which, unfortunately, met with any spontaneous enthusiasm. As the meeting dragged on, the group around the table grew increasingly irritated and bored with the proceedings. George Duncan, Metromedia's paternal negotiator, suddenly couldn't take it anymore.

"I don't understand this," he snapped. "I don't know why we're here! Why don't we do something? Why don't we take a simple name like 'Cellular One'?" As though scripted, the room fell silent. Murmurs of "That's great" then rippled around the table, accompanied by vigorous nods of assent; at last, consensus!

Then Duncan, suddenly pleased with himself, piped up again. "Wait a minute, wait a minute!" he exclaimed. "I've got a better one!" Faces around the table turned toward him expectantly. "How about 'Cellular One *Plus*'?" The hooting began immediately. Consensus again: What a dog! The group eagerly adopted Duncan's initial suggestion, and Cellular One became the name of Washington, D.C.'s first cellular service.

It's very likely that no one outside the D.C. metropolitan area would ever have heard the name Cellular One if it hadn't been for a second decision the group made. In a brilliant stroke, the partnership decided to license the name, making it available to other nonwireline systems essentially for free. The wirelines, many with their RBOC roots and Bell names, had the automatic advantage of regional name recognition, an advantage that threatened to overpower the nonwirelines' scattershot marketing strategies. But following the decision to license the "Cellular One" name, it gradually spread across the country, eventually gaining even greater recognition than any one of the names of the giant AT&T offspring. Though there was in fact no national "Cellular One" company, soon the ubiquity of the name had the effect the nonwirelines hoped: Consumers knew it and trusted it. At last, the nonwirelines had found an advantage of their own.

7

THE BOYS' CLUB

THURSDAY, DECEMBER 1, 1983, DAWNED CLEAR AND CHILLY in Manhattan. As the city slowly stirred awake, New Yorkers began to peruse the day's news in the *Times*: Brewery chairman Alfred Heineken had been rescued in Amsterdam after being held by Dutch kidnappers for three weeks. The Soviet Union was rife with rumors about its mysteriously absent leader, Yuri Andropov, who hadn't been seen in public for more than three months and was suspected to be seriously ill. And Ronald Reagan and his advisers had agreed to proceed with developing a controversial new missile-defense system known as "Star Wars."

In movie theaters across New York City, marquees advertised the hit films of the day: *The Big Chill, Terms of Endearment* and *Yentl*. Sean Connery was still playing James Bond, starring in *Never Say Never Again*. And just south of Central Park, a five-story brownstone that was a landmark of show-business tradition was about to play host to a small group of would-be cellular moguls.

The English Renaissance–style house at 57 East Fifty-fifth Street was home to the Friars Club, an exclusive fraternity of entertainers and businessmen who drank and networked within its walls and funded charitable ventures outside them. With its oak paneling, vaulted ceilings and studded leather chairs, the venerable old club was, in 1983, a man's domain—no women were admitted until 1988, when Liza Minelli was accepted, joining an elite membership roster that included luminaries such as Frank Sinatra, George Burns, Edward Albee, Jimmy Durante and Edward R. Murrow, among many others.

It was a club for only the most elite of show business and industry—so it was exactly the kind of place George Lindemann would claw his way into.

Lindemann, the brusque, volatile, multimillionaire chairman of Metro Mobile, embraced anything and everything that bespoke power, luxury or wealth; his tastes ran to racehorses and oversized sailboats. A tough and daring businessman, he had little use and less patience for anyone he deemed his social, intellectual or economic inferior.

So it's no surprise that, when Lindemann agreed to host a meeting among his fellow nonwireline applicants, the guest list was carefully pared down to include only the more influential applicants in the cellular race. He scheduled the meeting for the impressive, old-world confines of the Friars Club, a place where dark-suited businessmen could sit and talk in peace over a few cigars and cocktails.

The purpose of the meeting was simple. Throughout the fall, Lindemann and others had wrestled to arrange piecemeal settlements with the other nonwireline applicants. Countless telephone calls and dozens of meetings at airports, hotels and trade conferences had produced agonizingly slow progress toward settling a handful of markets; by the end of 1983, only eight of the top thirty nonwireline markets were settled.

The nonwireline industry was losing ground fast: The wirelines had settled all their markets months before; they were well ahead in building out systems—putting up the first cell towers, then adding more, or "building out," as customer demand increased—and they already had one system on the air, in Chicago. It was clear that if the nonwirelines continued to battle each other, they would all lose out to the common wireline enemy. And there was another concern: If the FCC did decide to hold cellular lotteries, the advantages these heavyweight players had in comparative hearings would be worthless. Clearly, it was time for the nonwireline "big boys" to have a talk.

The invitees took their seats: MCI's Jerry Taylor, Metromedia's George Duncan and LIN's Donald Pels were there, as well as representatives from Western Union, Millicom, Maxcell and Knight-Ridder, Inc. A few smaller companies were tapped too: McCaw's John Stanton, CellNet's George Perrin and Don DePriest of Charisma came to the meeting. Left off the invitation list were scores of even smaller applicants and one conspicuously big player: Graphic Scanning. This was an exclusive boys' club, after all, and there was simply no way they would let scrappy, hair-pulling, wrong-side-of-the-tracks Graphic join.

Barry Adelman, the attorney for Ram Broadcasting, took charge of the meeting. A tough, smart, competitive lawyer with a reputation as a hard-nosed negotiator, Adelman was a true anomaly in that he eschewed the trappings of power that most 1980s New York lawyers held dear. His office at Rubin Baum Levin Constant & Friedman in Rockefeller Center was small and disorganized, and he tended to come to work dressed in casual clothes rather than the standard '80s uniform of gray suit and Hermes power tie.

But Adelman had a keen legal mind, was personable and engaging, and perhaps most important, he had a sense of humor. The day of the Friars Club meeting, however, his good humor was being tested.

In the midst of the discussion, one voice kept piping up from the back, asking question after question. It wasn't that they weren't valid queries—in fact, they were unfailingly insightful—but the rapid-fire delivery and con-tinual interruption finally got on Adelman's nerves. After the tenth ques-tion or so, Adelman snapped.

"Who are you?" he barked at the brash, persistent stranger.

"I'm John Stanton," the young man answered.

"Well, that doesn't tell me anything," retorted Adelman. "Who is John Stanton?"

"I'm with McCaw," Stanton replied. Adelman had never heard of the company, which was still little more than a consolidator of small cable busi-nesses in the Pacific Northwest, but he grudgingly had to admit that the young man presented himself well. "He was impressive even then," Adel-man would recall later. George Lindemann, on the other hand, found noth-ing to admire in the cellular whiz kid.

"I'm one of the few people who didn't like [Stanton]," he said later. "I thought he was a verbose, crybaby jackass."

But Lindemann's disdain wasn't confined to just Stanton. He had little patience for anyone who didn't register on his finely tuned caste radar, and it galled him to have to deal with anyone lower on the business totem pole than he was. Even though he and Adelman had winnowed the list of invi-tees to the so-called big boys, there were still too many little fish in the pond to suit Lindemann. As the meeting drew to a close, he lit a tremendous cigar and abruptly turned to the man next to him, William Collins, of a small company called Cellular and Mobile Radio Systems, Inc. "Who in hell are you," he demanded, "and why are you here?!"

"God damn it, George!" responded Metromedia's George Duncan, who had invited Collins. "You've had too much to drink!" On this occasion, Lin-demann's affinity for midday cocktails resulted only in a rude comment or two. But before long it would come close to derailing the very settlement process he was now taking such pains to arrange.

The meeting ended in a cloud of cigar smoke, with no concrete agreements reached and no clear plan for how to proceed. But the outline of a solution—mass settlements of markets—had been put on the table, and it would not take long for someone to act on it.

———

NOBODY LIKED CARL ARON. It wasn't that anyone in the new industry really actively despised him, but the general consensus was that he was a charisma-challenged, opinionated windbag. But even those who wouldn't raise a finger to greet him in passing had to admit that he was frequently right, and especially so on the subject of cellular settlements.

Aron, a squat, curly-haired New York lawyer with an arrogant, professorial air, was the first and most vocal proponent of mass nonwireline settlements. An attorney at Rubin Baum, Aron had taken on the CEO job of Ram Broadcasting as a sidelight, but as the cellular industry heated up, he quit his legal career to run the company full time. With his former law partner Barry Adelman as his legal counsel, Aron had led Ram to apply in the first three rounds of the giveaway, and he had watched in dismay as comparative hearings dragged out interminably and the buzz about lotteries intensified.

Something needed to be done very soon, Aron believed, and he was not shy about telling every applicant within earshot what that ought to be. In the weeks leading up to the Friars Club meeting, he had quietly but messianically preached his gospel of mass settlements; Lindemann was one of his earliest converts, and Adelman took the message to the masses.

Shortly after the Friars Club meeting, Aron asked Adelman to draft a document laying out possible parameters for mass settlements. Adelman put together a first draft modeled after Larry Movshin's Indianapolis and Buffalo settlement agreements, then circulated it to the other players, who commented, critiqued and revised it throughout December and January. Though more and more applicants were becoming convinced of the need to settle as the lottery talk gained credence, it still was an uncomfortably large leap to make: Who wanted to make deals with the competition, after all? Would it be better to take a risk and try to win a market outright? And wouldn't it be difficult to run cell phone systems with partnerships?

What the "Grand Alliance" drive really needed was a compelling personality to take the lead—a person who could act as a unifier, someone who could assuage the fears of the disparate groups trying to partner. What it got instead was cold fish Carl Aron, a man who, according to George Perrin, had an "ego even bigger than his intelligence."

"Carl is a unique character," says Larry Movshin, "very eccentric, extremely bright. . . Unforgiving of fools and also, absolutely greedy of his position. And it wasn't bad, it was just—you know, if Carl saw a crumb on the table, he was going to try and get it."

"Carl had the kind of personality who could be the most incredibly tough, mean son of a bitch you'd ever met," says Perrin, "and yet he could sweet talk a bird out of a tree on the days he tried." It was a skill he would need if he was to succeed in corralling the squabbling nonwireline businessmen.

Following the Friars Club meeting, John Stanton had flown back to the West Coast and huddled with Ed Hopper, Craig McCaw and Wayne Perry to report on what had transpired. The Grand Alliance, the team concluded, was a threat to McCaw's cellular aspirations. "[W]e didn't want to join the Grand Alliance," remembers John Stanton, "because we thought we had better applications—maybe naive in hindsight."

Though Stanton and the rest of the team thought McCaw could win more by remaining independent, there were two compelling reasons why that strategy might not pan out. First, comparative hearings were being decided on factors that were, in Tom Gutierrez's memorably dry estimation, "minimal and contrived," with size of coverage area eventually proving the only real criterion. In a "size matters" scenario, McCaw's carefully prepared applications would have no particular advantage.

Second, McCaw's lawyers who had been dispatched to lobby the FCC were phoning from Washington with important news: It looked increasingly likely that the FCC would switch to lotteries. This would, of course, render McCaw's fancy applications worth no more than anyone else's: one chance in the lottery. Settling, it was clear, was the only way to ensure getting any part of a license.

Despite the compelling reasons for settling, the McCaw team was dissuaded by another factor. Thanks to MCI's arrogant intransigence, bullheaded entrepreneurs like Metrocall's Harry Brock and the natural distrust among applicants, settlements—even relatively simple ones between two or three partners—had so far proved discouragingly difficult to pull together. How likely was it that overbearing, unpopular Carl Aron could really bring these wary competitors together?

As Adelman's draft agreement circulated among the applicants and their lawyers, it looked at first as though McCaw's skepticism would prove accurate.

"You had fifteen players," remembers Adelman. "Each one of those players had their own lawyer. You'd send out a draft agreement and you'd get fifteen comments on the same paragraph with fifteen different views. . . I mean, [we couldn't] agree on the color of a pencil." Predictably, the applicants' highly paid communications lawyers felt compelled to earn their money, but this kind of fiddling and maneuvering threatened to stall, if not kill, the process.

Adelman had his own solution to the problem. "You sit there and you kind of look at the fifteen views," he mused later, "and 50 percent of the time, I'd leave the draft the way I sent it out."

———

TO THE AMAZEMENT OF MANY, the nonwireline big boys not only achieved consensus, they achieved it reasonably quickly—partly because of the rising crescendo of lottery rumors. On February 21, 1984, less than three months after the Friars Club meeting, representatives of more than a dozen applicants—including Metromedia, MCI, Metro Mobile, LIN, Western Union, Ram Broadcasting, CellNet, The Washington Post Company, Cox Cable and Maxcell—signed partial settlement agreements for all sixty markets in rounds II and III. The Grand Alliance was born.

But even as the ink was drying on the documents, Carl Aron remained troubled. In a lottery scenario, it wasn't clear whether the Grand Alliance settlement provided much of an advantage, thanks to the FCC's silence on the thorny issue of "cumulative chances."

Say, for example, that three out of five applicants in a given market formed a partial settlement, agreeing to merge their applications. If the FCC then switched to lotteries, would that partnership application receive three chances in the lottery? Or, as the commission's rules implied, only one? If the rules were reinterpreted so the answer was three, then the benefit of settling was huge: Each of those three partners now would share a three-in-five chance of winning the license. If any of their three chances to win came in, the partnership would get the license, with each partner getting one-third.

On the other hand, if the partnership application received only one chance, then their odds of winning fell to one in three, clearly inferior to the 60-percent chance they'd share if "cumulative chances" were allowed—and, some argued, inferior to the one-in-five chance of winning the whole license outright if no partnership settlement had been arranged at all.

As the lottery rumors had swirled, Aron and others had foreseen this potential problem—through the winter of 1983–84, as the Grand Alliance was still being debated, they lobbied the FCC hard to allow cumulative chances. Their argument was simple: Allowing cumulative chances would entice applicants to settle. And the more applicants that settled, the less work there would be for the FCC. A full settlement of any market—meaning, all applicants agreeing to join a partnership and merging their applications—meant that that market's lottery could be called off, as there would be no one competing against anyone else for the license. No lottery meant no petitions to deny the winner a license, which meant less work, faster implementation of cellular service and an end to the FCC's embarrassment over delays.

Getting any market fully settled would help, but Aron had still a bigger idea: What if *every single market* could be fully settled? Then there would be no need for either comparative hearings or lotteries at all—the businesspeople could simply wrest the process out of the FCC bureaucrats' hands altogether. And everyone would be assured of getting something for the hundreds of thousands of dollars they had spent on applications.

But Aron, Lindemann and the rest of the Grand Alliance had already pointedly excluded all the "little people" applicants from their club—and these applicants had already gotten wind of the Grand Alliance's efforts to squeeze them out. Aron was obviously not the right person to now make overtures to these suspicious small businesspeople. But who could?

Aron thought he knew: He picked up the phone and called Dick Sherwin. Though Graphic was widely despised in the industry, it was the most powerful applicant left out of the Grand Alliance, and its applications in all sixty markets guaranteed it a seat at every negotiating table. Aron pitched his mass settlement idea to Sherwin, then asked the key question: Would he be willing to pull together the second alliance? Sherwin demurred.

"I knew that Graphic couldn't be the spearhead of this thing," Sherwin said later, but he did have an idea who could. John Stanton, Sherwin saw, was the natural choice to head up the second alliance. Charismatic, energetic, smart and persuasive, he was the kind of person who could compel people to do what he wanted without setting off alarm bells.

"We needed a small player who could be molded and who was bright," remembers Sherwin. "He fit the bill. Because at the time McCaw was a very small player."

Sherwin contacted Stanton and outlined the proposal; Stanton and the McCaw team were immediately intrigued. With lotteries now a virtual certainty, McCaw's refusal to join the Grand Alliance had left it in an untenable situation: Suddenly McCaw was faced with a cellular landscape in which the newly formed Grand Alliance was virtually certain to win half the markets, leaving the crumbs to be divided among Graphic, McCaw and dozens of smaller applicants.

McCaw needed a way to get back in the game, and besides, the idea of helping spearhead a nationwide alliance—the so-called Counter Alliance—appealed to Stanton. Not only could he make a name for himself, but his prominence in the role of peacemaker would bring his company increased exposure and credibility among these dozens of small applicants—who might, after all, eventually represent acquisition targets for McCaw. The offer was tempting.

Stanton decided to begin slowly, by calling a meeting among all non–Grand Alliance applicants in Sacramento, Oklahoma City and three other Round II markets where McCaw had applied. He and Sherwin culled names and addresses of applicants from the FCC filings, and Stanton began a marathon session of cold calls, inviting applicants to come to Washington, D.C., for a meeting in April.

It was a motley group that showed up at the law offices of Becker, Gurman Lukas, Myers, O'Brien and McGowan on Washington's Thomas Circle for the meeting. Newspaper executives from the *Baltimore Sun* sat side by side with Florida real estate developers, a retired army general, a U.S. attorney, a soon-to-be disbarred communications lawyer and a Texas speculator in a bolo tie and cowboy boots.

"We didn't know who any of these guys were," remembers Stanton.

Stanton opened the meeting by talking about the five markets at hand, but soon his limited agenda was overtaken by more vocal, strident voices in the room. "Basically," Stanton remembers, "Sherwin was obnoxious at the other end of the table and started saying, 'Well, we ought to do the whole thing'"—meaning, settle every one of the sixty markets, just as Aron had suggested. Don dePriest of Charisma piped up in assent, followed by MRTS's Bernie Cravath.

But although Sherwin and others were convinced that forming this second alliance was the only way to counter the Grand Alliance's threat, others in the room were skeptical. Mostly small entrepreneurs and family businessmen, many lacked the kind of cold, calculating business judgment and broad experience of the seasoned executives who had met at the Friars Club. For many, the single cellular application they'd filed was a distraction from their bread-and-butter cable businesses or TV and radio stations. Some were suspicious of Graphic and the bigger companies represented in the room, and others were dismayed to find themselves sitting at a conference table with sworn enemies against whom they'd litigated license grants and pag-ing-signal overlaps for years.

Aron had managed to pull together the Grand Alliance, but would Stan-ton be able to do the same with the disparate, far-flung applicants who were left over? If not, McCaw, Graphic and others were destined to be cellular also-rans, losing the licenses for America's biggest cities to a powerful con-sortium from which McCaw had practically blackballed itself.

———

ON APRIL 11, AT A PUBLIC HEARING, the FCC at last announced its by-now-widely-expected rule change: It would henceforth distribute all cellular li-censes via lottery, including those for rounds II and III—markets thirty-one to ninety. It also declared that it would allow the "cumulative chances" that Aron, Adelman and others had so vigorously lobbied for, ensuring the Grand Alliance's huge advantage if the Counter Alliance did-n't pull together. With the stroke of a pen, the FCC suddenly imploded the monstrous structure of rules it had spent years building. Now, ab-solutely everything would be different, though the full ramifications of this new luck-of-the-draw environment would become clear only over the coming months.

Back in October 1983, when it first published the cellular lottery pro-posal, the FCC had invited comments from interested parties. Buried in the text of its pamphlet-sized Report and Order confirming the rule change (re-leased in May 1984), it published information on the thousands of com-ments, both pro and con, it had received in the intervening five months.

One commenter, Henry Geller, a former FCC official who went on to be-come director of the Washington Center for Public Policy Research at Duke University, suggested the FCC should auction off cellular licenses, selling them to the highest bidder rather than simply handing them out for free. Spectrum licenses governed the use of a valuable commodity, after all—one that belonged to the U.S. taxpayers, who had, it could be argued, been get-ting shafted for years by the government giveaways.

Suppose the government just decided to give away the rights to use—and charge others to use—the National Parks System? Voters and taxpayers would never stand for lotterying off the exclusive use of the Grand Canyon or Yellowstone. So why should they stand for having another priceless slice of public property given away in, of all things, a game of chance? But ordi-nary Americans couldn't have cared less about spectrum or how it was used. Spectrum was an intangible commodity, something a sliver of the population might have heard of in high-school physics classes and then quickly forgotten. There was no public outcry about the spectrum giveaway, and no real call for the use of auctions to distribute licenses. It wouldn't have done much good anyway—the FCC had no authority under the law to sell anything. Thanks in part to the chaos the lottery decision would spawn, that would eventually change.

And what of the decision to retroactively change the rules governing rounds II and III of the giveaway? The applicants from these rounds had prepared extensive, expensive applications in the belief that they would be judged in comparative hearings. Now the FCC was changing the rules in midstream—how could that be justified?

Commissioner James H. Quello didn't think it was. "I find it unreasonable and unnecessary to so drastically change the rules," he wrote. "Those who mistakenly relied upon the Commission's repeated assurances that lotteries would not be used in this service now find that they have spent significant sums of money to speculate in ping-pong balls."

But the decision had been made, and the Report and Order's language was curt and unsympathetic on the subject of the midstream rules change. "To the extent there is some 'unfairness' to applicants in markets 31–90," the document bluntly declared, "we find that it is far outweighed by the public benefits of using lotteries."

On the face of it, lotteries seemed like a reasonable idea. One of the chief complaints against the FCC was that it took too long to get things done, and the lottery was a sure way to speed things up. "We estimated that most of the construction permits for markets 31–90 could be issued by mid-1984, instead of late 1986," FCC chairman Mark Fowler told *Business Week*. "The time saved by using lotteries would thus greatly benefit the public." But three more rules issued that same day virtually ensured that the lottery process would devolve into frenzied turmoil; the Law of Unintended Consequences was about to wreak havoc on the new procedures.

First, the FCC declared that in future rounds, different applicants could file duplicates of the same application—no longer would they need to prepare unique engineering studies, marketing analyses and the like for every market. Because the applications were mere lottery chits anyway, there was no value in making everyone go through the trouble of preparing expensive, one-of-a-kind applications.

Second, the FCC relaxed the financial qualification rules, deeming it unreasonable to expect applicants to tie up capital for months in a speculative lottery investment where the money might never be called for.

Third, the FCC declared it would choose not only the license winner, but second- through tenth-place finishers, so that if a winner were found to be unfit to receive the license, it could simply be handed to the next in line. This ensured that the FCC staff wouldn't have to hold more than one lottery for each market—surely there would be at least one qualified applicant in each list of ten. But no one, it seemed, had anticipated the fact that naming second- and third-place finishers virtually guaranteed that petitions would be filed seeking to deny a winner the license. Why not challenge the winner? A victory meant getting the license, and a loss was of no consequence to anyone but the winner, who would lose valuable time in getting the license granted and the system built.

As with so many of the FCC's decisions, the new rules seemed on the surface to make perfect sense—but combined, they would engender horrific abuses of the process. The bureaucratic minds at the FCC wouldn't see this until it was too late, although a telling comment in Commissioner Quello's statement summed up the situation perfectly.

"[T]he benefits of using the lottery may well prove illusory," he wrote, "while its flaws are obvious and enduring." Soon enough, all involved would be forced to agree.

———

MEANWHILE, MORE AND MORE SYSTEMS were going on-line. In one city after another, new customers signed up and eagerly drove their cars to garages to get their phones installed. Technicians drilled antenna holes in roofs and trunk lids, and wired $3,000 briefcase-sized boxes of electronics under seats. After a day or two, the customer would drive out of the shop, dial home and shout, "You won't believe where I'm calling you from!"

"You can turn rush hour into the most productive hour of your day," trumpeted early ads for Cellular One in Washington, D.C. "It's as direct and as private as your office phone. Just pick up the handset, and call." Well, not exactly as private, of course—but it was still too early in the industry for electronic eavesdropping to have become an issue. It wasn't too early, however, for another contentious topic already to be making news.

In April 1984, the American Automobile Association announced its fear that cell phones could contribute to traffic accidents. Fifteen percent of all accidents, the AAA said, were caused by driver inattention—and car phones were an obvious source of distraction to drivers. To combat the problem, AAA made a series of recommendations: Drivers should "call when the car is parked," "assess the traffic situation before answering" the phone, "use a speakerphone instead of a handset," and have the microphone installed on the visor. The AAA's recommendations were the first salvo in a battle that would rage throughout the development of the cell phone industry.

In Washington, D.C.-Baltimore, the first market to have both the wireline and nonwireline systems on the air, the competition heated up quickly. Cellular One placed full-page advertisements in magazines and newspapers across Washington before Bell Atlantic got into the running. "Call around the Beltway, or around the world," the ads promised. "Invaluable communication for less than $3 a day." In gridlock-choked, automobile-dependent Washington, the car phone pitch was an enticing one, a fact the ads played up. "If you're an average Washingtonian," read one, "one hour and 14 minutes of every day are lost driving to and from work. . . . with a Cellular One phone, you could spend those hours communicating, instead of just commuting."

Hundreds of commuters bought the pitch. By the time Bell Atlantic got its system running four months later—with a ceremonial first call to comedian Bob Hope on April 10, 1984—Cellular One had signed up 2,200 customers. The company had been lucky in scooping up the early customers, but now that both systems were on the air, the pie-in-the-sky platitudes about the wonders of technology gave way to something a bit meaner.

Almost immediately, Cellular One attacked Bell Atlantic in print, going negative in its drive to capture the harder-to-get second tier of customers. "Which car telephone will you buy: Bell or Better?" asked one Cellular One ad, while Bell Atlantic bet on customers instead being drawn to the familiar Bell name: "Now you can get the telephone good enough to earn this," trumpeted the ads, with a Bell telephone logo finishing the sentence. And for the name of its service, Bell Atlantic chose "Alex," after Alexander Graham Bell—a naked ploy to capitalize on AT&T's iconic founder.

But this was not a competition that would be won on words. As *Barron's* succinctly put it in March 1984, "[E]arly signs are that competitive battles in the new technology will be fought with that old weapon—price. Dealers in Washington already have begun to trim the prices they charge for cellular car phones; what sold in December for nearly $3,000 was on sale last week for $1,999."

Indeed, it was immediately clear in Washington that the duopoly would have the effect the FCC had hoped: Two systems battling for customers led to lower prices than in markets where there was still only one system running. In Chicago, for example, Ameritech charged a monthly fee of $50, plus 40 cents per daytime minute and 24 cents per off-peak minute. Cellular One, by contrast, charged $35 a month, plus 40 cents per daytime minute and 20 cents at other times. And Bell Atlantic's "Alex" service charged $25 a month, plus 45 cents per peak minute and 27 cents per off-peak minute.

Though the Washington markets' prices were lower, cellular service was still considered a luxury item—with an average monthly bill of about $150, Cellular One service was not cheap. Still, many of the 2,200 who signed in the first four months of the service were by and large untroubled by the cost. For users who were able to do business as opposed to losing productive time in their cars, the cost was negligible.

"In my business," real estate broker Dee Carl told *Time* magazine, "I can pay for a cellular phone in one deal." Cellular One seized on that same point in ads that called the car phone an "ingenious tool of mobile management": "Why, you could earn the cost of a *year's* use in ten minutes with one well-placed call!" It remained to be seen whether ads, word-of-mouth and good old-fashioned buzz would propel sales of this still-exotic technology.

8

LE GRAND DEAL

Mark Hamilton looked at the tieless man sitting across from him and thought, "I didn't know anybody did this sort of thing."

An attorney in his twenties, Hamilton had already become disillusioned with the practice of law. "It often seemed to me," he recalls, "that the client was having more fun than the lawyers were. They were out doing stuff and lawyers were just sitting around and writing stuff down on paper." Bored with the work at his firm, he'd had a conversation with a fellow associate who told him about a fast-growing cable company that was looking for a lawyer. Soon Hamilton found himself facing McCaw executive Wayne Perry in a job interview.

"I just went up and sat in his office one afternoon just to kind of see what he was doing," says Hamilton. "Well, he was doing everything. He was being part lawyer, part businessman, he was telling people to do this, asking people to do that, talking to bankers in New York. And I thought it was unbelievable." Though Perry was a former tax lawyer, he wasn't practicing; instead he and his small squad of young executives were building an empire on the fly—a mesmerizing prospect for a buttoned-down lawyer such as Hamilton.

It was the summer of 1984, and the McCaw team was spread thin over three fast-moving enterprises: cable, paging and cellular. Though cable was the company's dominant business and was doubling in size annually, the little cellular division was growing quickly and wrestling with more and more issues, including building out their cellular systems. John Stanton, who had recently agreed to pull together the Counter Alliance, was being pulled in twelve directions at once; it was time to bring in some help.

"Your job," Perry said to Hamilton toward the end of the interview, "will be to follow this guy named John Stanton around and make contracts out of cocktail napkins." With that, Hamilton was hired—and just in time. When the McCaw acquisition machine got cranked up, it was going to need him.

———

IN THE SUMMER OF 1984, McCaw took the first tentative steps to buy its way into more cellular applications, trying to make up for its mistaken bet against the likelihood of lotteries. The first item on Stanton's target list was Knight-Ridder, Inc., a major newspaper chain that had filed in eight of the top ninety markets but had since soured on the cellular industry. With lotteries and settlements, there was now little chance of winning a license outright, and Knight-Ridder had no interest in complicated partnerships. Knight-Ridder wanted to sell, and McCaw wanted to buy; soon enough, the two sides were discussing a deal.

But the FCC rules stood in the companies' way: Though the commission had declared that cumulative chances were permissible in Carl Aron's Grand Alliance settlement, nobody had yet gotten two chances in a market by *purchasing* other applications outright. Under the current rules, if McCaw purchased a Knight-Ridder application for any market where McCaw had already applied, the FCC could dismiss both applications.

McCaw immediately began lobbying the FCC, harping, as Aron had, on the expediency argument: The commission was looking for ways to encourage everyone to settle, and McCaw was offering the perfect solution: cash. But the FCC, as usual, was slow in making a decision. Tired of waiting, the McCaw team made what Perry calls "one of the gutsiest moves" in the company's history—buying Knight-Ridder's applications before it was sure whether they'd be worth anything.

In Perry's estimation, the FCC had little choice but to allow the purchase of cumulative chances. After all, it had changed the rules of the giveaway in midstream; scores of angry businesspeople had seen their expensive applications converted to mere lotto tickets in the name of efficiency. The pressure was now on the commission to prove that the lottery change would really get the cellular systems up and running without more delay; cumulative chances would, McCaw argued, speed the process by reducing the number of combatants. Perry had sent McCaw's attorneys to the FCC with a message: "We're not going to do this unless you give us a wink and a nod that you're not going to screw us on this." That blunt plea brought marginal reassurance from the FCC bureaucrats. "We never got them to agree to give us two chances," says Perry, "but we did get the head nod that they wouldn't bounce us." McCaw would, at minimum, retain its original chance in each market.

Perry then approached Craig McCaw. "I just want to tell you what we're doing here," he said to his boss. "Stanton and I are going to buy this stuff. We may piss away this money. It may all come to naught, but it's a hell of a value." Craig gave Perry the go-ahead, and he and Stanton flew to Washington, D.C., to close the deal.

As it happened, those final negotiations took place in late June, and to the parties' chagrin it soon became apparent that the paperwork wouldn't be ready before the July 4 holiday. Anxious to close the deal, the two sides agreed to meet in the Covington & Burling law offices on Independence Day, a Wednesday, to sign the documents. It would have been a decidedly unfestive way to spend the Fourth, except that the firm's offices were just a few blocks from the Mall, where the Beach Boys were crooning their pop harmonies for an ecstatic throng of thousands.

As Perry and Stanton worked to finalize the deal's terms, the music wafting in the windows, they felt on top of their game. And well they should have: The McCaw team was buying the Knight-Ridder applications for a comparative pittance, partly because of an anachronistic FCC rule. In order to head off what it called "trafficking" in government licenses, the FCC maintained the legal fiction that its spectrum licenses had no monetary value, and therefore could not be bought or sold. In cases where one company wanted to buy another's paging licenses, the strictures could be overcome by couching the purchase as an adjunct to an operating business transfer; in other words, the buyer was paying for hardware, customer lists and other elements of the business, with the licenses thrown in. Never mind the fact that the purchase price was usually in excess of what these other assets would bring on their own; the FCC strictly enforced its ruse and for decades communications companies had had little choice but to adhere to it.

Because spectrum licenses had, in theory, no monetary value, the applications didn't either. And because Knight-Ridder had no operating cellular business to camouflage the purchase—these were applications, not even licenses, and certainly not working cell phone systems—the price had to be low to get past the FCC watchdogs. Stanton and Perry convinced Knight-Ridder that the FCC would only allow it to sell the applications for a mini-

mal price: whatever it cost to produce them. This was like giving someone
an airline ticket for the cost of the ink and paper it was printed on.

Knight-Ridder had applied in eight cities: Jacksonville, Orlando and West
Palm Beach, Florida; Charleston, West Virginia; Raleigh-Durham and Charlotte, North Carolina; Greenville, South Carolina; and Austin, Texas. The
price McCaw paid—about $1 million—would prove an absolute trifle com-
pared to what Knight-Ridder's share of those markets would be worth in
even a few months' time, when the value of cellular licenses everywhere
began their ascent.

Even more important, McCaw had once again broken new ground for the
industry, by convincing the FCC to bless the sale of a pending cellular application for cash. It was the first deal of its kind, and hundreds, then thousands more like it, would follow.

———

IF THE CRUSH OF APPLICATIONS HAD BEEN SUFFOCATING in the first three
rounds of filing, it was nothing compared to what happened following the
FCC's lottery decision.

On July 16, 1984, staffers braced themselves for the latest in the parade
of document dumps—Round IV, for the 91st–120th largest markets, cities
like Jackson, Mississippi, and Madison, Wisconsin. The first three rounds
had brought filings of 190, 353 and 567 applications, respectively. The
thirty markets of Round IV were much smaller (averaging some 350,000
people per city compared to 3 million per city for Round I markets) but the
battle-weary staffers knew better than to hope that would mean fewer applicants. Now that every applicant would have an equal lottery chance, it
was anyone's guess how many might leap into the fray.

And the equality factor wasn't the only thing enticing new applicants.
With the FCC's corollary decision to allow "duplicate applications"—essentially photocopies of standard engineering and marketing information—a
few small companies had prepared master applications and were offering
copies to all comers at cut-rate prices. While each Round I application cost
as much as $300,000 to research and produce, now Graphic Scanning's en-
gineering division, called Richard L. Vega and Associates, was churning out
applications for only $1,500 each.

To the staffers' dismay, 5,180 applications were delivered to the FCC on
July 16. If the Secretary's office had been clogged in earlier rounds, now the
entire building was jammed. "We took over a conference room that had
been a hearing room," remembers then-staffer Mike Sullivan, "and took

over another room, took over another room. And we had applications piled to the ceiling, in the hallways and everything else."

Though the applications had been reduced in size to a single three-ring binder with about an inch of paper inside, the sheer number of them overwhelmed the staff. "We had to get the building engineers to tell us whether the building was structurally sound for having all of these applications stacked up in boxes," remembers staffer Myron Peck. "It was a real zoo." Even FCC chairman Mark Fowler was roped into service; he was handed a stamp and ink pad and hurriedly stamped applications in.

Round IV opened up the cellular giveaway to small investors and the first vanguard of a new class of FCC applicant—pure speculators, who leapt at the opportunity to get in on any high-paying game of chance. By contrast, many of the big boys of the first three rounds didn't even bother to apply, having suspected there would be a flood of competing applications. With prognosticators guessing there could be fifty or more applications per market—meaning a one-in-fifty chance of winning the lottery—what was the point of even applying? Those smaller markets promised to be worth little or nothing anyway; how many people in Huntington, West Virginia, could realistically be expected to buy $3,000 cell phones? Better, thought Kluge, Lindemann and their brethren, to keep attention focused on the big markets, where the settlement game was still being played.

Of the 5,180 applications that were filed—an average of 170 per market—the FCC rejected at least 1,000 of them out of hand, for a wide range of sometimes trivial reasons—failing to put the market number on the cover, for example, or having misnumbered the pages. Despite that wholesale dismissal of 20 percent of the applications, there were still more than 4,000 for staffers to contend with. But life at the FCC had changed for the better: No longer would staffers have to pore over each document; once an application was deemed superficially passable, it was simply thrown into the lottery bin with the rest of them. Nothing could be simpler.

Or so the FCC thought.

THROUGH THE SUMMER OF 1984, Stanton and Sherwin continued to cajole their fellow applicants into the Counter Alliance. Though many were easily persuaded to join settlements, there were plenty of holdouts, footdraggers and wafflers.

Some were wary of the fast-talking, sometimes arrogant Stanton; some were simply averse to partnering with people they didn't know. Some were unhappy with the draft-settlement documents and insisted on their own partnership provisions. "There are always a couple of crazies," noted Ed Taptich caustically, "who say, 'We don't give a damn. . . We feel it's important philosophically to preserve somebody's opportunity to smoke green cigarettes with their left nostril, and so we're not going to join.'"

The trick was to get commitments from a large enough majority of applicants that the timid and stubborn would feel compelled to join too. "We figured if we got 80 to 90 percent. . . the other guys would really feel a requirement to come in," says Taptich. But although Stanton was traveling all over the country and working eighteen-hour days, the lack of a deadline precluded any sense of real urgency.

That all changed on August 31, 1984.

That day, the FCC announced it would hold the lottery for Round II markets on October 3 (only nonwireline, as the wirelines had settled long ago), and the lottery for Round III shortly thereafter. "Now," says Taptich, "the commission throws a switch, lights a fuse, and we've got a ninety-day time period running." In fact, there was less than five weeks to pull together complicated settlements of sixty markets among hundreds of wary would-be partners. It seemed an impossible task.

It might well have been an impossible task, for anyone except Stanton. Still in his late twenties, Stanton was a man possessed of an easy charisma and seemingly boundless stamina. "He had," says CCI Chairman George Blumenthal, "the energy of a bull." And Stanton had one other advantage in bringing together the disparate applicants: He had adroitly maneuvered his way into the chairmanship of Telocator, the cellular industry's Washington, D.C.–based trade association.

For many of the small paging operators who had applied in rounds II and III, a call from a random businessman hawking partnerships would have aroused skepticism. But Stanton was one of them, an industry spokesman, and his Telocator credentials helped sway suspicious small businessmen into joining the Counter Alliance. "I knew most of the people who were hard to get in," remembers Stanton, "the little paging guys, so I was in a much more legitimate position to call them up and say, 'You know, we'd like to be working with you. We'd like to get you in.'"

With the clock ticking toward October 2, Stanton, who always operated in high gear, went into overdrive. He arranged several meetings between the heads of the Grand Alliance and the Counter Alliance (jokingly dubbed "Solidarity" after Polish electrician Lech Walesa's labor union), and threw himself into bringing the lost sheep into the Counter Alliance's fold. If a catastrophic earthquake had wiped out half the country in those weeks, Stanton would have had a terrific chance of survival—he spent much of the time in airplanes, zipping around the country to meet with reticent applicants. "I probably covered 25,000 miles in a week and a half jumping around," he remembers.

By mid-September, Stanton had convinced scores of applicants to come to Washington to finalize the Counter Alliance's partnerships. The task was as easy to define as it was difficult to carry out: Sixty separate partnership agreements—one for each city in rounds II and III—had to be hammered out among scores of applicants. And, as with the Grand Alliance settlements, each Counter Alliance applicant had lawyers who insisted on justifying their high hourly rates by suggesting alterations, however small or inconsequential, to the partnership agreements. Negotiating one partnership between two parties is difficult enough; this was a virtual marathon of deal making, and time was running short. By the time Stanton had mustered everyone at the McKenna Wilkenson offices, there were only three weeks left until the lottery date.

"It was almost like a factory assembly line," remembers Ed Taptich. "There were two conference rooms that were continuously occupied. . . . A total of eight meetings a day. It went on for two weeks." When one market settlement was finished, weary organizers would stick their heads out of the conference room and call out the next market. The applicants for that market would then shuffle into the room to hammer out the settlement in their allotted two-hour time slot.

Initially, the settlement discussions could be contentious. "It was like buying a house," says Taptich. "'God damn it, if that isn't included, I'm not buying it!' You know, there was always something." But after the first few meetings, a funny thing happened: The same faces began appearing in subsequent meetings. For one thing, many applicants had applied in more than one market. Also, some lawyers were representing more than one client. After a while, everybody seemed to know the issues and know the drill.

"The same players—you know, 'It's 10:30 so this must be Dubuque'— were coming back," remembers Movshin. "At the end of the day. . . everyone would say, 'Okay, do you want this provision?' 'Yes.' 'Do you want this provision?' 'Yes.' You didn't have to describe it anymore. It was more a matter of taking one from column A, two from column B, and that became our partnership."

"It was," says Movshin, "like telling jokes by the number."

By mid-September, Stanton had accomplished the unimaginable: He had, with the help of Sherwin and the attorneys, convinced all but three of the remaining applicants to join the Counter Alliance. Thanks to Stanton's Herculean efforts, it was now possible for the fledgling industry to take its fate out of the hands of the FCC: The formation of the Grand Alliance and Counter Alliance made possible a 100-percent settlement for sixty of the largest cities in America.

After months of discussions, meetings, arguments and pleading, all that had to happen now was for the two alliances to merge—and it had to happen before October 2. This was by no means an easy task: The two alliances' agreements had major structural differences, and it wasn't at all clear whether the corporate Goliaths could agree with the rebellious upstarts over how the sixty cellular businesses ought to be operated.

The standard Grand Alliance document was drafted for a consortium of well-financed large operators; it restricted transfers of ownership and called for simple majority rule for decisionmaking. The Counter Alliance's document, on the other hand, favored free transferability of interests and supermajority rule, which encumbered partnership operations in order to prohibit one or two large-percentage owners from financially squeezing a minority interest holder. A Solomonesque compromise would be required to make the final merger—christened "Le Grand Deal" by participants—reality.

━━━━━━━

WHITEY BLUESTEIN HAD NEVER FELT MORE HATED IN HIS LIFE.

Seated in a room with other representatives from the Grand Alliance and Counter Alliance, he had listened attentively as the assembled lawyers and executives debated how the new settlement partnerships should be governed. Should decisions be made by simple majority vote, or by a two-thirds supermajority vote? The Counter Alliance agreement, designed to protect its "little guy" members, incorporated supermajority protection, and it looked as though a consensus was moving in the supermajority direction.

This was one issue the Counter Alliance representatives insisted they could not compromise on. Fearful that the more powerful and business-savvy Grand Alliance members would steamroller them after the mass settlement was arranged, the smaller Counter Alliance members demanded supermajority provisions, giving the little guys a veto.

Their argument was simple, and it was all about money. No one knew how the dozens of partners in a single partnership would raise the millions in capital needed to construct and operate these cellular systems. Any money that couldn't be borrowed (which could well be all of it) would have to be "called" from the partners. If one or two affluent Grand Alliance members bought up 51 percent of a partnership, they could conceivably demand cash or large management fees from their smaller, impoverished partners—a move that could force those partners into insolvency and out of the partnership.

The Counter Alliance's arguments were sensible enough, and the Grand Alliance members in the room had already begun murmuring their sympathetic assent when suddenly Whitey Bluestein spoke.

"MCI will not agree to the supermajority," he declared. "It's simple majority or we're not in." All eyes turned to Bluestein. Was that a threat? Was MCI really willing to scuttle the whole settlement for this one issue? If MCI did back out, it could mean the collapse of settlements and the certainty of lotteries for the many markets it had applied in. And while the alliances (with their multiple chances) would be statistically almost guaranteed to split the winnings, FCC red tape and the possibility of petitions and suits between the groups could hold up the distribution of licenses for months or even years. Everyone had come so far; why did arrogant, obnoxious, blowhard MCI have to come in and thwart everything at the last minute?

"Boy, I'll tell you, those people wanted to kill me," remembers Bluestein. "They wanted to run across that room and strangle me." But he had his orders from the MCI brass: Only a simple majority would do. Executives at the brash, independent company were afraid that supermajority control—where a mere 34 percent of "little guy" partners could veto decisions—would end up choking the business operations.

"I just remember the tension in that room when I said, 'We're not doing it,'" says Bluestein. With paranoia rampant among the smaller players and MCI—whose reputation preceded it—already making a "My way or the highway" declaration, everyone feared that the full-settlement dream might be out of reach.

With the two sides at loggerheads, it was time for MCI's partners to pull Bluestein out of the room. The lawyers huddled, struggling to find some middle ground. Suppose MCI got half and everyday operational decisions were run by a simple majority vote and large money issues—like budgets, borrowing money and capital calls—needed a supermajority? Bluestein reluctantly agreed to take the compromise back to his superiors.

As stubborn as MCI was, it couldn't afford to push the issue. If everyone else agreed to supermajority, MCI would be left out of the big alliance, and its one lonely chance in each lottery would make for terrible odds against the alliance's cumulative chances. And the alliance didn't want to see MCI drop out either, especially considering a new plan that was being hatched.

With a 100-percent settlement, the license in any given market would simply be divided evenly among all applicants. There was no wrangling over percentages, because all lottery chances were equal, regardless of company size or application quality: Six applicants in Toledo would each get one-sixth ownership of the license, period.

The idea that stoked the imaginations of the participants was the next logical step in the process: If the ownership of the licenses was already determined, then what was to stop everyone from trading their fractions for others' fractions, in order to gain control of one market? Why own one-sixth of Sacramento, one-fifth of Dayton and one-sixth of Charleston when you could make a few trades and get majority control of Charleston? Nobody wanted to own little slivers in numerous big, unwieldy partnerships—they all preferred to control a few markets. Settling all the markets made this next step possible—but if you elected not to join the settlement, you'd be left out in the cold.

The mob logic was too compelling, the alternatives too drastic. So MCI capitulated: It would accept a supermajority vote on big money issues, while ordinary operational decisions could be decided MCI's way—by simple majority. With this last impasse broken, Le Grand Deal was suddenly and surprisingly a reality. Against the odds, some 150 different businesspeople representing more than 700 different applications had agreed to merge into sixty partnerships.

A week and a half remained before the scheduled lottery. While Movshin, Taptich and Adelman scrambled to get the paperwork assembled for the massive pile of agreements, the members of Le Grand Deal turned to the next improbable event in the industry: They prepared to meet and trade their chits.

Never mind the fact that nobody officially owned what they were about to trade, or the fact that these license fractions had, in theory, no monetary value. These businesspeople had wrenched the process out of the hands of the FCC; they were on a mad, momentum-fueled push across completely uncharted terrain, and they weren't about to stop now.

9

THE BIG MONOPOLY GAME

AN AROMA OF PASTRAMI, SWEAT-DAMP COLLARS AND CIGAR SMOKE hung thick in the air at the Rubin Baum law offices during the last week of September 1984. For one week, the conference room smelled more like a New York City subway platform than the Fifth Avenue offices of a powerful law firm.

Inside the conference room, an extraordinary scene was taking place. Businessmen and lawyers, ties askew and brows furrowed, were milling about, calling out the names of cities like traders on a stock exchange floor.

"Who's got a Fresno for an El Paso? Or how about a Toledo? Anyone need a Toledo?"

"I've got an Oxnard-Simi Valley, anyone need one?"

"I'd take another Dayton; who's got a Dayton they can part with?"

With Le Grand Deal a reality, the applicants could now fulfill the next part of Carl Aron's vision: trading the many small bits and pieces of the licenses they'd received in the mass settlement in an effort to consolidate control in a few markets. Aron invited his Grand Alliance partners and some key Counter Alliance members to his firm to trade while they could; with a little over one week left before the scheduled Round II lottery date, there was just enough time for parties to trade their partnership shares before Larry Movshin and Barry Adelman would have to present paperwork to the FCC.

In theory, the process was simple enough—anyone could trade their fractions for any other fractions, and properties could change hands any number of times. But first the traders had to overcome a value problem: One-tenth of, say, Johnson City, Tennessee, was obviously worth less than one-

tenth of Salt Lake City, as Salt Lake was a bigger city—so trading based simply on the fraction of license ownership wouldn't work. Besides, there were
varying numbers of applicants in each market, so the ownership fractions
were different in each—how did one-thirteenth of Mobile, Alabama, size up
against one-seventh of Rochester, New York? The traders needed a way to
quickly and appropriately value each fraction.

They settled on one almost immediately, and from its first use at the
Rubin Baum "Big Monopoly game," it quickly spread, becoming the standard metric for the industry. There is disagreement among those who were
at Rubin Baum about who put forth the idea first, but all agree it was
adopted almost instantly. The measurement was called "POP"s, and it was
based on how many heads of population—hence the "POP"s abbreviation—
lived in a market's geographic coverage area. The population figures, traders
agreed, would be based on the 1980 census.

Orlando, Florida, for example, had a population of 700,000 according to
the 1980 census. Thirteen companies had applied for Orlando's nonwireline
license, so after the full settlement, each held a one-thirteenth fraction of
that number, or prospective ownership of 55,000 POPs. Canton, Ohio also
had thirteen partners, but its population of only 400,000 left each applicant
with a mere 30,000 POPs—just over half the number of potential customers
the same fraction of Orlando represented. Based on the $3-per-POP price
McCaw had recently paid Knight-Ridder for its applications, one-thirteenth
of Orlando's license was worth $75,000 more than one-thirteenth of Can-
ton's. Clearly, trading thirteenths for thirteenths made no sense—but trading POPs for POPs was a good superficial standard.

In theory, as the trading started, a POP was worth a POP, regardless of
which market it was in. But before long, the traders began applying other,
more subtle variables to determine how valuable certain markets really
were. Here the game got interesting: No one really knew what made a
"good" cellular market, but ignorance didn't preclude educated speculation;
a few value rules quickly surfaced.

First and foremost, control was worth a premium. A market—any mar-
ket—that you could gain supermajority control over was worth more per
POP than a minority interest in another, where you might someday get
squeezed by the majority. Next on the list of consideration was affluence:
The only people who owned mobile telephones in 1984 drove BMWs and
Jaguars, so Palm Beach, it was assumed, would have more customer
prospects than, say, Harrisburg, Pennsylvania. Then came growth rates.
The shrewder traders understood that the 1980 populations weren't static:

Salt Lake City, for example, was growing at more than 2 percent every year, which meant that in the four years since the 1980 census, it had added 80,000 "free" POPs. Other cities—Youngstown, Ohio, for example—had lost POPs over the previous four years. And finally, there was the oldest, most reliable measure of value: If someone else wanted it, it must be valuable.

Within a matter of minutes, after the first tentative trades began, a new problem arose: With dozens of players trading hundreds of fractions, how in the world would Adelman and Movshin keep track of it all? A one-seventeenth piece of Tucson traded at 10:15 A.M. might be retraded for a piece of Springfield, Massachusetts, at 10:20 A.M., giving it three different owners in a span of six minutes—who would keep ultimate track of who owned this piece, and the hundreds of other pieces, at the end of the day? Aron thought he had the solution: An employee of his at Ram had brought along a newfangled portable computer—the first many in the room had ever seen—to keep track of the trades.

The electronic marvel met with little enthusiasm, however; there seemed something a little too chancy about it. What if it malfunctioned? What if people needed concrete evidence of trades later—possibly to present in court? A file on a computer was pretty ethereal for an official record of trades. "Neither of us trusted that stupid computer," says Adelman. So he and Movshin turned to a more trustworthy method: pen and paper.

Adelman hurriedly wrote out one-paragraph trading slips—"napkin-size pieces of paper," remembers Movshin, "with 'I give you this many POPs and you owe me this many POPs.'" Little blanks were left for players to fill in the names of the markets being traded. And that was it. The free-for-all could begin.

———

IT WAS A SURREAL SCENE: Licenses to run the latest high-technology businesses were being traded in a process that would have been recognized in the bazaars of ancient Mesopotamia. Traders waved chits in the air and shouted to be heard; on all sides, the sounds of bargaining, bluffing and bullying clattered about the room.

"You'd trade in the mornings," remembers Bluestein. "People would either go out to lunch or bring sandwiches in. Some people would go out to lunch, get completely sloshed, come back in. You were always more productive in the mornings than the afternoon, but the wheeling and dealing would be going on."

Morning, afternoon and evening, the players milled about, plotting strategy, making calls, trading fractions, taking catnaps and talking business. Metro Mobile alone had three traders—George Lindemann, Jack Brennan and attorney Aaron Fleishmann. Not all were present all the time; sometimes they took part by phone.

"There was no structure to it," remembers John Stanton, "Carl tried to put structure in it, but you couldn't put structure in it, because of the personalities. You had a bunch of very, very smart guys in that room. . . some of the smartest people in telecommunications in the country."

As the week went on, the trading intensified. "This went on for days," says Bluestein, "and I remember we had these sessions in the morning and I walked out of the room because people were smoking big cigars, George Lindemann was just stinking up the place." Lindemann, Bluestein recalled, smoked cigars "that were just gigantic. I mean, they were like baseball bats." The sleepless nights and the foul air in the conference room combined to claim at least one victim: John Stanton spent so many consecutive hours in the smoky room that his contact lenses dried to his eyeballs; he had to be rushed to the hospital to have the lenses removed.

At the end of each day, most traders went wearily back to wherever they were staying to assess the day's activity and perhaps report back to the home office. "Every night I'd go back to my hotel room," says Bluestein. "On my little trashy Model 100—remember those? The first laptops? Three hundred dollars from Radio Shack? I'd sit there—it had a great little keyboard and a tiny LCD screen and an old 300-baud modem—and every night I'd [send the home office] a daily wrap-up." Others repaired to hotel bars to drink late into the night, and a few simply lay down to sleep in the conference room, anxious not to miss any trading opportunities. Barry Adelman, the nominal ringmaster, spent most nights at Rubin Baum.

"We'd sleep in the office or on a couch," remembers Adelman, "because people would wander in at all times of the day and night, dead drunk, and they'd say, 'I traded X for Y.'" Only the lawyers were there to play referee and record keeper, while the FCC staff droned on 200 miles to the south, oblivious to the drama.

Hanging over the proceedings was a kind of disbelief that all of this was actually happening. "I mean, we were all out in left field picking daisies," says George Perrin. "First of all, it wasn't clear to any of us at the time that the FCC was going to sanction this, and I remember a lot of us sitting around saying, 'I hope we're not wasting our time,' because it kind of felt illegal, but you know, we didn't know."

Out in the hallway, taking a breather from the ever-present cigar smoke, Bluestein remembers chatting with a couple of traders. "One guy says, 'You know, I've been in business for twenty years, and I hope to be in business for another twenty years. I've never seen anything like this in my life. Don't ever expect to see anything like this again.'"

Another trader had a different angle. "You know," he said to Bluestein, "if we were doing this in a motel room instead of a law firm on Fifth Avenue, we'd all be going to jail."

―――――――

As THE TRADING SLOWED, TRADING FODDER became harder to find and IOUs—offered when a trade left one side with a POPs deficit—were getting harder to pay. Traders were looking for specific pieces rather than just good markets, and someone who coveted a certain property might not have anything desirable to offer. Not surprisingly, a few traders began trading that universal commodity—cash—to get what they wanted.

Once the cash-for-POPs ice was broken, it took little time for more opportunistic players to follow suit—out came the checkbooks, and the trading chits were forgotten. This was a clear violation of the FCC's rules, which prohibited "trafficking" in spectrum licenses, but the players decided to forge ahead in hopes that the FCC would either overlook the purchases or rule them legal, perhaps out of mere expediency. It was a calculated risk: Aggressive consolidators like Metro Mobile and McCaw simply chose to believe that the FCC wouldn't scuttle the whole process for a tangential rule violation.

Not everyone had cash to spare, however. The few large players that had both currency and nimble management enjoyed a distinct advantage over the poor and the bureaucratic. To Bluestein's dismay, his orders from MCI had been very clear: No buying POPs. "I had no cash. . . What [the buyers] paid was a pittance, but I had none."

"Kluge and Lindemann alone probably were the only guys who had any real money among any of us," remembers Perrin. "They were money people and the rest of us were just, you know, sitting around thinking, 'Well, we're playing cards. I don't know what we're playing with.'"

But even those with cash didn't really know what they were playing with. "You have to remember that this was a time when nobody knew what the hell they were buying into," says Adelman. "'What the hell is a "cellular system"? Is it going to work? Is anybody going to buy this service?' If you looked at the prices, the prices in the early days were single digits—two or three dollars per POP. So, it's two dollars per POP, so it's two dollars and fifty cents somewhere else. What difference does it make? For fifty cents you're going to fight?"

Lindemann was unburdened by any such uncertainty. He declared that certain markets were worth certain per-POP prices because—well, because he declared it so.

"I remember Lindemann coming in and saying, 'Shit, [that market's] worth ten dollars a POP,'" says Perrin. "And everybody would say, 'Well, George, how'd you come up with that?' He said, 'Shit, don't you guys understand? You've got to put an artificially high value on it so everybody will justify the financing we want to get underneath it.' And I think it was the first time in a lot of our cases that the light bulb went on."

Perrin explained further: "You've got to set these values [high], because what you want [the lenders] to do is come back and multiply that dollar value times everything you own, and that gives you an implied equity value that's going to enable you to borrow on it. Lindemann said, 'None of us want to put any real money into this.' It was absolute genius."

But though the mercurial Lindemann was capable of truly visionary insights and remarkable business savvy, he nearly brought the entire carefully constructed house of cards down in one careless incident late in the week.

Every afternoon, the Monopoly Game would break for an hour or two for lunch. Players spent the time in a variety of ways, some going off in small groups; some, like Stanton, poring over population figures and demographic information and strategizing; and some, like Lindemann, indulging in lavish luncheons replete with preprandial cocktails and postprandial cigars. Some days Lindemann returned from lunch evidencing his enjoyment of a few midday drinks.

One afternoon, Lindemann returned to the Rubin Baum conference room in a state one player characterized as "loaded beyond belief." He announced that he had traded an interest in Sacramento, California. The problem was, he had already traded that same interest to Graphic Scanning's Dick Sherwin. It took only an instant for pandemonium to erupt.

"I went bullshit," remembers Sherwin. "I went absolutely berserk. I said, 'How dare you do this?!'" Lindemann responded, indignant, that he hadn't sold his Sacramento to Sherwin. "You did sell it to me!" Sherwin shouted at him. "Here's the piece of paper!"

At the sound of Sherwin's eruption, Carl Aron and Metromedia's George Duncan rushed into the room. As Sherwin spluttered out a stream of profanity, Lindemann good-naturedly called out, "I'm short one Sacramento. Who'll sell me a Sacramento?" But there were no Sacramentos to be had.

The Big Monopoly game was already a precarious enterprise. With hundreds of trades going on at all hours, handshakes and head nods serving as deals, little one-paragraph pieces of paper serving as contracts, and an absolutely essential underpinning of cautious trust, the whole endeavor threatened to implode if Lindemann—or anyone else—flouted the unspoken rules. If the traders couldn't rely on each other's word, then everything they'd done all week had been a waste of time.

Though he knew he was in the right, Sherwin also understood that the whole process was at stake. Reluctantly, he agreed to give up his piece of Sacramento to settle the problem. But in return, he got a guarantee: Aron and Adelman insisted, and the Metro Mobile team agreed, that Lindemann would no longer be allowed to trade without having his trading slips signed and approved by Lindemann's lawyer, Aaron Fleishmann.

At last, Friday, September 29 arrived—the day Movshin and Adelman had declared would be the end of trading. The Round II lottery date was now only five days away, and Movshin and Adelman somehow had to reconstruct who had ended up with what in the Big Monopoly game, to draft all the documents and get them to the FCC by Wednesday to stop the FCC lottery from going forward.

"Barry and I had to get together and figure out what the hell these folks had done," remembers Movshin. "They signed this master agreement that said, 'Here's what we've been doing.' And they attached all these trading sheets—a copy of every trading sheet, to the document."

Because every trade relied on every other trade, Adelman and Movshin structured the agreement so that "nothing would be done until the FCC had approved it, and then if any one trade was accomplished, they'd all occur." The reason was simple said Movshin: "We didn't want anyone backing out, because this was serious dominoes here."

The two lawyers set up a kind of record-keeping "war room," where they spent the next few days desperately trying to sort out who owned what. Their greatest fear was missing a trade and assigning an interest to the wrong party.

"If there's a mistake, we're dead," remembers Movshin. "We're the ones who [will be] blamed. So we called up each of the players, anyone who had been involved in the trading sessions, and said, 'Next week we're going to be going through and sorting out and making sure everyone is where they think they are. . . God willing, you are where you think you are. But, if we find a hole, you've got to take our call.'"

Every day, the two lawyers found holes, and every day they called the parties involved to straighten out who had traded or sold what. And in the end, an astonishing thing happened. "We never went to bed at night with an unresolved hole," says Adelman, "and the two most surprised people in the world were Larry and myself. Everything sorted out."

Still, there were a few players who believed they'd been stiffed somehow. "To this day, there are still some people who believe they are owed by somebody else," says Movshin. "Graphic Scanning still believes that McCaw owes them some POPs. It's a long-dead issue, but Sherwin still holds a piece of paper that he is convinced that Stanton owes him some POPs."

Movshin and Adelman presented the settlements to the FCC on Monday, October 1, and the grateful and relieved FCC staff postponed, then canceled, the Round II lottery. Two markets in Round III would still have to be lotteried, however, because a single applicant in each market had absolutely refused to settle. (When they had their lonely Ping-Pong balls tossed in the lottery bin along with the multiple balls of the Grand Deal, the alliance ended up winning both markets, leaving the stubborn holdouts with nothing.) On October 15, Movshin and Adelman presented the FCC the results of the Big Monopoly game, hoping for quick approval of the unorthodox settlement.

Only then could Aron, Movshin, Adelman and the rest look back at what had happened over the past couple of months and take it all in. Faced first with years of delay and legal battles, then with the uncertainty of lotteries, a group of businesspeople had banded together to beat a bureaucratic system. And they had done it by writing their own rules. "Nobody did anything except act selfishly," Aron told *Business Week*, "and it worked."

────────

THE GRAND DEAL AND THE BIG MONOPOLY GAME are unique events in the American business landscape. Even the most hard-nosed businessmen who took part in the settlements still describe them in near-mythical terms.

"There is a camaraderie among the people that were in the room," remembers Whitey Bluestein. "I think everybody had the feeling that what was going on in there was just unheard of, never to happen again, a once-in-a-lifetime experience."

"It was a historical event, and very few people recognized it," says Dick Sherwin. "A major event in the history of the economy."

Though the lawyers reported to the FCC that the market ownerships were settled with the end of the Big Monopoly game, the trading actually went on for months afterward. Although several dozen of the biggest and most ambitious cellular aspirants had made it to Rubin Baum, dozens and dozens of smaller players—single-market applicants and smaller family companies—hadn't known about the New York session. And for those who were there, the five days of trading hadn't been nearly enough time for the participants to fully consolidate regions. Fleishmann, Stanton and others, ignoring their lawyers' pleas and admonitions, kept swapping, buying and selling through the fall. "It went on nonstop for months," remembers Fleishmann. "It went on, it was weekends, nights. . . "

As the trading continued, Fleishmann helped concoct a spectacularly successful subterfuge: He huddled with MCI's Bluestein and the two agreed to collude. They would make some trades for each other, in order to conceal their companies' true aims. If Fleishmann badgered everyone looking for every piece of New Haven he could get, word would quickly spread and the price would go up. If Bluestein made a random trade for New Haven, however, Fleishmann's attempt to corner that market for Metro Mobile could be concealed.

Fleishmann and Bluestein's gambit worked perfectly—so well, in fact, that years later, most traders never realized they'd been had.

As time went on, trading got tougher and tougher. "It's kind of like mushrooms in the forest," says Bluestein. "The first time you go in, all the mushrooms are easy to see and you start picking 'em out. The next time you go back in, you have to dig around a little harder to get to 'em."

The continued trading might have been helpful for the companies, but for the lawyers in charge of the settlement deal, it was a problem. The FCC had agreed to stop the lottery based on the settlements Movshin and Adelman had documented in early October, but the process of finalizing ownership of the markets wasn't finished yet. The lawyers would have to submit formal transfer applications for FCC approval of all trades and sales, and the informal extension of the trading bazaar left them trying to document a moving target. Frustrated and fed up, the lawyers decided that their clients should schedule another trading session, after which Movshin would submit the final transfer applications and wash his hands of the situation.

A second Big Monopoly session was scheduled for the second week of December 1984. For ten days, the traders again milled about the Rubin Baum conference room, wheeling and dealing with competitors whom they now knew all too well. An exhausted Carl Aron insisted that the traders finish their business by Thursday, December 20, so he, Movshin and Adelman could get the final—really final—paperwork to the FCC. When the last trade was finished and the participants had all gone home for the holidays, Movshin and Adelman settled in for a few long weeks of assembling paperwork, building for the FCC the equivalent of a map of the American cellular landscape assembled from piles of trading slips. On January 15, 1985, they presented the FCC with the final list of who owned what in the thirty-first- to the ninetiest-largest nonwireline cellular markets.

By then, there was a huge disparity between those who had traded well and those who had blown their chance. The big winners—those who managed to assemble controlling majority stakes in regional clusters of markets—were Metro Mobile, MCI, Metromedia and a handful of smaller players like McCaw, Cellnet and Charisma.

Conspicuously absent from the list of controlling owners were Western Union and Graphic Scanning, two companies that had started the game in late September with larger piles of chits than anyone. In the beginning of September, Western Union looked like a behemoth compared to startup Metro Mobile, but by Christmas, Metro Mobile controlled ten major cellular markets, including Phoenix, Tucson, Charleston, Raleigh and Providence—while Western Union found itself controlling only lowly Mobile, Alabama.

———

BY THE END OF 1984, CELL PHONES were still on the relative fringe of American consciousness. Thirty-two systems were on-line in twenty-six cities, but only 91,000 customers had signed up for cell phones—fewer people than attended the Rose Bowl football game that year. Though the cell phone had a growing cachet as a hip, cutting-edge product—it was named the top product of 1984 by the *New Product Development Newsletter*, beating out the artificial heart, the Cabbage Patch Kid doll, and a new model station wagon—it wasn't easy to convince people it was worth its cost.

The wireline companies were building systems as fast as they could, raking in the easy first few thousand customers in each market, after which the pace of sign-ups slowed drastically. New York, Los Angeles, Chicago, Philadelphia, Detroit, Dallas, Houston and eleven other of the top thirty cities had wireline systems on-line, and the others would follow shortly. Meanwhile, the nonwirelines were building their handful of systems that had been settled, but more than seventy of the top ninety markets were either embroiled in comparative hearings or awaiting FCC approval of the mass settlement from the Big Monopoly game. Despite the remarkable achievement of bringing together Le Grand Deal, the wirelines' head start was already doing its damage.

Nynex Mobile, which went on-line in June 1984, would, for example, be on the air for nearly two years in New York City before its nonwireline competitor Metro One (a Metromedia and LIN Broadcasting–led partnership) got up and running. The first day the Nynex system went on-line, hundreds of eager customers lined up for service. *Time* magazine quoted Bart Robins, a cellular-installation manager at a car dealership, as being "exasperated. 'Everybody's got to be first. Me. Me. Me.'" These were the easy pickings; what would be left for Metro One when it finally got on-line two years later?

PacTel got its L.A. system up and running in time for the 1984 Summer Olympics, while the nonwireline side was hopelessly entangled in a nasty court battle over its license. And in Dallas, Southwestern Bell inked a high-profile deal to provide the Republican National Convention with fifty to one-hundred cell phones while the nonwirelines squabbled.

St. Louis, Minneapolis, Milwaukee, Buffalo and Indianapolis were the only markets in which the nonwirelines had gotten on the air within a few months of their wireline competitors in 1984. And in only one market—Baltimore-Washington, D.C.—the nonwireline had been the first on the air.

The 1984 Christmas-shopping season brought the first real marketing pressure on cell phone pricing; the cost of a car phone dropped to about $1,500. Two converging factors led to the price dip. First, when hundreds of early adopters flocked enthusiastically to buy the first phones, surprised local managers thought they were seeing the beginning of a boom. They optimistically placed larger equipment reorders, triggering the industry's first economies of scale: Manufacturers could make the phones cheaper in volume, and sell them cheaper in large lots.

Second, the marketers tried to lure new users with a cheap sticker-price. It made sense to sell a $2,000 phone for $1,500, because the new customer might easily bring in $1,500 in per-minute-usage revenue in twelve months—more than making up for the initial $500 discount. One by one, cellular companies ditched their old financial models, which had projected fat profits on hardware sales, as they realized that service charges could subsidize handsets. The real pot of gold, they saw, lay in per-minute charges.

Across the country, the makeup of companies' cellular teams began to transform. Once peopled by the engineers, financial analysts and lawyers who'd prepared applications, they became increasingly filled with salespeople, marketing experts and competitive operations officers. Creativity was the order of the day, with carriers dreaming up promotions, sales gimmicks and come-ons in an effort to convince a largely ignorant public that they should try out these newfangled phones. Operators hid high hardware costs by offering "packages" that included leased phones and a certain number of minutes per month—Cellular One and Bell Atlantic, for example, both offered a ninety-nine-dollar monthly lease in the Baltimore-Washington area.

Cell phone rental booths appeared at airports and in taxicabs. Some operators offered free service to news organizations that would use their cell phones in their helicopters. Manufacturers scrambled to develop phones with special features: Motorola and NEC touted memory and redial features, hands-free microphones became standard fare and Oki designed a phone that could automatically call the police if the car was broken into.

With the Grand Deal and the Big Monopoly game vaulting the nonwirelines into their construction and operations phase, hardware price wars and increased advertising were already pointing the way to higher penetration. For most of the big boys, the battle now was about getting customers for their systems in the top ninety markets. When the applications for Round IV markets—the 91st–120th largest U.S. cities—were filed in July, most big companies hadn't bothered to file. Now there was little to distract the new operators from getting systems going and getting customers signed up.

It was time for the shakeout to begin.

10

THE EXODUS BEGINS

EVEN BEFORE THE GRAND DEAL AND BIG MONOPOLY GAME, the seeds of exodus were taking root. Throughout 1985 and 1986, many of the companies that had struggled for the past two years to win, swap and acquire non-wireline properties would sell their holdings, trading a potentially lucrative—but uncertain—future for cash.

The sellers had two motivations: disillusionment and fear. Initially, many applicants hoped to gain control of whole regions, or at the very least their hometown licenses. But the FCC's persistent rule-changing and the unexpectedly large numbers of applicants pretty much dashed those hopes. Not only that, but applicants were growing cowed by the stark reality of how much these systems would cost to construct; one AT&T estimate figured it would cost $1 billion to build out wireless systems across the United States. While the wireline phone companies had $90 billion in annual telephone revenue running through their cash registers, nonwirelines like Metromedia, MCI and Ram traditionally relied on the banks for expansion capital—and what bank would lend that kind of money to an unproven industry based on some science fiction technology?

The money problem was sharpened by the settlement partnerships' provisions allowing the majority to "call" the minority partners for cash—and to carve up the shares of any partner who failed to pay on schedule. After all the wrangling it took to get a piece of a license, it could be taken away again with relative ease if a partner didn't have ready money. For many, the risk was too great: Better to sell now, make some money and get out clean.

With ownership of most of the top ninety markets decided, through either settlements or comparative hearings, the nonwireline field now divided in a new way: into predators and prey. The surprising thing was who ended up devouring whom.

―――――

For Western Union, the end began practically at the very beginning. For Jim Ragan, the company's point man on cellular, the first sign was an unexpected phone call he received on October 4, 1982, not three months after the Round I applications had been filed.

Ragan was in Washington, D.C., helping wage Western Union's battle in the Round I paper war, when a friend in the industry called him. "Congratulations!" the caller offered, to which Ragan, confused, responded, "For what?"

"You've just bought E. F. Johnson," said the friend. Unbeknownst to Ragan, Western Union had that morning announced its purchase of the E. F. Johnson Co. of Waseca, Minnesota, a supplier of mobile radio transceivers that was now developing a line of cellular equipment. With car-mounted cell phones, switching equipment and other products in the pipeline, E. F. Johnson was hoping to compete with Motorola, Ericsson and other hardware suppliers for the new cellular business. Trouble was, the company's car phone was, in Ragan's words, "a dinosaur," and its infrastructure equipment was so bad that in 1983 a Western Union employee who was researching system hardware for the Buffalo, New York, market recommended the company use Motorola equipment rather than its own E. F. Johnson brand.

Incredibly, no one had consulted Ragan and his cellular team on whether the $132 million deal was a good one. Under the direction of CEO Robert Flanagan, Western Union had simply forged ahead with the purchase.

"That's news to me," a stunned Ragan managed to respond to the caller, even as he turned over in his mind the myriad ways the deal was a bad one. "I damn near died," he remembered later, "because I saw the consequences of that loud and clear. As long as we were a pure systems guy, we could play the field on equipment manufacturers. . . but once we were into the manufacturing business, we were a competitor and. . . as we would try to make alliances, everyone would be suspicious." Worse yet, financial analysts quoted in an August 1984 *Data Communications* article noted that the price was "extraordinarily high for a company that could be slaughtered by the Japanese, AT&T and Motorola." It was immediately obvious that the deal was a mistake, but the real ramifications would occur two summers later, when Flanagan made an E. F. Johnson–related decision that would completely gut Western Union's promising cellular strategy.

In the meantime, Western Union's technological ineptitude was at last catching up to it. The company's lifeblood had long been its steady stream of cash from telegrams and telex, but the newfangled fax machine was poised to decimate those businesses. Then, just as new personal computers began appearing in offices, Western Union set out to spend $1 billion in largely borrowed capital on Easylink, a new "electronic mail" business that promised to whisk messages electronically for hundreds of miles, after which they'd be delivered by hand over the last urban mile. And in February 1983, the company's Westar VI satellite—expected to be a source of scores of millions in revenue for the company—was lost in space. In the meantime, E. F. Johnson was, as Ragan had predicted, performing abysmally in the cellular equipment market.

Something had to be done, and quickly, so Flanagan made a move: He ordered Jim Ragan to swap jobs with the head of E. F. Johnson. Rather than leading Western Union's quest for cellular licenses, Ragan would now be in charge of whipping the hardware division into shape, in an effort to garner better equipment sales.

Flanagan's timing could not have been worse. He ordered the switch in the summer of 1984, at a time when Western Union held application fractions in seventy-two of the nation's top ninety cellular markets—a position second only to Graphic Scanning. The Grand Alliance and Counter Alliance were about to merge, and the Big Monopoly game was weeks away. Western Union's portfolio of 3.28 million POPs could, if shrewdly traded and then operated, easily wipe clean the company's long-term debt of $470 million.

"It was so obvious and so straightforward. You could see the multipliers," remembers Ragan. "All of us who were working on the program felt that we held the key to saving [Western Union]. . . [if] we could hang in there long enough until it came time to sell out." But just as the trading was about to begin, the entire business was handed to a manufacturing man, who had not only failed at his last job, but understood nothing about the cellular industry. Former Western Union employee Michael Sullivan observed at the time that the company "has been robbed of all the accumulated knowledge of the past three years by the substitution of the second string. It may take a year for the new team to 'come up to speed.'"

Ragan was aghast. "That was a terrible mistake," he remembers. "I never should have [agreed to the switch]. I should have just stood up and said, 'No.' But Bob was the boss. . . He had a lot, near-term, riding on E. F. Johnson."

When the Big Monopoly game and continuation of trading took place in the fall of 1984, the magnitude of Western Union's ineptitude became clear. Western Union never showed up, leaving its chits to the charitable ministrations of Lindemann, Aron, Kluge and the other traders. When the dust settled, Western Union had been traded out of the second-largest number of markets into a single majority stake: thirteen-sixteenths of Mobile, Alabama. Michael Sullivan remembers it "was just a joke. Ragan was out of it. Nobody was managing it. I think they just didn't go to the meetings."

Its opportunity for financial salvation now lost, Western Union faced a slow descent into oblivion. Before the summer of 1984 ended, Flanagan had been ousted in a contentious board meeting and replaced in a takeover attempt by Curtiss-Wright Corporation CEO T. Roland "Ted" Berner, a curmudgeonly, egotistical lawyer-turned-wheeler-dealer in his midseventies. Berner, an old-style executive with a reputation for belittling subordinates and falling asleep in meetings, had absolutely no clue about cellular. Almost immediately, he declared that Western Union would focus on Easylink, its fledgling e-mail system, and that the cellular assets were for sale: With comically misplaced enthusiasm, he crowed to a New York television audience, "Even my desk is for sale!"

Over the next two years, Western Union sold its cellular assets at fire-sale prices as the company careened along the path to bankruptcy. The stock slid from a 1983 high of forty-seven dollars to single digits. The thermostat in the headquarters building was turned down and all employees were socked with a 10-percent pay cut the week before Christmas 1984. Desperate for cash, the company sold E. F. Johnson in April 1985 for $38 million—nearly $100 million less than the nominal price Flanagan had paid for it just thirty months earlier.

On October 1, 1985, Western Union announced the sale of its cellular partnership interests in Los Angeles, Milwaukee and Indianapolis to American Cellular Telephone Corporation (ACTC)—a company controlled by Carl Lindner and Harper Sibley, two Western Union directors who had learned about cellular from Ragan. The sale covered nearly 1 million POPs, more than 70 percent of which were in the nation's finest cellular market, Los Angeles. The price: just over $9.6 million in cash, or some $10 a POP. Within four months Lindner resold the same properties—tripling his money with the sale of L.A. at $30 a POP. Within four years, the three big stakes sold to Lindner would be worth more than twenty-five times what Berner had dumped them for.

By the end of 1988, virtually all of Western Union's cellular portfolio was gone. Even Bob Flanagan now acknowledges the company's mistake. "On balance," he says, "the deals that Jim made would have turned Western Union into an extremely profitable company if we had simply stood still and done nothing for a couple of years."

But Ragan traces the downfall back to an earlier day. "I go back to the day that the decision was made to buy E. F. Johnson," he says. "The jig was up, and it was just a question then of trying to salvage what you could." The portfolio of POPs Ragan had built on a shoestring budget of $5.9 million had— even at premature fire-sale prices—brought in some $60 million, certainly one of the company's best investment returns of the twentieth century.

In the end, the company salvaged very little beyond that. By 1990, it had sold its leased lines, satellite, nationwide paging and cellular businesses. And in a final, colossal gaffe, Western Union sold off hundreds of miles of crucial urban conduits beneath the streets of Manhattan, Chicago, Boston and other major cities, surrendering for a pittance priceless rights of way that would springboard the next decade's fiber-optic telecommunications industry.

By December 1990, Western Union's stock was headed for a low of twenty-five cents a share. When AT&T purchased the company's telex and e-mail business, there was virtually nothing left of the once-proud Western Union. In September 1994, at a bankruptcy court–supervised auction, the company's worldwide money-transfer business was sold, bringing the 140-year history of America's first telecommunications firm to a whimpering end.

"I mean, there's a company that at every critical juncture made the exact wrong decision," says MCI's Whitey Bluestein of Western Union's truncated foray into cellular. "I never understood those guys, but they weren't players at all. They weren't players."

"It was a real tragedy," remembers Jim Ragan. "Western Union could have been a major, major player. . . I can sum it up for you very simply: Western Union blew it."

━━━━━━━━━

THOUGH WESTERN UNION'S FLAMEOUT was the most spectacular, it was certainly not the only collapse among the early players. In a modest office complex in Rockville, Maryland, Peter Lewis was watching his dream of operating a cellular system slip through his fingers.

MRTS had fared well in the first three rounds of the FCC's giveaway. Lewis's little firm held pieces in forty-seven of the sixty markets in rounds

II and III in addition to its stakes in Washington-Baltimore and Tampa and Miami—3.3 million POPs in all. Better yet, while other applicants had only been spending money on the new industry, Lewis and Bernie Cravath sold their firm's engineering expertise to a few dozen would-be applicants for upwards of $150,000 per application, bringing in more than $1 million in much-needed cash.

But Lewis's profitable application business soon went flat. When the FCC switched to lotteries in the spring of 1984, the service Lewis was selling—specialized applications preparation—became a low-priced commodity essentially overnight. Soon after the lottery announcement, Richard L. Vega and Associates, a Graphic Scanning subsidiary, began peddling applications for less than $5,000 apiece—a mere 3 percent of what MRTS had been selling them for. Before long, the price plummeted even further—down to $1,500 per application. The lottery decision effectively killed Lewis's cash cow, leaving MRTS with a bloated payroll and throwing the company into financial turmoil.

The timing was disastrous: MRTS's need for cash was about to grow exponentially. The company's success in getting license pieces meant it would quickly have to come up with its partnership share of the money to run the systems. The Grand Deal would hasten the distribution of licenses, which meant that capital calls for system construction would come sooner rather than later. In Cravath's estimation, MRTS needed to come up with as much as $20 million in the months ahead to meet those capital calls. Where would they get that kind of money? For all its promise, cellular was still a risky bet, and $20 million was beyond what Cravath could expect to get from friends and relatives. The only hope lay in selling equity.

Trouble was, MRTS was a tiny company, with no operating track record and capital requirements that were too small to attract a top-tier Wall Street firm. After months of searching, Cravath was finally able to engage a Cleveland-based investment firm to raise capital, boosting everyone's hopes that financial salvation was at hand. But the firm promised more than it could deliver and when it failed to stir any investor interest in the cellular story, the deal died. With it died the long-held dreams of Peter Lewis.

The only remaining alternative, Cravath determined, was to sell MRTS's cellular assets. For Cravath, the pragmatic businessman, the decision was difficult but unavoidable. But Lewis was little persuaded by pragmatism or logic. Lewis "didn't want to sell," remembers Cravath, but "I just didn't know what we could do if we didn't sell."

Even worse, as Cravath struggled with the company's looming insolvency, he also determined that all of MRTS, including its cellular assets, would have to be sold. Selling only bits and pieces would result in double taxation, first to the corporation and then to Lewis, Cravath and the other stockholders; if they sold out piecemeal, Cravath figured, after taxes they'd be lucky to end up with thirty cents on the dollar. Selling the entire company was the smarter way out. Peter Lewis, bitter and disgusted at his company's impending collapse, refused to speak to his partner, reducing their communications to messages ferried up and down the office hallway by a colleague.

At first, Cravath—taking a cue from the prices McCaw paid in the recently announced Knight-Ridder deal—talked of selling the entire company for what amounted to three to four dollars per POP, a practical giveaway. But because the properties were mostly in the less-valuable Rounds II and III markets and were geographically scattered across the country, Cravath had trouble finding someone with deep-enough pockets and enough interest in the properties to buy them all.

Cravath approached Metromedia's George Duncan, Metro Mobile's George Lindemann and Metrocall's Harry Brock, all of whom declined. Smaller investors who were interested in the properties couldn't scare up the money to buy the whole company. With the Big Monopoly game about to begin, Cravath abandoned his tax-saving plan and sold a block of the MRTS properties, everything west of the Mississippi, to McCaw's John Stanton. He then went into liquidation mode, selling the balance of the assets as fast as he could strip them out. Four months later the liquidation was complete. MRTS, the corporate embodiment of young Peter Lewis's dream, was history. Though the sale had left Lewis a millionaire, he was now not only disappointed, but jobless.

But the real losers in the MRTS sale were those who passed up on buying at the prices Cravath had first offered. In September 1984, Metrocall's Harry Brock had declined to buy the whole package for Cravath's asking price of $8.5 million. By February, a mere five months later, Cravath had sold the pieces individually for a total of nearly $14 million: Brock—and the others who passed on the sale—had let a quick $5.5 million windfall simply slip away. And that was only the beginning: In little more than five years, the price for the top ninety markets would reach $150 per POP or more, making MRTS's round II and III markets worth upwards of *$500 million*. And anyone willing to risk $8.5 million in the fall of 1984 could have claimed it.

—————

IN RETROSPECT, IT'S EASY TO CASTIGATE the companies that sold out too early. Looking back on the spectacular ascent of license values through the mid-1980s, it seems obvious now that cellular, which allowed Americans to do two things they love more than almost anything—talk on the phone and drive—would be a slam dunk.

But back in 1985 that was far from clear. Huge construction and marketing costs, the flattening of growth rates following the initial boom in each city, the skepticism of pundits and analysts, the expense of the phones—all these factors contributed to a general uncertainty about whether the industry would really take off. Cell phones were still widely seen as status symbols and a frivolous fad. Cellular was so much of a risk that even arrogant, hard-charging, we-can-run-it-all MCI eventually got cold feet. Though CEO Bill McGowan saw cellular as a local phone service his company could at last dominate, two unrelated events conspired to drive the upstart out of the business altogether.

The first event traced its roots all the way back to the Round I filing, to a decision that seemed frivolous at the time. It involved the nonwireline applications for the Los Angeles license—potentially the most valuable market in the country.

A string of partial-settlement agreements had winnowed the number of applications down to two—one for a partnership made up of MCI, Metromedia and Graphic Scanning, and the other for a partnership of five applicants (including Western Union), dubbed Los Angeles Cellular Telephone Company, or LACTC. This wasn't particularly unusual—partial settlements were taking place across the country—but what was strange was that both sides ended up using the exact same engineering, thanks to a consultant's having switched sides in midstream. The engineering plan called for twenty-three cell-tower sites to be situated in and around the city.

This was a problem—how could either side hope to get the upper hand in a comparative hearing if the applications were essentially identical? Just a few days before the Round I filing, lawyers for LACTC found themselves scrambling for a way—any way—to distinguish their group's application. As they pored over the engineering and attached maps, someone had pointed to a lonely little slab of land out in the Pacific Ocean, about twenty miles southwest of L.A.: Catalina Island. A sparsely populated vacation community, Catalina had only one claim to semifame: Less than a year before, in November 1981, Hollywood starlet Natalie Wood had mysteriously plunged from the deck of her husband Robert Wagner's boat and drowned in the dark waters just off its coast. Now the lawyers saw in Catalina a desperate last chance to somehow set their cellular application apart.

The LACTC team quickly called in engineers, who drew a twenty-fourth cell site on the application's maps, plopping it down on Catalina Island. This made little commercial sense; a cell site on the remote, hilly island would likely cost three quarters of a million dollars or more to construct, and the island hosted only a relative handful of cars to equip with cell phones—in fact, there were strict rules limiting the number of cars allowed on sleepy Catalina.

With only a few days to the filing deadline, there wasn't time to incorporate the new cell site into the channel plan, alter the application's subscriber assumptions, or make any other changes. But the LACTC team decided to gamble anyway: It stuck the cell site out there, hurriedly tracing on their maps a wobbly amoeba shape over Catalina Island, a decision MCI's Bluestein dismissed as "stupid. I mean, why would you engineer something until you just over-engineer it?"

Judge Walter C. Miller, a career bureaucrat who had gotten his law degree at night school, presided over the comparative hearing. After sifting through the mountains of applications, petitions, attachments and other paperwork, he made his decision in February 1984: Despite the fact that the applications were nearly identical, he declared that the MCI/Metromedia application was "clearly comparatively superior to [that of] LACTC." Per the fashion of the times, LACTC immediately appealed the decision.

Both sides knew the appeal had a good chance of winning, as LACTC's application had a larger coverage area (thanks to that single cell site on Catalina Island) than MCI/Metromedia's did. They also knew that the time wasted in fighting over the appeal would harm whoever ended up with the license, as the wireline side had long ago settled and Pactel was already building out its system. In view of these two factors, LACTC proposed that the two battling nonwirelines simply settle the market fifty-fifty.

But MCI, true to form, would hear none of it. They had won fair and square; why give in and split it evenly now? Though Metromedia's Stuart Subotnick urged its partner, MCI, to agree to the settlement, MCI insisted on a special condition—one that would ensure it got the better end of the deal. As they had in the Cleveland settlement meetings, MCI's representatives insisted that the company should own and operate the cellular central-office switch in return for a percentage of revenues—a clumsy attempt to skim extra profits from the partnership. The settlement talks collapsed, and the appeal went forward.

When the full commission then considered LACTC's appeal, it ruled that LACTC's greater coverage area—meaning, that twenty-fourth cell site randomly stuck on Catalina Island—rendered its system superior. Tossing Judge Miller's decision aside, the FCC awarded LACTC the license, stripping the stunned MCI/Metromedia partnership of one of the most valuable licenses in the country. "It was really the first game of chicken," recalls Tom Gutierrez. "It was a $600 million gamble." And MCI had lost. "There was always a feeling that L.A. was the crown jewel," remembers Bluestein. "L.A. gave you the critical mass. It wasn't Kansas City and Pittsburgh and Minneapolis and Denver that were going to do it—no, L.A. was what we needed to do it." The loss of the license was a devastating blow—"the defining moment" for MCI's cellular ambitions, as former MCI executive Dan Akerson recalls. It was soon followed by another, making up the one-two punch that would knock the company out of cellular.

Back in 1974, MCI had, like the Justice Department, filed an antitrust lawsuit against AT&T, charging the company with unfair business practices. In 1980, a jury had awarded MCI $600 million—which was automatically tripled by law. The verdict, which was immediately appealed by AT&T, left MCI management salivating over the prospect of a $1.8 billion windfall from its arch nemesis. In January 1983, a federal appeals court upheld the verdict—but rejected the size of the award. More than two years later, a final decision was made on the amount of the award, and when it came down, it was a shocker.

On May 28, 1985, a jury awarded MCI $37.8 million, automatically tripled to $113.3 million—a pittance compared to the $1.8 billion MCI had won earlier, and absolutely miniscule compared to the $5.8 billion it had sought. Suddenly, in the spring of 1985, MCI found itself with its presumptive war chest empty, its most valuable cellular property lost and the cellular construction budget rising. ("The capital requirements were eating our lunch," recalls Akerson.) It would take uncommon, even reckless, optimism to go deeper in debt to fund a cellular dream.

"At that point," says Bluestein, "MCI made a decision that we needed to stick to our knitting, go back to the core business"—long-distance telephone service. Cocky from the start, certain of its rightful claim to the best cellular markets, MCI simply gave in, deciding in the summer of 1985 to sell its cellular and paging division, Airsignal. The surprising thing was who would end up buying it: the upstarts from the Pacific Northwest, McCaw.

Thanks in large part to a random, ill-planned cell site drawn hastily on a competitor's application, MCI would effectively hand over its invaluable cellular portfolio to McCaw—which would use it to springboard toward industry dominance.

Metromedia's Stuart Subotnick said later that "MCI should have been big in this business. They blew it. . . they were so entrenched in their thinking, and it had to be their way or no way, and it's a shame."

But Metromedia was yet another company that sold out too early.

BY THE EARLY 1980s, centimillionaire John Kluge had established himself as a daring, unusually creative businessman.

Kluge, described by the *New York Times* in 1983 as "one of the great entrepreneurial geniuses of the media business," had built Metromedia through a cornucopia of eclectic investments. The new cellular and paging acquisitions were layered atop television and radio stations, a TV-production studio, the Harlem Globetrotters, long-distance services, a limousine business and a billboard company. The entire mix was leavened by the inventive tax strategies of CFO Stuart Subotnick, Kluge's invaluable consigliere and the designer of some of Metromedia's most impressive financial deals.

Wall Street sometimes had difficulty deciphering Kluge's strategies. While profits and the company's stock price generally grew, rising some ninetyfold between 1974 and 1983, Kluge adroitly took advantage of every price dip to increase his own holdings in the company. Rather than using his own cash, Kluge operated a long-running stock repurchase plan, which used corporate cash and debt to buy back shares, shrinking the number outstanding by nearly half, and eventually raising his ownership from single digits to nearly 25 percent by 1983.

At first, investors loved the news of Kluge's foray into paging and cellular. But a few new deals he and Subotnick engineered—a mammoth taxdriven lease deal for New York City transit buses, followed by a devilishly complex spinout of Metromedia's billboard assets—left investors confused and analysts wary. As Kluge's wealth multiplied, so did his critics.

By June 1983, Metromedia's stock had reached a split-adjusted fiftyseven dollars a share—up from the equivalent of forty-three cents nine years earlier—and Kluge was still on the move. Metromedia continued to acquire paging companies and their cellular applications, rushing to fill in the smaller urban holes between Philadelphia and Boston. But with the stock market moribund (the Dow stood at barely 1,000) and Metromedia "drowning in debt," as one analyst put it, criticism mounted and Metromedia's stock price began to flag, dropping by more than 50 percent to near twenty dollars a share in December 1983. Much of the sell-off was attributable to two critical *Barron's* articles by Baruch College accounting professor Abraham J. Briloff. A longtime critic of unorthodox accounting practices, Briloff castigated Metromedia for "questionable practices" in accounting for Subotnick's creative (and perfectly legal) manipulation of the tax code. As controversy swirled and the stock price plummeted, Kluge, described by the business press as a "brilliant cheapskate" who liked to "buy low and fix 'em up," saw the greatest buy of his long business career: his own company.

After a two-week whirlwind of behind-the-scenes maneuvering in the late fall of 1983, Kluge made his move. On Tuesday, December 6, Kluge, Subotnick and two other executives announced an offer to purchase all of Metromedia for a nominal $52.50 per share or $2.2 billion. The fine print showed a cash offer of $30 per share, a nice 20-percent premium over the stock's price, plus an additional $22.50 in debt securities—an innovative twist promptly labeled by *Forbes* as "a leveraged leveraged buy out." The financial community was stunned by the offer. Shock soon gave way to disbelief. Where could Kluge possibly get that much cash?

Kluge and Subotnick again dumbfounded their critics. In a matter of weeks, they lined up all they needed with a complex combination of private investors, venture capital and a massive pile of fresh bank debt. The deal structure, laden with interest deductions, cost the U.S. Treasury more than it did any of the participants. When the smoke cleared, Kluge himself actually walked away with cash in his pockets, letting Metromedia's new lenders pay for some of his old stock and options.

By the time the FCC approved the deal four months later, as the details slowly came to light, *Forbes* deemed it "little short of brilliant," going on to note that, "when it comes to magic, the late, great Harry Houdini had nothing on John Kluge." By September, before the first interest payments came due on the company's massive bank loans, Kluge agilely swapped out the conventional loans with a new series of junk bonds managed by Drexel Burnham's Michael Milken. The junk bonds deferred interest payments out for years, buying valuable time to turn assets into cash or cash flow.

With no more public shareholders, bankers or securities analysts to answer to, Kluge entered the fall of 1984 in charge of his own destiny, just as the Grand Alliance and Big Monopoly games were taking shape. Within twelve months, he would be well on his way to converting one of Metromedia's least understood assets, its cellular applications, into its most valuable.

When Kluge took Metromedia private, it was generally perceived that he had used borrowed money to buy a broadcast company. In fact, he'd gotten a huge wireless business thrown in for free. He now owned nearly 93 percent of a multibillion-dollar empire—provided he could pay off those junk bonds.

No one understood Metromedia's assets better than John Kluge, and he wasted little time in selling off the most attractive ones, using the cash to nurture his cellular newborn. First to go were the television stations, sold to Rupert Murdoch, who would use them to launch his FOX TV network. The $2 billion deal wiped out virtually all of Metromedia's debt less than ten months after Kluge had taken the company private—and he still owned radio, billboards, entertainment, paging and the formative cellular businesses. The TV deal had taken him, in two short years, from "merely megarich. . . to super megarich," according to *Forbes*. The TV sale was followed by billboards ($710 million), entertainment ($30 million) and radio ($300 million). In all, Kluge had pulled in $3 billion in cash in little more than twenty months, a key step on his journey to being named the richest man in America in 1989. Metromedia was—to the amazement of everyone but Kluge and Subotnick—suddenly flush with cash, and still they held cellular licenses covering some 36 million POPs. And Kluge wasn't done selling yet.

As LARRY MOVSHIN AND BARRY ADELMAN, the legal managers of Le Grand Deal, feverishly prepared the final Big Monopoly list for delivery to the FCC in early January 1985, one FCC judge was preparing a document of his own—one that would further cripple Graphic and hasten its ultimate collapse.

On January 9, FCC Judge Thomas Fitzpatrick issued his initial decision in the ASD affair. Peppered with phrases of indignation and dismay, the 173-page document was an unmitigated disaster for Graphic Scanning. Graphic was, the judge wrote, the "real party in interest" behind the rash of copycat paging applications filed back in 1982. The company had not only "exhibited a lack of candor," but it had "intentionally misrepresented material facts to the Commission." And Fitzpatrick singled out Barry Yampol personally, writing that he "must be held a party to these concealments and misrepresentations."

The decision declared that Graphic and the four shell companies Yampol had set up were unqualified to hold paging licenses. And that wasn't the worst of it: The FCC's Michael D. Sullivan, now the mobile services division chief, told the *Los Angeles Times* that "every license Graphic and its subsidiaries hold is at risk." Though many doubted the FCC would impose such a draconian penalty, the commission could strip not only all of Graphic's licenses, but all its applications—meaning all its cellular interests. Graphic could possibly be left with nothing.

Barry Yampol had effectively been ousted as CEO already, but he still manipulated the company through his position as its chairman and largest stockholder. He immediately ordered an appeal of the decision, and within weeks, he announced a plan to sell some of Graphic's assets. For Yampol, who had spent his professional life hoarding spectrum, this was a desperate act. Though this wasn't the first time he'd announced such a plan—in 1984, disappointed at Graphic's low stock price, he'd threatened to auction off the company's spectrum assets—he'd never actually done it. But this time the company was in desperate straits: The stock price was low, cash was scarce, cellular construction costs loomed, and now Wheatley and the company's weak executive team had to negotiate a settlement of the ASD ruling with a suspicious FCC staff. Graphic was injured, bleeding in the water; soon enough the sharks began circling.

In a huge concession to the troubled company, the FCC decided in the spring of 1985 that Graphic could sell its cellular interests, as the annual report put it, "free of any condition relating to the ASD proceeding." Over the next two and a half years, Graphic liquidated its massive cellular portfolio for a paltry $287 million, all of which promptly went back out to the company's lenders. In the meantime, Yampol was finally ousted for good by a group of Wall Street vulture investors, who engineered a takeover of the struggling and leaderless company. Graphic limped along for five more years, slowly cannibalizing itself as management sold off Yampol's priceless portfolio to McCaw and others, finally selling the last remnants of the company to Bell South in September 1991.

This was the unceremonious end of what began as the most brilliant cellular strategy in the business. Yampol understood before anyone else that the most important thing in the new industry would be getting a seat at the table in every cellular market. By applying in every market, he guaranteed his company an absolutely dominant role. Then he destroyed his own future by committing an act of unfathomable greed and stupidity.

Yampol was, in Subotnick's words, the "smartest guy in this whole business." Movshin echoed that view, but with a caveat. "He really was one of the few people that saw that spectrum never lost value," said Movshin. But "his brilliance occasionally was transcended by his personality. Because he was smarter than everyone else, he really didn't tolerate fools easily. And he viewed people that were pretty smart as fools."

In the end, the only lesson Yampol taught the industry he'd helped pioneer was a cautionary one: Greed trumps brains.

NOT EVERYONE ON THE NONWIRELINE SIDE SOLD OUT, of course—many companies held on to their partnership interests, built the systems and began selling cell phones. A few, like Metro Mobile, not only went into business in their markets, but they kept buying up others' interests, expanding their spectrum holdings. But only one worked up to a flat-out buying spree, purchasing from Graphic, Metromedia, Western Union and anyone else who would sell: McCaw.

McCaw's purchase of Knight-Ridder's cellular applications in the summer of 1984 marked the beginning of an acquisition phase that grew in intensity through the Big Monopoly trading sessions and beyond. By the summer of 1985, McCaw's cellular assets would double in size, growing to 6 million POPs. "We probably did thirty or forty deals for 100–200 interests between July '84 and July of '85,"remembers John Stanton. "There was a tremendous amount of interests we were buying. . . It was deal after deal after deal." And this was only the beginning.

Throughout the '70s, while Craig McCaw was building his cable company, he had given his team extraordinary autonomy in doing deals. Speed was the defining strategy: Putting purchases through a rigid, hierarchical decision-making process would only have slowed things down, hindering the McCaw growth engine. In the cellular game, Craig McCaw again allowed his team—Stanton, Wayne Perry, Ed Hopper, Mark Hamilton and others—to move on deals as quickly as possible, without having to wait for anyone's specific approval.

For the most part, Craig trusted his team to get the job done. The quintessential "big picture" guy, a dyslexic who had no patience for long memos and little details, he mostly kept out of the nuts and bolts of the acquisitions. One memorable episode related to the San Francisco market demonstrated the wisdom of that strategy.

The San Francisco nonwireline license—one of the most valuable in the country—had been awarded to a partnership of five companies. McCaw, CellNet, Communications Industries (CI) and Graphic Scanning each owned 23.5 percent, and Associated Communications owned 6 percent. The ink had barely dried on the settlement documents before some of the partners began negotiating to buy the others out; McCaw soon upped its ownership to 47 percent by agreeing to buy Graphic Scanning's 23.5 percent of San Francisco, along with its interests in San Jose, Seattle, Tacoma, Portland, Sacramento and San Antonio. Next, Perry and Stanton set their sights on majority control: They wanted to purchase CI's partnership stake.

CI CEO Clayton Niles was willing to sell—the per-POP prices being bandied about were certainly high enough. But he was suspicious of the rag-tag team from Seattle; they had neither the balance sheet nor the public prestige of the type of company that Niles, who was something of a senior statesman in the communications industry, wanted to be associated with. An impatient, impetuous man by reputation—he supposedly would prowl around the CI offices at night, throwing away anything his senior managers had left on their desks—Niles made his decision quickly. He turned the McCaw team down flat.

When Hopper and Perry told Craig McCaw about their inability to sway Niles, Craig's response was equally swift, according to Perry. "You just don't know how to deal with these people," he said. "I'll take care of Clayton." Shortly afterward, Craig flew his plane to Dallas to meet Niles.

Though no one disputes that Craig McCaw is an exceptionally intuitive and intelligent person, anyone who has dealt with him also knows he is a bafflingly oblique communicator. He speaks in abstract pronouncements, and the intent behind his verbal meanderings can be frustratingly opaque. Craig's declaration was met with no little skepticism among his team: They couldn't imagine their diminutive and boyish CEO, with his limited nego-tiating patter, persuading the aloof and aristocratic Niles to sell—especially after McCaw's best deal-makers had failed. With a mixture of anticipation and bemusement, they awaited his return from Dallas.

The Monday morning when Craig returned, Perry and Hopper were wait-ing for him. Craig walked through the door and headed straight for his of-fice, as his team searched expectantly for some sign of how things had gone. At the door of his office, Craig paused and turned to his team.

"Those guys are mongoloids," he muttered, then entered and shut the door behind him.

Craig's fruitless foray to Dallas was one of the more amusing stories from the San Francisco market shakeout, but the most significant development had happened a few weeks earlier. For the first time in the cell phone industry, a wireline company tried to buy a nonwireline property: On January 8, 1985, Pacific Telesis, a West Coast RBOC, announced its intention of buying Cell-Net's 23.5 percent of the San Francisco license. In order to avoid competing with itself, it announced it would sell its small share of the wireline license.

The ramifications of this announcement were explosive. If PacTel—and by extension, any other wireline company—were allowed to purchase non-wireline licenses, the character of the infant cell phone industry would be transformed. PacTel and its sister RBOCs had huge asset bases, enormous cash flows, and the ability to outbid almost any company in the world. What hope did tiny McCaw—or any other of the comparatively small non-wirelines—have to grow their cell phone businesses if they had to compete with these monster companies?

The McCaw team understood instantly that PacTel's move was a harbinger of wireline domination if the FCC chose to permit it. They reacted immediately: On February 1, McCaw asked the FCC to rule the purchase impermissible. Wasn't it flouting the whole purpose of the duopoly to allow wirelines to control both systems in a market? Hadn't the FCC gone to great pains to ensure the nonwirelines half the cell phone business? There was no incentive, they argued, for the RBOCs to provide good, cheap cell phone service, when that would just cut into their wireline profits. Allowing the PacTel nonwireline purchase would allow two potentially collusive partners to "compete" in the same market. It would be a step backward, McCaw argued, for the industry.

A week later, McCaw filed suit in California Superior Court in an attempt to block the sale. McCaw appeared to be marshaling the nonwireline forces against the wireline incursion. But there was another side to the story, a subtext that all but ensured McCaw would come out ahead regardless of how its lawsuit played out.

If McCaw's lawsuit succeeded, the ambitious Seattle upstarts wouldn't have to compete with the deep-pocketed wirelines for half the licenses across America. On the other hand, barring wirelines from buying non-wireline licenses carried a calculated risk. In its search for financing to buy cellular interests, McCaw needed to be able to show lenders and equity investors an "exit"—bankers wanted assurance there were well-heeled buyers who could bid for McCaw's properties if the company were forced to liquidate. If McCaw succeeded in having all the major telephone companies disqualified as nonwireline license owners, it could jeopardize its own efforts to raise capital. Still, in this scenario, all nonwirelines would be equally hindered—so McCaw decided to press on with the lawsuit.

Regardless of the outcome, the lawsuit provided one clear benefit to McCaw. The San Francisco case kept the industry in disarray, which caused prices to stay relatively low—and McCaw spent the next two years acquiring as quickly as it could at bargain prices. Then, when McCaw lost the lawsuit in 1986, ironically its prospects soared. Now that the rich wireline companies could buy, the properties McCaw had steadily, stealthily been buying up were worth far more than what Stanton and his team had been paying for them.

"In the end," said Ed Hopper, "we lost but we really won."

And now the wirelines were free to devour the industry at will.

———

AS THE FATE OF CELLULAR LICENSES WAS MULLED OVER in boardrooms and courtrooms, the industry's marketing side busily tried to ensure there would be enough customers to make the debate more than merely esoteric.

Earl "Mad Man" Muntz, an eccentric used-car salesman in Los Angeles, made the news in February when he offered a Hitachi model cell phone for under $1,000. Though most phones had cost around $3,000 two years before, now there were multiple models of differing sizes and prices. The "briefcase phone" or "bag phone," a two-pound box the size of a lunch pail, was introduced; Hammacher Schlemmer's model cost $2,995. Walker Telecommunications Corp. unveiled the smallest phone yet: a one-pound phone, about the size of two cigarette packs laid side by side, which could fit into a suit pocket (but not a shirt pocket). It also cost about $3,000.

There were more options: Voice Control Systems introduced a hands-free, voice-activated phone which would operate, the company claimed, regardless of the user's "age, gender, accent, tone of voice or elocution." Companies began offering voice mail service to customers, for a monthly fee. And insurers, recognizing that these cell phones were a major investment for some, offered insurance plans: full replacement coverage for around thirty dollars a month.

Cell phones began showing up wherever companies could place them. Amtrak announced plans to install cellular phones on its Metroliner trains running between New York and Washington, D.C. Phones appeared on Washington state ferries running to Bainbridge Island. A contestant in the Cannonball Rally, an around-the-clock cross-country road race, made news when he transmitted updates on the race to a radio station via a cell phone. And an Associated Press story reported that "cellular phones are now used by fishermen on their boats, on-the-scene reporters, travelers with flat tires and medical emergency crews. Cincinnati's Providence Hospital provides cellular telephones to rescue squads previously limited to talking to a two-way radio dispatcher."

But although cell phones were becoming cheaper and gaining more widespread use, they still were seen as status symbols. In a profile, the *Los Angeles Times* reported breathlessly that although "Post-*Splash*, Pre-*Cocoon* Ron Howard continues to drive his unwashed Volvo 760"—a sign of humility from the director and former child star—"he recently installed a cellular car phone, the closest thing to a visible bauble of his seven-figure success." And the *Seattle Times* reported that "The latest status symbol is a small black 'pigtail' antenna on your car, indicating you've got a cellular telephone inside."

With increasing cell phone sales came a new electronic phenomenon: radio scanners. The *San Diego Union-Tribune* reported in February 1985 that "Radio scanners that allow electronic Peeping Toms to eavesdrop on cellular telephone conversations are selling like hotcakes, and officials say the public should be careful about discussing highly confidential matters on such phones." In April, legislators in California proposed outlawing eavesdropping on cell phone conversations. And in March, AT&T and Bell Atlantic announced plans to test encrypted transmission of voice and data over cell phones.

The safety aspects of cell phones received glowing coverage through 1985, with *Newsweek* reporting that growing numbers of motorists were calling from their car phones to report drunken drivers. Regional highway authorities began installing cell phones along long stretches of roads, for emergency calls. And during the devastating Malibu fire of 1985, when more than 5,000 acres were incinerated, a cell phone–equipped van made the rounds so residents could call when their land-line phones were no longer operative.

Yet cell phones didn't receive universal acclaim. Complaints grew about drivers paying more attention to their phones than to the road. And as companies built out their systems, residents began protesting the cell towers that suddenly loomed above the trees. These towers, 150 feet or more of industrial-looking metalwork, some bearing FAA-mandated red or white strobe lights, were eyesores, and neighbors began banding together to try and block them from their neighborhoods. In some cases, compromises were made—fueled by monetary compensation. In San Diego, for example,

PacTel was allowed to lease land for a cell tower on a corner of a high-school football field. In return, PacTel not only paid rent, but also built two new restrooms for the school.

By the end of 1985, there were 102 systems on the air in eighty-five markets, serving a total of 340,000 customers. The total penetration of the U.S. population was approaching 0.2 percent. Most customers leased their phones rather than bought them, and the mind-boggling variety of plans led one newspaper to comment, "One almost needs to be an accounting wizard to evaluate all the various 'customized' packages." There were different prices for phones, installation, per-month fees and per-minute fees, and all manner of discounts and calling plans.

As the systems were turned on in America's ninety biggest cities, the battle for those licenses continued. Now that the wirelines were trying to buy the nonwireline side, the stakes had changed dramatically.

But while the big boys continued their jockeying for the largest markets, something strange, even incredible, was happening in the smaller markets. The spectrum rush was gearing up, and some very unlikely people were lining up to take part.

PART TWO

11

THE TRUCK DRIVER TRANSFORMS

LORRAINE PELISSIER WASN'T AT HOME when her husband got the April 1986 call that changed their lives. In an instant, Bob Pelissier had gone from truck driver to cellular entrepreneur, controlling—with his little, three-man partnership—the cellular license for Manchester-Nashua, New Hampshire. He could hardly wait until his wife got home so he could tell her the news.

"Oh my god," were Lorraine's first words. "What are we going to do now?"

"Well," Bob responded jovially, "You better start climbing poles, and I'll hand you the wire!"

Lorraine was at home, though, when Bob got a second call regarding the license. This time it was the representative of a company that was following the lottery, looking for license winners to buy out. The caller offered Bob more than a quarter of a million dollars, a sum that would have made back many times the $37,500 he'd spent on his applications. Lorraine listened as Bob discussed the offer, then politely declined and hung up the phone.

Lorraine stared at her husband.

"What's the matter, honey?" Bob asked.

"What right does a truck driver have to turn down that kind of money?" she asked in return.

"Let me tell you," he responded, "if somebody's offering you that kind of money right off the bat, what do you think it's really worth?"

THIS WAS THE SPECTRUM RUSH: a mad scramble by ordinary Americans to get in on the FCC's big lottery giveaway, followed by a hurried corporate crusade to buy out the winners. It all started with the handful of hucksters and scam artists who lured Middle America to the government casino with promises of great wealth—even though the only "great wealth" they really cared about was the pile of cash they raked in by selling tens of thousands of applications.

The Grand Deal and Big Monopoly game were unusual, even remarkable milestones in the American cell phone industry. But with the advent of the application mills, the industry moved from the realm of the merely remarkable to that of the truly bizarre.

12

TAKE THE MONEY AND RUN

AL SCHNEIDER WAS IN A BAD MOOD.

He had agreed to have lunch with his business partner, Nicholas R. Wilson, in hopes that a trip to Night Town, one of their favorite restaurants in Cleveland, would cheer him up. By the end of lunch, though, it was apparent the strategy hadn't worked. So Nick came up with another idea. They paid their bill and headed to their next destination, about a half-mile away from the restaurant.

Within minutes, Nick and Al were standing on the showroom floor at Jaguar Cleveland, eyeing the gleaming 1985 Jaguars and Porsches. Nick, a flamboyant Englishman with a taste for fancy cars and less-fancy women, was at home in the showroom; he prowled around the cars, sizing them up as Al admired two shiny new Porsches—one red and one black—in the middle of the floor.

"Why don't we get a pair?" Nick suddenly asked, his clipped British diction lending weight to what was, on the face of it, an absurd suggestion. Al looked blankly at him, but Nick was serious. They wouldn't pay for the cars themselves, of course—their company, The Cellular Corporation, would take care of that. Why not just fill out the paperwork, have a check brought down from the office, and drive those babies off the lot right now? Al could have the red one, and Nick would take black.

As he pulled out of Jaguar Cleveland in his new red Porsche, Al Schneider thought, "This can't be happening." It was a common refrain among Wilson's associates, especially during the spectrum-rush years.

There are plenty of choice words one could use to describe Nick Wilson, but one is used consistently by friends and detractors alike: charming. A trim, sandy-haired, charismatic Englishman in his early forties, Wilson had a quicksilver tongue and a disarming manner. Despite a reckless hedonism and disdain for details that threatened all of his business undertakings, Wilson found as many ways as anyone to successfully manipulate the FCC rules for huge profits.

A native of England, Wilson came to the United States in 1966 following a whirlwind romance with the daughter of a prominent Cleveland banker. When the couple married, Wilson's legal status was secure and his entree into Cleveland society assured; he then launched a mercurial business career. His first year working in America, the twenty-four-year-old Wilson found his way into retail stock brokerage with the help of his father-in-law. A natural salesman, Wilson earned a then-gargantuan $104,000 his first year in the business. By 1974, Wilson had gravitated from workaday stock brokerage to a faster-paced world: selling newly created options on the financial markets listed on the Chicago Board of Options and Exchange.

But soon Wilson's run as the English gentleman of Cleveland society ended: First, he lost the patronage of his influential father-in-law when his marriage collapsed and he quickly remarried—to a belly dancer named Nancy who worked at the Grecian Gardens nightclub. Then, he was sanctioned by federal securities regulators for accepting an illegal commission— a Rolls-Royce, presented by a grateful client. No one would have known about the car, except that Wilson, an irrepressible showman, couldn't contain his pride: He posed for a photo that made the *Cleveland Plain Dealer*.

In the decade that followed, Wilson slid into the dodgy, high-margin underworld of thinly traded stocks and private equity deals, selling contrived securities under the euphemistic description of "investments." Among the products he peddled were stock in a company with plans for three-wheeled, bubble-shaped minicars (the ostensible solution for the oil crisis of the late '70s) and "The Perfect You" (a personal computer system to create profiles for health club customers). He was a pariah in respectable Cleveland society, but Wilson did well enough to buy himself a rundown mansion in the affluent waterfront suburb of Lakewood.

Then one day he had a chat with an old friend from his early days in Cleveland, attorney Albert Schneider. Schneider was managing some investments in cellular, a business, he thought, that could lure his friend back from playing so close to the edge of securities trading laws.

"Nick, here's a perfect product," Schneider told Wilson. "What you'll do is, you'll sell the individual his very own application for a cellular telephone license, and it's a nonsecurity. You can mark it up as high as you want, it doesn't make any difference." Nick's interest was piqued, and Schneider wasn't through yet. "I've got this consultant, Peter Lewis," he told Wilson—the same Peter Lewis whose company, MRTS, had recently collapsed—"He'll do a credible application, and for the first time in your life, you'll have a legitimate product."

This was all Wilson needed to hear—it sounded perfect! With Lewis on board to do the engineering, all they would need was a sales force to get the product out. "I've got these guys in California that are really great," Wilson told Schneider excitedly. "They could sell ice cubes to Eskimos." With that, the pair began planning for a trip to California to meet Wilson's "guys": Joe Steingold and Earl Serap.

In late August 1984, Wilson, Schneider, Steingold and Serap met in Marina Del Ray and hashed out the details of a new joint venture. Through Schneider, Peter Lewis had agreed to prepare master applications for five Round V markets at a cost of $150,000 apiece plus a fee of $500 for every copy the sales force sold. With Steingold and Serap out front making sales pitches—and taking responsibility for any unfulfillable promises—Wilson and Schneider planned to sit back and provide application preparation services, safely insulated from any potential securities laws irregularities. The partners hoped to sell hundreds of applications at $15,000 each; after expenses they'd split the profits.

There was only one problem. Serap and Steingold, who would have to convince investors to buy into the cellular dream, were themselves unconvinced of it. What kind of sucker would pay for a lottery ticket to win some science-fiction high-tech business? Despite Schneider's assurances that cellular was the real deal, Serap and Steingold decided they needed a sales gimmick: They'd make Uncle Sam pay for the lottery tickets.

Instead of charging $15,000 per application, as they'd originally discussed, they would charge $45,000—but with a couple of important hitches. The applicant would pay $15,000 up front, and the remaining $30,000 would be in the form of a promissory note. Then, Serap and Steingold would advise the applicant to write off the entire $45,000 as a tax-deductible investment expense, saving each applicant more money in taxes than the $15,000 he'd spent.

This still wouldn't be a bargain for applicants if they had to pay the $30,000 promissory note, but another twist in the scheme took care of that. The $30,000 note wouldn't be collected unless an applicant won a license—in which case they'd have plenty of money to cover it. Despite the fact that it was a blatant violation of the tax code, the scheme had a quasi-legitimate, something-for-nothing ring to it that Serap, Steingold and Wilson knew would appeal to their usual class of customers.

With the promise that the applications were essentially free, Serap and Steingold were now convinced they could move their "product." The first full-scale application mill, American National Group (which later became American National Cellular, or ANC), was born.

Round IV applications had just been filed in July 1984, and the FCC had yet to announce when the Round V filing—for the 121st–135th largest cities (such as Erie, Pennsylvania and Montgomery, Alabama)—would be held. In theory, the FCC was taking time to figure out how to stem the overwhelming flood of applications. In practice, its dithering gave application mills time to sell thousands of them. The year and a half that passed between the Round IV and Round V filings gave marketers like Serap and Steingold plenty of time to spread the lottery gospel to every corner of the country.

American National began marketing almost immediately, but equally quickly, the enterprise threatened to fall apart. A mere two months into the partnership, Serap and Steingold refused to honor their agreement, complaining about Peter Lewis's high rates and Wilson and Schneider's service fees. The partnership split: Serap and Steingold set out on their own, while Nick Wilson and Al Schneider quickly formed their own Cleveland-based mill: The Cellular Corporation, or TCC.

Just like that, there were two application mills where there had been one. Both ANC and TCC adopted the tax–write-off strategy, hired groups of telemarketers, and spewed brochures and ads all over the country in an effort to round up customers. Operators at 800-numbers lured customers with promises that "Cellular's just a vehicle to turn $10,000 into five to ten times that amount!" Investing in cellular was all but a sure thing, they implied—just buy a lottery chance, join in a settlement group comprised of fellow applicants, and everybody gets a piece of the pie. That's what had happened in the Grand Deal, after all—why shouldn't the same thing happen now? With hundreds of customers banding together to share lottery chits, they had an excellent chance of winning at least one market, and everyone would share the spoils. Besides, with an instant tax write-off, you risked nothing; it was like using the casino's money at the craps table.

Other mills sprouted up, most notably one run by a pair of hucksters out of San Francisco. Ex-lawyer Quentin Breen and part-time college professor Anthony T. "Terry" Easton sold thousands of applications through several enterprises they organized (loosely categorized as General Cellular Corporation, or GCC); they and the other mills cranked out applications as fast as they could through the winter of 1984–85.

For the most part, the "entrepreneurs" selling applications couldn't have cared less whether their clients ever won anything, or even had a remote chance to win. As long as the application fees were rolling in, their bank accounts would be fattened regardless. One salesman, Wladimir Naleszkiewicz, took that logic to its most extreme conclusion. He took hundreds of thousands of dollars from lottery hopefuls, spent it heedlessly—much of it on marketing expenses, in hopes of selling still more applications—then discovered at filing time that he didn't have enough cash left to cover the FCC's filing fees. So he filed a few with the money he had left, then simply chucked the rest of the applications—more than a thousand of them—in a dumpster. Fortunately, he was caught; he pleaded guilty to two counts of mail fraud. Meanwhile, his hapless clients watched their dreams of cellular riches evaporate with no hopes of refunds.

It wasn't long before word of the applications frenzy made its way back to the FCC. The mills were selling applications to people who had no idea how to run a cell phone system, and more important, no intention of doing so. This was exactly the sort of rampant speculation that spectrum-lottery critics had predicted. Something had to be done to stem the flood.

On May 3, 1985, the commission declared that it would allow no more pooling of chances. This decision would, the bureaucrats reasoned, take away the mills' big selling point: With no shared chances, each applicant's odds of winning a market had just plummeted from near-certain odds to a 1-in-500 shot in the dark. It looked, for a brief, shining moment, as though the FCC had outwitted the mills—and that it might finally get the troubled spectrum-licensing process under control.

━━━━━━━━━━

AT NICK WILSON'S MANSION, Schneider, Wilson, and a handful of TCC employees and hangers-on gathered in the first-floor living room, which had been converted into Wilson's office. (He avoided at all costs the company's real office, in the rat-infested Ace Shoe Company building downtown.)

In a scene common to offices across the country, the group congregated around the water cooler. Unlike most water coolers, however, this inverted five-gallon jug was filled with chilled, eighty-proof vodka. Throughout the day, Wilson would pour himself a swig (usually into a wine glass) regardless of whether the sun was on the way down or the way up. Stenciled on the jug's side were the words "Minnehaha Water Company," and as Schneider recalls dryly, "That water cooler was good for some 'ha has.'"

In the six months that TCC had been running, applications sales had been brisk. Wilson's ragtag team of Al Schneider, accountant Greg Neely and a growing band of quasi-independent marketing agents led by Kent Maerki watched smugly as hundreds of thousands of dollars poured into the TCC bank account. But now the FCC's no-pooling rule change was threatening to shut TCC down. And worse yet, refunds would be out of the question—Wilson had already spent much of the customers' money.

TCC's only hope lay in what appeared to be a single, tiny loophole in the FCC's new rule. And the more Wilson pondered it, the more he realized it offered a way out—a way the rule could be twisted to his advantage. With growing excitement, he laid out his plan.

The FCC initially intended to express its "no pooling" rule through a simple, blanket ban: One applicant or partnership could own only one chance in any market. Under no circumstances would anyone be allowed to hold multiple applications, or ownership interests in more than one application.

But this created a problem: What if a stockholder of a public corporation filed his own application in a market where the corporation had filed? Under an absolute blanket ban, both applications could be tossed out. But with potentially thousands of stockholders to worry about, it was impossible for a corporation to know whether it was in violation of the new rule. This would never do, the corporate lobbyists argued. And the FCC agreed.

So the FCC came up with the so-called 1-percent rule: An applicant for a given market would be allowed to own a less-than-1-percent share in another application for that same market. Because a shareholder's stake in a big public company was unlikely to exceed that threshold, the 1-percent rule was seen as a quick and easy fix.

Then Wilson had his epiphany: The 1-percent rule left him just enough of a loophole to keep his application mill running. He would have all his TCC customers join a giant "Alliance Group." Whenever a TCC customer's application was chosen in the lottery, the nominal winner would, according to the terms of the alliance, own at least 50.01 percent—a controlling majority—of the license. The other 49.99 percent would be owned by the remainder of the alliance partners (all owners of identical applications for the same market)—and as long as there were at least fifty of them, they would each own less than 1 percent.

The more customers Wilson could entice into his alliance, the better their statistical probabilities were for winning lotteries. And for the vast majority of TCC customers that didn't win markets outright, they could make back the money they spent on their applications by owning their tiny, less-than-1-percent fractions of markets other TCC applicants won. The barely legal pooling of chances Wilson envisioned virtually ensured TCC customers would share in several wins, thus assuring an almost certain profit.

It was, Wilson gleefully calculated, practically a sure thing. And that's how he told Maerki to market it. Soon enough, similar schemes sprouted across the country: In New Jersey, a company called Cellular America, working in partnership with ANC, advertised the same plan, even running it by the FCC for approval. In a Keystone Kops–style exchange, the FCC bureaucrats couldn't figure out what to make of the scheme. When Cellular America's Justin Kolb presented a copy of his company's agreement to FCC Mobile Services Division chief Michael Sullivan, Sullivan blurted, "This is an outrage!" But William Adler, deputy chief of the FCC's common-carrier bureau, reacted differently. "Really?" he asked Sullivan. "I thought it was okay. I told him he could do it." With the 1-percent rule successfully sidestepped, the mills were again free to fuel the spectrum rush.

Still, for the majority of Americans who in 1985 had yet even to see a real cell phone, the "sure thing" pitch clanged like cheap tin. Why would you send thousands of dollars to some random marketing company to get in on a newfangled business you knew nothing about? Of all the get-rich-quick schemes people were bombarded with, this one seemed pretty far-fetched— how could it be legal to promise the government you can run a cell phone system when you're really just looking for a quick buck?

ANC's Serap and Steingold knew their product, even with its tax shelter come-on, was still a hard sell. They understood there was no reason consumers should trust them—so they hired someone Americans had trusted for a long time to help flack their product: talk show host Mike Douglas.

Nearly two decades after his show left the air, it's difficult to remember just how popular and influential Mike Douglas was in his heyday. With his soothing, benevolently paternal chitchat and his comfortingly predictable TV presence, Douglas was a man Americans eagerly welcomed into their living rooms each week for twenty-one years, until his show was canceled in 1982. In an age before Rosie O'Donnell and Oprah Winfrey perfected the confessional, emotions-bared talk show, Douglas ruled the genre with an understated wit and easy manner.

For an initial payment of $25,000, Douglas agreed to tape a half-hour infomercial for ANC. It was a decision he would soon profoundly regret.

"You and I have an equal opportunity to compete with the corporate giants for a piece of the multibillion-dollar pie!" crowed Douglas in the ads, which ran on the Financial News Network cable channel. Serap also appeared in the ads, which declared that *Barron's* "had devised a formula showing that a cellular license may be worth up to $20 per person in the larger markets"—a reference to a *Barron's* article that had recently speculated on the worth of the Houston, Texas, cellular market. Though the ad correctly paraphrased *Barron's*—and though the per-POP price for markets would soon far exceed $20—this bit of apparent puffery would create big trouble for ANC.

The pitch worked. Across the country, ordinary Americans like Bob Pelissier saw the ad and reacted: This seemed too good to be true, but if Mike Douglas was pitching it, it couldn't be a scam! To Serap and Steingold's delight, millions of dollars started rolling in.

The mills were now getting plenty of attention, and before long some of it came from an unwelcome source. In the spring of 1985, FCC officials—long accustomed to receiving respect from the companies they regulated—became peeved at ANC's blatant manipulation of the rules. The FCC called on a fellow agency, the Federal Trade Commission, to investigate the mills for possible abuses.

This was too much for Al Schneider. With his new red Porsche, his law license and his reputation still intact, Schneider hurriedly disassociated himself from Nick Wilson and TCC. Meanwhile, TCC and Peter Lewis also parted ways, thanks mainly to Lewis's stubborn insistence on charging $500 per application while prices were falling across the country.

As the FTC came knocking, digging through files and records in TCC's office, it was sober, blindly loyal Greg Neely—who had known and worked with Wilson since his days peddling "The Perfect You"—who was there to greet them with meticulous records and infinite patience. But at ANC's offices in California and Arizona the Fed's suspicions would be harder to answer.

Chief among the FTC's complaints were two claims TCC and ANC made. First, the mills implied that the lottery was a "sure thing"—Kent Maerki, who handled marketing for TCC through his company called "Spectra" (and who was accused of violating Alabama securities laws in 1984), even told investors, "We have reserved the Reno market exclusively for Spectra representation and clients"—an impossibility in a fair lottery. And second, ANC's intimation that Round V markets would be worth twenty dollars a POP, based on the *"Barron's* formula," was, in the eyes of the federal investigators (who knew less about cellular than even Steingold or Serap), patently misleading. There was no guarantee the smaller markets would command those kind of prices, the FTC maintained, and to claim otherwise was fraudulent.

"Even if you're selected for a license," the FCC's Sullivan told the *Wall Street Journal*, "it doesn't guarantee you anything except spending a lot of money setting up a cellular system. You might do better gambling in Las Vegas."

Despite the FTC investigation, the mills continued their frantic pace of marketing and selling applications. Thanks to Greg Neely's careful book-keeping, TCC never got in any serious trouble; the company was reprimanded and instructed to put a disclaimer on its brochures indicating that its applications were a "high-risk" investment. ANC, on the other hand, soon began to unravel under the FTC's scrutiny.

Convinced his company was careening toward trouble, ANC chairman Earl Serap fled the country, taking with him more than a million dollars from ANC's bank accounts as the company blithely declared he'd gone on vacation. As it turned out, Serap's fears were well founded: In August 1985, Arizona Assistant Attorney General Chuck Johnson filed a civil suit claiming ANC had violated state securities and consumer-fraud laws. Johnson also filed an administrative complaint against Mike Douglas, demanding that the entertainer hand over the money ANC had paid him. Embarrassed by the negative publicity and potential legal troubles, Douglas insisted he hadn't known the true nature of the company or its aims; he declared that he believed he was filming a "training video" rather than an advertisement. It was a humiliating turn for a man who had traded for years on his impeccably trustworthy image.

In November 1985, the FTC froze ANC's assets and ordered refunds for its customers, a decision that had tragic, unintended consequences. With the accounts frozen, the employees disbanded and the lawyers and engineers stopped work midstream on customers' applications. Hundreds of unfinished applications—applications that had already been paid for by ANC customers—sat unfiled in ANC's darkened offices.

In ordering ANC to reimburse its customers, the FTC felt it was rescuing would-be victims from a scam. But what the investigators didn't realize was that their actions would end up costing those would-be applicants hundreds of thousands—maybe even millions—of dollars, for a reason the well-meaning bureaucrats didn't anticipate.

A TWENTY-TWO-FOOT RENTAL TRUCK slowly made its way into the asphalt parking lot of a federal building in Gettysburg, Pennsylvania, on February 4, 1986. When it stopped, the driver got out, looked around, and with feigned disconcern sauntered up to the front entrance, a single cellular application for Tucson, Arizona, in his hand.

The man filed the application, then headed back out to his truck, glancing furtively around to see if anyone was paying undue attention to him or his cavernous vehicle. Satisfied that no one seemed to notice or care, he then beckoned cryptically up the road, where another truck was waiting. Having fulfilled his role as decoy, John Landy stepped over to the other truck as it pulled up, and walked with its driver, Greg Neely, around to the back to open the cargo bay.

The second truck was stuffed to bursting with cardboard boxes holding thousands of Round V applications. With all the intrigue and threatening talk coming out of the FTC and FCC, Nick Wilson had decided not to take any chances. Paranoid that he or his employees could get restrained or even arrested, he had devised a plan to detect whether the FCC—or even an ANC goon, angry that Wilson was still in business while ANC had been shut down—was lying in wait for them. When Landy filed the Tucson application without incident, he decided they were in the clear. "We were concerned, very concerned, for no reason," Wilson said later. "We were just overly cautious."

A year and a half after the Round IV filing, the Round V filing dates had finally arrived. The FCC, knowing it was about to be inundated yet again with applications, declared that applicants should file not at the cramped headquarters building in Washington, but at a government warehouse in Gettysburg, Pennsylvania. The bureaucrats were right: More than 8,000 applications were filed for the fifteen Round V markets (an average of 533 per market)—a 300-percent jump over the 5,180 applications filed for thirty markets in Round IV (an average of 172 per market). No matter what the FCC did, it seemed that the frenzy over cellular-spectrum licenses increased exponentially.

The FCC's Michael Sullivan finally decided there was only one way to keep the number of applications from completely exploding: Give everyone less time to prepare them. With licenses for one hundred eighty-five more cities and towns (metropolitan areas, or MSAs in FCC parlance) to distribute, Sullivan convinced the commission to rush the filing deadlines for the coming rounds. Under Sullivan's plan, all the MSA filings would be finished by May 23, only three months away, and the lotteries would be held only a few weeks after each filing. It was perhaps the smartest decision by any Mobile Services chief in the history of the spectrum rush.

Despite the FTC's warnings and press criticism of the mills (the *Washington Post*, for example, published scorching editorials exhorting consumers to stay away from cellular licensing—never mentioning that its parent company had been involved from Round I on), the number of applications kept growing in each filing.

With Peter Lewis gone, TCC turned to a blue-collar, self-taught engineer named Eldon Heinz to do the applications' engineering. John Landy remembers that the eccentric Heinz—a tall, heavy-set, perpetually disheveled techno-geek—fit in well with the odd band of sycophants that flocked around Nick Wilson. "He would just kind of show up and do applications for a while, and then he would disappear," remembers Landy. "We used to call him 'Elvis.'"

Once, Landy asked Heinz, a college dropout who used to work in a TV-repair shop, how he had learned the esoteric art of radio-engineering design. According to Landy, Heinz replied, "'I went down to the dime store and bought myself a folder and took a bus to Washington [to the FCC], and that was about it.'" In preparing his "professionally engineered" maps, Heinz eschewed mathematical modeling and draftsman's tools: He would simply place a drinking glass upside down on a federal topographic map to trace his best estimates of cell coverage areas.

Before the new lottery rules had opened the gates to the proletariat, the idea that a nonprofessional such as Eldon Heinz would do engineering for cellular applications would have been heresy at the FCC. For decades, the group involved in communications and its regulation had been a selective, insular society. An informal guild of well-paid engineers and lawyers cornered the market on FCC-related work, and the commission itself encouraged the view that a certain level of sophistication was required to function within its arcane rules. It was like a gentleman's club: Those who were in the inner circle behaved with the proper decorum; those who attempted to circumvent the system—people such as Barry Yampol, and now Heinz—were as guilty of disrespect as of anything else.

Once Heinz had prepared his slapdash engineering, the rest was a matter of filling out a relatively simple FCC form and running it through a photocopier. Luckily for the mills, the streamlined lottery rules had simplified the process.

"After a while," says Landy, "a monkey could fill out an application. This is not brain surgery here. If you do them enough, anyone can do them." Soon, in the rush to get applications out, Landy himself began teaching people how to do them. At one point, Landy recalls, "We made 14,000 applications in a week."

And the money kept pouring in. Wilson, says Greg Neely, "was spending it as fast as he could, as it came in. I mean, literally, it was just ridiculous." Never one to deny himself any kind of indulgence, Wilson structured his life as a continuously rolling party, attended by an ever-present band of toadies and hangers-on that included twin brothers convicted of marijuana trafficking as well as young women who would disappear with the boss for a few hours at a time. He drank copious amounts of vodka, ate at the best restaurants, visited the gaming tables of Las Vegas, bought himself and Nancy all manner of expensive playthings and never looked too closely at what Neely was doing with the business and the books. In fact, he preferred to know nothing at all about the operational details of the company.

Wilson's lawyer, Bill Franklin, once said that Wilson "couldn't organize. . . a two-car funeral himself. He depends on other people doing all the detail work." This became abundantly clear to Greg Neely one afternoon when he enticed Wilson to come see how applications were put together.

The scramble to meet a filing deadline was on, and Neely asked his boss to come down to the office. "Wouldn't you like to have actually done it yourself," he asked Wilson, "at least part of it so you'd understand really the nuts and bolts, what it is we really do?" Reluctantly, Wilson agreed.

Like a patient tutor, Neely showed Wilson the different parts of the application, the exhibits and appendices and signature pages. They were an almost comical pair: the suave, impeccably tailored, smooth-talking Wilson sitting hunched over a three-ring binder with the rumpled Greg Neely, a troubled former Vietnam vet whose last job before TCC was doing the books for a Chuck E. Cheese pizza franchise. After showing Wilson how to thoroughly double-check each application in minute detail, he showed him how each should be packed into a box to be trucked to the filing center. Neely then left the room for a moment, and when he came back, Wilson was gone.

Neely figured he had gone to the bathroom, but Wilson never returned. After a while, Neely called Wilson's wife, Nancy. "He came back and packed up and was muttering something about you getting on his back," she told the stunned Neely. "He just went to the airport. He's catching a plane to San Francisco."

"He just got the hell out of Cleveland," Neely later marveled. When they later talked, Wilson told him, "Greg, believe me, you were far better off that I was gone. When I realized that I would be responsible if that [application] was late, I couldn't take that responsibility." Wilson wanted to be as far away from the reality of the applications business as he could.

With Neely managing the applications preparation, the checks continued to stream into TCC's bank account. In the spring of 1986, as the FCC rushed one filing deadline after another, TCC sold applications at a breakneck pace. At the same time, starting in February, the FCC began holding its lotteries for Round V and beyond. Now there were dozens of lucky winners who had big decisions to make.

━━━━━

THIS WAS THE MOST INCREDIBLE THING OF ALL ABOUT THE MILLS: Even their most inflated sales pitches turned out to be essentially true. By pooling chances and providing every customer with a small percentage of any other customer's winning lottery score, ANC and TCC *did* virtually guarantee their customers a return on their investment. And the per-POP price of the markets won *did* end up worth the *"Barron's* formula" price of twenty dollars and beyond, eventually surging in some markets up to triple digits. ANC's promises of markets commanding twenty dollars a POP, the target of the FTC's wrath only months earlier, soon looked laughably understated. And the FTC's decision to freeze ANC's assets and thwart the filing of hundreds of applications meant only that the would-be applicants the FTC was trying to protect lost out on the big windfall.

As McCaw's Mark Callaghan notes, "It was funny. At that time, they were saying that this was the investment opportunity of the future. 'Investment of your lifetime! Invest in these things, they'll be worth $50–100 a POP!'. . . That was [considered] a ridiculous claim. Well, in fact, it was true." But when the FTC undertook its investigation in the winter of 1985–86, that was not yet clear.

As part of their investigation, the FTC's gumshoes invited affidavits from "experts" who claimed the Round V markets would never be worth the touted $20 per POP. One of those "experts," incredibly enough, was John Stanton. Back in 1982, when Stanton prepared his first financial projections for the yet-unformed cellular industry as an Ernst & Whinney consultant, he had calculated that many big-city markets would easily be worth many times that figure; these were the projections that got him in the door at McCaw. Stanton was the one person who clearly foresaw how much cellular spectrum promised to be worth, but now that McCaw was on a buying spree, he was better served by downplaying those numbers.

Most Round V markets, Stanton told *Communications Daily,* "would be difficult to make profitable as a stand-alone business," and furthermore, he went on, "the market of buyers for those interests will be fairly small." This latter assertion was true, but it was worth noting that at that time, McCaw's acquisition team was gearing up to cover the country, buying license fractions from whomever would sell, at prices they hoped would be wild bargains. The last thing Stanton needed was to have huge alliances of hundreds of "little people" owning the licenses McCaw coveted; Stanton was more than happy to encourage the popular belief that the licenses were worth very little.

Stranger yet was the case of Ellis Thompson, an early ANC customer who claimed he'd been duped. A star witness for the FTC, Thompson hurriedly rescinded his testimony in the spring of 1986 when he learned that he'd won the Atlantic City, New Jersey, license, thereby assuring himself of a multimillion-dollar windfall.

In the months following the shutdown of ANC, the FTC sold off artwork and furniture from the company's abandoned offices in an effort to raise enough money to reimburse ANC's customers. But when it began sending out checks in mid-1986—after the lotteries had been held and winners announced—it found that many were reluctant to accept the money. Bob Pelissier was one of those who had no complaints against ANC.

"He might have embezzled a lot of money and hurt a lot of people," Pelissier says of Serap, "but he did what we required of him for us.'" When he received a $4,000 check in the mail from the FTC, Pelissier says, he tried to return it.

"I called them back and I says, 'You don't understand, the company that represented us. . . they did a good job for us as far as we are concerned,'" remembers Pelissier. "'They did everything required of them. So we're not entitled to this money. I want to give it back to you.' And the guy just said, 'The government never makes mistakes.' So that was that."

━━━━━

FORMER FCC MOBILE SERVICES DIVISION CHIEF Kevin Kelley later looked back on the cellular lotteries as "the greatest gambling game that ever existed." With the benefit of hindsight, it's easy to agree with that statement. But many of the smarter business minds at the time deemed entering the lottery a waste of time and money.

Many of the early-round applicants didn't bother applying in the lottery rounds, even though the applications were so cheap to prepare. Their reasoning was sound: The flood of applications from the mills meant the odds of winning were hundreds to one. And the jackpots were hardly impressive:

With customer penetration in the new industry still low, and per-POP values correspondingly cheap, smaller markets were unlikely to be worth much at all. To anyone who thought they knew the industry, it was obvious that the lotteries were a bum investment.

That left the greenhorns. The odds promised by the mills and their settlement groups sounded irresistible: It was, as Mike Douglas had pitched it, the "opportunity to compete with the corporate giants for a piece of the multibillion-dollar pie." And the people who bought this pitch—the same people who habitually bought keno tickets, "authentic" signed decorative plates, and zirconium "diamelle" rings—were untroubled by questions that never occurred to them. Would license values rise? Who would finance construction of the system? Would owners of minority license fractions—which many of the mills' customers would soon be—get paid full value for their tiny slivers?

In the end, wise men looked like fools. Customer penetration went nowhere but up. Per-POP prices rose. Minority fractions sold at discounts, but values were so high that they were still profitable. And the know-nothing gamblers who entered the lottery walked away with profits, while the sensible businessmen who had abstained gawked jealously from the sidelines. The "diamelles" had turned out to be worth real diamonds.

It's clear in retrospect that the cellular lottery was, as Mike Douglas had declared, "the opportunity of the century." As Kelley put it years later, "Keep playing. Play it every time and play it often. If you find a game like that, go borrow money from your grandmother and play it. That's the way the mathematics of these things worked out.

"Whatever the numbers were, I mean, it was a winning deal. How can you stop people from playing a game like that?"

13

THE RUSH IS ON

SNOW BEGAN DRIFTING TOWARD THE STREETS of Washington, D.C., around noon on Monday, February 24, 1986. Before the evening rush hour was through, five inches of powdery flakes would cover the nation's capital.

While bike messengers and pedestrians struggled to navigate the thickening snow on M Street, a few dozen people waited nervously in Room 856 of the drab black building on the corner—the FCC headquarters. In the front of the room, an old-fashioned lottery drum—the very same machine used to select unlucky new soldiers in the Vietnam War draft—twirled about. As numbered Ping-Pong balls jounced around inside the clear plastic hopper, Round IV applicants watched expectantly to see who would win the cellular licenses for America's 91st–120th largest cities.

A year and a half had passed since the Round IV filing day, just three weeks had passed since the Round V filing in Gettysburg, and the mills were now spewing applications for Round VI across the land. The giveaway was in high gear, but the days of exclusive, backroom wheeling and dealing in smoky New York conference rooms were gone. The lottery had opened up the cellular game to any random person willing to risk his money—and in Room 856 on this snowy February day, the first lucky winners were about to cash in at the government casino.

The faces were different in this round, but the spirit of Le Grand Deal prevailed. Looking to increase their chances of winning, most Round IV applicants had joined forces in three new settlement groups, two of which arose from the remnants of the Grand Alliance and Counter Alliance, and a third that was formed by a group of newcomers. These groups—unimaginatively named CTC, CellTelCo and CSP—were poised to take most of the Round IV markets on behalf of their members.

What these big partnerships would then do with their licenses was, for the moment, an unanswered question. But a few of the more aggressive partners had their own ideas. And soon after the lottery was finished that snowy February day, they began maneuvering.

AS A LAWYER-TURNED-SMALL-BUSINESSMAN, I was too poor and too late to join in the first three rounds of the cellular giveaway. But when the FCC announced its switch to lotteries in the spring of 1984, I knew I wanted in. Having recently made some money on FCC paging licenses with my brother-in-law and new business partner, Graham Randolph, I was a convert: Spectrum, I had decided, was worth whatever risk the lotteries and the cost of system buildouts posed.

That spring, in fact, I had been convinced enough to make an overly ambitious stab at buying out the MRTS license pieces that Bernie Cravath was then trying so desperately to sell. Lacking anything like the $8.5 million Cravath was asking, I had scrambled to find investors. I traveled up and down the Atlantic seaboard from New York City to Norfolk calling on business acquaintances, venture capital funds and several big newspaper chains. Every time I urged a wary executive to trust in the value of spectrum represented by those settlement partnerships, my pleas were met with mute disbelief and even incredulity. After six weeks of fruitless proselytizing, I was forced to give up, relegated to watching from the sidelines as the value of the licenses leapt, making Cravath, Lewis and their partners an additional $5 million within months.

My MRTS frustration only strengthened my determination not to miss out on the next rounds of the spectrum giveaway. With the 1984 lottery announcement, it was suddenly easier and cheaper (though not as easy as the mills would soon make it) to get into the game. Graham and I hired an engineering firm to prepare applications for all thirty of the Round IV markets. Then, on July 16, 1984, we stuffed Graham's station wagon full of them, drove down to FCC headquarters, and double-parked as we hurriedly carried boxes up to be stamped in. Within weeks, we learned to our dismay that the FCC had received more than 150 applications in each of the thirty markets. Facing miserable odds of winning a license outright, we reluctantly agreed to pool our chances with eighteen other applicants in a settlement group.

When the Round IV lottery was held that snowy day in February 1986, our settlement group, CTC, won four of the thirty markets: Napa and Stockton, California; Lancaster, Pennsylvania; and Newport News, Virginia. Now it was time for the CTC partners to meet and decide what to do next. I drove up from Charlottesville to Washington, D.C., with our investor, Leonard Dreyfus, for what would be one of the biggest meetings so far in my young business career. I hoped to trade our shares in three of the markets for a bigger stake in Napa, but Leonard and Graham were voicing doubts. We decided just to wait and see how things played out.

We made our way to Fifteenth Street in downtown Washington, where we were ushered into the conference room of a plush law firm. Inside, a dozen or so strangers milled about, chatting quietly and sizing each other up as they sipped coffee from Styrofoam cups.

As we would soon learn, CTC was an eclectic assembly of singular personalities: There was Richard Landy, a sophisticated cable-TV and radio investor who'd made a modest fortune as George Lindemann's early partner in Vision Cable. Across the table was Sandra Cox, a statuesque, gum-chewing Texan with brightly polished fingernails and a high crown of stiffly teased, bleached blonde hair. There was a quiet, laconic African American with the improbable name of Early D. Monroe; a stocky, combative attorney named Steven Kafee, who arrived in a neck brace thanks to a weightlifting injury; and a cowboy-booted businessman named David Smith. Graham, Leonard and I took our seats as the meeting began.

As I looked around the room, it occurred to me that something was amiss: The crowd seemed small. CTC had eighteen partners, and several of those had, like us, multiple representatives, including lawyers. By my calculation, there should have been at least three dozen people in the room. Where was everyone?

Larry Movshin called the group to order, introduced himself and announced the agenda. The first task, he declared, was to elect a chairman to conduct the meeting. At this, a tall, sandy-haired young man (who had, I noticed, breezed in moments before, appearing to be in a great hurry) stood beside Movshin at the end of the long conference table. He cleared his throat and introduced himself. His name was John Stanton.

In measured, quiet tones, Stanton spoke. McCaw, he said, had already purchased the interests of a majority of the partners in all four of CTC's markets. It would therefore be natural, he continued, for a McCaw representa-

Italian inventor **Guglielmo Marconi** roiled a skeptical scientific community 100 years ago when he declared that radio waves could travel around the curve of the earth. His 1901 experiment proving him correct made history; it also showed that one day wireless phones could make and receive calls over distances.

(Courtesy The Guglielmo Marconi Foundation, USA, Inc.)

By the time this 1973 photo was taken, the idea of a "wrist telephone" had already thrilled Americans for nearly three decades, starting in 1946 with the appearance of comic strip detective Dick Tracy's "2-Way Wrist Radio." But despite high consumer interest and the fact that the "cellular" communications concept was developed back in 1947, FCC foot-dragging delayed the first commercial cell phone system until 1983.

(© 1973, *The Washington Post*. Reprinted with permission. Photo by Harry Naltchayan)

The cell phone industry launched just as AT&T broke up, and at first it wasn't clear whether Ma Bell or the seven new Regional Bell Operating Companies would get the cellular business. The decision was made on AT&T Chairman **Charles Brown's** watch; foolishly, the telephone behemoth simply handed the business to the RBOCs. As one executive later put it, AT&T was "more interested in the Yellow Pages at the time than wireless." It would pay tremendously for that indifference, later buying its way back into the business at an astonishing price.

(© 1982, *The Washington Post*. Reprinted with permission. Photo by James K. W. Atherton)

Having announced an open competition to win one of the two cell phone system licenses designated for every U.S. city, town and rural area (the other li-

cense would go to the local telephone company), the FCC was stunned at the volume of applications it received. Would-be cell phone companies packed their applications with charts, studies, diagrams—anything to give them an advantage in the "comparative hearings." Little did the FCC staffers know it, but this was only a trickle compared to the flood that would come.

(© 1982, *The Washington Post*. Reprinted with permission. Photo by Frank Johnston)

Looking at Motorola's "brick"—the first commercial handheld cell phone—it's not surprising that many observers doubted cell phones would ever become popular. Expensive, heavy, unwieldy and with a laughably short battery life, the "brick" seemed little more than a toy for showoffs.

MCI Chairman **William McGowan**, a driving force behind the breakup of AT&T, fought to position his company at the forefront of the cellular industry. His cocky self-assurance gave investors confidence, but within MCI's ranks, an emerging corporate arrogance threatened to undo the company's cellular efforts.

Former Army officer **Peter Lewis** was one of the few early applicants not backed by a company or big investors. Lewis was a pioneer in the cellular business, a fearless, creative tactician who excelled at finding unorthodox ways to profit from the FCC giveaway. But his cellular career would end in disgrace when he finally bent the rules a little too far.

(© 1997, *The Washington Post.* Reprinted with permission. Photo by Dayna Smith)

At the top end of the scale among first-round applicants was multimillionaire **John Kluge**, a classic 20th-century entrepreneurial baron who oversaw a sprawling empire of media businesses. Though the retirement-aged Kluge already had more money than he could spend, a huge new country estate and a new wife, he impulsively decided to gamble on the cellular industry—a gamble that would make him the richest man in America.

(Photo by Matt Gentry / *Charlottesville Daily Progress*)

Used to illustrate a 1984 *Washington Post* story about the newfangled "car phones," this photo demonstrated one of cell phones' earliest selling points: safety. In the industry's early years, phones were marketed as business tools and safety items; it seemed almost heretical to suggest that people might want a wireless phones just for chatting. "It's not going to be something you and I put in the car to call home and say we're on the way home for dinner," declared one FCC official.

(© 1984, *The Washington Post*. Reprinted with permission. Photo by James A. Parcell)

Mercurial, intuitive, combative **Barry Yampol** was the most controversial figure in the telecommunications industry. He understood before anyone else how valuable radio spectrum was and how big the cell phone industry would become, so he made sure his company, Graphic Scanning, applied for every single cellular license the FCC made available. His competitors were furious, partly from outrage at his maneuver, but mostly because they hadn't thought to do the same thing themselves.

(*New York Times* Pictures)

Boisterous, abrasive **Dick Sherwin** was Yampol's point man in dealing with the rest of the industry. As the steward of Graphic Scanning's cellular assets, he was in charge of the largest pile of cellular spectrum controlled by any one company. Unfortunately, his boss's penchant for shortcuts and duplicity would end up decimating the company.

(Courtesy Dick Sherwin)

When he walked into a small Seattle-based cable company in 1982, 26-year-old consultant **John Stanton** was just looking for another client. When he walked out following a feud with Craig McCaw six years later, McCaw Communications was the dominant force in the cellular industry. Though Craig McCaw would receive most of the credit for the phenomenal rise of the company, it was Stanton—who transformed himself from hourly consultant to billionaire in less than two decades—who orchestrated much of the company's strategy behind the scenes.

(Photo by Mike Siegel / *The Seattle Times*)

From humble beginnings as young Craig McCaw's tax lawyer in the mid-'70s, **Wayne Perry** became his boss's right-hand man, eventually heading nearly every one of McCaw's many ventures. Perry, Stanton and Ed Hopper designed most of the deals that propelled McCaw to the head of the industry.

(Courtesy Wayne Perry)

From a tiny cable TV company in Centralia, Washington, **Craig McCaw** fashioned a telecommunications powerhouse built on little more than borrowed money and epic chutzpah. An awkward, introverted anti-mogul who once famously declared "I want to be the Wizard of Oz," he put together the greatest team of deal-makers in the young industry, then set them loose to build an empire.

In the early days, cellular was a speculative industry with huge up-front capital costs; finding financing was an unending struggle, and many companies succumbed when they couldn't find enough to fill the coffers. When Wall Street's old-line money men failed to drum up the financing McCaw needed, the team turned to junk bond king **Michael Milken**. How could he, they asked, get them the money when no one else could? "Why can some people pole vault 19 feet and others only 14?" Milken snapped back. "You guys needed brain surgery and you went to a bunch of veterinarians." Milken found money for other cellular operators as well, including John Kluge's Metromedia.

The "grandfather of the cellular industry," **Wayne Schelle** was involved in the new industry from its very beginning. He helped run one of the first experimental systems in the late '70s, ran his own cellular company and investment banking firm, and then ran the first experimental PCS system in the early '90s. He also pioneered "phone-in-a-box": allowing a customer to walk into a store and buy a phone, rather than waiting for hours or days for credit approval, paper processing and system delays.

As cell phones grew in popularity, more and more cell towers began sprouting up across the country, drawing anguished protests from citizens and neighborhood groups. In response, companies have begun disguising the towers, hiding them in church steeples, grain silos, and even fashioning local flora – from palm trees to saguaro cactuses.

(The Larson Company, Camouflage Division)

Slick, charming, utterly amoral **Nick Wilson** saw his chance at riches when the FCC began giving away cellular licenses by lottery. Intended to cut back on the paperwork and delays of the comparative hearings system, the lottery decision opened the floodgates to Americans hoping to get a piece of the telecom industry: Anyone could apply, regardless of whether they had the first idea of how to run a cell phone system. Wilson opened an application mill, The Cellular Corp., and hawked FCC applications at inflated prices to anyone who would buy them, even throwing in a dubious tax-dodge to entice more customers.

(Courtesy Greg Neely)

Seventies TV icon **Mike Douglas** filmed an infomercial for one of the application mills, pitching the FCC license giveaway as "one of the greatest business opportunities, not only in your lifetime, but of the century!" Thousands of Americans who saw the ad on cable TV sent their money to the mills, enriching hucksters like Nick Wilson and throwing the FCC giveaway into complete chaos.

(© 1973, *The Washington Post.*
Reprinted with permission. Photo by James A. Parcell)

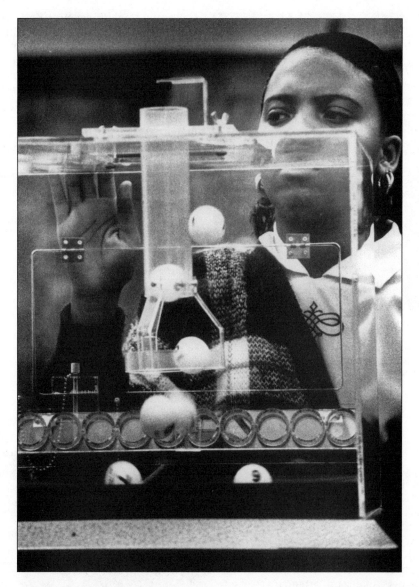

"[Cellular] is a valuable service needed by the public," FCC Commissioner Joseph Fogarty declared in 1982, "and it shouldn't be decided on a roll of the dice." Yet the FCC went ahead with cellular lotteries, initially employing the same Ping-Pong ball drum that was used to select unlucky new soldiers in the Vietnam War draft. Thanks to lax financial rules, the lottery was essentially open to anyone—and the "pig farmers and hairdressers," as one cellular executive called them, wasted no time buying their lucky lottery tickets.

(Photo by Justine Frazier for *The Washington Post.*)

California truck driver **Bob Pelissier** saw the Mike Douglas infomercial late one night when he couldn't sleep. Enticed by the pitch, he talked it over with his wife **Lorraine**; the couple took out a loan against their house and bought a chance in the lottery. When the Ping-Pong balls were drawn, Pelissier—who had never run a business and never seen a cell phone—had won part of the cell phone license for Nashua-Manchester, New Hampshire. Now he had two choices: build a sophisticated cell phone system within six months, or sell the license piece to someone who could.

(Courtesy Robert Pelissier)

As the lotteries continued, Craig McCaw sent **Scot Jarvis** (left) to track down the winners and convince them to sell their licenses. Jarvis jetted frantically back and forth across the country, meeting with nurses, retirees, schoolteachers, mailroom attendants—people who, in many cases, had no real idea what they'd won. With his combination of boyish charm and business wiles, he succeeded in winning people's trust—and getting his hands on their licenses. **Scott Anderson** (right) somehow kept track of and papered the myriad deals.

(Courtesy Scot Jarvis)

When hundreds of cellular applications began pouring into the FCC from rural Tennessee zip codes, staffers suspected a scam. To the surprise of almost no one, it turned out that country hustler **Mack Johnson** was behind the barely-legal applications flood. Johnson earned his reputation as the man who discovered more ways than anyone to manipulate FCC rules for profit—and in the process, he made enough money to buy a lakeside home, a private jet and just about anything else he wanted.

(Courtesy Mack Johnson)

Jim Murray (left), a country lawyer-turned-entrepreneur, learned what radio spectrum was in the shabby garage office of a paging company, then applied for paging and cellular licenses. **Mark Warner**, a young political fundraiser at the beginning of the cellular industry, went from sleeping in his car to earning millions as a speculator in licenses. Together with two partners, Murray and Warner co-founded Columbia Capital Corp., the first investment banking firm dedicated solely to mergers and acquisitions in the burgeoning market for FCC cellular licenses. Columbia, now transformed into a venture capital firm, manages in excess of $1.5 billion in investments, and Warner is running for governor of Virginia.

(Photo by Warren Mattox)

FCC Chairman **Reed Hundt** (right) presided over the Commission's switch from lotteries to auctions, in a tenure marked by spectacular successes as well as dismal failures. A high school classmate of Al Gore and law school classmate of

Bill Clinton, Hundt enjoyed the spotlight and missed no opportunities to promote himself. **William Kennard**, seen conferring with Hundt at a hearing about spectrum auctions, became chairman on Hundt's departure.

(© 1994, *The Washington Post*. Reprinted with permission. Photo by Ray Lustig)

tive to chair future meetings. No one should feel any pressure, he assured us, as McCaw "welcomed partners" and planned to be "fair." But if anyone else in the room was ready to sell his percentage to McCaw, Stanton had cash at the ready. With his understated, self-confident style and disarmingly pleasant manner, Stanton had us lockjawed. The message was clear: McCaw was in charge.

We were stunned. The official lottery results hadn't even been published by the FCC yet, and already McCaw had outmaneuvered us, gaining control of our CTC partnership. McCaw's blitzkrieg purchase of a majority in each of the four markets from its old Grand Alliance partners had completely blindsided the newcomers, including us. When Stanton concluded his little speech, recalls Graham Randolph, "It hit the fan." Stanton had effectively "announced he was going to pay us $6.86 per POP. . . and pick up your checks when you went out the door, because they had ink on them that was going to evaporate if we didn't get them quick." In an instant, my naive plan to consolidate our winnings into a 20-percent stake in Napa had vaporized.

Having said his piece and thrown the room into confusion, Stanton quickly departed. Movshin, who had been the de facto leader before Stanton's bombshell, did the same. And there the rest of us sat, temporarily mute and unsure of what to do next.

Reactions among those left in the room were mixed: Graham was furious, Monroe was resigned, Landy wanted retribution and I found myself marveling at the ingenuity of these unknowns from Seattle. There was, however, one thing we had in common: We didn't want to sell at McCaw's price. We formed a little group of holdouts, then began shopping for other cellular operators who, in search of trading chits, might give McCaw some competition and drive up the prices.

Our strategy worked. Over the coming months, we slowly negotiated the prices upward to eight dollars, then nine dollars per POP rather than the six dollars and change Stanton had offered. The burgeoning yuppie haven of Napa was our great bargaining chip; when we threatened to sell Napa to McCaw's sworn enemy, the hated wireline PacTel, McCaw reacted instantly: What did we want? When we asked for thirteen dollars a POP, we secretly worried we had overreached. Though there had been rumors of controlling pieces selling for ten or twelve dollars, and press speculation (quoted by application mills like ANC) that giant markets might be worth twenty or more dollars, no market we'd heard of had yet sold for more than nine dollars. But McCaw's answer was swift and simple: Done!

Even as our partners congratulated each other on the group's patience and negotiating skills, I found myself wondering: What did McCaw know that we didn't? Why were they so willing to pay what seemed an outrageously high price? Sure enough, McCaw's bold gamble paid off; our joy turned to dismay as we watched license prices quickly soar, raising the value of our Napa license twenty-fold over the next few years. We were merely among the faces in the growing crowd of suckers who sold out too early to the McCaw machine.

ACROSS TOWN, ANOTHER SANDY-HAIRED YOUNG WHEELER-DEALER was preparing to spring his own surprise announcement.

Mark R. Warner was only thirty-one in the spring of 1986, but he was no gawky amateur. With his huge, toothy grin and aw-shucks manner, the athletic young Harvard Law School graduate was able to balance his monumental ego with a homespun charm. Though his ambition and self-confidence became legendary—he would run for the U.S. Senate by age forty—somehow Warner managed to turn every conversation into a cozy, just-you-and-me chat.

Working as a fundraiser for the Democratic party, Warner deftly brokered his contacts with wealthy businesspeople on one side and young Washington communications lawyers on the other to carve out a slice of the cellular industry for himself. In Round III of the giveaway, Warner had convinced a few wealthy Connecticut acquaintances to apply and had helped them through Le Grand Deal. And when two competing bidders for the Charlotte, North Carolina, market—Metro Mobile and the Providence Journal Corporation—came calling, Warner had stepped into the breach as the seller's agent, playing one against the other.

The young deal-maker watched in bemused amazement as his client's one-twenty-second interest in the license (a mere 29,000 POPs)—one of the few remaining available pieces after others had been snapped up first—rocketed in value from $200,000 to more than $1 million in a matter of weeks. Warner got a percentage of the profits, the better part of a year's pay for a few hours work. Lesson learned, Warner was determined to repeat his brokering success; luckily he had already helped a few more friends apply in the upcoming Round IV.

Like most Round IV applicants, Warner's clients pooled their chances in one of the three big settlement groups. CellTelCo, which was, like CTC, a loose amalgam of strangers, had collectively won ten of the thirty Round IV markets.

Shortly after the lottery, the Washington lawyers called together their clients, and nearly a hundred CellTelCo partners convened in a ballroom at the Westin Hotel in Washington. The purpose of the meeting was to discuss joint action and governance, but Warner had other plans; he brazenly convinced the lawyers to give him a spot on the agenda, and plotted the move that could springboard a new, lucrative career.

Mark Warner was the picture of self-confidence as he strode to the front of the room, but underneath his suit jacket, he was sweating. As the dozens of businesspeople rustled through their papers and shifted in their seats, he began to speak.

"We've won ten markets," he began, in his booming baritone, "and what we have to do now is decide whether we're going to build the markets or sell the markets."

"We need to be in this together," Warner continued, his adrenaline rising, "and you need to have a single agent. . . . What you all need to do is to sign me up as your broker." He then related the story of the Charlotte-market sale and his client's remarkable windfall, warning that if CellTelCo didn't agree to hire him as its broker, "some of you are going to get $6 a POP, and some of you are going to get a whole bunch of money, and the rest of you are going to get screwed."

As Warner spoke, the mood of the gathering shifted from polite boredom to an excited buzz. "It was so loud," Warner recalls, "it was almost like a revival meeting at one point." Who was this guy? And why should the CellTelCo partners turn over their deal making to him? He looked young enough to be a student, yet this Charlotte deal gave him a veneer of credibility—few others in the room had a clue about the value of what the partnership owned. Still, the natural first impulse of those in the room was to hold tight to their pieces and control their own destinies; Warner would need every ounce of his considerable charisma and charm to sway the group.

Warner stood at the front, waiting for the ruckus to die down. He had prepared a short document for each of the partners, with a paragraph stating that the undersigned agreed to pay him 5 percent of the sale price if he brokered a deal the partners later accepted. As their agent, he would only make money if they did. A few tense moments passed, as Warner stood uncertainly at the front of the room, wondering whether someone was about to call his bluff. After all, he was only one deal more experienced than any-one else there, and the audience was stacked with far more astute business-people than he. Sure, he had a law degree to bolster his credentials—yet he'd never taken the bar exam and hadn't practiced law for a single day. As the silence hung unbroken, Warner feared his plan was about to flop.

But then a voice came from the back of the room.

Gus Mijalis, a Louisiana native with a down-home style and blunt char-acter, piped up, "God dammit, Mark, I think we should do it with you." He stood up, walked down the aisle to the front of the room and laid his signed agreement on the table in front of Warner.

It was as if a spell had been broken. One by one, and then in a stream, the rest of the partners brought their agreements to the front of the room. "The whole thing could have fallen apart for me," Warner remembers, "if some-body hadn't kind of pulled the trigger and said, 'Okay, we don't really know Warner and we don't really know each other, but we've got to do this.'"

When all the partners were signed up, Warner was free to sell: He had just made himself into the cellular industry's first—but certainly not its last—cellular broker. Almost immediately, suitors came calling. McCaw, whose appetite for cellular properties was growing more voracious by the day, wanted to purchase most of the CellTelCo markets. In order to boost the price, Warner badly needed what we at CTC also desperately sought: com-peting buyers. But most major operators were either distracted with system buildouts or pessimistic about smaller market prospects; it looked at first like McCaw would have free reign over the small-market landscape. Fortu-nately, a competitor arrived: paging and cellular veteran Wayne Schelle, who was launching his own startup cellular operation, First Cellular Group.

What followed was an object lesson for federal policy-makers. Warner held an auction, selling six markets for more than $20 million and garner-ing more than $800,000 in fees for himself—a spectacular windfall for someone who just months earlier had spent nights sleeping on the floors of friends' apartments, or in the back seat of his 1965 Buick Special. McCaw wound up with Madison, Wisconsin ($9.50 per POP) and Corpus Christi, Texas ($9.06 per POP), and Spokane, Washington (nine dollars per POP), while Schelle took Lakeland, Florida (ten dollars per POP); Columbia, South Carolina (eleven dollars per POP); and Shreveport, Louisiana (eight dollars per POP).

To many, the very idea of Warner's auction was a travesty—not because Warner was breaking any laws or deceiving anyone, but because the U.S. government had given away the public radio spectrum for free, and now the winners were promptly flipping it for a huge profit. The winners hadn't even been required to offer proof that they ever intended actually to build a cellular system. And besides that, they had been handed these invaluable licenses not because they deserved them, but because they'd won them in a lottery, of all things.

At the FCC, staffers grumbled anew that the process was a farce, and that the commission was being played for a fool. At the time, the FCC had no legal authority to hold auctions themselves. Though a small handful of policy theorists had occasionally suggested changing the policy, it would be nearly a decade before the FCC could do what Warner had done. In the meantime, hundreds of lucky winners continued to get rich on the backs of U.S. taxpayers.

———

THE QUICK CASH-OUTS ENGINEERED BY settlement group members attracted a few grumbles of dissent, but the FCC's overall reaction was one of resignation—especially compared to the controversy soon sparked by the maneuverings of the CSP settlement group.

The main characters in CSP could have walked off the pages of a Tennessee Williams play. There was Haynes Griffin, a short, arrogant butterball of a man with horn-rimmed glasses, a Princeton degree and a nasal Southern twang. There was Steve Leeolou, a blow-dried, all-American boy who gave up his job as a star TV anchor to get into cellular (reducing his mother, a telephone operator for Publisher's Clearinghouse Sweepstakes, to tears). There was Richard Preyer, a part-time tennis instructor, freelance writer and general layabout, the son of a North Carolina congressman. And then there was Lee Lovett.

Lee Lovett was a Washington attorney, though with his gold jewelry, European-tailored suits and aggressive style, he came across more like a hyperactive mob underboss—especially compared to his colleagues in the buttoned-down world of communications law. Once described by a colleague as the "F. Lee Bailey of the communications bar," Lovett was like a marionette master—able to manipulate his young business protégés, Leeolou and Preyer, and a handful of other would-be cellular entrepreneurs into selling his services for him, and able to manipulate the FCC's rules to fit his needs. He also made a career of prancing right on the edge of business propriety, until he finally got too close.

Lovett and his law firm already had a modest applications business going when Leeolou and Preyer showed up and agreed to sell applications for him.

They had enjoyed modest success in rounds II and III: They entered the Big Monopoly trading with a couple of North Carolina applications, and came out with a substantial minority stake in a couple of cellular licenses in the Pennsylvania rust belt around Scranton and Allentown. Emboldened by their success, they named their company Vanguard Cellular, recruited fuel-oil salesman Haynes Griffin as full-time CEO, and eagerly set out to sell more partnerships on Lovett's application services. Round IV was coming, and the fledgling businessmen were ready to cash in on the continuing giveaway.

Leeolou and Preyer set out across the South in an old Subaru station wagon in the winter of 1983–84; for months, they peddled applications for $175,000 to groups of friends and relatives while taking a mere 2 percent of sales for their efforts. The bulk of the money and occasionally a share of the equity went to Lovett, ostensibly as prepayment for his future legal services in shepherding the applications through comparative hearings.

But the comparative hearings would never take place, of course: A few months before the Round IV filing, the FCC had declared its switch to lotteries. Suddenly, the $175,000 applications Leeolou and Preyer were selling could be had for a fraction of that. The North Carolinians panicked. They would have to refund everyone's money! No one would stand for having shelled out tens of thousands of dollars for a 1-in-100-chance lottery ticket!

Lovett scoffed at their panic. Relax, the lawyer told them, this will all work out. Never mind the fact that every reputable communications lawyer in Washington had known for months that the lotteries were inevitable; this was, Lovett declared, not his fault: The FCC had changed its rules unfairly in midstream.

The North Carolina promoters had two choices: They could either sue Lovett for malpractice to recover some of his $2.5 million in prepaid and totally unnecessary legal fees, or they could find a loophole that would keep everyone's cellular hopes alive.

Not surprisingly, Lovett suggested a loophole. Each of the expensive partnerships could, he proposed, take their single big application (which was yet to be filed), blank out the name of the applicant, copy it, and give individual copies to each partner to file separately. Now a partnership of twelve would have twelve applications instead of one. So far so good. But one problem remained. These dozens of partners were all passive investors—bank executives, lawyers, doctors, oilmen, farmers and the like. Leeolou and Preyer had convinced them to file in groups, but the prospect of filing alone, then possibly being solely responsible for getting a cell phone system up and running, was daunting for many of them. What did a dentist or lawyer know about cell phones, anyway?

Lovett had another answer, but this one would stretch the rules, becoming the first (but certainly not the last) major scam perpetrated against the FCC in the cellular-spectrum rush. In Round IV, the FCC rules allowed applicants to band together in settlement groups—but only *after* they had filed their applications. Why not, Lovett suggested, simply agree in advance to pool everyone's chances—all those individual applications Lovett had just run off on the photocopier—back together again as soon as they were filed, with each partner owning the same percentage they'd originally held in the $175,000 application? Left unspoken was the fact that the plan would also benefit the Vanguard team in another way: If the twelve applications were put together again, Lovett, Leeolou, Preyer and Griffin could have equity in the operating company, something they couldn't do with twelve separate applications.

This was clearly a violation, but the Vanguard entrepreneurs, believing they'd received the consent of an FCC staffer, plowed ahead with their plan. Now the partnerships were still intact—but instead of having one application per market, they had many.

Thanks to Lovett's scheme, nearly a quarter of all the Round IV applications had ties to Vanguard. When the Round IV lottery day came, Vanguard's settlement group, CSP, won 7 of the 30 markets, including Jackson, Mississippi; Reading and York, Pennsylvania; and Little Rock, Arkansas—whose winning partnership included a young attorney named Hillary Rodham Clinton. Her purchase of a stake in that Round IV–Little Rock application would prove to be one of her shrewder investments (though not quite as impressive as her infamous cattle futures windfall).

CSP's seven wins in the Round IV lottery served only to pique the ire of the other two settlement groups who saw Vanguard's subtle rules-tampering as a major violation, even a fraud. The FCC, they insisted, should throw out all the offending applicants, including dozens who had innocently joined CSP after Lovett implemented his scheme. Their outrage wasn't based entirely on principle, of course: Wholesale dismissals of CSP applications would result in the elevation of second-place finishers from CellTelCo and CTC into the winners' spots.

Leeolou, Preyer and new Vanguard head Haynes Griffin had a fight on their hands—and they were facing it without Lee Lovett, who was convicted of mail fraud in August 1985 and subsequently spent three months in prison, gave up his law license and withdrew (albeit with millions in profits) from all his cellular partnerships. CellTelCo and CTC, armed with evidence gathered by private investigators, were determined to get their hands on the CSP licenses. What they got instead was a snarled, intractable legal tangle that held up construction of all seven of the contested markets.

As Yogi Berra might have observed, it was déjà vu all over again: As in the comparative hearings' paper war, there was complete license gridlock. Despite the nonwirelines' determination to deny the wirelines head starts in these new markets, the FCC's first preannounced lottery had created little but chaos. And it was anybody's guess how long it might take to clean it up.

As squabbling over Round IV markets heated up, the filing dates and lotteries came at an ever-faster clip, thanks to Michael Sullivan's order to hurry things up. The Round V lottery was held on April 21, 1986, a mere two and a half months after the filing, and the filing dates for the remaining 155 cities came in rapid succession after that.

With every spin of the lottery drum, more and more "little people" were striking gold in the spectrum rush. Truck driver Bob Pelissier's partnership won Manchester-Nashua, New Hampshire. Former Miss Louisiana-turned-businesswoman Lynn Noble Hawthorne won Spokane. Deep-sea divers, secretaries, preachers and nurses suddenly found themselves majority owners of cellular licenses—and all thanks to the luck of the draw. Few of these applicants actually made the trip to Washington to watch the lottery-drum spin, but for those who did, there were some exciting moments.

Washington attorney Carl W. Northrop was at the FCC on April 21 for the Round V lottery. His application for the Trenton, New Jersey, license— one of several hundred applications for that market—had been assigned lottery number 009. Northrop sat in the front row, watching as the lottery machine whirred and spit numbered balls into three slots to spell out a number.

"This machine had some age on it," remembers Northrop, "so the thing would kick around, and the ball would get stuck in the tube, and *whirrrrr*, it'd come off the top." Northrop watched the first two balls for the Trenton market come up: two zeroes in a row! Now he had a one-in-nine chance of winning Trenton, which, thanks to its strategic positioning between New York and Philadelphia, promised to be worth millions.

"I'm starting to get a little excited," says Northrop, "so then the third ball starts to come up and it gets stuck in the tube! It gets stuck in the tube but I can see the number, and it's a nine. And I just went crazy! I went absolutely crazy: 'We won, we won!'

"And the ball comes up, and [the lottery official] looks at it and she says, 'Six.' And she turns it over and puts it down.

"After that," says Northrop, "I never went to another lottery again."

The Trenton lottery was notable for another reason as well: In the audience that day were Nick and Nancy Wilson. Among the thousands of applications for Trenton was one bearing Nancy's name. A few twirls of the drum after Northrop's crushing disappointment, Nancy Wilson's number came up as the third-place finisher in Trenton. Some may have been disappointed at placing third, but Nancy was euphoric: In no time, Nick had her convinced that they could sue and have the first- and second-place finishers dismissed, after which the license would be hers.

Nancy was, in fact, so thrilled at her apparent good fortune that when it came time to name the boy she and Nick adopted, she chose the name "Trenton." Fortunately, the name has its own merits (and equally fortunately, Nancy didn't place third in Erie or Kalamazoo, both Round V cities), as Nancy never did end up with the Trenton license.

———

IN THE DAYS FOLLOWING THE ROUND V LOTTERY, Bob Pelissier might have thought he'd won a popularity contest instead of a cellular license. Suddenly he had a host of new would-be best friends: salespeople hawking multimillion-dollar cellular hardware systems, aggressive lawyers, brokers offering to help him sell out, marketing firms and a host of con artists and parasites all looking for a piece of the Pelissier windfall.

Across the country, lottery winners such as Bob and Lorraine began getting more phone calls and mail than they ever received before. New letters and trade publications began arriving, many bearing articles targeted at a small new breed of American nouveaux riches: the cellular-lottery winners.

The most strident of the newsletters came from disguised sources closely tied to the application mills. Nick Wilson's TCC launched the "Roamer One News Bulletin"; San Francisco–based General Cellular Corp. began publishing its "MTC Report"; and both were later emulated by Dean Lovett, Lee Lovett's son, who published "The Cellular Equity Mismatch," billed as "the newsletter that looks out for the 'little guy.'" These handouts ostensibly offered unbiased advice on how to maximize lottery profits. But behind the supposed altruism lay more devious motives.

As of May 23, 1986—the last filing deadline for U.S. cities (or MSAs, in FCC parlance)—there would be no more work for the application mills. True, the FCC planned to lottery off rural markets (RSAs) at some point, but as of yet there were no rules and no scheduled filing dates. The mills' founders—people such as TCC's Nick Wilson, and GCC's Terry Easton and Quentin Breen—were loath to see their easy cellular money evaporate; they began trolling for new ways to milk the system.

Their advice to license winners was simple and direct: Don't sell out now. Per-POP prices, the newsletters proclaimed, have climbed from three to twenty to forty-five dollars and beyond. They'll keep climbing, to $200 or more—even, claimed a few wild prognosticators, up to $500. Selling now meant missing out on huge prices. The smarter option was to build and operate.

If the purpose behind their scheming was subtle, their methods were not. The newsletters demonized the potential buyers and shamelessly plucked the populist heartstrings with lines like, "Mr. Deep Pockets (unlike our typical lottery selectee, who has a bank account resembling ours) can afford to play expensive games, and he may." The March 1987 issue of "Cellular Equity Mismatch" even profiled an offer made on Pelissier's Manchester-Nashua market, blasting a law firm for making a below-market offer for an anonymous client. "The only thing to do for our fat piggies is to stop playing games, start making profits and share them like good boys," blared the newsletter, "and should the fat piggies stay greedy (and make below-market offers)," they would "end up at the slaughterhouse."

Now came the real pitch: The newsletters' authors were ready to offer help in the form of "management advice." Nick Wilson formed Cellular Management Services (CMS), an ostensibly independent company run by Wilson protégé John Landy and convicted drug smuggler Robert Neff, with offices conveniently colocated with Wilson's. GCC offered its own stock in trade for cellular licenses, so that lucky winners could let Breen and Easton "professionally manage" their systems while the licensee relaxed in confidence, retaining the "upside" growth in the form of GCC stock.

Meanwhile, the growing number of operating companies seeking to buy licenses struck back, with phone calls and letters of their own. The winners who waited to sell, they proclaimed, risked losing everything: Those who kept their licenses would have to borrow millions to build their systems, after which they might be killed by falling rates and low revenues once competition kicked in.

For many of the small-time winners, this battle for their souls was dizzying. Often, decisions were made based on gut instinct or a pleasant phone conversation, rather than on the true merits of the option. Some of the suitors were more successful than others; one of the most persuasive of all the buyers was Leroy Carlson, the chairman and CEO of Telephone and Data Systems. But even with his formidable powers of persuasion, Carlson met his match—at least temporarily—in the stubborn California truck driver, Bob Pelissier.

Leroy Carlson was one of the cellular industry's unforgettable characters. A disconcertingly tall, wraithlike man in his midseventies, Carlson was, with his knobby bones, big teeth and floppy ears, a study in exaggerated proportions. His disarming, soft-spoken manner belied his insatiable avarice; despite his already formidable net worth, he wedged his gangly frame into economy-class airline seats nearly every day as he crisscrossed the country looking for acquisitions for TDS, an aggregator of small rural telephone companies.

Carlson—who had made himself a multimillionaire with his first company—had honed his skills with decades upon decades of acquiring companies big and small. Any reasonable observer might have expected a lopsided mismatch when, hours after the lottery on April 21, 1986, he set his sights on acquiring the Manchester-Nashua, New Hampshire, market.

But Bob Pelissier didn't want to sell. He believed the pitch that prices would only rise, and he'd read about other winners who were building systems with the aim to sell later. "God darn it," Pelissier remembers thinking to himself, "if these other applicants can do it, then so can I." And so he would—with the help, ironically enough, of Leroy Carlson.

Pelissier's first step was to sign up for a five-day cram course in cellular offered by the University of Wisconsin, after which he began visiting other cell system owners in markets far removed from his, looking for advice on running a system. Meanwhile, Carlson plotted his end-around. The truck driver owned only 25 percent of his partnership, which in turn owned 50.01 percent of the Manchester-Nashua license. So while Pelissier had been designated the nominal managing partner, his total ownership percentage of the license was only 12.5 percent.

Quickly and quietly, Carlson moved to acquire as much of the other 87.5 percent as he could. TDS approached Pelissier's octogenarian partner, James Jenkins, who owned 50 percent of the partnership (giving him 25 percent of the license). Like many less sophisticated ANC and TCC customers, Jenkins had barely understood what he'd applied for, and he was more than happy to sell out immediately.

"I got the suspicion that [Jenkins] just thought he was buying stock," remembers Pelissier, "because when we told him what happened when we won, he came unglued. He says, 'What do you mean? We don't have to build a telephone company!' And we says, 'You do! You do! And you're the one who runs it because you are the one that owns 50 percent of the company!'" Shocked at the suggestion, and anxious to get out of an obligation he hadn't fully understood, Jenkins sold almost immediately to TDS.

Before they knew what had happened, Pelissier and the third partner, Jalal Hashtroudi, found that half their partnership was now owned by TDS. While they were still digesting that news, Carlson began buying up the dozens and dozens of small partners who owned the other 49.9 percent of their license, eventually inching his way from 25-percent ownership up to nearly 75 percent.

So it was that when Pelissier sat down to talk with his partners about how to build New Hampshire's second cellular system, he sat at a table with a cadre of engineers and executives from U.S. Cellular Corporation, the TDS subsidiary. This was a curse and a blessing: With TDS as a partner, Pelissier had professional engineering help in building and running the system, but he was in a shotgun marriage, left with only one buyer and little negotiating leverage.

Still he held on. While many of the "little people" who won licenses sold right away, Pelissier kept his percentage for seven years, watching as the market heated up and increasing numbers of Americans bought cell phones. When he sold, the former truck driver and his wife—two of the many who struck gold in the spectrum rush—found themselves millionaires.

―――――

LIKE OTHER MCCAW EMPLOYEES WORKING on the cable business, Scot Jarvis had heard of cellular phones, but he wasn't altogether sure what McCaw's cellular division really did. He got his first lesson one afternoon in 1985 at the Shumway mansion in Kirkland, Washington, where Wayne Perry was giving a talk to a small group of the company's senior cable-TV employees.

"This is your cash flow," intoned Perry, as he drew a cartoonish pot of money on a white board at the front of the room. "This is the cash flow that cable creates." Perry turned and drew a circle a few inches from the money pot, then scribbled furiously, coloring it completely black.

"This is the black hole that's called cellular," he continued, absolutely deadpan. "We just pour this pot of money into the black hole, and you just keep refilling the pot, and we just keep pouring it over here into the black hole. And at some point this will actually start filling up its own pot, and we'll go find something else to do."

Jarvis had been with McCaw for only a few months when he got the call to switch from cable to cellular. A handsome, ambitious University of Washington graduate, Jarvis wasn't sure he wanted to derail his career in cable; McCaw was, as he recalls, "a cable company, with this little teeny group of paging, which had this little teeny group of cellular." Moving from the cable side to the cellular side was, he figured, "like going from the big horse down to the smallest horse of the organization." But because his cellular assignment was to last only six months, Jarvis agreed to it.

His first assignment was to take a plane trip to Washington, D.C., with John Stanton. There, Stanton would introduce Jarvis to many of the main players, show him the ropes, and then, as was standard procedure in the freewheeling McCaw organization, he would set him loose to make his own deals.

In his short time at McCaw, Jarvis had already found himself amazed at the level of autonomy he was allowed. Everything seemed to move at warp speed in the growing company, and decisions that would, at any other company, require several tiers of upper-management approval were made in the ranks with seeming abandon. One early cable deal in particular stands out in Jarvis's memory.

"I remember calling my mom once," Jarvis says, "and telling her, 'I'm on my way down to sign an agreement to buy $1.1 million worth of cable system, and I'm having no help from anybody and I'm nervous. Who are these guys that would just let some kid go negotiate these things?' But that was the McCaw way. Throw a man in, and if he makes a mistake don't let him do it again."

That kind of autonomy could not, of course, be granted to just anyone. The McCaw team vetted any potential new hires very carefully, with more attention focused on psychological evaluation than on academic transcripts. Jarvis, like most of McCaw's new hires, ran a virtual gauntlet to earn a spot at the company: He took an IQ test, a Myers-Briggs Type Indicator® test, and was evaluated by a psychiatrist; he also endured about ten interviews, with all levels of staff, before McCaw finally hired him.

"It made me want to work there," says Jarvis, "because it was difficult to get in." And now he had been drafted for the fastest-moving, most unstructured division of all.

The flight to Washington with Stanton was an education in itself. Stanton had so much energy, Jarvis recalls, that he was "bouncing off the walls. He could hardly sit down long enough to explain things to me, and then he'd have to walk around and get all over the plane and terrorize the flight attendants. He just had way too much energy to sit down."

Stanton was able to focus long enough to draw Jarvis a map of the United States on a napkin. "It was an incredible map, all from memory, of who owned what licenses and what we were trying to buy," remembers Jarvis. Stanton, in his trademark rapid-fire way, was "just dumping information. He's very bright, and very articulate, and he always spits when he talks." By the time the plane landed in Washington, Jarvis had the barest of bare-bones understanding of McCaw's cellular strategy. Now it was time to meet the experts, and try to act like he knew what was going on.

In the midst of the kind of summer storm that drenches Washington with powerful bursts of sudden rain, Jarvis was shepherded from law firm to law firm along the city's K Street corridor, where he was introduced as McCaw's new cellular guy. It was, Jarvis remembers, "my first trip to Washington, D.C., ever in my life, and now suddenly I'm brilliant because I've done some acquisitions in cable TV, which have nothing to do with cellular." He felt like an impostor in his new role, but worse was yet to come.

The biggest meeting of the day came at Covington & Burling, three blocks east of the White House, where cellular veteran Wayne Schelle had convened a gathering of all the main players in the Vanguard-CSP imbroglio. Schelle, who was anxious to purchase several of the contested Round IV markets, knew someone had to convince the squabbling sides to settle their differences to free up the licenses.

Schelle was the picture of middle-aged gravitas, with his bulbous nose, fleshy ears with floppy lobes, and wispy tufts of hair straggling across his balding pate. Long a hired hand at other paging and cellular companies, Schelle had helped run the nation's first nonwireline experimental system in Washington and, though he was already seen as something of a cellular godfather, he was now struggling to launch his entrepreneurial career. He wanted those Round IV markets, and he believed he knew a way to free them from their legal entanglement.

As several dozen wary executives from all three sides of the battle eyed each other across the huge mahogany table, Schelle took the floor, speaking above the staccato drumming of raindrops against the picture windows eight stories above Pennsylvania Avenue. The licenses at stake were worth tens of millions of dollars, he told the assembly, and no one would benefit from holding them up in litigation. The only thing this pointless squabbling had accomplished was to assure the telephone companies a huge head start. As he spoke, Schelle adopted the cadences of a charismatic preacher, a man in love with his own voice. *We need to spend today resolving our differences*, he told the assembly, *and get started on the path towards redemption.*

It was time, right here in this room, to find a way around the gridlock and to save everybody from yet another wireline head start.

Jarvis sat uncomfortably in his chair, dripping wet from the rain—it didn't rain like this in Seattle, it just got misty!—and trying to look suitably mature in the only tie he owned. He'd grown a mustache to try and hide his youth, but sitting there with his hair dripping wet—"I felt like a duck who wanted to shake," he remembers—he was unprepared for what happened next.

Schelle, fully relishing the spotlight and reveling in his elder statesman role, next made a suggestion to the besuited and still dubious crowd. If the contested markets were sold for cash, he declared, then the money could be divided among the warring sides, allowing everyone to claim victory. This would be the quickest and least messy way of solving any and all disputes.

As he spoke of the need for cash, Schelle, walking with a slight limp from an old football injury, moved his portly frame around the length of the conference table. He came to a stop behind Scot Jarvis's chair and put his meaty hands on the young man's shoulders. Jarvis felt his face go pale.

"This is Scot Jarvis, from McCaw," Schelle declared to the group. "He's the man who'll take care of all our issues. Scot, why don't you say a few words?"

Jarvis's first thought was: *These people are all old enough to be my parents. And they know a ton more about all this than I do.* He turned to Joe Walter, another McCaw employee who had joined him for the meeting and knew even less than he did, and croaked, "Joe, do you want to start?" Fortunately, Walter was able to stall for a few minutes while Jarvis struggled to collect his thoughts. After a few moments of Walter's banalities, Jarvis spoke.

"We are willing to participate in this," he began carefully. "We're very interested in acquiring licenses. . . If you're interested in selling, we're certainly willing to talk to you." And he announced his phone number to the assembled. Immediately, conversations began buzzing around the table. Could McCaw really afford to buy all these markets too? Where were they getting the money? Was this some sort of elaborate scam? The meeting broke up with participants still mumbling in consternation.

But the fact was, Wayne Schelle had called it right. Within a year, McCaw would, in its ever-expanding acquisitions quest, buy out not only many of the contested licenses, but also Schelle's still-nascent enterprise. And Jarvis, now properly broken in, would lead the charge.

14

PIG FARMERS AND HAIRDRESSERS

STANDING IN HIS WET SUIT ON A ROCKY LEDGE at the Columbia River Gorge, peering down at the choppy water beneath him, Scot Jarvis was thinking about anything but cellular telephone licenses.

It was a brisk Sunday late in the summer of 1986, and Jarvis had come to the river to work on his windsurfing technique. As the Oregon wind whipped along the gorge by the rock outcropping where he stood, Jarvis tossed his board, sail and mast into the river, then leapt in after it, his feet tucked under him as he fell in a slow arc toward the water.

He never saw the rock just below the surface, but the instant he splashed into the river, he felt a searing pain shoot through his foot. Treading water, he lifted his leg and peered at it as cool water streamed off; a small, neat puncture wound marked the top of his foot. Annoyed at his bad luck, and anxious not to spoil a day of windsurfing, Jarvis stayed out on the river that day despite pain that seemed unusually intense for such a tiny wound.

Now the cellular race was even farther from his mind; the nagging pain drove other thoughts away. But for Jarvis, who over the next two years would crisscross the country trying to buy cellular licenses, even this seemingly peripheral incident would play a role in his work.

McCaw had moved from its modest offices in Bellevue—where John Stanton had, only four years earlier, come looking for a job—into posher accommodations, the new Carillon Point office complex in Kirkland, on the shore of Lake Washington.

Now the growing ranks of McCaw employees could park in their own parking lot, rather than hunting for curbside spaces on the streets of Bellevue. The handsome brick building offered a tranquil view of Lake Washington and the marina where Craig McCaw kept his boat, and in the nearby park, the energetic young workaholics could take lunch-break jogs. For quick breaks, the hamburger joint next door, Kidd Valley, became a favorite place to grab a milkshake.

With its cable business thriving and its cellular division growing by the day, McCaw was beginning to attract notice. In the new cellular industry, where everyone was still trying to figure out what things were worth and how to make money, it was impossible not to notice these upstarts from the Northwest, with their aggressive style, their speed and tenacity in signing deals, and their undisguised ambition to buy up everything on the map.

Craig McCaw presided over the growing company from his modestly appointed office, but as he'd always done, he essentially left his troops to their own devices. As often as not, Craig would spend his most productive time in pursuits that looked to others like a kind of detached, unfocused reverie. Often he could be found gazing out his office window, or he would suddenly take his plane or his yacht off for a solitary ride. At times, he would startle his employees with odd non sequiturs uttered in a mumbling, off-hand fashion as he passed them in the hallway. Those who interacted with their aloof CEO soon built up short catalogues of curious encounters, which were whispered about and traded over lunches.

Craig had given Wayne Perry and John Stanton the go-ahead to buy up licenses as quickly as possible, but he assiduously avoided any involvement in the details. For Scot Jarvis, who was the company's point man for buying up the smaller markets of Round IV and beyond, it was Wayne Perry who offered guidance.

A tall, sturdily built tax lawyer with a warm, engaging manner, Wayne Perry was, along with John Stanton, one of the prime architects of McCaw's cellular strategy. He was "a soul of the company," says Jarvis, as well as a charming foil. "He has an aura about him and an attitude about him that's extremely positive," remembers Jarvis. "You could go in, have your list of things that you wanted to talk about, sit down with Wayne and have him tell you 'no' on every one of them and still walk out feeling great."

On one wall of Perry's office hung a large map of the United States, so he and the team could keep track of which markets were available, which they'd bought and which ones they had their eye on. And on Perry's desk was another tool for keeping track of McCaw's purchases.

"On my desk, I had a corral," remembers Perry. "I went out to the Woolworth's store—like a Woolworth's store, but we don't have Woolworth's here. . . And I bought this little package of farm animals and a fence. And I had my secretary go out and name all the small markets that we didn't already own. I took all the farm animals with the names of these markets out here and said, 'They don't go into the corral until we have a goddamn contract.'"

"So they'd come in with their contracts," says Perry, "they'd show me the contract, and they'd move the pig in the corral." Years later Scott Anderson, who worked with Jarvis on acquisitions, recalled the plastic animals as a major motivator: Perry's desk was in plain view of every employee, investment banker, visiting executive and janitor, and everyone knew that Jarvis and Anderson had been charged with herding the animals into the corral. The young, competitive and driven duo was determined to round those animals up.

Getting the pigs into the corral was easier said than done. Dozens of completely random people across the country had been selected as lottery winners, most of whom were members of sprawling settlement groups. The nominal winners, many of whom, like Bob Pelissier, had no business experience, then owned 50.01 percent of the license while hundreds of minority partners owned the other 49.99 percent.

Most of the big players like Metro Mobile and Metromedia felt these smaller markets—cities like Yakima, Washington; Tyler, Texas; and Monroe, Louisiana—were hardly worth the effort it would take to buy them. But the McCaw team already understood three things as they were just dawning on the rest of the industry. First, as Stanton's early business model had predicted, thousands of new customers were signing up monthly, indicating that current per-POP prices were far lower than what the markets might ultimately be worth.

Second, they saw an arbitrage opportunity to buy for fifteen dollars per POP and resell to the public for twenty-five dollars per POP through an IPO. In June 1986, CCI had been the first cellular company to go public, and its share price of $12.50 indicated a per-POP valuation of $21. In its ongoing search for fresh capital, McCaw was planning a public stock offering, and CCI's valuation convinced Perry that more POPs meant a higher market value and more cash for growth. If Perry was right, McCaw's IPO would turn these new POPs into instant cash: The more markets the team bought, the better.

Third, the McCaw team realized that without the smaller markets in between the larger ones, there was no way to provide continuous cellular coverage for people who were traveling from one place to the other—a critical component of Craig McCaw's evolving vision of regional wireless systems.

The smaller markets, says Perry, "take a gabillion hours and they're very hard to do, but they're very important. Because if you have Seattle but you don't have Bremerton and you don't have Bellingham, you have a very poor system. You've just got to have them." So Scot Jarvis and attorney Scott Anderson became the core of a busy small-market acquisition team: Jarvis jetted around the country trying to convince lottery winners to sell to him, and Anderson helped negotiate and paper the deals. The team worked under the nominal leadership of Craig McCaw's brother, John McCaw.

Though the pace Jarvis and Anderson set from the summer of 1986 through 1988 suggested a random frenzy of buying, there were in fact some strategy guidelines they tried to follow. "If you think of [McCaw's] big markets as the sun, we were trying to add Mars and Mercury and keep going out in the solar system," says Jarvis. "The further away they got [geographically], the less interest we had" in a particular market.

In addition to location, there were a few more criteria the team used to evaluate markets' desirability. Once again, the "Mercedes factor" played a part: Markets where there was a greater percentage of residents with luxury cars were assumed to be more promising. Jarvis studied each market's "Socio-economic status indicator," or SESI score, which theoretically indicated which markets were likely to yield the most cell phone customers. "Frankly," he says, "our target market at that time was kind of yuppies or urban professionals, usually male. . . We actually seriously considered the SESI score as something of value. But we later realized it really didn't have any value whatsoever."

Whatever nominal research Jarvis and Anderson did on the markets, it didn't slow them down in their land rush.

"If we had any money, we bought something," says Perry. "You know, you have an eight-year-old kid and you give him his allowance and he will buy whatever amount of candy he has equal to the money in his pocket. And that's how we were with cellular. 'Oh, here's another buck, let's go buy something.'"

There was nothing magical or mysterious about the way Jarvis went after the markets. The FCC would make public the list of winners, and Jarvis would get on the phone.

"I would cold call," he says, "and start striking up a conversation and letting [the winner] know who in the heck we were, because we were a private company and no one had ever heard of us before. . . . I had a tendency not to call the people [directly], but to call the attorneys first. Because the attorneys didn't really like us calling the people first."

With their phones ringing incessantly, many winners turned to their attorneys to help sort out the quick-buck artists from the important new business contacts. McCaw set up an 800 number where winners as well as minority owners could call to ask questions. Mark Callaghan manned the phone during the height of the buying spree, educating and negotiating with hundreds of callers. "A lot of folks, we were the first person who had ever talked to them about this license that they owned. . . They'd bought this thing and they were told they'd be able to put their grandchildren and their great-grandchildren through college on this investment. Well, we had to educate them that in fact, they ended up with a minority piece of a small market, they didn't have liquidity, and this was the current market price."

As always, speed was essential to McCaw's strategy. It sometimes took longer than the team liked to convince a reluctant buyer—"Jarvis would do footwork and footwork and footwork, and then when it came time and it was necessary to bring in the big guns, John [McCaw] would fly in, have a three-hour meeting and then be gone," says Anderson—but no one was faster at nailing down agreements.

McCaw's purchase of the Santa Rosa, California, market was typical. The license winner had been in negotiations with George Blumenthal of CCI, who expected to close the deal. "We were basically about to sign a contract," remembers Blumenthal, "and [the license winner] calls us up and says, 'I just accepted an offer from McCaw. They wired a million dollars into my account.' Without a contract or a piece of paper. That's something we never would have done."

These were the nuts and bolts of the acquisition strategy, but the real story is in the people whom Jarvis and Anderson bought licenses from. These "little people," many of whom lived in backwoods hollows, centuries-old farmhouses, trailer parks, modest condos and split-level homes with picket fences, made quite an unusual contingent of newly minted businesspeople.

As the team scoured the country, Anderson remembers, "I'd flip on CNN and, you know, they would say, 'Well, somebody fell down a well in blah-

blah-blah city, and you'd think, 'Oh, that's in MSA number 122' or whatever. 'That's on the highway to Indianapolis.'" And Jarvis, more often than
not, had been there, or was on his way there, or had stuck a "go there" pin
in his map.

⸻

JEANINE HOCHHALTER WAS A TALL, CHESTNUT-HAIRED NURSE working at a hospital in Half Moon Bay, California, when she won the cellular license for
Salem, Oregon. She had seen the Mike Douglas infomercial on TV, sent her
money in and beaten the odds.

Soon after Hochhalter's win, Scot Jarvis called her up at the hospital
where she worked, and began trying to convince her to sell McCaw the
Salem license. "She didn't trust me from the start," remembers Jarvis. "I just
couldn't get her to warm up and trust me. I don't know why. I'm not a snake
oil salesman or anything. I'm a nice guy. But I couldn't get her to warm up
at all." Hochhalter, who had—like Bob Pelissier—hired Washington attorney David Hill, put off her persistent suitor for months before finally agreeing to meet Jarvis in Salem to have a look at the market she'd won.

Salem, an unassuming city of 250,000, didn't seem like a tremendously
attractive market, but in fact McCaw wanted it badly. "We were desperate
for it," Jarvis recalls. McCaw operated Portland, while the RBOC U.S. West
owned the wireline licenses in both Salem and Portland, giving the wireline
the crucial marketing advantage of being able to advertise a larger home-
service area.

There was nothing arbitrary about Jarvis's suggestion to meet Hochhalter
in Salem—he'd done his homework, and knew that downtown Salem was
suffering from urban blight brought on by the flight of consumers to strip
malls at the edges of town. Once in Salem, the pair took a little drive down
the city's main street. As Jarvis knew it would be, the largest department
store downtown—a looming Frederick and Nelson—was boarded up.

"God, that looks awful," Jarvis remarked as the car crept along the street.
But Hochhalter was not so easily swayed. Perhaps downtown was a shell,
but there were plenty of stores in the strip malls, she pointed out. And so
went their drive, Jarvis pointing out signs of decay and Hochhalter pointing out pockets of prosperity.

"It was kind of comical," remembers Jarvis, "because we both knew what
we were doing and we were both being somewhat serious about it."

Jarvis had gone to Salem that day harboring fantasies of calling Wayne
Perry with news of another multimillion-dollar cocktail-napkin contract.

Although he never got Hochhalter's handshake on a price, the trip proved worth the effort. She was now inclined to sell and McCaw was the first buyer in line. It was now just a question of price.

Within weeks, Jarvis was in Washington, D.C., staring across sloppy piles of paperwork on David Hill's desk. Hill knew enough about the latest cellular deals to turn down Jarvis's opening bid, a per-POP price in the low teens. But within a few weeks, Jarvis had his market, at a price of just over sixteen dollars per POP.

Though happy to have his market, Jarvis was disappointed at having to pay a price above his target. "In the long run," says Anderson, "we still made a lot of money on it, but it was very upsetting at the time, when fifty cents [per POP] was a big deal negotiation. . . We knew realistically that if we got it for under $20 a POP, we were well within our Kill Zone.

"But we were young," Anderson says with a smile, "and wanted to outperform our superiors' expectations."

Closing the deal was a feather in the caps of Jarvis and Anderson, but for the nurse from Half Moon Bay, it meant something far more significant. Her response to ANC's Mike Douglas infomercial had netted her some $2 million. She'd never have to do a shift in the ER again.

———

LEE CHARLES AND NEVA BROOKS, an elderly retired couple in Century City, California, had seen the Mike Douglas infomercial too. With their attorney, Martin L. Sturman, out of town and unable to advise them, they had decided to withdraw some of their savings and get in on the cellular "sure thing." When Sturman returned, he listened with horror as they told him what they'd done before berating them for their impetuous move. Then, to his great surprise, the couple won the license for Visalia, California.

Not long afterward, Scot Jarvis called to discuss a possible license purchase. When Sturman, still skeptical of this whole cellular fairy tale, asked him how much the couple's 50.01 percent was worth, Jarvis casually responded that he was authorized to offer $500,000. Stunned, Sturman blurted, "How much?" Jarvis repeated his offer and invited Sturman to come to Seattle at McCaw's expense to discuss it; the lawyer agreed and soon set off to negotiate for his clients. He got Jarvis up to more than $700,000—then added that he'd like McCaw to pay for him to travel to Washington, D.C., to sign the deal, as he hadn't been in a while and wouldn't mind a return visit.

"There were some people we had to worry about fishing out on us, because this was a time of rising cellular prices," remembers Jarvis, "but [Sturman] we didn't worry about—he was more interested in getting his trips."

Lee and Neva had a different request of Jarvis: They wanted him to come visit them at home and go out for lunch. "We're not going to finish this thing until you visit," Neva crowed to Jarvis, who happily complied. He flew to Orange County, visited the couple in their modest ranch-style home in Century City and went out for a lunch of chicken salad at a nearby restaurant. An aggressive, ambitious businessman, Jarvis also knew how to charm a client: He chatted politely with the pair, nodding courteously and listening attentively, the perfect gentleman. The couple was very taken with the pleasant young man, and shortly after he flew back to Seattle, he received a little thank-you note in shaky, grandmotherly handwriting.

Back in the frantic, high-intensity bustle of Kirkland, news of Jarvis's Visalia purchase was met with enthusiasm: Another check in the win column! Better yet, the price was an outrageous bargain, barely 25 percent of that month's going per-POP rate—and for a premium California market to boot. In just a few short years, the Visalia price would soar to more than thirty times what Jarvis paid the elderly couple.

Jarvis might have felt a guilty pang at buying the market at such a bargain, but in reality he had little to regret. The deal had been struck fair and square with the seller's legal counsel—and shame on Sturman if he'd been so starstruck by his client's apparent profit that he never bothered to investigate the value of what he was selling. Also, the deal was not unusual for the times, when no one really knew what cellular licenses were worth and willing sellers made the market.

Lee and Neva Brooks were, in Jarvis's words, "as pleased as punch" to have won the lottery. They had cashed in on their good fortune with a minimum of stress and worry, and now they had plenty of money with which to enjoy their twilight years.

At their lunch, Jarvis had mentioned his upcoming wedding. To his surprise, the now-wealthy elderly couple sent him a Lenox crystal bowl for the big day.

━━━━━━━━━━

JARVIS MAY HAVE MADE FRIENDS IN THE VISALIA TRANSACTION, but not everyone saw the McCaw negotiators as nice guys. And Jarvis didn't always get his markets.

George Crowley, a tall, debonair, smooth-talking businessman with a mane of longish, deep auburn locks, was one of the few license buyers to outhustle McCaw for a market they wanted. Crowley's recollection of the McCaw modus operandi is considerably less charitable than that of Lee Charles and Neva Brooks. Stanton's usual style, he once remarked, was "trying to lowball everybody and just bully 'em with 'I'm McCaw and you'd better sell to me, and there are no other real buyers out there.'"

In fact, the McCaw team was desperate to get good prices, even though they believed that even the highest prices they were paying in 1986–87 were wild bargains. "The bullish view was that we were buying at twenty dollars and they were worth seventy dollars," remembers Scott Anderson, "and, you know, Craig, in his wilder flights of fancy, thought it was worth much more than that, as you can see by what he paid a few years down the road."

"You'd negotiate and negotiate and negotiate, and play all these games, and go out and make phone calls and fake phone calls and everything else to buy some market for twenty dollars per POP," remembers McCaw's Robert Ratliffe, "and you'd think, 'Oh my God, I got completely beaten up.' And I'd get home, and John [McCaw] would say, 'Well, I would have let you go to $28, but I wanted you to get it and I told you you had to get it for $16.'"

Many analysts and businesspeople couldn't understand McCaw's optimism—or its seemingly quixotic buying spree. These towns were tiny! And cell phones were expensive! What in the world was McCaw hoping to gain by spending so much money on a bunch of nowheresville markets?

"There was no operating history, so you couldn't value them like a normal business," says Mark Callaghan. "We were buying these on a speculative basis, based on a vision and some modeling, but there was no operating history then to prove that that in fact was going to play out."

As the months went by, McCaw's foresight became clear: Prices went nowhere but up. "Initially, we thought $20 [per POP] was too much to pay for Santa Barbara," says Mark Callaghan. "That was early-on modeling, and we said, well, that was the limit. That was the maximum. And six months later, thirty dollars seemed to be okay. Six months after that, forty bucks seemed to be okay, so we were constantly upgrading our models as well."

In the midst of the spree, Jarvis almost never had to call back to Kirkland to get Perry's okay to spend more money. In fact, says Anderson, it was the other way around.

"You know Jarvis, how competitive he is," says Anderson. "He always wanted to get them cheap. So it wasn't usually a problem where he'd have to call back for more authority. It was more where he would call Wayne and say, 'Don't make me spend another two bucks because [the sellers are] really bastards and I don't want to do it.' And Wayne would say, 'Go ahead and get it.'"

Regardless of the price he ended up paying, Jarvis almost always got his market. There were, of course, a few notable exceptions—and one of them could be traced back to Jarvis's fateful leap into the Columbia River.

———

THE MORNING AFTER JARVIS'S ACCIDENT, he boarded a plane to Boca Raton, where he was scheduled to meet the Daytona-license winner, a retired Ohio state policeman named Eugene Folden. On the plane, he knew something was very wrong with his foot—it was so swollen, he could barely fit it into his wingtip.

When he arrived in Boca Raton, he met Folden for dinner at a seafood restaurant with a view of the Atlantic. His shoe unlaced, he limped to the table and sat down gratefully, practically dizzy with pain. This was Jarvis's first trip to Florida, he was at a pleasant seaside restaurant, and Gene Folden was ready to talk business; at any other time, Jarvis would have been completely in his element, ready to charm the seller and make a deal. But tonight, it wasn't to be.

"I'm not doing as well as I should have in terms of keeping the conversation going," remembers Jarvis, "when my eyes are rolling into the back of my head. We didn't hit it off as well as we should have." Still, when he left the restaurant, he thought he and Folden had reached a kind of understanding. At the very least, thought Jarvis, he'd persuaded Folden not to sell without getting McCaw's best offer.

Jarvis flew to Washington, D.C., that night, and when he arrived, he realized he could ignore his foot no longer. By now, the swelling had crept halfway up his shin; the lower part of his leg looked like a gigantic German sausage. He made an appointment for George Washington University Hospital the next morning, and as he sat on the examining table after much poking and prodding by a doctor, he suddenly fainted, breaking his glasses and tearing a gash in his forehead that would require stitches to close. Still, the doctor could find no apparent reason why a tiny puncture wound should give Jarvis so much trouble. Jarvis got a prescription for antibiotics and was sent on his way.

Meanwhile, the Daytona negotiations ebbed and flowed between McCaw staffers and Folden's lawyers, while Jarvis, relying on his hazy memory of that pain-filled dinner, trusted Folden would phone him with a final chance to buy Daytona. When Jarvis learned Folden had sold to Crowley without calling him for a final bid, "I was shocked," he says. "I was totally blown away. I couldn't believe that I had lost it. You know, you just beat yourself up. Because I hadn't lost one yet." But before that happened, Jarvis at last found out what was wrong with his foot.

Three weeks after the accident the swelling had finally subsided, and Jarvis was left with a small scab that refused to heal on the top of his foot. Wearing flip-flops while sanding his floors one afternoon, he suddenly noticed something sticking up from the scab. Peering at his foot, he was shocked to see part of a snail shell protruding from the scab. "The snail was probably alive when it went into my foot," says Jarvis, "and my body did not react to a live snail very well. . . Isn't that weird? We lost Daytona Beach because of that little snail."

Adding insult to injury, Crowley says that Daytona was one of the best markets around. "I will tell you that there is probably no city in America that has more roaming traffic at the end of May than Daytona Beach, Florida," he says. "I mean, when guys are coming to Daytona for the Daytona 500 or for Bike Week or any of that stuff, and we're charging 85, 95 cents a minute and we have no cost to those guys coming through. . . we had a toll gate out on the Florida highway! Everybody going right down south has to go through Daytona Beach, and anytime you pick up the phone, bang! We got ya! Three bucks and ninety-five cents a minute. And it was all to the bottom line."

Years later, McCaw, under heavy competitive pressure to round out its Florida presence, bought Daytona at price of more than $25 million—nearly $200 per POP; Crowley had paid less than $14 per POP for it.

Another market McCaw lost to Crowley was Waco—an event that Crowley calls a "major embarrassment" for McCaw, which had a large presence in Texas cellular markets. Not long after Crowley bought it, he received a call from Mark Warner, asking if Crowley would meet John McCaw for lunch to talk about selling the license. "We're not interested in selling it," Crowley told him, but he reluctantly agreed to at least meet for lunch. Warner came by Crowley's Washington, D.C., office and the two headed off in a cab.

"Where the hell are we going?" asked Crowley as the cab left the city on westbound Interstate 66.

"To the airport," answered Warner.

"Why? Where are we having lunch?" persisted Crowley.

"Chicago," Warner responded glibly.

Craig McCaw's private jet was at Dulles International Airport, ready to take the pair to Chicago. On landing, they headed for the restaurant in the Ritz Hotel on Michigan Avenue, where they found John McCaw seated at the corner table. After a few minutes of one-sided conversation, Crowley says, McCaw tried to intimidate him into selling the Waco license. But the exhibitionism and the heavy-handedness backfired. A consummate show-off himself, Crowley was little impressed by ostentation, and he was far too confident a businessman to be cowed by John McCaw's bluster. Crowley stormed out of the restaurant.

"I told Wayne Perry this story," recalls Crowley, "and he just got the biggest kick out of it, because it was vintage John McCaw, trying to over-whelm you with the private plane and the lunch at the Ritz and buppa-de-buppa-de-bup. . . And then, when you don't give him the right answer, he tries to intimidate the shit out of you. He basically said, later on, he said, 'We'll bury you in Texas if you guys don't sell to us.'"

But Crowley was far from buried. As he did with Daytona, Crowley and his venture-capital backers built the market and went into business, then later sold Waco to McCaw for more than $20 million, some $140 a POP. Just a half-dozen years earlier, he had paid $1.6 million, a mere $19 a POP, for the controlling interest.

———

THEIR WRANGLING WITH CROWLEY ASIDE, the McCaw team met with far more success than failure. Sometimes Jarvis even managed to have a little fun in the negotiations, such as the time he faced off against another won-der boy of the industry, Mark Warner, over the Jackson, Mississippi, market. Though he would occasionally handle projects for buyers like TDS or McCaw, Warner enjoyed working for sellers where he could demand stead-ily escalating prices, sometimes setting new industry records while he helped "make the market" in cellular licenses.

Warner, by now a full-fledged, smooth-talking broker of cellular licenses, dealt many times with the buyers from Kirkland. From their first meeting, he and Jarvis had developed a friendly mutual respect—both were young, com-petitive dealmakers who relished haggling over every nickel in negotiations.

Meeting in the Petroleum Club, an elegant club for high rollers high atop the lone skyscraper in Jackson, Mississippi, Warner and Jarvis made one of their more memorable deals.

Warner and his partner, Robert Blow, represented a partnership of oilmen and bankers—a veritable Who's Who of the Jackson business community.

Warner and Jarvis had already haggled at length by phone over the license, and they had agreed on a general price. Both sensed a deal was inevitable, but still they needed to go through the motions—after all, Warner and Blow had a 5-percent fee to justify. So they agreed to fly to Jackson and complete the deal in front of the sellers.

At the Petroleum Club, the usual pleasantries were soon followed by business posturing: Though the two sides were close to agreement, dickering continued over whether McCaw would cough up fifty cents more per POP. Warner and Jarvis haggled as the fidgety clients looked on, occasionally interjecting comments. Finally, Warner turned to his side of the table.

"Please leave the room," he told his clients. "Let us see if we can try and convince Scot." Nervous and tense, the group shuffled reluctantly out of the room. Now only Warner, Blow and Jarvis were left at the table.

The negotiations ended almost as quickly as they began. If Jarvis wouldn't pay fifty cents, then how about twenty-five? Within seconds, they had agreed to the deal. That, unfortunately, left a new problem.

"We've done this in five seconds," Warner remembers thinking. "If we go back out there and say the deal's done, they're going to say, 'Oh, shit—we've left money on the table.'" His clients would surely believe Warner had given in too quickly. So Warner, Blow and Jarvis, convinced the clients were listening at the door, decided to put on a little show: They suddenly began shouting and cursing at each other.

"Jarvis, God damn it!" Warner screamed, "You've got to do this! We came all the way out here! These people aren't going to sell for this!"

"You know we can call Roy [TDS's Leroy Carlson] right now and get that price!" bellowed Blow, as the three of them struggled not to laugh.

"Don't you call Roy, you son of a bitch!" shrieked Jarvis, a huge smile on his face.

For twenty minutes, the trio staged a spectacular fight; when Warner and Blow emerged from the room, their faces were red, their hair was mussed, and their shirts were disheveled. "We've got a deal," Warner announced huskily to his shocked clients. And another market was McCaw's.

MOST DEALS WEREN'T QUITE THAT MUCH FUN, though Jarvis did find it generally entertaining trying to convince people to sell. One sale in particular he remembers with a tart chuckle, partly because it involved people Jarvis hated dealing with more than any other: Nick Wilson and his cronies. "You just felt like you ought to take a shower right after meeting with those guys," remembers Jarvis. "It wasn't like they were bad people face-to-face; you just knew something wasn't right here."

It had taken him a while, but Wilson had finally figured out that the product he was selling was the real deal. Tax schemes and huge applications profits aside, Wilson now wanted to make some money on the licenses themselves. So when the filing deadlines for the later rounds arrived, Wilson had made sure that he submitted applications for his friends, family and staff. And he'd included a little surprise document in the packet of papers he'd gotten each applicant to sign.

When TCC's mailroom attendant, Frank Avallone, won the license for Johnstown, Pennsylvania, Avallone was ecstatic. Scot Jarvis came calling almost immediately, offering him a tidy sum for his license. In no time, Jarvis was on a plane out of Cleveland with what appeared to be an iron-clad contract.

His plane had barely touched down in Seattle before Jarvis got a call from TCC's lawyer. The attorney cautioned that his client, Nick Wilson, held a signed document giving Wilson a right of first refusal to buy Avallone's license. Jarvis was chagrined, and Avallone was stunned—his huge windfall could simply vanish. But Wilson was, in his own twisted way, merciful: Hungry for quick cash, he hurriedly capitulated to a new offer from Jarvis. Leaving millions of dollars of unrealized value and his own professed dreams of operating a cellular system on the table, Wilson agreed to a quick payoff of some $100,000—75 cents per POP—to tear up his little document. With that, McCaw could close its purchase, and Avallone had little choice but to be perversely grateful to his scheming boss.

When another of Wilson's applicants won the license for Bremerton, Washington, Jarvis and his team already knew who they were dealing with. Bremerton lay across Puget Sound from West Seattle, and when the McCaw team invited Wilson to fly out to Seattle and take the ferry to Bremerton to look at the market, Wilson happily agreed. A great lover of all manner of expensive vehicles, Wilson loved fancy boats most of all—in fact, following the Johnstown sale to McCaw, Wilson had used his windfall to buy a boat. So when he showed up for the ferry trip to Bremerton with Scot Jarvis, Wilson came prepared.

He showed up in a blue blazer with a gold patch on the breast pocket, white trousers and a jaunty little cap, ready for a day out on the high seas. What he didn't realize was that Jarvis, as he'd done in Salem, had already scoped out the scenery. He knew the ferry docked in a seedy wharf area near abandoned naval facilities—an area where, in Jarvis's words, "even the tattoo parlors were boarded up." As Jarvis guessed, Wilson was dismayed at the squalor, and the next day, in negotiations with John McCaw, he agreed to sell the Bremerton license for $8.30 per POP.

Typical of Wilson, he hadn't had the patience to do his homework. As Jarvis knew, Bremerton's affluent middle-class population was skyrocketing. And even without this fat base of cellular customers, Bremerton held critical strategic value for McCaw's Seattle system. Bremerton might have been a long ferry ride away, but as any engineer could have told Wilson, it was only a millisecond away from Seattle via radio waves. Any cellular tower in Bremerton shot a clean easy signal across the water into West Seattle, easily serving McCaw's customers there. Finally, Bremerton had one other strategic value: Craig McCaw badly wanted to own his hometown markets.

All told, Wilson smugly departed Seattle oblivious of the millions of dollars he left behind if only he'd exercised a little patience and discipline. Instead, he was already dreaming of bigger boats, faster cars and perhaps his next trip to Las Vegas.

———————

EVERY ONE OF THE DOZENS OF LICENSE WINNERS had their own stories, but some were a bit odder than others.

McCaw's Bob Ratliffe went to Kansas City to meet a seller who called himself "the Fat Man." When Ratliffe arrived at the airport, the Fat Man led him to a superstretch limousine covered with radio and TV antennae. The two went to dinner at the Savoy Grill, and when Ratliffe made an offer of $700,000 for his percentage, the Fat Man ebulliently declared that he would buy dinner for everyone in the entire restaurant that night. According to Ratliffe, John Stanton reported that in another meeting, at the Fat Man's office, this unlikely cellular licensee stared just past Stanton's head the whole time, watching porn videos on a television behind him.

Another of Ratliffe's stranger conquests was the license held by a woman named Ruby Jean. When Ratliffe got lost driving to her house from the airport, he called from his cell phone and she told him the directions, ending with, "We're the lavender chalet with the largest motor home you've ever seen in the driveway." When Ratliffe showed up, he made his way past the lavender rocks spread across the yard in front of the Swiss-style chalet and knocked on the door.

Ruby Jean answered, and when she saw it was Ratliffe, she exclaimed, "Oh, you give me a kiss!"

"It was like I was the guy in the millionaire TV show, and I brought the check for $2 million," remembers Ratliffe.

———

NOT ALL THE STORIES ENDED HAPPILY. One family in rural Silverlake, Washington, saw their unprecedented success in the lotteries decimate their relationships in a King Lear–like fashion.

Five family members stretching over three generations—a grandfather, his two sons and two grandchildren—won a total of six licenses in the lotteries (after mortgaging everything they could to buy applications), a truly remarkable run considering the many thousands of applications filed. But their good luck was overshadowed by wrangling, bad faith and lawsuits—first between the family and competing operators, then among the family members themselves. Before long, father had sued son, brothers were battling, and bitter allegations of drug use, fraud and theft kept teams of lawyers busy for half a decade. In the end, the money the family made seemed a poor salve for the wounds the wins had produced.

And there were other strange stories. When one older man fell seriously ill after the lottery, his son, who had the same name, represented himself as the lottery winner and made arrangements to sell the license without his father's knowledge until his fraud was discovered. One man who had an epileptic seizure during a negotiation struggled to sign a contract as he was carried out on a gurney. One elderly woman who died on a Saturday was discovered to have signed a contract with McCaw the day before. And a scion of a wealthy American family—a man whose fortune was already secure—won a remarkable three licenses after buying applications from one of the sleaziest bucket shops around. His windfall: nearly $50 million.

A pair of preachers in Columbus, Georgia, set up a business called "Sonrise Management Corp.," exhorted their parishioners to apply for licenses, then, when they won, set up cellular companies named after books of the Bible, such as "Corinthians Cellular," "Acts Cellular" and "Revelation Cellular." The pair did well enough in the cellular-spectrum rush that they then encouraged their flock to apply for low-power FM radio station licenses. They sold expensive partnerships across the South, fattening their own bank accounts with no intention of building stations. A later investigation found that Sonrise bilked more than 800 people out of $16 million.

The scheme might never have made the news, save for a bizarre incident involving one of Sonrise's attorneys, Thomas Root. One sunny afternoon in 1989, Root was flying his private plane from Washington, D.C., to Rocky

Mount, North Carolina. Midway through the flight, air traffic controllers realized something had gone horribly wrong: The plane was on autopilot, cruising without purpose along the East Coast with Root unconscious at the controls.

When the plane at last ran out of fuel, it crashed into the Atlantic. Rescuers who pulled the injured Root from the wreckage were astonished to discover that he had a bullet wound in his stomach—a wound that eventually was determined to have been self-inflicted. At the time of the incident, Root and Sonrise were under investigation for the preachers' scheme. After he recovered, Root pleaded guilty to state and federal charges, and today he is serving out his seventeen-year sentence in a state prison.

As sad as Root's story is, he fared better than another of the conspirators. One of the preachers, a man named Ralph Savage, shot himself in the head when he, too, was sentenced to seventeen years in jail. In all the stories of greed, gambling and gall that came out of the spectrum rush, few can match the sheer pathos of the story of Sonrise.

15

A HUSTLE HERE, A HUSTLE THERE

IN A MEETING ROOM OF A BETHESDA HOTEL, a few miles from the FCC head-quarters, an odd-looking scene was unfolding.

Several dozen people, mostly African Americans, were queued up behind a table. As each person got to the front of the line, a young man standing to the side would hand him or her three twenty-dollar bills. The person would turn and hand the money to the man seated behind the table, then lean over to sign a stack of photocopied documents. Task accomplished, the signer would drift out of the hotel and into the wintry night, most likely unsure of what exactly he'd just agreed to do. And the man behind the table would hand the bills back to his assistant to start the process again.

Though he'd lost both MRTS and his lucrative cellular-engineering business, Peter Lewis wasn't yet finished prospecting for gold in the spectrum rush. The group of strangers blindly signing documents in the late winter of 1986 were his new clients, and in many ways, his latest scheme was his most creative yet.

Thanks to mills like TCC and GCC, the price of applications had plummeted to $50 or less, squelching Lewis's applications-preparation business. The well had run dry; Lewis, who was already a millionaire several times over thanks to his first two forays into cellular, had been forced to close up shop.

But then he had an idea. Though there was clearly no more money in the applications-preparation business, there certainly was in the licenses themselves. Why not entice as many people as possible to apply at a minimal

179

cost, then charge them hefty consulting and service fees if they won any-thing? Preparing applications was practically as easy as pushing the button on a copier, after all. What did Lewis have to lose?

Lewis set immediately to work, placing clip-out coupon ads in the *Washington Post*, purchasing cable-TV spots and hiring workers to slip flyers under car windshield wipers in parking lots across the Washington metro area. "FREE U.S. GOVT. LOTTERY," blared the flyers in capital letters, "MAY MAKE YOU VERY RICH IN BILLION DOLLAR CELLULAR CAR TELEPHONE INDUSTRY!!" Interested parties were invited to come to seminars Lewis scheduled in area hotels.

At the seminars, the assembled sat rapt as the sharply dressed Lewis coolly made his pitch. The government was running a giveaway, he told them. Anyone could win valuable license to run car phone companies in places like Sheboygan, Wisconsin, and Midland, Texas. Best of all, it would cost only sixty dollars to enter the lottery—three dollars per application for twenty markets. And if anyone didn't have sixty dollars, he reassured the crowd, he'd lend it to them—hence the young man recycling the three twenty-dollar bills at the table.

To the assembled, this lottery sounded absurd. Then again, this was a government that paid farmers not to grow crops, bought herds of dairy cows to artificially inflate milk prices and spent millions of dollars trying to protect something called a "snail darter." Was a spectrum lottery really any more bizarre than that?

More than 350 people thought it wasn't. They bought Lewis's pitch, and just like that, he was in the cellular game once again.

———

HUNDREDS OF MILES AND A WORLD AWAY, a few photocopiers in tiny Crossville, Tennessee, were perilously close to overheating as they pumped out thousands of FCC application pages. Dozens of residents of rural Crossville, which billed itself "The Biggest Small Town in the South," were ready to stake their claim in the big government giveaway.

As Peter Lewis was doing in Washington, D.C., the architect of Crossville's applications blitz—a country hustler named Edward M. "Mack" Johnson, well known at the FCC for previous spectrum-related scams—wanted to stuff the lottery box with as many applications as possible. Johnson knew the good folk of Crossville would have no idea what to do if they won a cellular license; any winners would have no choice but to turn to him for help. Besides, good old Southern loyalty would surely come into play—

the people he helped apply, Johnson believed, were certain to include him in their windfall out of a simple sense of genteel indebtedness.

Mack Johnson was a slight, high-strung young man with an extraordinary nose for making big money quickly—particularly where it involved radio spectrum. He displayed this talent early, when he took a job managing a new Crossville-based radio station at age seventeen. Though the going rate for managing an AM station at the time was, in the words of one veteran, "$200 a week and all the records you could steal," Johnson volunteered to work for even less—provided he could have a piece of the station's profits. Barely old enough to vote or buy a beer, the skinny youngster cleared $100,000 his first year as station manager.

And that was just the beginning for this budding entrepreneur. The station did well, but Johnson wanted more: Deciding that the best way to increase listeners and ad revenue was to increase the little station's power, he flew to Washington, D.C., and walked into the FCC to learn how to do it.

As they had with the enthusiastic young Peter Lewis, the FCC staffers took a liking to this ambitious youngster, and they were more than willing to help him fill out the paperwork and figure out the technical requirements. "You don't need to know what you're doing," said Johnson later. "You just go from office to office and tell them you don't know what to do, and they'll sit you down and fill it out for you."

Though Johnson never went to college, he got his education "at the FCC, from their engineers," he says. It was an education he'd twist to his tremendous advantage—and to the FCC's singular frustration.

Armed with his new education, Mack Johnson launched a career that was most unusual, especially for a young man from the hinterlands of East Tennessee: He took advantage of every FCC spectrum giveaway he could. At first, he applied for radio station licenses himself, with the idea of building and squeezing cash flow out of rural stations. But before long, he realized there was an easier way to make money off the FCC's license giveaways.

In the mid-1970s, when cellular telephones were still playthings for Bell Labs scientists, Johnson began running an application mill. He roamed the South, promoting himself as an "engineer" with special expertise in preparing FCC applications, first for AM radio, then FM radio, then UHF television licenses. This bold young huckster would prepare an FCC application for anyone willing to pay his fee—and customers proved very easy to find. "There's always someone who wants to be the big shot in town," Johnson would later remark, such as "the local undertaker who wanted a radio station in his town."

"We just declared ourselves the application store," says Johnson. "We were the self-appointed salespeople for the FCC." Since he did all the work himself, it cost him only a few hundred dollars to prepare the forms—but because the radio and television stations might someday be worth hundreds of thousands, he could charge tens of thousands of dollars for a few hours' work. For Johnson, it didn't matter whether any of his applicants ultimately won a license, or even whether they really needed one; the main thing was, the work was easy, the money was rolling in—and the profit margins were sinful.

There was only one problem: The FCC made available only a limited amount of radio and television spectrum, a situation that naturally constrained his business. But then, in 1983, the FCC opened up a whole new block of spectrum, intended for something called low-power television (LPTV). This was just what Johnson needed. Advertising his new company, Edward M. Johnson Associates, as "the nation's largest communications consultants firm" ("No one challenged it," Johnson bemusedly observed years later), he excitedly began flacking applications for the new licenses. Using automated word-processing equipment, he'd plug in variables for frequencies, geographic names and tower locations, and produce a professional-looking application for $50 or $60—which he'd then turn around and sell for $5,000 to $6,000. With his new business partner, a fellow broadcaster and natural salesman named Robert Blow (the same Robert Blow who would later partner with Mark Warner), Johnson was soon grossing $200,000 to $300,000 per month.

The flood of LPTV applications stunned the FCC. What the bureaucrats had assumed would be a straightforward, reasonably quick license distribution among a handful of qualified applicants suddenly threatened to become a fiasco. Overwhelmed by the volume of paperwork, the FCC declared it would choose the license winners by lottery—the first one ever held by the commission.

Staffers were dismayed not only at the mountain of applications, but also at the dawning realization that one man was responsible for as many as 80 percent of them. They'd taken the time to teach Mack Johnson how to apply, and now this opportunistic young hustler was turning it back on them by spewing out applications to anyone who wanted to take a gamble. This, to put it mildly, wasn't how federal license distribution was supposed to work.

Johnson's applications were slapdash—one, for example, contained geographic coordinates locating a prospective transmitter tower in the middle of a high-school football stadium—and the FCC soon began dismissing them wholesale, before eventually shutting down the whole LPTV-lottery plan in consternation. By then, Johnson had already banked a million or more in fees, and, over Blow's objections, he refused to refund any of it. Incredibly, though Johnson's plan was the foreseeable result of mixing greed, a little ingenuity and a patently flawed system, the FCC completely missed the object lesson the LPTV debacle offered. Had the bureaucrats been paying attention, they might have realized what would be in store when they later switched to lotteries in the fledgling cellular industry.

Johnson began putting together applications in the earliest rounds of the cellular giveaway. The more money he made, the greater was his appetite for more chances, more licenses, more cash. When the FCC switched to lotteries, Johnson prepared a few dozen applications for clients, but he was dismayed at how many mills sprang up to copy his LPTV processing mill. Their prices were low and their marketing resources intimidating; Johnson saw no profit in doing the same thing. Worse yet, with so many applications being filed, the chances of Johnson's handful of applications winning were diminishing.

Frustrated, Johnson decided there was only one way to better his odds: by filing applications in the names of friends and family, and hoping that the extra dozen or so chances in each market might bring success. Then, in March 1986, he took that idea a step further. "If fifteen applications for friends were a good idea," Johnson recalls thinking, "then more ought to be a better idea." Why not just give away as many applications as he could get people to sign? More chances in the lottery drum meant more chances of a Crossville winner; why not give away enough applications to sway the statistical probabilities?

Thanks to his earlier schemes, Johnson knew his name was anathema at the FCC; realizing it was best to keep his connection to this plan a secret, he enlisted a trio of Crossville residents—Thomas E. Looney, Dean Bennett and Mike Miller—to help him peddle the applications. "Never try to sell anything," Johnson instructed the trio; they should only give the applications away, trusting that any winners would offer them a part of the windfall. He then recruited a few engineering students from a local two-year college and a couple dozen high-school students to help him assemble the applications.

The trio's efforts were wildly successful. Local businessmen, lawyers, salesmen and bank presidents signed their names to applications, as did the high-school basketball, baseball and football coaches. Had they stopped to think about it, these good citizens might have realized there was something perverse about a high-school football coach from rural Tennessee declaring to the U.S. government that he was ready and able to build a multimillion-dollar cell phone system in Idaho or Puerto Rico. But Looney, Bennett and Miller were respected members of the community. If they were behind it, applicants assumed, the plan couldn't be against the law. Or could it?

Though the plan stretched the FCC rules to the limits of absurdity, ultimately it could be argued that, when it came down to the legalities, Johnson and his "salesmen" were doing nothing wrong. Unfortunately for Johnson, one member of his team had too little faith in the nuances of the plan. Insurance agent Dean Bennett understood that he was meant to give away the applications for nothing in return, simply trusting that his "customers" would remember him if they won a license. But that was a bit too vague for him. So he typed up a letter for those he described as his "less trustworthy friends" to sign, promising Bennett 90 percent of any winnings realized from the lottery.

The existence of this letter was an egregious violation of the FCC's "real party in interest" rules, which made clear there could be only one application per person. With the deal on paper, Bennett was now clearly the real party in interest behind multiple common applications. If a single one of these letters made its way to the FCC, Johnson's carefully constructed scheme would unravel.

On April 28, 1986, a Federal Express truck rumbled into the parking lot at the FCC's warehouse in Gettysburg, Pennsylvania, and the driver unloaded more than 5,000 applications with ties to Crossville—about 100 in each of 50 markets. With only 400 or so total applications filed in each market, Crossville hopefuls stood a one-in-four chance of winning any given market. And with fifty markets up for grabs, it was likely Crossville applicants would win at least twelve markets on lottery day.

When the lottery drums stopped twirling, Lewis and Johnson saw that their plans had paid off well. Fourteen Crossville-related applicants—including Dean Bennett's secretary, an assistant football coach at Tennessee Tech and a junior bank officer (who won Arecibo, Puerto Rico)—had won markets that promised to be worth $50 million or more. Seven of Peter Lewis's clients were winners, including a retired postal worker, an aircraft factory worker, and a bus driver from Washington, D.C. All told, Lewis's winners had claims to nearly 800,000 POPs—$30 million worth of cellular licenses at 1986 prices. All over Tennessee and Washington, D.C., new winners asked the same question: "What do I do now?"

The euphoria in Crossville didn't last. Two observers—an FCC staffer and a former employee of the GCC application mill—independently discovered that large numbers of winning applications came from the same zip code. This was strange enough, but compounding their surprise was the fact that the zip code was for a tiny Tennessee hamlet of only 6,000 residents. Clearly, something strange was going on. Similarly, it soon became clear that a number of winning applications had roots to Peter Lewis—and that some of the applicants appeared to have no idea at all what they'd won. Were Lewis and Johnson the real parties-in-interest behind these twenty-one winning applications? If so, competing applicants had a huge opportunity to lay claim to the $80 million in cellular licenses they'd won.

The ensuing string of events plunged things further into chaos. The FCC sent investigators to Crossville, the press picked up the story, and Mack Johnson filed lawsuits charging he was being defamed. A federal grand jury was impaneled, disgruntled late-place finishers filed petitions to have the suspect applications dismissed, and all across Washington lawyers quietly salivated at the prospect of the juicy fees awaiting them. In Crossville, Johnson's fate was sealed when a "Deep Throat" informant gave the FCC a copy of the 90-percent agreement. And in Washington, Peter Lewis, in a rage at what he considered a witch hunt, angrily accused the FCC of targeting him and his clients because of their race.

The twenty-one licenses won by Lewis and Crossville applicants were soon stuck in a legal quagmire the likes of which had never before been seen at the FCC. Not only were the winners of these twenty-one markets suspect, but so were many of the markets' second-, third- and fourth-place finishers, who were also tied to Lewis or Crossville—making them as unfit to challenge for the licenses as the winners were to hold them. In each of the contested markets, the first clean runner-up, no matter how far down the chain, would have to discredit each of the suspect applicants in front of him, one by one, before the FCC could award the disputed license.

A resolution, assuming one could be reached, appeared to be years away at best. Meanwhile, valuable markets would sit unbuilt as the wirelines stormed in with their systems.

———

In spring of 1987, the principals of a new boutique investment-banking firm—Schelle, Warner, Murray and Thomas Inc.—met to discuss how the firm might find fresh opportunities in the mushrooming cellular industry.

The last MSA lottery had been held in December; with the cellular-spectrum giveaway on hold until the Rural Service Areas, or RSAs, were distributed, we were hoping to find other ways to make money in the evolving industry.

Wayne Schelle, Mark Warner, Gary Thomas and I had founded the firm six months before, after independently enjoying entrepreneurial success in the cellular spectrum rush. On this day, we were meeting with Bob Blow— once Mack Johnson's business partner, he had split with Johnson over business and ethical issues, and now he was a partner of Warner's. Blow had a provocative idea: We should, he suggested, try to solve the Crossville fiasco for the FCC. The plan Blow offered that day sounded like a particularly diabolical circle of hell—but it was one that could potentially prove fabulously lucrative for us all.

The concept was straightforward, but the execution promised to be horrifically complex. First, Blow said, we should get McCaw to commit to purchasing the contested licenses at a certain price. Then, using the money McCaw promised, we could buy out the tainted license winner—as well as any tainted second-, third- and fourth-place finishers, if necessary. Finally, we could buy out the first clean finisher, and then turn the license over to McCaw. As long as we could buy out everyone for less than what McCaw promised to pay for the license, we'd come out ahead.

But how could we pay off three, four or even five parties with the money McCaw offered for a single market? The tainted finishers faced the likelihood that the FCC would strip them of their licenses; they had plenty of incentive to take whatever buyout they could get. As for the clean runners-up, we'd have to convince them that going along with our complex plan would save them the money and time it would take to fight the tainted winners. Finally, we'd have to convince the FCC to go along with our plan. Blow's idea made sense, and I suggested we try to do the same thing with the seven Lewis markets. Though initially reluctant, my partners agreed. In the space of half an hour, we'd nonchalantly committed ourselves to a task that would consume us for nearly the next two years.

We began slowly, negotiating individually with the dozens of amateur speculators who'd won—people who had no reason to trust a bunch of cold-calling, suit-wearing, smooth-talking deal-makers like us. We were in for many months of difficult work; not only was each individual deal comprised of headachy details and tedious repetition, but we forever faced the looming threat that some FCC bureaucrat or a couple of stubborn applicants could scuttle our hard work. Was it even worth it to try?

It seemed preposterously ambitious to think that the five of us could circumvent what looked to be at least eight to ten years of upcoming litigation. Still, if we pulled it off, the rewards could be staggering. There were some 2 million POPs in those twenty-one markets, and our plan was to clear five dollars or more per POP.

Over the next eighteen months, we undertook a dealmaking marathon, gambling several hundred thousand dollars of our own money on legal fees and borrowing another half-million from McCaw. We paid Peter Lewis hundreds of thousands of dollars for "past-due consulting services," and the Crossville applicants willingly signed on to accept $100,000 apiece for their dubious claims on cellular licenses worth millions. As we'd figured, they decided it was better to take a small fraction of what the licenses were worth than to risk getting nothing at all.

The scope of the buyouts led to some serendipitous moments for unsuspecting applicants. Los Altos, California, resident Frank Mirgon, for example, had spent tens of thousands of dollars on applications and hadn't won a single market—the closest he'd come was fourth place in Charlottesville, Virginia, and fifth place in Sheboygan, Wisconsin. Incredibly, when we dug down through the list of finishers for those two markets, we found that all the applicants ahead of Mirgon were tied to either Crossville or Peter Lewis. Years after his disappointing finish, Mirgon got a phone call offering him millions for applications he'd long since thought were worthless.

In a year and a half of pleading, negotiating and cajoling, we managed to settle nineteen of the twenty-one markets. And by the spring of 1989, the FCC had, to our relief and amazement, approved more than sixty separate contracts we'd negotiated with five dozen applicants, three buyers and a handful of other parties. As the millions of dollars in payments passed through our bank accounts, we managed to hold on to more than $10 million of it, together with minority ownership in several of the markets that would later prove to be worth millions more. Once again, as it had in Le Grand Deal and the CSP imbroglio, pragmatism prevailed over procedure: Businessmen had wrested control of the licensing process from the FCC, and now nineteen new cellular systems were ready to go on the air.

In these years, as the '80s wound down and the cell phone boom of the '90s loomed, the real action in the cell phone industry had precious little to do with the phones themselves. As my partners and I discovered, there were numerous opportunities to make money in this new industry, in ways that usually weren't immediately apparent.

Nick Wilson, Peter Lewis and others who ran application mills became rich men thanks to the spectrum rush. Lawyers billed untold millions of hours fighting Sisyphean battles—as one anonymous FCC official told *Business Week*, "A lot of lawyers have sent their children through college on frivolous filings." Business novices like Jeanine Hochhalter and Bob Pelissier made more money than they'd ever dreamed of. And dealmakers like Mark Warner, Bob Blow, Wayne Schelle and I were able to claim a share of the action.

But all this money had to be coming from somewhere. There were several companies buying up a majority of the markets during these frenetic days, but none moved so aggressively or spent as much as McCaw. For many industry observers, the real object of fascination was not all the "little people," the scams or the frantic deal making. It was a simple question:

Where was McCaw getting all that money?

16

MORTGAGING THE HOUSE OF CARDS

RAISING CAPITAL FOR A CELLULAR BUSINESS WAS A STRUGGLE in the early years of the industry. With no operating histories, no reliable usage estimates and huge up-front capital needs, everything about the industry was highly speculative. Additionally, most nonwireline cellular companies were young, undercapitalized and run by unproven operators; it's no wonder the traditional banking industry wanted little to do with them. Rounding up enough cash to compete was a difficult business at which few excelled, and none excelled like McCaw.

The costs of competing in cellular were astronomical. Applying and battling for licenses, building multimillion-dollar systems, hiring management teams, and paying for splashy marketing campaigns all consumed cash—and much of it had to be spent "up front" before the revenues could follow. McCaw's fellow nonwirelines understandably played cautiously, unwilling to have their companies swamped in debt. But whenever Craig McCaw could find someone willing to lend to him, he would take the money; he seemed never to doubt that the returns would follow.

"I am normally accused of being one of the more highly leveraged players around," says Metro Mobile's George Lindemann, "but compared to Craig, I was the most conservative guy out there."

Fortunately for Craig McCaw, his uncanny ability to hire exceptional employees brought him some of the smartest, most creative deal-makers in the country—people like Ed Hopper, Wayne Perry and John Stanton. From the earliest days of cellular, the McCaw team excelled on two fronts: They were able to put together purchases that fueled Craig's evolving vision of a world without tethers, and then, more remarkably, they found creative ways to finance what they'd bought.

Early on, McCaw's cellular division (which was then little but an applications department) was run on whatever spare change could be found under cable's cushions. By the fall of 1983, the tiny cellular group faced a huge problem cloaked in a huge opportunity: In a matter of months, Stanton had snatched up enough properties to more than double the spectrum produced by McCaw's original cellular applications. Having established a watershed business strategy for the new industry, Stanton aggressively replicated the model: He contracted to buy up dozens and dozens of fractional application interests created by the Grand Alliance process.

But by January 1984, the bills were coming due, and it wasn't clear how McCaw would pay them. Craig McCaw still saw himself as a cable-TV operator; these cellular spectrum deals were exciting, but there certainly wasn't enough cash filtering down from cable to pay for them. Hopper and Stanton would have to figure out a financing strategy, and quickly.

Ed Hopper telephoned a friend at California-based newspaper-publishing firm E. W. Scripps; what followed was the first in what would be a long line of creative financing schemes. Stanton structured the deal, and it was a subtle masterpiece: Stanton convinced Scripps that the value of McCaw's new cellular business would be directly proportional to its spectrum ownership. For $12 million, Scripps would receive anywhere between 15 percent and 40 percent of McCaw Cellular's equity, depending upon which spectrum licenses McCaw could acquire in the ongoing nonwireline shakeout. Before anyone else in the industry had heard the term "POPs"—in fact, before anyone had even considered using population coverage as a proxy for spectrum value—Stanton designed a deal in which Scripps's ownership percentage would decline as the number of McCaw's POPs rose.

While fair in principle, Stanton's deal structure triggered a consequence unanticipated by Scripps. McCaw suddenly had a huge incentive to acquire as many POPs as possible; thanks to the structure of the deal, McCaw would benefit by using the new money not to build cellular operations, but to buy more spectrum—McCaw would effectively use Scripps's own money to dilute its ownership. It was a brilliant double dip.

Stanton's financial legerdemain was soon eclipsed by that of his mentor Ed Hopper. In the cable industry, Hopper knew, vendors for the infrastructure equipment sometimes financed the system operators' purchase of their hardware. This was a relatively safe bet for the vendors; cable had been around for nearly two decades and prior experience all but guaranteed that the revenue generated by the new systems would provide more than enough cash flow to pay back the debt.

Why not, Hopper reasoned, ask cellular equipment vendors to do the same thing? There was, of course, no track record to ensure the vendors would get their investment back, but there was another incentive for them to provide financing. The vendors competing for market share in this brand-new industry—companies like AT&T, Ericsson, ITT and Motorola—all wanted to stake out their territory. In addition, Hopper argued, there was the razor-for-razor-blades theory: Whichever manufacturer sold the big central switch would then be assured of future millions by selling numerous cell site radios as the system expanded. For the hungry manufacturers, getting in on the ground floor would be, Hopper reasoned, more than worth the risk of providing financing.

As fellow nonwirelines fretted over the cost of buildouts, Hopper made his pitch to the vendors. Not only did he want 100-percent financing, he told them, but he also demanded that they lend McCaw 20 percent more than the full cost of their own hardware to cover the "soft costs" associated with building out systems, such as engineering, construction, services, marketing and the like. It was a bold move for little McCaw to ask 120-percent financing from these behemoth equipment makers, but Hopper believed he could sway them.

Hopper was the only guy at McCaw who could take this on, remembers Wayne Perry. "We couldn't go to AT&T," he says, remembering early PR difficulties caused by the McCaw team's relative youth and inexperience. "We were young whippersnappers. But Ed could go. A little gray hair worked."

Before long, Hopper had engineered a two-horse race between AT&T and ITT. He deftly played them off each other, convincing the executives at AT&T that ITT was about to walk away with the business. Pitting the inventors of cellular technology against one of their biggest telecom competitors was a shrewd gambit: ITT, which had yet to sell a single cellular system, badly wanted a toehold in the new industry; AT&T wanted just as badly to keep them out.

In March 1985, AT&T agreed to Hopper's terms: Ma Bell would provide 120-percent financing. The deal was a boon not only for McCaw, but soon for the entire nonwireline cellular industry. The first and largest hurdle everyone faced was to get a system on the air, and now Hopper had created the model of how it could be done. Within a matter of days, Ram Broadcasting's Carl Aron had pulled off a similar coup with Ericsson to finance the Detroit system, and in the following months every manufacturer followed suit. McCaw's nonwireline competitors who'd bailed out of cellular thanks to lack of cash—companies like Peter Lewis and Bernie Cravath's MRTS—now watched in dismay as, too late for them, the biggest reason for their premature exit was eliminated.

The equipment deal, wrote a *Forbes* reporter, "broke the whole race open." Now McCaw and the rest of the nonwirelines could compete with the deep-pocketed RBOCs. Wayne Perry calls it "Ed Hopper's single greatest contribution to the cellular industry."

Years later, even Hopper remains amazed at the accomplishment. "The Scripps deal and the AT&T deals were impossible deals," he says. "You just couldn't do them, but we did." With a source of start-up capital now assured, most nonwireline operators breathed sighs of relief and settled down to constructing their systems. In Kirkland, however, the upstart McCaw team saw the vendor-financing solution as an invitation to grow.

———————

AS MCCAW PLUNGED EVER DEEPER INTO CELLULAR, one of its biggest competitors started edging its way out. Metromedia had abruptly entered cellular in the spring of 1982, and now, in the spring of 1985, John Kluge was already contemplating his exit.

One afternoon late that spring, Kluge met with several of his top advisers—CFO Stuart Subotnick, cellular chief George Duncan and economist Thomas A. Domencich—to discuss what kind of hardware to buy for their New York system. They had two options: Buy cheaper hardware from Motorola and face potential expansion limitations, or pay millions more for Ericsson or AT&T equipment that could serve a larger customer base. The team had laid out the pros and cons of each side; now it was up to Kluge to decide.

The CEO's answer was brief and illuminating. They would buy Motorola, Kluge told them, because he didn't plan to stay in the cellular business for long, and the inferior Motorola equipment would be sufficient for the short term.

"Cellular is a business of the '90s," Kluge told his surprised team. "It's the '80s now, and I'm 70 years old." Simply put, Kluge foresaw the day when the skyrocketing growth in cellular values would flatten, and he planned to move on before that happened. Why spend money on a future that wouldn't profit him? Domencich was stunned—Kluge had bet his entire company and most of his personal fortune on the move into cellular, and suddenly he was again announcing an abrupt change of course.

A year after that surprising pronouncement, Subotnick gave Kluge the perfect catalyst for following through on it. A former tax lawyer, Subotnick had calculated that he and Kluge could save hundreds of millions of dollars in personal income taxes by liquidating everything left in Metromedia— which essentially meant cellular.

After some rough calculating, Kluge and Subotnick determined that if they could get $1.5 billion for the whole package of cellular plus paging, they'd sell. The number was arbitrary; with current paging-industry values running at $1,300 per subscriber, they worked backward to figure out how much they needed for their cellular POPs in order to reach their $1.5 billion target. The figure they came up with was $40 per POP—50 percent higher than the best price paid yet for control of a cellular license. The price had very little to do with present or future values of cellular; it was simply what Kluge and Subotnick wanted to get based on their personal goals.

Had the wirelines been prohibited from buying nonwireline properties, it's doubtful Kluge would have found any buyers. But once the FCC and the courts had ruled that PacTel could purchase part of the San Francisco non-wireline license, the game was open to all. Not surprisingly, the two suitors who stepped up to bid were both RBOCs: Southwestern Bell and PacTel.

Though Kluge first began talking about a potential sale with PacTel, Southwestern Bell gained the edge by negotiating swiftly and definitively. A Southwestern Bell team swooped in, had a quick look around at operations, and made a preemptive bid: $1.65 billion for the package. Pactel CEO Sam Ginn, given a chance to meet or exceed the bid in twenty-four hours, was agog at the number; unsure whether Kluge was bluffing or not, he declined to match it. When the record-breaking sale to Southwestern Bell was announced in July 1986, the press and the industry went wild. No one could decide who was the genius and who was the fool.

"Southwestern paid through the nose. A ridiculously inflated price," Paine Webber analyst Jack B. Grubman sniffed to *Business Week*, and when Southwestern's stock slipped on the news, it seemed Wall Street agreed. *U.S. News* took a more sanguine view: "[T]o judge by the June 30 pact. . . big investors are now convinced the business can fly."

Most analysts couldn't figure out what Kluge's ultimate strategy was. "Puzzled?" asked analyst Alan J. Gottesman in the *New York Times*, "If you've watched Metromedia for a long time, the point of puzzlement has passed. . . Whatever [Kluge] does works out real well. You always assume there was a good reason, and you usually find out later that it was a good move."

Though $45 a POP was a record-setting price in mid-1986, it would seem a ridiculous bargain just six short years later, in the spring of 1992, when those same POPs would sell again at seven times that price—validating Kluge's prescient observation that cellular was a business of the '90s.

One unexpected twist in the deal showed that, even on the rare occasion when Kluge isn't the smartest guy in the room, he seems to be the luckiest. Despite his determination to exit cellular altogether in 1986, a last-minute hitch arose: Kluge's partner in New York and Philadelphia, LIN Broadcasting, threatened to legally undermine the deal, leaving Kluge with no choice but to hold onto his interests in those two cities. Accordingly, the contract with Southwestern was shrunk to $1.2 billion for everything but New York and Philadelphia. Kluge was disappointed, but that would prove to be short-lived: When he sold those interests a half-dozen years later, he would make another $2 billion—more money than he'd made on the entire original cellular portfolio. Even when he wasn't trying, John Kluge had a knack for making money.

The Southwestern Bell deal had huge impact on the industry. It was the first real sign that the RBOCs would move to snatch up any spectrum the nonwirelines put on the market. CCI's George Blumenthal remembers feeling "depressed, because all of the industry was disappearing around us. . . [W]e had always assumed we'd have more time to buy licenses."

On the other hand, the $1.2 billion price tag meant that overnight, everyone's cellular properties were valued at forty-five dollars per POP. Despite Blumenthal's regrets, the deal was a huge boon for CCI, which had just two weeks before become the first cellular company to go public. CCI had bought its POPs for prices ranging from two dollars up to the teens and twenties; suddenly they could expect the price of their stock to reflect Kluge's new benchmark. Blumenthal's net worth would more than triple over the next thirty months, as CCI's stock rose from its offering price of $12.50 (the equivalent of $21 per POP) to over $40 (the equivalent of over $100 per POP). And as the wirelines continued to buy, the prices continued to rise.

Also in the spring of 1985, at the same time Kluge was plotting his exit from cellular, MCI executives in Washington, D.C., were planning to do the same thing.

Thanks to two developments—first, its surprising loss of the L.A. license in a comparative hearing; and second, the disappointing sum awarded by a jury in its antitrust lawsuit against AT&T—MCI had decided to refocus on its core long-distance business. "We were either going to be a great long-distance company or a great wireless company," remembers former MCI President Dan Akerson, "but we couldn't be both." In early 1985, MCI put its cellular and paging subsidiary, Airsignal, up for sale.

Ed Hopper decided McCaw ought to buy it. One afternoon, Hopper walked into a meeting of what he remembers as "a very tired bunch of troops." The cable division had just acquired a large cable company called Midwest Video, and McCaw's executives had barely had a moment to catch their breath.

"Just at that moment," remembers Hopper, "I come walking in here and say, 'Hey, I've got this MCI deal!' And I'm looking around the room and everybody is thinking, 'How are we going to handle this? Oh, God almighty!'" Sure, the McCaw employees were an ambitious bunch, but purchasing Airsignal would be orders of magnitude larger than anything the company had ever done before. Where would they get the money? Craig McCaw, too, was unconvinced it was a good move.

To Hopper, it was a no-brainer to at least throw in a bid. "If McCaw doesn't want this," he remembers telling Craig, "I'll go get it. . . I'll raise the millions and I'll go do this damn thing."

Airsignal's cellular portfolio was impressive: Its license interests covered 7 million POPs in twelve cities—places like Minneapolis, Denver, Sacramento and Salt Lake City. Though a purchase would cost well over $100 million, Hopper surmised that a per-POP bid far cheaper than McCaw's internal model values might carry the day. "Ed was absolutely convinced that we could get it done," says Stanton. "I don't think the rest of us thought it could happen. The amount of money [it would take] was enormous." And complicating matters further, MCI would prove a reluctant dance partner.

Hopper had been in earnest when he threatened to go after Airsignal himself and at first Craig, still viewing himself as primarily a cable operator, encouraged it. But as Craig watched his most trusted senior adviser start planning to buy all that precious spectrum, he abruptly changed his mind. Though his executives were split over whether it was a good idea, the depth of Hopper's conviction eventually swayed him. Craig decided McCaw would go for it.

John Stanton immediately set to work valuing McCaw's bid. When the executive team met to hash out a price, much debate ensued; the number of variables was enormous. After agonizing over every conceivable facet of the deal, Stanton suggested that McCaw submit a sealed bid of $156 million.

"No, John," blurted Wayne Perry. "That just looks too ephemeral. Let's make it $156,623,000," he suggested, picking random numbers. The team agreed, and Hopper submitted the bid.

The trouble was, MCI executives were leery of dealing with anyone they thought might not be able to come up with the money. When Cleveland-based CCI had inquired about bidding, the company's executives were tut-tutted by MCI's investment bankers, who told them, remembers George Blumenthal, "Oh, MCI only wants to talk to people with money." As Hopper put it, MCI was impressed enough with McCaw's bid—"They thought they were just putting the pants on these crazy people from McCaw," he says—but their second reaction was less enthusiastic: "'Who is this outfit, anyhow? They're crazy enough to pay these big prices, but can they come up with the money?' That was their issue."

It wasn't especially surprising, then, when the McCaw team learned they'd lost: A *Newswire* story reported that MCI had agreed to sell Airsignal to Mobile Communications Corporation of America, a Mississippi-based paging and cellular operator that had recently received a big equity investment from Bell South. What was surprising, though, was the price of the deal: $156,623,000. "We knew. We knew. More than anything, we knew that number," remembers Wayne Perry. "They had just shopped our number." Not only had McCaw lost, it had lost in a most disappointing way: thanks to unethical negotiating practices by MCI.

In the end, though, the MCI-MCCA deal fell through, a victim of the MCI board's animus toward Bell South. Though the sale was technically to fellow nonwireline MCCA, the deal MCCA had recently reached with Bell South effectively meant the properties would fall to the RBOC. MCI's Bill McGowan had spent his career battling AT&T and the Baby Bells; he was not about to give them a leg up in the cellular industry.

As soon as the news got out that the MCCA deal had collapsed, McCaw raced to bid anew. This time MCI, no longer in a position to be quite so picky about its suitors, agreed to a deal. Now all the McCaw team had to do was figure out where they would get $156 million. "We didn't know how to pay for it," remembers Stanton. "We just flat didn't know how to pay for it." Thanks to regulatory delays, McCaw would have about a year to figure it out.

MANY THINGS HAPPENED IN THE COURSE OF THAT YEAR, between June 1985 and July 1986: The application mills went into gear, the FCC held its cellular lotteries and many of the early nonwireline companies got out of cellular.

But the year was notable at McCaw for another reason: Craig McCaw was absent for much of it. Already famous for his willingness to delegate authority—"Scot [Jarvis] at age twenty-four was doing deals for tens of millions of dollars without even looking at Craig," remembers Barry Adelman with incredulity—Craig had another hands-off quirk. He took sabbaticals for weeks, even months at a time, checking in only sporadically and trusting his team to run things without him.

"[Craig] took three sabbaticals in my first four years at McCaw," remembers Stanton, "which I viewed as inspiring, something I've always wanted to do." Sometimes Craig took time off for personal reasons, to sort out his thinking or simply get away. Other times, such as his December 1985–September 1986 sabbatical, health reasons figured in as well. The reticent CEO didn't say much about what was ailing him in 1986, and protective McCaw executives would say little more than that he had "throat trouble."

The McCaw team was in contact with Craig during his sabbatical, but Wayne Perry had been named acting president, and most decisions were made internally. "John and Wayne were pretty much running the show," says Larry Movshin, "and when [Craig] came back, he was kind of viewed as a very aloof, almost a mystic-like person that no one ever saw."

When Craig returned, the dynamics at the Kirkland offices suddenly shifted. Something else was different, too. In his time off, Craig seemed to have reached a turning point in his thinking. For the first time, he was now focused primarily on cellular, rather than cable.

Craig had entered the business world in cable television. His father had been a cable pioneer, Craig and his brothers had spent their teenage summers stringing cable and selling subscriptions in Centralia, and the Twin Cities cable company had been the sole legacy left when their father died. Even as the cellular division grew, McCaw had always been primarily a cable company; cable was the core of Craig's business life.

But when Craig returned from his sabbatical in the fall of 1986, he made the decision many considered unthinkable for him: He put McCaw's cable division up for sale. The decision, remembers Wayne Perry, was "very hard on Craig. . . it was emotionally very hard to do."

"He was considered a big up-and-coming player in the cable industry," remembers Perry, "and we were [ranked number] 22 [in size] at the time. Everybody expected us to be top ten. I mean, it was just ordained that we would be top ten." But cellular, Craig now realized, was where the true growth potential lay. Throughout 1986, as both the cable and cellular divisions chased acquisitions, Wayne Perry saw a growing divergence in values: For every cable deal McCaw considered, they found "a plethora of cellular deals, which were absolutely no-brainers to beat the deal."

There was no shortage of interest when McCaw put its cable properties up for sale in November 1986. Jones Intercable, Comcast and American Television & Communications Corporation all came calling. At first the strongest interest came from Jones, which sent a team of analysts to McCaw headquarters to study the systems' accounts. Then McCaw got a call from a representative of Jack Kent Cooke.

With his slicked-back hair, red-meat-and-cigars life style, thoroughbred horses and sprawling Virginia estate, Jack Kent Cooke was an old-style mogul. The owner of the Washington Redskins and New York City's Chrysler Building, Cooke reveled in the luxuries money brought. He also loved the art of the deal; already a billionaire, Cooke approached new business deals with a gamer's relish.

For the notoriously claustrophobic Cooke, the first step was the most difficult: He decided to fly from northern Virginia to the Pacific Northwest to meet Craig McCaw face-to-face. Unable to stand being cooped up in his private plane for too long at a time, Cooke would periodically order the pilot to land at the nearest airport; he'd then amble stiffly down the steps to the runway to collect his nerves. The long, frustrating trip was immediately worth it, though—when he got to the McCaw headquarters, Cooke was instantly impressed with what he saw.

"[He] was enthralled with our organization," remembers Perry. "He couldn't believe all this young talent we had. . . Boy, he was really excited."

Sensing Cooke's appetite, Wayne Perry suggested that the McCaw team huddle out of the room before naming a price. Perry then outlined the tactical situation. The best course for McCaw was to convert the cable operations to cash as quickly as possible. But the cable industry was notorious for slow closings—long, drawn-out contract negotiations; copious due diligence studies (which Jones was now doing); and finally, months or even years waiting for federal and local government approvals.

What if, Perry suggested, they could convince Cooke to contract quickly and pay quickly? McCaw could promise to continue operating things for Cooke, leaving the local government approvals to happen after the closing. If Cooke would take the risk, McCaw could give him a lower price, yet profit by using Cooke's cash to quickly snap up more cellular bargains. Nobody had ever closed a cable deal without having municipal approvals first, but why not try? Craig quickly nodded assent.

Returning to the room, Perry suggested a "no tears" negotiation: there would be no letter of intent or preliminary agreement; a contract would be prepared and parties could either sign or not. If they had a deal, Perry said, McCaw could pick a closing date as soon as federal approval was received, leaving the dozens of local governments with no power to hold everything up. Cooke loved the idea, and when the price was named, he bit. As the team of Jones Intercable accountants droned on through columns of numbers down the hall, Jack Kent Cooke smiled his trademark toothy grin as he shook hands with Craig McCaw, sealing the deal on the spot. Just like that, he bought the McCaw cable operations for $755 million.

The price set an industry record. With 433,000 cable subscribers in forty-two markets, McCaw's cable properties had commanded $1,740 per subscriber. And the negotiation had taken a single day. Both Cooke and McCaw reveled in the speed of the deal, with Perry later mocking Jones Intercable for having "47,000 accountants up the kazoo. . . Jones' knuckleheads [were] going around still doing their due diligence" while McCaw and Cooke were shaking hands in the next room. No tears indeed.

Just like that, McCaw had another $755 million in its coffers. Much of it, however, was already committed—to cellular system build-out expenses, mounting operating expenses, and the company's favorite pastime: acquiring still more markets.

As 1985 gave way to 1986, McCaw continued to look for the rest of the money it needed to close the MCI deal; meanwhile, they used every available ploy to slow down the regulatory approvals that were preconditions to closing. "In the end," remembers Scot Jarvis, "MCI really didn't think we were going to be able to pull it off, because we had delayed enough that it looked like, 'Oh, these guys don't have the money.'. . . They really didn't think it would close."

Ed Hopper had an idea of how to get the money, but he knew it would be a hard sell to convince the investor. Trading on his straight-shooter reputation and long experience in cable, he approached McCaw's old cable-system partners, Affiliated Publications, Inc. Initially reluctant, the conservative *Boston Globe* publishers were swayed by Hopper's arguments, and the

two sides began to talk seriously about a more than $100 million invest-
ment in McCaw Cellular. It would be a huge leap of faith for a cautious firm
used to the dependable cash flows of cable.

But an Affiliated commitment came with a price: Given the huge amount
of money needed, Affiliated would end up owning a controlling majority
stake in McCaw's cellular division. Craig McCaw, ever leery of ceding control, was reluctant to do the deal. Still, he let Hopper continue talks with Affiliated, and the two sides drew nearer to a firm commitment. More than
once, when MCI executives grew nervous about whether McCaw could
come up with the money, Hopper trotted out Affiliated's balance sheets to
assuage their fears. "Affiliated Publications," says Hopper, "kept us in the
deal."

Even as Hopper negotiated with the Affiliated executives, the McCaw
team explored another avenue: America's new junk bond market. In the
spring of 1986, McCaw was approached by Salomon Brothers, one of Wall
Street's respected old-line firms, which promised to help raise $225 million.

Assuring McCaw they could pull it off, the Salomon bankers did several
months of preliminary work, then set up a two-week road show during
which the executives crisscrossed the country making their cellular pitch.
When the road show ended, Perry and the rest of the McCaw team learned
to its dismay that the Salomon bankers had succeeded in raising only $2
million: It was a catastrophic, unequivocal flop. And now the MCI closing
date was fast approaching.

Then Wayne Perry made a move he'd long been tempted to try: He called
the junk bond king, Michael Milken. On Friday afternoon, with Salomon
virtually conceding failure, Perry hurriedly arranged a Sunday visit with
Milken. Though many New York bankers would likely be found in the
Hamptons on a Sunday, Perry knew the workaholic Milken would have a
regular day at his Beverly Hills office.

The McCaw team knew that Milken's reputation was less than impecca-
ble. In fact, at a recent Affiliated board meeting, the chairman had waved
around a copy of *Fortune* with Milken's picture on the cover and declared,
"We should not do business with this man." But controversial was not the
same as criminal—three more years would pass before Milken's 1989 in-
dictment for securities fraud and racketeering—and McCaw now badly
needed Milken's help. Perry, Stanton and CFO Rufus Lumry flew down to
California to meet him.

That Sunday afternoon, as the McCaw trio sat expectantly in a Drexel
conference room, a secretary suddenly appeared and placed a bowl of pop-

corn on the table. This was the signal that Milken was about to appear: During meetings the hyperintense Milken liked to scoop handfuls of the salty snack into his mouth, talking through his crunching. For the hundreds of supplicants who came to Milken during his heyday, this popcorn ritual took on a legendary air.

Shortly after the popcorn was brought in, the junk bond king walked in and took his seat. At first, it seemed Milken would rather chat than talk business. Instead of broaching the topic at hand, he started by musing on the amount of time U.S. students spend studying in comparison to their counterparts in other countries. It was an odd beginning, a strange way for a driven personality like Milken to expend his strictly budgeted time. But then he quickly got to the point.

Training his deep-set, dark eyes on the trio, Milken launched into a detailed recitation of where his Salomon Brothers competitors had taken the McCaw executives over the past two weeks, who they had approached for financing and why they had been unsuccessful. "My god," Perry thought, "he knows where we've been!" As Milken reeled off the list of the road show's failures, the McCaw team sat dumbfounded.

"How much are you asking for?" Milken abruptly demanded, though he already knew the answer. Told McCaw was seeking $225 million, Milken replied, "The first thing we'll do is increase the size of the deal. We'll go for $250 million."

This seemed preposterous. Salomon Brothers had just tried and failed to raise even a fraction of the amount McCaw sought. Now here was Milken saying he'd get even more, and in an even shorter time. How, Stanton asked, could Milken possibly pull it off?

"Why can some people pole vault nineteen feet and others only fourteen?" Perry remembers Milken snapping. "You guys needed brain surgery and you went to a bunch of veterinarians." Milken's hubris was apparently limitless, but so too was his ability to attract money others couldn't find. Sitting face-to-face with Milken, Perry was convinced he could raise the money.

On hearing Perry's report of the meeting, Craig McCaw made a decision: McCaw would go with Milken, and all talks with Affiliated should be terminated. Hopper was livid.

"Craig fell in love with Michael Milken and jilted our partners," he said later. "I thought Craig treated [Affiliated] very shabbily." For weeks, Craig had allowed Hopper to string Affiliated along, reaping the benefits of their verbal agreement; then, at the last minute, he failed to live up to what Hopper called his "moral obligation" to do the deal.

For Craig McCaw, the decision to go with Milken was a simple business calculation. Years after witnessing the dissolution of his deceased father's empire—a painful process in which strangers had the power to make decisions that profoundly affected his family—he opted to take the risk of fresh debt rather than cede control to Affiliated. If feelings were hurt, so be it.

But for Hopper, Craig's action had crossed a line, and the old-school cable veteran was embarrassed and angry at his CEO's actions. "That point," Hopper recalls, "was the beginning of my decision to leave [McCaw Cellular]." Over the coming months, he would transition out of the company he had helped build from scratch.

The McCaw executives had left Milken precious little time—only a few weeks to find a quarter of a billion dollars. As June 1986 gave way to July, nearly a year had passed since MCI and McCaw had agreed to the deal. If McCaw didn't wire the money to MCI by July 3, MCI could declare McCaw in default and, at the very least, renegotiate the sale price. With per-POP prices climbing steadily and potential competitors looking for ways into the blossoming industry, this would be disastrous for McCaw: The company would almost certainly end up paying hundreds of millions more for the deal, or even lose it completely.

As if this mammoth deal wasn't enough for McCaw to swallow, the cellular team was organizing a mind-boggling array of concurrent deals, the failure of any one of which could seriously impact the rest. McCaw was, in the words of Mark Hamilton, playing a "three-dimensional chess match." While Hamilton and Stanton dealt with a skeptical MCI in Washington and Wayne Perry agonized over the details of the Drexel closing in New York, both teams were quietly slipping off for anteroom telephone calls or shuttling across town for hasty meetings on two secret new deals.

Six weeks earlier, soon after landing Milken's financing commitment, Perry and Stanton had recklessly launched a big new purchase: the acquisition of 9 million POPs in the Deep South, including control of Birmingham, Knoxville, Memphis, Nashville, Jacksonville, Orlando, Louisville and other cities belonging to a partnership between the Maxcell and Charisma companies. Thanks to bitter distrust among the Maxcell and Charisma partners, Stanton and Perry had negotiated a bargain price of seventeen dollars per POP. Now, Perry was surreptitiously shuttling back and forth from the Drexel offices to the purchase negotiations; because of clauses in the yet-to-be-closed bond deal that appeared to prohibit such a purchase, Perry was anxious to keep the acquisition secret from Drexel. But buried in the fine print of the bond deal, Perry knew he had a loophole that would save him when he disclosed the new purchase—after getting the Drexel money in hand.

Meanwhile, in Washington, McCaw was planning another confidential deal. Unbeknown to MCI, McCaw planned to resell Airsignal's paging properties almost immediately after purchasing them; the cash from that sale would help pay for the simultaneous Maxcell-Charisma deal. And not only was McCaw planning to "flip" the paging, but the buyer of the vast majority of the systems was none other than MCCA—the company the MCI board had refused to do business with.

All four deals—the Drexel bonds closing, the MCI deal closing, the Maxcell-Charisma purchase and the paging sale—had to happen at essentially the same time. As the four deals hung in the balance, an unexpected announcement threatened to unhinge them all.

On July 1, 1986—two days before McCaw planned to close the Airsignal deal—the Metromedia–Southwestern Bell deal was announced. The price of forty-five dollars a POP was two and a half times more than what McCaw planned to pay in the yet-unsigned Maxcell-Charisma deal—and roughly four times the net price of the yet-unclosed Airsignal cellular properties (taking into account the resale of paging). With this announcement, it was suddenly clear that McCaw was getting dirt cheap prices: Suddenly, the temptation for both sellers to walk was huge. With only two days to go until closing, McCaw desperately needed to get its financing, or risk losing two tremendous bargains.

The crucial day, July 3, started badly. Stanton and Hamilton arrived at MCI headquarters that morning to find what Hamilton called "absolute chaos": MCI had gotten word of McCaw's resale of the paging properties to MCCA, and the executives were livid. One, a key MCI executive, was "rampaging like a bull elephant," according to Hamilton, and the rest were "just going absolutely crazy." Stanton and Hamilton did their best to calm the angry MCI team; they succeeded in establishing a shaky truce, but one thing was clear—McCaw had better deliver the money before sunset. The bankers at Drexel-Burnham had assured McCaw that their bond sale had closed the day before, but everything was reliant on the vagaries of multiple wire transfers.

As Stanton and Hamilton sat cloistered in a conference room with impatient and irritated MCI executives, the clock ticked past 2 P.M., the time when banks' wire rooms close for the day. No news came, and the clock ticked slowly onward: 2:30. . . 2:45. . . 3 P.M. The group sat in nervous silence.

Finally, at 3:25 P.M., the phone call came: The final wire to MCI's account had gone through. "We opened some champagne," remembers Hamilton, "then got on a plane and headed back home for July 4." The McCaw team had pulled off not only their biggest cellular deal yet, but four crucial deals at once.

The Airsignal purchase was, as Hopper put it, "a hell of a coup." It instantly doubled the size of McCaw Cellular, making it the largest nonwireline cellular company in America. What's more, it would soon become clear that McCaw had gotten the Airsignal POPs at fire sale prices. In the coming months, when McCaw closed the two sales of the paging properties, it made back nearly half of the $156 million it had paid for the cellular plus paging. McCaw had effectively paid some $80 million—less than $10 per POP—for 7 million prime cellular POPs, at the same time Southwestern Bell was paying $45 per POP to John Kluge. In comparison to Southwestern Bell's deal, McCaw had gotten a $230 million discount.

"We thought we had taken McCaw to the cleaners," Akerson later recalled. "We could not have been more wrong."

The events of July 3, 1986, catapulted McCaw onto the national financial scene. The MCI-Airsignal purchase, the Drexel financing, the Maxcell-Charisma purchase and the cable sale had propelled McCaw laterally from the top twenties in cable to number one in cellular—and they were just getting started. Before the year was out, McCaw started a new cellular subsidiary that owned McCaw's southern properties (a subsidiary financed by Affiliated, who was kept in the loop by Hopper), and that was followed by the purchase of Kansas City and a contract (later challenged) to buy Milwaukee. All the while, prices spiraled upward, soon surpassing Kluge's record price of $45 per POP.

McCaw's portfolio was impressive, but it pushed the company's capital structure to the limits: Bankers increasingly weren't satisfied letting such a huge enterprise live off borrowed money alone. McCaw needed equity capital, money that required no interest payments, if it wanted to keep growing. As 1987 began, Craig McCaw essentially had three choices for his company: stop growing, give up a big chunk of his company to a financial investor like Affiliated or Scripps, or sell a much smaller chunk to less picky public investors hungry for a way into the spectrum rush.

For the very private Craig McCaw, the choice was more difficult than it might have been for most businessmen. He had always relished the ability to run his company as he pleased, keeping its financial details private. Going public would mean the loss of the flexibility Craig treasured—but it would also mean cheap cash. In the end, the chance to keep growing and the lure of easy money won out.

The lesson of CCI's IPO hadn't been lost on the McCaw team. Despite Kluge's $45-per-POP sale and other similar transactions, POPs were still cheap: McCaw's spectrum treasure chest included millions of POPs bought for low prices, in markets like Sacramento and San Antonio (purchased at $18.50 per POP); Las Vegas (purchased at $16.50 per POP); Memphis, Nashville, Orlando, Jacksonville (purchased at $17 per POP). Why not sell a share of all these cheap POPs to the public at the high prices an IPO would bring? The arbitrage was irresistible.

And why stop there? If the market was valuing POPs in the forty-dollar range, why not buy as many as possible—even in small, supercheap markets—before going public? There was no good reason not to; this was the reasoning behind sending Scot Jarvis on his manic mission in 1986–87 to buy up the "little people," buying anything and everything low so it could be resold high.

"Wayne [Perry] just turned me loose and said, 'Get everything you can,'" remembers Jarvis, "which is how we ended up with some properties that a lot of people wondered about. He just said, 'Get it, get it, get it, get it,' and every time I'd call home and say, 'I think I can get this,' Wayne would say, 'Get it.'"

By the summer of 1987, just before the IPO, McCaw owned licenses covering 35 million POPs in 94 markets—nearly twice as many POPs as the second biggest nonwireline, LIN Broadcasting, which had 18 million.

Initially, McCaw's IPO prospectus called for an offering of 10.5 million shares at a price between seventeen and eighteen dollars. But as the offering date approached, demand from prospective purchasers pushed the share number and price higher; on August 21, 1987, McCaw opened trading at $21.75, selling just over 13 million shares. The stock traded up to $25 a share before the market closed that afternoon. To jaded Internet and optical-fiber investors accustomed to 400-percent leaps on offering dates, a run-up of 50 percent over the cover price might look modest. But by 1987 standards, McCaw's soaring opening was proof of a voracious public appetite for cellular.

In a simultaneous offering, McCaw closed a second Drexel junk bond deal, selling $600 million worth of bonds—also a 50-percent increase over the original plans to sell $400 million.

In a single day, McCaw had, after paying off earlier debts, increased its war chest by some $600 million. Once again, McCaw had skillfully refinanced, converting its house of cards into a solid spectrum treasure house. Clearly, the

IPO and bond offering were smart business moves, but like so many great companies, McCaw was also blessed with exceptional luck. Just six weeks later, on Monday, October 19, the U.S. stock market crashed, with the Dow Jones Industrial Average losing 508 points—22.6 percent of its value—in a single day. The crash wiped out several of McCaw's competitors' plans for cellular IPOs.

"Black Monday" decimated the market in general, but it was particularly bad for cellular stock offerings. What had been Wall Street's hottest investment trend was suddenly shunned after the crash as an excessively speculative industry. Fearing a recession was on the way, many analysts predicted cell phones would be the first item cost-conscious Americans dumped. "People are going to get rid of car phone service costing $100 a month a lot faster than regular phone service," Shearson Lehman Brothers analyst John Bain told the *Toronto Star*. And forget about any new customers signing up for service.

It looked like a good time to avoid cellular investments—which, of course, really meant it was the best possible time to do exactly the opposite. With uncertainty at a high and would-be purchasers crippled financially, prices—which had been soaring—shrank back. Still, no one was buying. No one, that is, except McCaw. And not only was McCaw buying, but the company was paying record prices for coveted markets.

In January 1988, McCaw stunned the industry by paying the Washington Post Co. a record price of $81 per POP for the Miami market. Once again, Craig McCaw seemed to be single-handedly pushing prices higher and higher; he alone seemed to have no concerns about whether the properties were really worth that much. As they had before, industry observers could only shake their heads, wondering what Craig McCaw knew that everyone else didn't.

━━━━━

IT WAS AN ORDINARY FRIDAY AFTERNOON MEETING in November 1988 when the uncannily smooth relations among the McCaw team finally shattered.

For four years, a group of highly intelligent, aggressive, ambitious young executives had worked at maximum intensity in a fast-moving, unpredictable new industry. These executives were, for the most part, men in their twenties and thirties who were used to being the cleverest guy in the room; there was no shortage of egos in the group. Yet the team enjoyed "a very good atmosphere," remembers Mark Hamilton. "Nobody ever yelled at each other. You really never got angry." But this particular Friday was different.

Seven or eight executives had gathered to discuss strategy for the coming year. In preparation for the meeting, Stanton had drafted a long memo detailing the strategy he thought the company should follow. As Stanton himself noted later, "Craig didn't tend to work that way. Craig didn't tend to write or read—or spend a lot of time on a ten-page memo—because Craig's a visionary." Not only that, but Craig is dyslexic, and his aversion to reading or writing anything longer than a few paragraphs was well-known in the company.

Craig wasn't inclined to read the memo; he had his own ideas about where the company needed to focus, and they were very different from Stanton's. In the past year, the company had sprinted so madly after new markets that it didn't have the resources left to provide good systems and customer care. Craig's modus operandi, the strategy he'd used in building his cable empire, was to provide great service and charge high rates. And now, in the cellular rush, operations were sloppy, service was bad, and as a result, there was tremendous customer churn. As Craig saw it, things were getting out of hand; it was as though he was losing control of his own company.

When Stanton presented his memo, Craig erupted. As the group watched in shock, the normally soft-spoken and cerebral CEO began shouting at Stanton, angrily criticizing his performance and berating him for a catalogue of real or imagined transgressions. For an instant, Stanton was stunned into silence. But then, to his colleagues' alarm, he suddenly launched a counterattack, accusing Craig of having made some operational decisions—including a few acquisitions in California and Hawaii—for his own self-interest rather than the good of the business.

The shouting intensified, and the rest of the group could only watch, aghast, as Stanton and Craig flung wild accusations at each other. Then, suddenly, Stanton had had enough. He stormed angrily from the building, leaving the group sitting in awkward silence. "It was," remembers Hamilton, "just one of those things that was dreadfully uncomfortable." Hamilton hurried out after Stanton, and the two walked in a nearby park, trying to dissect what had just happened.

Though Craig was the CEO, John Stanton was, in many ways, the heart and soul of the cellular operation. All through the McCaw headquarters, employees tried to sort out what the clash meant. "The whole company was abuzz with it," remembers Scott Anderson. And everyone had an opinion.

"My sense of it," says Anderson, "was, Craig said one day, 'Look, John, this is not your sandbox, it's my sandbox. And if you can't take direction from me, get the hell out.'"

Another executive took it a step further. "From my perspective," he says, "Craig was a little bit jealous. I think it was his company, and he had had the ideas and that kind of thing initially, and Stanton was becoming a big leader in the cellular business. . . At the core, it was probably a clash of ego."

In his own recollection, Stanton echoes that view. "I had a huge ego at the time," he says, "and probably still do. I had viewed myself as having built a lot of the operations. I'd hired a lot of folks. And, you know, we sold the cable division and Craig . . . got involved in the cellular business really for the first time. He'd been away for most of '86."

For a long time, Stanton's level of autonomy in cellular had worked well for Craig. But his legendary ability to let the executives run things had its limits, and now he wanted to reclaim control. "Craig felt like, I think, that I had . . . railroaded this conclusion into how we were going to go without enough input from him," says Stanton.

The next morning, Hamilton was sitting at his desk when Craig walked by for a chat. "Well, gosh," Hamilton remembers him saying, "I don't know what we should do. I probably said some things I shouldn't have. Maybe John just needs some time off." Following Craig's lead, several of McCaw's senior executives had taken sabbaticals; in this case, it seemed the easiest and most sensible thing to do. Hamilton agreed.

Within days, Stanton was gone. No one knew it at the time, but he would never work full-time for McCaw again.

"In the end, I was fed up," says Stanton. "You know, I said, 'I'm done.' I'd just gotten married. I just wanted to spend a little bit more time at home and less time doing this, and I was tired, beaten and tired." He spent much of the next six months skiing in Breckenridge, Colorado, and, in his words, just "vegging out."

What Stanton left behind was an organization transformed—a handful of cellular applications worth several hundred thousand dollars had, under Stanton's manic drive, blossomed into some 40 million POPs in nearly 100 different cellular systems, all in less than five years. While McCaw's non-wireline competitors had struggled to build two or three system networks, Stanton, Perry and Hopper had used financial alchemy—employing a dizzying array of acquisitions, debt and equity—to build a company valued at some $2.5 billion. And now two of those three masterminds were departing.

"[Stanton] had built McCaw," says Scott Anderson, "but it was always going to be McCaw. It was never going to be Stanton Cellular Communications, and that always bothered him a little bit." Soon enough, Stanton would start his own company. And perhaps not surprisingly, his achievements in telecommunications would eventually rival those of his old boss Craig McCaw.

17

CATCHING THE THIRD WAVE

IN A CITY FILLED WITH NOTABLE LANDMARKS, the stretch of Twenty-first Street between Sixth and Seventh Avenues in New York City doesn't hold much cachet for most visitors. But for one particular group of people, this was a well-known spot: Like a telecom Bermuda Triangle, this block mysteriously swallowed cellular signals, cutting off urban chatters in mid-sentence.

More and more cell towers were going up across the country, but still there were spots in otherwise well-covered cities where users routinely found, to their immense frustration, that their calls were dropped. Despite millions spent on engineering, cellular signals were unexpectedly absorbed by some buildings, ricocheted off others and elsewhere seemed simply to be sucked up in an ethereal quicksand of dirt and leaves. Dead spots became regular topics of conversation among users, who also habitually traded information on pricing plans and new phone models. As one businessman told *Newsday*, "It's one of the things you do when you stop for gas and you see another antenna. You go over, compare services and equipment and where they break down."

Of course, the presence of a curlicue "pigtail" antenna on a car didn't always guarantee that its owner knew anything at all about cell phones. Seizing on the American mania for status symbols, a few companies began marketing fake antennae for would-be cell phone users to stick on their cars. A company called Faux Systems marketed the "Cellular Phoney": a fake antenna and coiled cord attached to a cardboard phone replica, priced at just

$9.95. The company's tag line said it all: "It's not what you own. It's what people think you own."

Clearly, cell phones were still a status symbol despite their gradual move toward the mainstream. One reason is apparent in a 1987 Cellular Telephone Industry Association (CTIA) survey which found that fully 70 percent of cell phone users made more than $50,000 per year—well above the national average of $18,426. A mere 23 percent reported earning less than that, and 7 percent declined to answer the question. A *Cellular Marketing* magazine survey categorized the users by profession: 20 percent were doctors or other professionals, 27 percent were sales and marketing personnel, 21 percent worked in real estate and 7 percent were in service industries.

In traditional marketing terms, new-product purchasing moves through several classes of buyers. The first wave is known as the "innovators": these are the users who buy new gadgets as soon as they become available. The second wave is known as "early adopters": the users that sign up in the first two or three years after a new technology is available, while it's still an expensive niche product.

It was at this point in the marketing cycle that many analysts predicted cellular would stall, blocked by an immovable price barrier. Prices could only fall if usage rose—but, paradoxically, usage wasn't likely to rise unless prices fell first. If this chicken-and-egg cycle could be broken, and the third wave of customers bought into cellular, then prices for hardware and service should both plummet, and cellular would take off. But many doubted that would happen.

Not only did it happen, but it happened faster than anyone had predicted. "Everything went wrong in the right way," remembers CCI executive George Blumenthal. "Demand was far greater [than we had expected, and] the price of phones collapsed to a few hundred dollars."

Few of the industry's entrepreneurs were better equipped to decipher the trends than the leadership at CCI, where the executive suite was occupied by two mathematicians, Bill Ginsberg and Barclay Knapp, and securities analyst George Blumenthal. They soon made a science of analyzing cellular numbers from their systems' operations. And what CCI learned was sometimes surprising.

"Everybody said the same thing," remembers Blumenthal. "Who would be the people using the phone? Well, the doctors, lawyers and Indian chiefs driving to work in the morning and driving home in the afternoon." The assumption was that usage would peak during the morning and evening rush hours, and fall off during the normal workday.

This assumption made sense. Yet it was, as Blumenthal puts it, "totally wrong. One hundred percent wrong."

The graphs charting CCI's analysis showed a mountainous bulge of users increasing toward the middle of each workday between 10 A.M. and 4 P.M.— a time when most industry experts had expected customers to be seated in front of a desk with a wired phone. These unexpected usage patterns were more than just a pleasant surprise. In Blumenthal's opinion, they "made the cellular industry."

"The fastest-growing segment in the cellular car phone business is blue-collar workers," Metro Mobile sales and marketing manager Joanne Loniewsky told the *New York Times*, which had noted the changing demographic in an earlier article. "When cellular mobile telephones were introduced four years ago," reporter Calvin Sims wrote, "they were gadgets only of the rich and powerful. Now everyone from drug dealers in Miami to the taco vendor in Rockefeller Plaza has one." Not only were these small businesspeople subscribing in unexpected numbers, but their average monthly usage was much higher than most financial models, including CCI's, had projected.

The unanticipated usage pattern not only created system revenue far in excess of early projections, but it had a secondary economic benefit as well. Virtually all industry models showed a growing need for infrastructure hardware as system usage rose. But this heavy usage at unexpected hours meant that user traffic was spread more evenly throughout the business day. As a result, system capacity was used more effectively, helping cut back on capital demands needed to meet rising usage during the first few years of operation. Even so, the huge waves of new customers would create capacity problems as early as the late 1980s.

As usage soared on the unexpected popularity with the working class, prices fell and phones became smaller, which led the third wave—the "early majority"—to begin buying in the mid-1980s. In response to increased usage, carriers experimented with lowering airtime rates, which led more optimistic observers to believe that a boom was coming. As Bart Robins of Potamkin Communications told *Newsday* in 1986, "When [the price] hits 25 cents to 15 cents a minute, you'll see housewives with phones in their cars." This would be the fourth wave—the "late majority"—and it would come in the 1990s.

The remarkable popularity of cellular left many red faces in its wake. The best known among these, Washington-based analyst Herschel Shosteck, was quoted throughout the early '80s decrying the initially low subscriber numbers, lack of cellular profits and imperfect technology. Cellular, in his view, would never be more than a niche product, partly because, he erroneously declared, prices were not likely to fall lower than their 1986 levels.

In the earliest days of cellular, Shosteck had predicted that there would be just over 500,000 users by 1990. When the one-millionth U.S. user was signed up in October 1987, just four and a half years after the service was introduced, industry officials were jubilant. By comparison, it had taken twenty years to reach 1 million regular telephone users, and thirteen years to sell a million television sets in America.

By the end of 1987, there were 1.23 million U.S. cell phone users, 44 percent of which had signed up in the previous year. Today, many of the statistics on those users seem surprising: Fully 93 percent of mid-'80s users, for example, were men. And only 7 percent had portable handheld phones—the rest had car phones. Sixty-four percent of users carried insurance on their cell phones. And the primary factor in choosing a phone, according to respondents, was not price but quality of coverage.

But the unexpected surge in sales brought with it a host of new problems. Though the earliest articles about cellular technology had glibly declared that reception would be as good as, if not better than, landline technology, the reality was proving far different. The solution to spectrum shortage that cellular technology had promised was proving illusory: When the thousands of unanticipated customers began dialing during those peak hours, the carriers soon found they had too few towers and too few radios to handle the flood of traffic. As Michael Murphy, editor of the *California Technology Stock Letter*, told the *San Francisco Chronicle* in 1986, "It's not like sitting in your living room unless your living room is in Guatemala. You are knocked off the air all the time. It's terrible." For a while, it looked like the cellular industry would prove a victim of its own success.

Ironically, the cell phone industry gained tremendously from misfortune. The worse the mishap or difficulty, the better the publicity when a cell phone helped someone overcome it.

Heart attacks, hurricanes, assaults, auto accidents—by the late 1980s, newspapers were reporting scores of unhappy incidents in which cell phones saved the day. A rape suspect in Maryland was collared when a bystander, hearing screams, dialed the police on his van's cell phone. Chicago emergency rooms began using cell phones in ambulances to send digitized electrocardiogram data to the hospital, aiding doctors in quickly diagnosing heart attacks. Hurricane Elena battered the Gulf Coast, knocking out numerous landlines, but the Red Cross and police could keep in touch via cell phones provided for free by the local carrier.

The more people used cell phones, the more uses they devised for them. Representatives of Grucci Inc., a company that designed and undertook fireworks displays, told *Business Week* they'd switched to cell phones for coordinating detonations, as walkie-talkies had too much interference. Traffic-monitoring services, such as Harrisburg, Pennsylvania's "Traffax," set up special numbers for cell phone users to call. An offshore network of cell phones was installed to expedite communications between oil-drilling platforms in the Gulf of Mexico. Country clubs installed cell phones on their golf carts. And Cleveland's Cuyahoga Community College registered students in shopping malls by sending their information back to a campus through a computer connected to a wireless phone.

As the new cellular companies got up and running, they struggled with how to market their new product—was it a luxury accessory, a business tool, a time saver or a safety device? And what was the best way to reach the expanding base of customer prospects—by newspaper, radio, TV, billboards, direct mail, or sponsoring a little league team? Across America, the carriers tried everything, marketing by trial and error.

Learning as they went along, companies spent millions of dollars on marketing and ads, to mixed results. In 1987, for example, McCaw spent $61 million on marketing, but added only 100,000 customers. At some $600 per customer, it was costing nearly a full year's revenue in some markets just to lure new users to the service.

Often marketing money seemed foolishly wasted. When one company sponsored a hot-air balloon race across San Francisco Bay, for example, two ended up in the water, one landed on a small island and one crash-landed in Tiburon, starting a fire. The only balloon that made it across the bay landed in a garbage dump in nearby Richmond, and when the pilot tried to call for help, he had to trudge to a pay phone to do it—his cell phone wasn't working. Another California company tried to lure upscale users, promising that its phones would appeal to "the sort of person who would appreciate a Bartok symphony." Unfortunately, as a reader pointed out in the *L.A. Times*, Bartok wrote no symphonies.

Most new users learned about cellular not through marketing, but via another, more old-fashioned method: word of mouth. Fully 48 percent of users in a 1987 CTIA survey said that was how they'd first become aware of cellular, compared to 16 percent who cited radio ads, 14 percent who cited display ads, and 11 percent who'd been approached by a sales representative. One Pactel representative took the word-of-mouth strategy to heart when she found herself in a California traffic jam: She lent her phone to frustrated drivers in nearby cars, then handed them her card and invited them to purchase one.

———————

At first glance, the terms "couch potato," "junk bond," "kissy-face," "Walkman," and "cellular telephone" don't seem to have much in common. But in 1987, they all received a notable honor: They were added to the Third College Edition of *Webster's New World Dictionary*.

If not yet a household word, the cell phone was now edging its way into the American lexicon. Cell phones were now appearing in films, even playing pivotal roles in some. In the thriller *The Freeway*, a serial killer called a radio talk show from his car phone to reveal the location of his next victim. Today, this plot device would attract no notice, but as late as the summer of 1986, the idea of calling a radio show from one's car was so novel the *L.A. Times* ran a short piece on it. The article quoted one station manager saying his deejays received a cell phone call "maybe once a month."

Though the great majority of cell phones were for cars—the term "car phone" was still used as a catch-all phrase for cell phones into the early 1990s—manufacturers were steadily shrinking the size of handhelds. Pocket-sized phones that worked reliably at affordable prices would, they knew, promise a vast new market. Hauppage, New York–based Walker Telecommunications Corporation came out with its 15-ounce "Pocketphone," priced at $3,295 in 1986; Mitsubishi offered its 18-ounce DiamondTel 90X in 1988.

Though intended to be carried around in a suit pocket, these handheld phones were still hopelessly clunky compared to the sleeker models of the '90s. A contemporary look at *Business Week*'s December 5, 1988, cover photo of Craig McCaw holding a "state of the art" phone evokes a sense of comical nostalgia: This paperback novel–sized phone, with its rigid antenna, looks huge today. With their high prices, hefty bulk and limited battery life—most models would go dead after little more than thirty minutes of conversation—it was little wonder that consumers weren't flocking to portables.

Car phones, on the other hand, were coming off the assembly lines by the tens of thousands. As manufacturers put more and more phone circuits onto single integrated circuit chips, prices moved steadily downward—from

$700 in 1987 to $299 in some markets at the end of 1988. The lower price was part of a larger strategy: Companies like McCaw, pressing to sign up more users, began paying bounties to agents for new customers. These agents, like service resellers, would pass on part of the subsidies in the form of discounts, and the prices would fall. In this way, the industry edged ever closer to the holy grail of the $100 cell phone, a level at which many experts believed ordinary Americans would begin buying in earnest.

As 1987 came to an end, McCaw Cellular was by far the largest cell phone company, with 37 million POPs nationwide. Next in line were six of the seven Baby Bells, which were now free to bulk up their portfolios with both wireline and nonwireline spectrum licenses: Southwestern Bell, PacTel, GTE Mobilnet, Bell Atlantic Mobile, BellSouth Mobility and Nynex Mobile had licenses covering between 16 million and 25 million POPs. The second-largest nonwireline came next: LIN Broadcasting, which claimed 16 million POPs in some of the country's best markets, such as New York, Dallas and Philadelphia.

Three hundred forty-six systems were on-line, providing service to 1.23 million users who ran up an average monthly bill of $97. So far, the industry had spent $2.2 billion in building out America's cell phone systems, and more than a billion dollars in revenue had been generated. And the FCC giveaway was not over yet.

18

LAST CALL AT THE CASINO

THREE YEARS HAD PASSED SINCE NICK WILSON bought Al Schneider a new red Porsche with his application mill's money, and though Schneider had disassociated himself professionally from Wilson, he still stayed in touch with the charming British huckster. And Wilson, as it turned out, was more than happy to brag about the plans for his latest FCC scam. There was one final group of cellular lotteries to come, and Wilson had already begun raking in money from a new batch of clients.

One evening in the spring of 1988, I had dinner with Schneider, Mark Warner and Bob Blow at the Jockey Club, a venerable old Washington, D.C., dining spot bedecked with hunt-club artifacts, knotty pine paneling and equestrian paintings. The industry had changed a great deal since its early days, and our lives had changed along with it. Warner, Blow and I were now in the cellular mergers-and-acquisitions business full time, having founded Columbia Capital Corp. with ex-Providence Journal Cellular President David Mixer. We spent our days helping license winners sell to the big operators, and doing deals with the new industry's players, large and small.

It was a balmy evening, so Al Schneider and I decided to stroll along the quiet, late-night streets of Washington back to his hotel. As we walked, our talk turned to the FCC's next cellular giveaway. The frenzy of MSA lotteries was finished; the FCC had distributed cell phone licenses for almost all the 306 MSAs, and the winners—from big companies down to the "pig farmers and hairdressers"—were either selling their licenses or struggling to build and run new cellular companies. At the FCC, there was a momentary lull:

Though it still had to distribute 428 pairs of licenses covering America's rural service areas (RSAs), the commission had yet to announce its rules for filing RSA applications.

It was clear to everyone that the MSA lotteries had been a failure. On all sides—from big cellular operators to FCC staffers to members of Congress—observers had grown fed up with the wild speculation and abuses of the lottery system. As it had done unsuccessfully in the past, the FCC would once again have to change its rules to try to restore order.

Rumors flew that spring as to how the FCC would change its rules, and one of the most credible was that the FCC planned to toughen its financial requirements for applicants. During the MSA giveaway, the FCC had required only that applicants provide "reasonable assurance" that they had the financial ability to construct a cellular system. Would-be applicants quickly discovered that equipment vendors would provide them with financial assurance letters subject to their winning the license, a situation that effectively meant anyone could apply and win.

But now FCC commissioners were discussing whether to require each applicant to provide a written "firm financial commitment" from a legitimate source of capital, such as a letter of credit from a bank. Securing a firm commitment to lend or invest a couple of million dollars in a rural cellular system in western Georgia or southern Nevada would be no easy task, the commissioners reasoned—what better way to keep the speculators out of the RSA lotteries? With stricter financial requirements, then only legitimate businessmen could apply; this would, the FCC hoped, prove to be the death knell for the mills.

As I walked Al Schneider back toward his hotel, I mentioned that these tougher financial rules might be disastrous for his old friend Nick Wilson.

"Oh, Nick's not worried," replied Schneider. "He's got it wired. He's been selling applications for months."

"How could that be?" I asked, surprised. "He doesn't even know what the requirements are yet. And how would he get around the financial letter problem?"

Schneider laughed. "He's got this friend in Canada who runs a 'bank.' Nick's got a deal with him to issue letters of credit for all of TCC's customers."

Now I was even more surprised. "You mean, every TCC client will get a letter of credit, regardless of financial ability?" This was an economic absurdity—many of Wilson's customers were, I knew, congenital gamblers and financial neophytes; some of these people would have trouble even getting a used-car loan.

"Sure," Schneider responded. "Nick doesn't care, and he says the 'bank' will be impossible to investigate, because it's outside the U.S.—the FCC will just have to take their word for it."

Tricky Nick Wilson was back in business. And, as we would soon discover, the bank letters were not the only scam he had planned for the RSA lotteries.

⸻

AT FIRST GLANCE, IT LOOKED AS THOUGH the 428 rural service areas would be practically worthless as stand-alone cellular businesses. The RSAs encompassed the long stretches of farmland, desert, mountains, forests and fields that lay between the metropolitan service areas; in many cases, relatively few people lived in these areas, and fewer still could be expected to spend hundreds of dollars a year on cell phone service.

Granted, the most heavily populated RSAs had several hundred thousand potential customers each, but most had far fewer. The least-populated RSA, for example, covered a mere 12,000 POPs, which were spread out over hundreds of thousands of sparsely populated square miles in northern Nebraska. At the time, 2-percent penetration was the industry's Holy Grail, but that seemed laughably inadequate for these smaller markets. Two percent of 12,000 was only 240 customers, after all, and that was far too few to offset the huge costs of building out a system to serve them—especially considering that the sprawling area the RSA covered would require more cell towers, making for a higher buildout cost. Why even bother to compete for a license covering so much land and so few POPs?

By themselves, many of these markets were worth little. But by taking a step back and assessing the broader picture, it was easy to see that in other ways, they were quite valuable.

First, many of these RSAs adjoined metropolitan areas. In cellular's first decade, users were trapped within invisible boundaries drawn around cities. With no rural areas and few of the suburbs built out, any cell phone user who strayed too far from the handful of cell towers around the urban ring would lose his signal. This was a major irritant, one that became especially notorious for vexing businesspeople traveling between New York and Washington on Amtrak trains. Though the four-hour trip up the eastern seaboard was a prime time to get some work done, passengers on the train knew they had to get any phone conversations in before leaving the Washington area or while rolling into New York. There just weren't any cell towers on the long stretches in between.

Second, some of America's most desolate stretches of countryside did actually harbor large crowds of people; they didn't live there, but they moved constantly along the thin strips of Interstate highways that cut through the RSAs. As more and more cars began sprouting pigtail antennae, pressure grew on the carriers and the FCC to ensure cellular users could talk while traveling along Interstate 5 between L.A. and Sacramento, or Interstate 65 between Indianapolis and Chicago, or Interstate 95 between Jacksonville and Daytona Beach.

And there was a third factor that promised value in the RSAs: The RBOCs were getting combative. These big phone companies, which had been handed half of the licenses in America, operated systems covering multiple states—far bigger regions than any one of their nonwireline competitors covered. In the race for customers, the companies soon began competing by advertising their larger coverage "footprint," promising customers that their cell phones would operate over a multicity region. Comparative coverage maps quickly became a key marketing tool, as two-city calling regions grew to three or more, and rate plans gradually covered entire regions like "Southern California." But still, where enemy borders met—where one RBOC's region abutted another, or where Metro Mobile operated beside Metromedia—cell phone service ended abruptly in a cacophony of static. The race was on to build regional "footprints" because even if the rural customers were few, the "footprint" expansion could be used as a sales pitch for more urban customers.

Finally, carriers were still learning about the unanticipated phenomenon of "roaming." When the FCC subdivided the United States into 306 metropolitan license areas, little thought was given to the traveling businessman who might subscribe to cell phone service in Dallas and want to use his phone in Houston. In the absence of a common government-imposed technical standard, it was likely that the Dallas and Houston systems would use different types of equipment; while the two systems could easily "talk" to any given car phone, they initially couldn't talk to each other in order to record and bill the call. This made billing difficult.

Under pressure from the carriers, hardware manufacturers soon developed a common software interface to fix the problem. In addition, the carriers built two big "clearinghouse" banks—one for the phone companies and one for the nonwirelines—to balance and exchange revenue. And what revenue it was! To nearly everyone's surprise, that Dallas-based salesman was perfectly willing to pay two or three dollars for each day he used his phone in Houston, plus ninety cents per minute for the talk time—double his home rates in Dallas. Better yet, it cost the Houston carrier nothing—no marketing expense, no sales commission—to get this high-paying customer. Roaming revenue became a huge profit maker for every carrier.

As more and more cellular companies signed roaming agreements, allowing customers from one city to use their phones on another carrier's system in a different city, the pressure increased to enable everyone to use their phones on the highways in between. This was where the RSA licenses came in.

THE McCAW TEAM UNDERSTOOD THE WORTH of the RSAs immediately, and they wasted no time maneuvering to get them. Before the FCC announced its RSA lottery rules, McCaw made a heavy-handed attempt to convince Congress and the FCC bureaucrats simply to hand over all the RSA licenses to whoever owned the adjacent MSAs. The licenses would ultimately end up in the operators' (read: McCaw's and the big wirelines') hands anyway, argued the company's lobbyists; why go through the charade of lotteries again? Why force McCaw to scramble around and buy more licenses from people who had no intention of building systems in the first place? Why enrich the speculators at the expense of the honest businesses?

Some on Capitol Hill and at the FCC were initially swayed by McCaw's argument, but when word of the ploy leaked, the application mills reacted with vehemence. Why should the McCaw brothers, now paper centimillionaires, simply be handed these licenses? What entitled them to a government subsidy of their business? Even Nick Wilson, realizing the threat to his applications cash cow, made a lobbying trip to FCC headquarters (after hurriedly fortifying his courage with four straight vodkas in the bar at the nearby Mayflower Hotel, according to a colleague). Meanwhile, the applications mills mobilized thousands of past and would-be speculators, who bombarded Congress and the FCC with mail and phone calls—outraged citizens protesting any abridgment of their "rights" to play the federal lottery game.

Sensing a political fiasco, McCaw's Washington supporters hastily dropped their plans for special legislation, and the FCC announced it would push ahead with lotteries. The crescendo of "taxpayer" lobbying was so great that the commission even capitulated on its previously announced tough financial requirements—adopting halfhearted standards that invited a plethora of copycats for Wilson's phony bank scheme. The mills, many headed by now-familiar faces, were back in business again.

Wilson's TCC, still essentially run by bookkeeper Greg Neely, peddled applications (with the phony bank letters) as fast as it could sell them. And General Cellular (GCC), which had sold more applications than any other mill in the MSA rounds, roared back into business. Prices started high, but soon began to erode as competing mills vied for business.

The RSA lottery rounds also brought in a new class of applicant. Ever since Round IV of the giveaway, bigger companies and serious operators—the "smart money"—had stayed out of the lotteries. The combination of poor odds and an uncertain future for cellular had kept many out of the game, opening it up for the hordes of small-time speculators and other "little people," who had applied in droves.

Now, for the first time, both the smart money and the little people were applying for the same markets. John Stanton, who was no longer working full-time for McCaw, applied (and won a market) in a partnership with his friends and family. (On hearing the news that by-now-wealthy Stanton had won, McCaw attorney Barry Adelman told him, "John, there is no God if you won a lottery.") Other McCaw executives, like Wayne Perry, Scot Jarvis and Scott Anderson, did likewise. TDS chairman Leroy Carlson's daughter Prudence won an RSA market. Deep-pocketed members of some of America's wealthiest families—Reynolds, Chase and Heinz, for example—applied, as did many industry insiders such as Mark Warner, Bob Blow, Harry Brock and executives from many of the operating companies. And, along with my old Round IV partner, Graham Randolph, I applied in every market.

What attracted knowledgeable speculators back into the game was simple arithmetic. POPs were trading at near triple-digit figures, cellular operators had impressive cash flow numbers, and the suburbs and interstates promised to be rewarding markets. Not only that, but the odds of the RSA lottery looked great—a 1-in-500 chance (the expected number of applications per market), repeated 428 times (the number of markets) was almost even-money odds. Paying $20,000 or $30,000 for a near-certain chance to make $1 million (or perhaps much more) was too good a game to miss.

A total of 288,258 applications were filed for the 428 RSA markets—an average of 673 per market. The lotteries were held over a fifteen-month period between September 1988 and December 1989. Once again, nervous gamblers gathered at the FCC to watch Ping-Pong balls clatter fatefully around the hopper. Time after time, as winning numbers were plucked out, novice businesspeople found themselves suddenly making fortunes on the backs of U.S. taxpayers.

This time, both the smart money and the mills had gotten it right. As *Forbes* reported in December 1989, just after the last lottery, "Little more than a year ago, most industry analysts thought the nation's rural POPs would fetch no more than $40 each. But today, rural cellular licenses are changing hands at prices that work out to about $85 a POP on average."

For many early winners of demographically superior RSAs, *Forbes* proved accurate, and before the year was out, our firm had represented clients selling a dozen or more RSAs for prices in excess of $100 per POP. Only time would tell whether the 12,000 POP licenses that covered more prairie dogs than people might someday do as well.

IN 1989, THE COW PASTURES AND CORNFIELDS near Dulles Airport looked much as they had a century before. Nestled between frenetic, cosmopolitan Washington, D.C., to the east, and the bucolic, gently rolling Blue Ridge Mountains to the west, the land around Dulles was generally undisturbed. But it lay at a volatile crossroads.

Within five years, this area would suddenly find itself the locus of explosive development. The Internet boom would transform these verdant Virginia hills into a bustling high-tech settlement, with companies like America Online, UUNet and WorldCom staking their claims to the area. By the late 1990s, "Dulles" was no longer a place but a concept: the Silicon Valley of the East.

That all lay in the future in August 1989, when a brand-new conference center opened just in time to host a most unusual gathering. The Westfields International Conference Center, a sprawling facility located a few miles south of Dulles in little Manassas, Virginia, was the site of an unexpectedly large assembly of RSA lottery winners. The gathering had been billed as an "educational" conference for winners and applicants in the yet-to-be-completed RSA lotteries; the promoters had basically hoped to make a few bucks if they could assemble a hundred or so curiosity seekers. Instead, to their amazement, around 500 hopeful applicants and new license-holders descended on Westfields for two days of schmoozing by equipment vendors, lawyers, brokers and buyers, in a teeming bazaar that one participant likened to a junior version of Michael Milken's "predators' ball."

Though similar buying and selling had gone on for a half-dozen years throughout the FCC giveaway, never before had so many license winners assembled in one place. Knowing nothing about cellular except what they'd heard in the hyperbolic sales pitches and read in the newsletters they got from the mills, many winners were convinced that per-POP prices would continue to follow the remarkable upward trajectory they had traveled since 1985. Everyone had heard the tales of license values doubling, tripling, quadrupling over a period of months, and many of the speculators, especially the mill clients who held one-tenth- and even one-thirtieth-partnership interests (sometimes representing only a few thousand POPs) were determined to realize the same remarkable gains themselves. When experts in the field dispassionately analyzed the potential cash flows of these rural systems and tried to explain why that wouldn't happen, the winners rebelled.

In a packed Westfields conference room on a Friday afternoon, Wayne Schelle approached the podium to speak as a crowd of 400 or so buzzed expectantly. By now an industry legend, as the builder of the country's first nonwireline system as well as a cellular company of his own, the portly Schelle took his spot at the front of the room. He gazed self-importantly at the assemblage over his half-moon reading glasses and made an unequivocal pronouncement: The RSA winners should sell their licenses. Now. Building cellular systems, he told the crowd, was a difficult and expensive undertaking, and prices would simply not rise enough in the coming years to make the effort worth it.

As he spoke, a few low grumbles arose from the crowd. This quickly grew into a groundswell of muttering, and then someone in the back yelled, *"Booooooooooo!"* A disappointed chorus joined in. Dozens of skeptical winners (not to mention lawyers, equipment vendors, consultants and others hoping to profit from dealing with naive "little people" license holders) quickly hooted Schelle down, believing this had to be spin. They thought that it was obvious that license values would go up—that's what they'd always done!

Practically everyone in the room could recite the anecdotal evidence. Two years earlier, PacTel had bought Detroit for $45 per POP. Four months after that, BellSouth had paid more than $60 per POP for MCCA. And one month after that, both those deals looked like screaming bargains when Comcast had offered $130 per POP for AmCell. Before 1988 was over, my firm negotiated a purchase/trade deal between Vanguard and Palmer Communications involving lowly Portsmouth, New Hampshire and Macon, Georgia at values in excess of $140 per POP. Then, to top it all off, two months before the Westfields gathering, McCaw had bid $275 per POP for a public stake in a half-dozen top-ten markets.

It seemed to the punters at Westfields that, as usual, smooth-talking "experts" were trying to fix the game and somehow fatten their own coffers. But this crowd would have none of it.

The speaker after Schelle, a man by the name of Charlie "Chicken" Jones, stood up and gave the crowd what it wanted. He'd led a partnership that had won the MSA license for Santa Barbara, California, Jones told the assembly, and then—despite strong pressure from McCaw—he'd refused to sell it. Instead, he'd abandoned his accounting practice, moved from Georgia to California to build and run his cellular company, waited while values rose, and then got the "big bucks." The Chicken had outsmarted the McCaw fox! Now the crowd was on its feet, whooping and cheering at this populist fable.

Unfortunately for the winners, Wayne Schelle's unpopular message was closer to reality. Chicken Jones and his partners might have made a lot of money, but there were two unusual explanations. First, Jones happened to win a market that Craig McCaw particularly wanted. Craig had a vacation home in Santa Barbara; he was willing to shell out more than the usual amount because he wanted to control the cell phone system where he'd be making so many calls himself. It was just the type of purchase John Stanton had angrily decried in his shouting match with Craig.

Second, Jones's price went up, thanks to the widespread ignorance about cellular operations and resulting skyrocketing values in the industry's early days—the "good old days" that were, Schelle knew, over.

In fact, values would soon begin to drop—particularly for smaller and rural markets—thanks to a number of factors. In the early '90s, recession would hit the United States, and the stock market would stumble. The savings-and-loan debacle would wreak havoc on the economy, generating new banking regulations that virtually prohibited banks from loaning money to even the best cellular-operating companies—the potential buyers these Westfields speculators were counting on. And, more simply, unless a new wave of cellular subscribers came along, values had risen to almost as high as system profits could justify. Even assuming continued growth in customer numbers, and employing the most optimistic estimates of rates and average monthly usage, there was simply no way license values could grow geometrically the way they had over the last four years.

Convinced that the gloomy expert prognostications were a ruse, many at Westfields refused to sell—a decision they would more often than not regret later. Meanwhile, they set about borrowing millions of dollars to build systems and pay consultants as they faced years of work until values recovered. These stubborn winners still made money, but many would have done better had they taken Schelle's advice, cashed out and invested in the stock market.

"The problem with these people," McCaw's Scott Anderson summarized dryly at the conference, "is that they've confused luck with brains."

ONE COULD HARDLY BLAME THE RSA WINNERS for imagining endlessly expanding pots of money in their future: In the spectrum-rush days, it seemed impossible to lose money in cellular spectrum. Selling a license made money. Holding and then selling made more. How could anyone lose?

The success stories were everywhere, and their lessons were not wasted. McCaw, Metromedia and Metro Mobile had dozens of emulators, companies such as Comcast, Century Communications, CCI, Vanguard, AmCell, Crowley Cellular, Price Cellular, Atlantic Cellular and General Cellular. In places such as Greensboro, Atlantic City and Bethesda, groups of entrepreneurs assembled collections of licenses, usually for smaller MSAs, and set out to build their own cellular conglomerates.

At CCI, a combination of work ethic, ambition and a modest dollop of venture capital allowed the executives to build the nation's first public cellular company. Likewise at Vanguard, the cellular team's hustle and tenacity overcame legal problems, second-rate markets and occasional management blunders to create another public success. But remarkably, a handful of smaller startups managed to blow their opportunity in cellular completely—a seeming impossibility in an industry where both holding and selling produced enviable returns.

Take the example of a group of investors from the windblown prairies of western Texas. In the town of Lubbock, a group of twenty or so prominent local citizens banded together to form a cellular company, which came to be called Cellular Information Systems, or CIS. When the lotteries were done, the group had won nearly 1 million POPs in places like Lubbock and Tyler, Texas; Fort Smith, Arkansas; and Duluth, Minnesota. All told, their licenses would soon be worth anywhere from $60 million to $80 million, on practically no investment.

Some founders wanted to sell out for cash, but the majority wanted to build a cellular enterprise. All they needed was cash and some management.

They got the cash from a wealthy stranger, New York cable-TV investor Richard Treibick. An arrogant, cigar-smoking, egotistical blowhard, Treibick soon seized voting control, moved CIS to his Fifth Avenue offices, and began billing his private jet to the fledgling firm. So great was his hubris that when he once met with Craig McCaw at the Beverly Hills Hotel to discuss the license for Abilene, Texas, he took the opportunity to lecture Craig for two hours, telling him what the future of cellular would be and never mentioning Abilene. At the end of the meeting, Craig turned to Scot Jarvis and said simply, "I will never do business with that man."

At first, Treibick dismissed dozens of acquisitions opportunities that would have given CIS critical mass while POPs were still cheap. Finally, in 1989, he leapt into growth mode at the top of a temporary RSA price bubble, paying over $60 million in borrowed cash for woefully rural markets. Treibick's errors were legion: He continued to borrow heavily, botched a small IPO, ignored internal budgets, responded to a cash crunch by firing the sales staff and reneged on contracts with consultants. Under his leadership, CIS was the only cellular company in America with negative subscriber growth.

Within thirty-four months, Treibick had led CIS from IPO to bankruptcy court. The leading citizens of Lubbock watched in dismay as their dream—once worth nearly $80 million—paid out in untradeable stock certificates quoted at 25 cents per share.

In San Francisco, GCC application-mill founders Quentin Breen and Terry Easton created a "roll-up," where the mill's customers could trade their newly won licenses for stock certificates. By the time the customers discovered that GCC had spent what little money Breen and Easton could raise, there was nothing left to cover the cost of buildouts; again, lucky license winners found themselves with almost nothing to show for their wins.

Failed cellular companies, which were generally brought down by inept management, were by far the exception to the rule. For the most part, investors in cellular found themselves making money almost no matter what they did. And for some, like Nick Wilson, the money they could make honestly was never quite enough.

━━━━━━━━━

Attorney David Kaufman was out drinking with colleagues after a long day at the Westfields Conference when he got a whispered invitation from Allan Kane, one of Nick Wilson's cronies and the leader of a winning TCC partnership.

"Can I come by your suite later?" Kane asked quietly. "I want to show you something tonight. It's very secret." Kaufman, intrigued, quickly agreed.

Sometime after midnight, Kane and his secretary came to Kaufman's hotel suite, where Kaufman and his law partner Rick Brown were waiting. The foursome sat down, and Kane pushed two documents across the table. Kaufman and Brown quickly read through the documents, their surprise and curiosity mounting. Tipsy from the three or four drinks he'd consumed, Kaufman found himself wondering if the documents he held were for real.

"Can we have copies of these?" Kaufman asked.

"No," Kane responded, pulling the documents back across the table. "It's highly confidential. I only let you read it because Greg Neely asked me to let you see it."

Neely, the Vietnam veteran and former Chuck E. Cheese bookkeeper who was now president of Nick Wilson's The Cellular Corp., was looking for a second opinion on the legality of Wilson's latest brainstorm. The document Kaufman was reading was the fruit of a complex scheme that involved Wilson, TCC, Neely, one badly conflicted lawyer and literally hundreds of applicants who were either ignorant, greedy or both.

In its ongoing quest to shut down the mills and curtail speculation in the lottery, the FCC had declared that there would be no more sharing of chances, period: no more 1-percent rule, no more multiple chances to win. Reluctantly, the mills had complied—with the exception of Nick Wilson's TCC.

Even before the FCC declared its RSA rules, Wilson had instructed his mill's marketers to sell applications by promising customers they'd be pooled together into settlement groups. When the FCC declared this new rule change, Wilson cared about only one thing: How could he get around these new rules so he wouldn't have to return the millions of dollars in customers' money he'd already taken in? After all, he'd spent most of it already.

As he always did, Wilson came up with a scheme. It was called the "Mutual Contingent Risk Sharing Agreement" (soon shortened to "Risk Sharing"), and it was, as Kaufman instantly determined, a blatant violation of FCC rules. Essentially, Wilson's customers agreed to share the risks and rewards of their applications, rather than the applications themselves. It was nothing more than a semantic trick; according to Wilson, splitting *profits* was not the same as splitting *ownership*. But even Wilson understood this was reaching too far. He set the plan in motion, then turned the reins of TCC over to Neely and departed for California, where he could live comfortably on the money he'd distributed to himself from TCC's accounts.

When Kaufman got a look at the "risk sharing agreement" at that late-night meeting, he knew instantly that Kane, Neely and their cohorts were legally obligated to disclose the scheme to the FCC. Within weeks, acting as Neely's attorney, Kaufman did so. As soon as news of the scam became public, protests flew from hundreds of angry applicants who had honestly spent thousands on their applications and had come up empty. Once again, as had happened far too many times in the FCC's bungled license distribution, more than two dozen valuable licenses (for potentially lucrative markets such as Hilton Head, South Carolina, and Squaw Valley, California) would be tied up in litigation for years to come.

Eight long years would pass before the problem was finally resolved—and then, the resolution would cause more outrage than the original scam had.

IN DECEMBER 1989, the giveaway at last came to an end. More than seven years after accepting Round I applications for America's largest cities, the FCC had finally, sloppily, distributed all the spectrum it had designated for cellular (with only the risk-sharing mess and a few similar cases left to be cleaned up). "God bless the FCC," summarized attorney Richard Rowlenson, "Round after round, every procedure they developed for awarding cellular [licenses] was flawed, seriously flawed. And each one seemed to be more flawed than the one before it." But at last, the spectrum was distributed.

This was the legacy of the spectrum rush: No matter how many times the FCC tried to tweak its rules, inventive and sometimes unethical entrepreneurs found ways to get around them. Whenever the commission was able to plug one hole in the dam, someone immediately figured out a way to poke another one.

"To be fair to the FCC," Mark Warner remarked later, "here you have a bunch of government bureaucrats trying to figure out a process on one side. And on the other side you have 50 companies and 500 of the highest-paid lawyers in the communications bar in Washington all trying to figure out a way around the rules. . . It's not any wonder that the scales were tipped against the guys at the FCC." (Ronald Reagan once expressed the same basic sentiment more succinctly: "The best minds are not in government. If any were, business would hire them away.")

Not everyone saw the relationship as antagonistic. Attorney Jonathan Blake commented that the FCC and the business community did an impressive job of figuring out how to adjust to the flawed systems available.

"It was as if we were assembling one of those complicated toys that have instructions to insert tab (a) into slot (a) and they don't exactly fit," says Blake. "Our job was to adjust both sides—government regulation and conventional business attitudes—so that the toy that then became cellular could be assembled."

In less than a decade, from 1982 until 1989, the cellular landscape had changed to the point where it was unrecognizable. In the early '80s, many of America's most highly respected corporations and businesses—companies like General Electric, ITT, RCA, Westinghouse and IBM—had treated the upcoming license giveaway with disdain. A group of smaller companies—MCI, Western Union, Knight-Ridder, the *Providence Journal*, Scripps Howard and the like—had dabbled early in the spectrum rush and had bailed out. But now, at the end of the decade, it was clear what they were missing out on: By 1990, 5.3 million cell phones had been sold in the United States, and the subscriber base was growing at a phenomenal 67.5 percent per year. In six years, annual industry revenue had grown from zero to $3 billion.

The FCC had given away a total of 1,468 cellular licenses, half to the wirelines and half to the nonwirelines. Each half covered 249 million POPs—the population of the United States at the time—for a total of 498 million POPs. To get an idea of what these licenses were worth, we can do a little bit of math using analysts' figures on value.

In 1989 Donaldson, Lufkin and Jenrette reported that the average value of publicly traded cellular companies was $108 per POP, while the average "private market value" of POPs had risen to $229. At those prices, those innocuous-looking pieces of paper the FCC handed out were now worth in the aggregate between $54 and $114 billion. And all anyone had needed to do to get a piece of this remarkable wealth was ask for it.

There was more money in the mix. Thousands of new jobs were created for salesmen, installers, technicians and managers. Cellular hardware sales were climbing. Meanwhile, millions more were being spent monthly on advertising, marketing, consultants, radio engineering, lawyers and, last but not least, investment bankers—firms like ours that helped big companies convince speculators to sell, or helped speculators get top dollar from operators. As the billions of dollars worth of government licenses passed from one hand to another, many millions fell to the few experts who could help the process along.

Though the federal giveaway was now over, the spectrum rush continued. As the '80s gave way to the '90s, McCaw and the wirelines bought up more properties, fighting to assemble those coveted larger marketing foot-prints. Before long, a couple of new technologies would edge their way into the cellular marketplace, changing the industry landscape again. And while the maneuvering continued, customers continued signing up for wireless phones in an ever-rising flood.

It had taken a decade for cellular to get a foothold in American society. Now a new decade was starting, one in which everything about the indus-try would seem to change at warp speed.

PART THREE

19

THE NATIONWIDE FOOTPRINT

THE NEW FACE OF CELLULAR BEGAN WITH A PREDICTION in a New York City elevator back in 1986.

Craig McCaw and Wayne Perry had gone to see Donald Pels, the CEO of LIN Broadcasting. With major stakes in New York City, Philadelphia, Los Angeles, Dallas and Houston, LIN owned some of the best cellular spectrum around; the company could easily have been a major force in the new industry. But unlike McCaw, LIN had simply applied for the big markets, walked out of Le Grand Deal with its fractional ownership of the licenses, and made few attempts to grow. It was as though Don Pels was intimidated by the frenetic pace of the new industry.

At the time Perry and Craig joined Pels for lunch, McCaw was charging into its acquisition phase, snatching up cellular licenses in every corner of the country—buying, in Perry's words, "Yakima and Elephant Breath, Wyoming, anything that isn't nailed down"—in the belief that the value of markets would go nowhere but up. Craig McCaw saw a future in which all Americans had wireless phones; Pels, on the other hand, was unsure whether there would be significant numbers of cell phone customers outside New York and Los Angeles. He was even uncertain whether LIN's fractions of cities like Philadelphia, Houston and Dallas would be worth very much.

As they talked over lunch, Perry recalls, "Don leans back and says, 'I really think we're convinced now that Houston is big enough to support two cellular companies'"—Pels's own limp version of cellular optimism. Perry, aghast at the LIN chief's shortsightedness, sat dumbstruck while Craig, he recalls, discreetly rolled his eyes. When lunch ended, Craig and Perry got into the elevator. As soon as the doors closed, Craig turned to Perry and made a declaration.

"Someday," he said, "we will have to take control of LIN. These people cannot be in charge of the destiny of our industry."

———

IN 1986, THE IDEA OF LITTLE MCCAW BUYING giant LIN Broadcasting seemed farcical. But only two years later, with a successful IPO, billions in junk bond financing and a sprawling portfolio of increasingly valuable cellular properties, McCaw was on its way to becoming a cellular powerhouse. Only one thing held it back: Unlike LIN, which had a few properties in huge metropolitan areas, McCaw had dozens of properties—but all were in smallish markets. Aiming to buy big cities like New York, L.A., Dallas and Chicago was a sensible goal for an obvious reason: These were lucrative markets. But Craig wanted them for another reason.

Though most big operators were now advertising bigger and bigger "footprints" of coverage, the breadth of this coverage generally extended no farther than the next city up the road. Craig McCaw envisioned something grander and more complete: a "nationwide footprint." Why shouldn't cell phone users be able to use their phones all over the country? Why not make it possible for a New Yorker to receive a call on his phone in San Diego? Craig knew that his long-held vision of "calling a person rather than a place" couldn't come true unless seamless nationwide coverage was available.

Though this seems like an obvious idea today, even a decade ago it was viewed as an impractical dream. First, there were hundreds of operators scattered across the country. If the FCC had simply given all the cellular-spectrum licenses to one company—as most European governments had done—it would have been simple to build a nationwide network. But ownership was scattered among wirelines and nonwirelines, competing businesses that would rather charge excessive roaming fees than work with neighboring operators to lower prices and improve coverage.

Second, the system hardware across the country was made by different manufacturers and had different specifications. Ericsson switches, for example, were just now being configured to communicate with Novatel switches in certain markets, while in others, operators were slow to adopt this new software. Finally, many operators, leery of fraud, were unwilling to allow roamers from far away to run up long-distance bills. The national cellular landscape was, in short, a chaotic mess of competing technologies and conflicting interests. With no immediately obvious financial incentive to do so, no one dreamed of undertaking the massive task of putting together a nationwide system. Except Craig McCaw.

In general, Craig McCaw is given too much credit for the unparalleled success of McCaw Cellular. Without Ed Hopper, John Stanton, Wayne Perry, Rufus Lumry, later arrival Steve Hooper and others who made deals, took risks and at times nudged their boss in directions he didn't necessarily want to go, the company would never have become the cellular powerhouse it did. But on the matter of the nationwide footprint, Craig deserves any accolades he gets. Simply put, he saw before anyone else the potential and the necessity of putting together a seamless nationwide system.

Though Craig was initially derided for his idea, technology improvements slowly began lending credibility to his plan. By the late 1980s, the manufacturers began supplying cellular switch software upgrades that allowed cellular operators to connect their multiple brands of switches together. Now, Bell Atlantic's Philadelphia customers could use their phones on New York's Nynex system, allowing these wirelines to better compete with LIN, which operated both the Philadelphia and New York nonwireline systems.

Coincident with the switch software upgrades, new tracking and billing software made it possible to charge users on their regular monthly bills when they used their phones in other cities. In areas with heavy regional competition—the New York to Washington corridor, for example—carriers made roaming simple by dumping the complex "roaming codes" or intercept operators they'd first required customers to use. And in some areas, carriers even did away with roaming charges altogether, giving up the lucrative charges in hopes of better holding on to their customers.

But even with these incremental changes, the wireless world was still too balkanized to form a truly nationwide service. On the wireline side, the RBOCs were too entangled in state and federal regulation—not to mention the legal complexities of proposing to share revenue under the restrictions of the AT&T split up—to attempt building a common nationwide network. On the nonwireline side, the 734 licenses were so thoroughly scattered among competing companies that only one company had even a remote chance of assembling enough of them to do it: McCaw.

Craig McCaw's quest began on the heels of McCaw's August 1987 IPO, when the company announced it had acquired substantial stakes in the next four largest public cellular companies, including 6 percent of Metro Mobile and 9.8 percent of LIN Broadcasting, for a total of $400 million. The investment community was perplexed by the moves: McCaw had borrowed so much already that it wasn't clear how the company would meet next month's payroll, much less find the billions it would need to go after other big public carriers.

For several years, McCaw's public stock portfolio reflected nothing more than Craig playing knight-errant, with fortuitous results—the value of the four stocks rose nicely. But only one of the four made critical sense to Craig's big vision. Two years after his pronouncement in the elevator, McCaw decided he had to buy LIN. Unfortunately for him, Don Pels was determined not to sell.

———

ONE AFTERNOON IN THE FALL OF 1988, someone saw TCI president (and McCaw board member) John Malone walk out of the Bank of New York with a shortish, mustachioed man.

This wouldn't ordinarily have been a noteworthy event, but a rumor had been going around that McCaw was looking to make a major purchase, possibly of LIN. The chance sighting of John Malone and Craig McCaw leaving the bank led to a phone call, which led to more phone calls, which led to LIN's stock quickly jumping five points.

As it turned out, the mustachioed man with John Malone that day wasn't Craig McCaw, but a member of Malone's financial team who happened to look something like Craig from a distance. But the rumors about McCaw and LIN failed to subside, goosing LIN's stock—and convincing McCaw it should cool it for a while until the excitement died down.

After McCaw had acquired 9 percent of LIN earlier in the year, the company had, in May 1988, adopted a "stockholder rights plan" designed to thwart any takeover attempts. In response, McCaw decided to keep plans for its offensive against LIN under deep cover.

"It was top, top secret," remembers Bill Hogland, a J. P. Morgan banker hired by McCaw to analyze a prospective deal. "We got a call from [CFO] Rufus [Lumry], who said, 'I want to talk to you about something very, very off the record, very top secret.'"

Mark Callaghan remembers that the company set up a "safe house," complete with an apartment for out-of-town consultants, where the proposed takeover could be discussed in secret. "They actually took a few analysts and told them, 'You're not going to see your family for six months, and you can't talk to people.'"

As rumors flew on Wall Street, McCaw's analysts secretly gathered at the safe house in Kirkland, a few blocks away from McCaw headquarters. Hogland and his associates told McCaw they were worried. "We had some real concerns looking forward that [McCaw] was going to get halfway into this takeover, and somebody was going to be able to just take them to the edge beyond which no one would finance them," remembers Hogland. It would be better, the analysts suggested, to get some more money on board first.

"That," says Hogland, "is where the idea of BT came up."

British Telecom, the mammoth former government monopoly from the UK, had been looking for a way to get into the U.S. cellular industry. When McCaw went looking for money in the fall of 1988, investment bankers put the two companies together.

But the discussions, Mark Hamilton remembers, "were excruciating. Just day after day of point-by-point stuff, back and forth. . . It kind of seemed like a negotiation with the Russians or something, where [they said] 'We're going to try and get every single point and we really don't care what you get,' that sort of thing."

Initially, discussions focused on an investment of less than $10 million, but soon it became clear that British Telecom wanted a bigger stake. After several months of tedious talks, a deal was announced in January 1989: For a $1.5 billion investment, British Telecom would receive a 22-percent stake in McCaw and the right to appoint four directors on McCaw's nineteen-member board. The deal was a good one for McCaw—it represented a per-POP value of $140, and it sent McCaw's stock soaring.

As always, though, Craig McCaw was paranoid about ceding even partial control of his company to anyone. After the final British Telecom agreement was reached during a meeting in New York, Craig walked with John Stanton and Mark Hamilton up Park Avenue toward their hotel on Sixty-third Street.

"How do you feel?" Hamilton asked him.

"I'm not really sure," replied the diminutive CEO. "I guess it's something we have to do."

Though many observers assumed McCaw wanted the British Telecom money for building out systems and paying down debt, the truth was more audacious: This was the money Craig needed to buy LIN.

THOUGH RELATIONS APPEARED CORDIAL ENOUGH on the surface, there was a sandpapery antipathy between Craig McCaw and Donald Pels. True, a hostile takeover wouldn't require any warm feelings between the two companies, but Craig wanted to keep an open line of communications, and he knew he wasn't the guy to maintain the link. He asked his brother John to step in for him.

By all accounts, John McCaw and Don Pels developed a respectful, reasonably friendly relationship in the dozen or so times they met over the spring of 1989. So when McCaw decided to make its unsolicited tender offer to buy LIN, John McCaw insisted on delivering the news personally to Pels, who was at the time in Paris for the French Open. When John McCaw, letter in hand, surprised him in the lobby of his hotel, Pels reportedly smiled, exclaiming, "There's John!" to his wife. Then, in an instant, his smile vanished as he understood the reason for McCaw's visit.

The offer was a record-setter. McCaw offered to pay $5.8 billion, or $120 per share, for LIN: This worked out to a staggering $285 per POP. Once again, McCaw was pushing the envelope on values: When the rest of the industry thought $10 a POP was excessive, McCaw paid $20. When $50 seemed a stretch, McCaw shocked everyone by paying $70. And now, in the summer of 1989, McCaw was declaring that POPs were worth $285. LIN's shares leapt on news of the offer.

The McCaw offer proved difficult to evaluate. Not only did LIN own fully built-out systems in America's largest markets, the company's stock price included television stations as well as hundreds of millions of dollars invested in cellular infrastructure. And the value of all this had to be adjusted for corporate debt. But no matter how the analysts parsed it, McCaw's offer was stunning.

"Given the regional, geographic and operational nature of the cellular business," Craig wrote in his letter to Pels, "the logic of combining our two companies is compelling. For that reason, we are willing to offer the highest price per POP in the history of our industry." True to form, McCaw had only a fraction of the money it was offering: Of the $5.8 billion proposed price tag, McCaw had a mere $1.3 billion on hand.

LIN responded less than two weeks later by declaring McCaw's offer "inadequate," noting that the potential outcome of pending litigation hadn't been considered in the price.

The litigation related to Metromedia's sale of its cellular holdings to Southwestern Bell in 1986. John Kluge had hoped to sell all of Metromedia cellular in that deal, but Pels blocked him from selling Metromedia's New

York and Philadelphia properties. At that time, LIN and Metromedia each owned half of the New York and Philadelphia nonwireline systems. Pels aspired to own all of both markets. But he wanted a cheaper price, so instead of matching the RBOC's forty-five dollars per POP, he offered only forty dollars—a move he would come to regret.

To Pels's surprise, Kluge had responded by taking the two markets off the table altogether. Afraid of losing an opportunity, the chagrined Pels suddenly decided he'd really like to buy them at forty-five dollars per POP; he duly raised his offer. But it was too late: Kluge now refused to sell. LIN responded by suing Metromedia, and the case had been tied up in court ever since.

If LIN won, it could purchase Metromedia's half of New York and Philadelphia at the 1986 price, $45 per POP—fully $240 per POP less than what McCaw was now offering for LIN's properties. This would mean an instantaneous $2 billion windfall for LIN. On the other hand, if Metromedia won, it would be free to sell the properties at current prices—and not necessarily to LIN. In that case, far from having a $2 billion payday, LIN would either have to shell out billions to buy the markets, or relegate itself to sharing New York and Philadelphia with whomever the new owner might be.

On July 30, 1989—a mere ten days after rejecting McCaw's bid—the final court decision on the litigation was announced. LIN lost. The impact was immediate: The company's stock fell. McCaw, seeing a chance for negotiating leverage, then nudged the stock lower by revising its offer down to $110 a share, the equivalent of $261.25 per POP.

For the next several months, McCaw and LIN dodged, feinted and bluffed as offers, counteroffers and rejections flew. Determined either to defeat McCaw's takeover bid or, failing that, to get the absolute top dollar in a deal, Pels and LIN's investment bankers began courting other suitors. In a double slap at McCaw, they approached the RBOCs, knowing not only that this would raise Craig's jealous ire, but that the RBOCs were rich enough to be able to outbid McCaw at will.

Craig McCaw's dream of building the nationwide footprint was absolutely dependent on getting LIN's major markets; if they were swallowed by an RBOC, they'd be gone forever—and there was no way he could get his hands on the wireline licenses for those markets. Suddenly, the battle's intensity had ratcheted up another notch.

On September 11, 1989, Craig's fears were realized: BellSouth and LIN announced a merger. The deal offered LIN stockholders shares in a new joint entity called LIN Cellular, plus a one-time twenty-dollar cash-dividend payment. Financial analysts scrambled to evaluate the bid, pegging its value at $98 to $110 per LIN share—a bit lower than McCaw's then-pending bid. But it had, the analysts noted, a couple of advantages: First, Bell South offered a tax-deferred way for the LIN shareholders to stay in the growing cellular game. And second, Bell South had the cash it needed to close the deal.

In Kirkland, the team was devastated by the news. It looked as though high-flying McCaw had just lost its most important battle.

THREE WEEKS AFTER THE BELLSOUTH ANNOUNCEMENT, the McCaw team began a second, seemingly unrelated major negotiation—but this time they were the sellers rather than the buyers. So important was this proposed deal that Craig McCaw had asked John Stanton, who was now running his own small cellular company, to come back temporarily and work on it. So it was that on the evening of Monday, October 2, 1989, Stanton, Don Guthrie, Barry Adelman and Scott Anderson found themselves in a New York law firm, engaged in an all-night negotiation that stretched their imaginations to the limits—but not for the usual reasons.

Stanton was negotiating a deal to sell 1.3 million of McCaw's POPs in Kentucky, Alabama and Tennessee to Contel, the country's second largest non-Bell telephone company. Negotiators from both companies had already pulled two all-nighters, meeting for seventeen hours on Saturday, September 30, and for nineteen hours on Sunday, October 1. Monday was Yom Kippur, so meetings were postponed until evening, when the group again came together in hopes of at last sealing the $1.2 billion deal.

To the relief of the exhausted Contel negotiators, things were wrapped up reasonably quickly. By about 8:30 that evening, the deal was essentially done; all that remained was for the parties to sign. Unnoticed by the Contel team, John Stanton pulled out his cell phone and made a quick call to Wayne Perry, who was at that moment in another conference room across Manhattan. "Put them off," said Perry. "We're not ready yet."

Thus began one of the odder episodes in McCaw's corporate history. The company whose motto had always been, "Sign 'em quick, close 'em slow" now needed to delay signing a contract. "We have to find something to negotiate," Stanton whispered to Adelman. So, although the contract was finished, Adelman approached the Contel team with an unusual demand. "You know," he said, "there's not a legal opinion in here from your firm."

"Barry," came the reply, "why do you need a legal opinion? We're paying you in cash." It was, Adelman knew, an absurd request. But he insisted.

"I need a legal opinion," he whined. "It's a big deal. It's a billion, two-hundred-million dollar deal. It might be a small deal for you guys, but it's a big deal for us. I want an opinion that this transaction is approved by your board, I want an opinion that you're duly incorporated . . ." His requests were, Adelman acknowledged later, "the worst kind of crap that you can imagine." The Contel team protested, arguing that Adelman's demands were ridiculous. But eventually, Adelman convinced them he would not yield; grudgingly, the negotiators agreed to insert the language in the contract.

Adelman pulled Stanton to one side. "Call Wayne," he said. "They're going to add one sentence, and it's going to take ten minutes. But I bought you an hour on that stupid argument." Stanton immediately called Perry, but the news was the same as before. "We're not ready," Perry told him. Again the McCaw team had to stall.

When the Contel lawyers brought in the new language, Adelman snapped, "You know, that's not good enough. I want to see the form of opinion and attach it to this contract"—a completely unnecessary formality that would easily consume another hour. As the frustrated lawyer stomped off to draft the opinion, the rest of the Contel team looked on in bewilderment: Why didn't they just sign the deal?

By the time the superfluous opinion was finished, it was after 11 P.M. "Okay," said the lawyer, "now we're ready."

"I've got to read it first," declared Adelman.

"Well, here it is," the lawyer replied.

"No, no, not this sentence," said Adelman. "I've got to read the contract."

"Barry," pleaded the exhausted and thoroughly irritated attorney, "It's a hundred pages long. What do you mean, you've got to read it?"

"Well," said Adelman, "we've made changes during the course of the day. I haven't sat down and read it cover to cover. It's a big deal for me. I need to read it and make sure it's internally consistent."

With that, Adelman retreated to another room. Stanton followed, and the two of them again called Perry. Again, they were told to delay.

Hours passed as Adelman sat in the side room "reading" the contract. The Contel negotiators, who'd thought they had a deal at 8:30 the previous evening, were close to mutiny as the clock ticked past 2 . . . then 3 . . . then 4 A.M. As Adelman hid in the room, they knocked repeatedly, shouting "Are you finished?"

"John," Adelman finally pleaded at 5 A.M., "I can't tell them I'm not finished reading this. They already think I'm a moron. Now they're going to think I'm illiterate." He thought for a minute, then looked again at Stanton and said, "Maybe you should go hide."

"What?" asked Stanton. "What do you mean?"

"I mean, go hide," responded Adelman.

"Where?" asked Stanton.

"I don't care!" hissed Adelman. "But don't show up again until Wayne says you can sign."

Stanton slipped out of the room and disappeared. A moment later, Adelman emerged, saying, "Okay, the contract's fine. We can sign."

"Where's John?" asked one attorney.

"I don't know, I thought he was with you," responded a straightfaced Adelman. With that, the irritated, nearly delirious group commenced a search for Stanton, checking the men's room, other conference rooms, calling his hotel room. There was no sign of Stanton—until he walked nonchalantly into the conference room nearly two hours later, at 7 A.M. At last, Wayne Perry had given them the go-ahead. Now they could sign.

The Contel troops were elated, partly because the marathon negotiating ordeal was at last over, but also because this agreement represented the largest acquisition in Contel's twenty-eight-year history. At $1.2 billion, it was sure to headline the business pages, heralding Contel's arrival into the pantheon of major cellular operators. A press release trumpeting Contel's achievement was already prepared, and the team couldn't wait to send it out.

After Stanton signed the deal, the McCaw team gathered their notepads, pens and briefcases, ready to go home. Suddenly, Stanton handed a piece of paper to the Contel team and remarked, "By the way, here's the press release we've done, because we've signed another agreement concurrently with this one."

As the Contel team crowded around the press release to look, Stanton said quietly to Adelman, "Elevator, now. Before they read it." And the McCaw team fled.

The press release—and the headlines that soon would result from it—were not about Contel at all. They trumpeted instead a surprising new twist in McCaw's pursuit of LIN: McCaw had bought Metromedia's half of New York for $1.9 billion, and it was using the $1.2 billion from the Contel sale to help pay for it. This explained Stanton and Adelman's bizarre behavior: They didn't want to sign the deal until they were absolutely sure the Metromedia purchase was done. If the Metromedia deal had fallen through for any reason, McCaw would have scotched the Contel deal as well. McCaw wasn't in the business of selling spectrum, after all—unless a sale was simply a means to buy more.

Contel, says Scott Anderson, never had a clue what McCaw was up to. "They were frustrated," he recalls. "They'd been up all weekend. I think the Contel guys had the sense that John Stanton was sort of taking them to the cleaners, so they were jittery anyway."

"We did not win a lot of friends or influence a lot of people in that negotiation," recalls Adelman with a laugh.

But the rest of the business world was impressed. In a single stroke, McCaw had changed the balance of power in its battle for LIN.

MCCAW'S INCURSION INTO NEW YORK made things very sticky for LIN; the analysts who believed, as one wrote, that the deal was merely a "face-saving maneuver" missed the true genius of the move.

Though LIN had lost its lawsuit against Metromedia, it still retained the right of first refusal on the New York market. Craig McCaw knew that his offer to Metromedia would put pressure on LIN and BellSouth to exercise that right. If LIN did buy Metromedia's half of New York, it would drive up the cost to BellSouth in the recently announced merger. On the other hand, if LIN didn't buy, BellSouth-LIN would end up partners with McCaw in New York, probably in perpetuity—a discomfiting thought for the RBOC.

Until the McCaw announcement, it had been safe for BellSouth to assume that Metromedia's half of New York would be for sale someday, and that the cost to Bell South could be deferred until the future. Now, BellSouth had three unpleasant options: Give up on controlling New York, pay up to match Craig McCaw or walk away. Craig knew that if the RBOC walked, Don Pels would never have the guts to buy New York on his own.

"Clearly, we couldn't lose," remembers Mark Hamilton. "It was a brilliant stroke. It really put the pressure on Pels, because he couldn't just sit back and say, 'I've got a great little company here; everything's fine.' He had to make a decision."

What followed was a high-stakes game of chicken. On October 10, McCaw announced a new bid of $125 per share for 22 million LIN shares, which would give McCaw just more than 50-percent ownership of LIN with the option to buy the remaining shares over time. Again, McCaw was doing the unexpected, flanking BellSouth instead of meeting them head-on. Responding to critics who carped that McCaw didn't have enough cash, Craig was offering to buy half now and half later. The offer promised more cash per share than the BellSouth merger (which promised mostly stock) and promised to get it more quickly to LIN's shareholders, but not all stockholders would get bought out. The offer created the threat of a race between competing LIN stockholders to sell out first—a situation the McCaw team hoped would disrupt Pels's last vestiges of control over his stockholders.

McCaw's bold moves worked: The LIN-BellSouth merger was temporarily derailed, and the LIN board was forced back into considering a sale to McCaw. Through the fall, McCaw and BellSouth continued to vie for LIN. If it came down to a pure battle of wallets, BellSouth had the clear advantage. But like its Baby Bell brethren, BellSouth was hobbled by one fear that overrode that ability: It was extremely reluctant to damage its reported earnings or to reduce its quarterly dividends, two numbers that were sacrosanct to its conservative stockholders.

On October 27, BellSouth sweetened its bid for LIN by upping the cash portion of the offer from $20 to $42 per share, for a total offer that analysts valued at $115 to $125 per share. LIN would also borrow $1.9 billion more to exercise its rights to the other half of New York. The two companies couldn't help showing signs of pain brought on by the new bid: "We're taking on more debt than we would have liked," a LIN executive confessed to the press, a hint to McCaw that the endgame was in sight. McCaw promptly countered by upping its offer for the first half of LIN's shares to $133 a share.

Each successive shot was covered with glee by the analysts, who took perverse joy in trotting out bloodthirsty metaphors: "McCaw is really turning the screws," declared Piper Jaffray & Hopwood's Thomas Friedberg in the *Wall Street Journal*. "The gloves are off and they're fighting bare-knuckled," announced Frederick Moran of Moran Asset Management, Inc.

The day of reckoning was fast approaching: A LIN board meeting was scheduled for Saturday, December 2, 1989, and the company had asked BellSouth and McCaw for their best and final offers. The McCaw team met in Kirkland that Friday night to fashion one last—hopefully irresistible—offer.

In the conference room by Craig McCaw's office, the group assembled with Lazard Freres investment banker Steven Rattner. This was it: How much could McCaw pay? What kind of creative structuring might appeal to the board? Was McCaw in danger of going completely overboard—of paying far too much for LIN in its desperate bid to outduel BellSouth?

As the group animatedly discussed its options, a strange thing happened: The lights suddenly went out. Thanks to a reserve generator, auxiliary lights around the edge of the room came on, and one direct halogen light shone down on the table, illuminating Craig McCaw's face as he leaned over the papers spread out in front of him. "It was sort of surreal," remembers Mark Hamilton. "You felt like you were in *Dr. Strangelove* in some sort of control room." In the dim glow of the reserve lights, Craig McCaw announced his decision: McCaw would offer a staggering $154 per share, or the equivalent of $320 per POP.

There was simply no way the LIN shareholders would allow the board to refuse McCaw's lucrative offer—and BellSouth, ever concerned with earnings, wouldn't raise its bid. The next day at the LIN board meeting, the directors, recognizing they had no choice, recommended accepting McCaw's bid. Finally, incredibly, McCaw had won.

Don Pels had a reputation of being a less-than-visionary CEO—as Metromedia's Stuart Subotnick once said of him, "I happen to like Don; he's a nice guy, but he's an accountant, and everything was negotiated down. . . Some people know how to say 'no' all the time, and Don was one of those guys." But the very intransigence that preserved LIN from either growth or shrinkage as cellular values rose also serendipitously proved the perfect strategy for Pels to extract a bank-breaking price for his company.

As *Forbes* noted after the McCaw-LIN deal was announced, "To create a national cellular telephone company able to compete with the Bell companies, McCaw had no choice but to strain his company to the bursting point to control LIN. And Don Pels knew that. By playing McCaw off against BellSouth, Pels was able to cut LIN's shareholders (including himself, with 1.6 million shares) a very fine deal."

The price LIN's shareholders got for their cellular POPs was a record. And McCaw got three things it desperately wanted: major markets, the real possibility of constructing a nationwide footprint and stature among the elite global wireless powerhouses. "That transaction made McCaw," remembers CCI's George Blumenthal, a sentiment echoed by Scot Jarvis, who later said, "Frankly, we didn't become a major player until we bought LIN."

In just eight years, this little cable company from Washington state had come to dominate the cell phone industry. Now it was poised to change the face of that industry—and in the process, to change the way Americans communicated. Yet even the seemingly supercertain Craig McCaw, so unassailable in his convictions about the future of cell phones, harbored doubts. One day shortly after the LIN deal, Blumenthal remembers him remarking, "You know, I think I'm sorry I did this transaction."

Buyer's remorse aside, McCaw had at last broken into the really big leagues. And as press coverage of the company and its inscrutable CEO increased, observers across the country found themselves wondering: *Who, really, is this guy?*

━━━━━━━━

THE ENDURING IMAGE ASSOCIATED WITH CRAIG MCCAW is one he unwittingly branded himself with in 1987. It happened at a company retreat in Snake River, Idaho, when he and other executives were asked to talk about what their goals were.

"I want to be the Wizard of Oz," announced Craig.

When one executive present at the retreat leaked the exchange to the press, business reporters and competitors gleefully dissected this odd response. What in the world was that supposed to mean? Sure, Craig McCaw seemed like a clever enough businessman, but eccentricities this pronounced were simply too delicious to dismiss. Craig, some none-too-delicately suggested, was a kook.

The "Wizard of Oz" quote was splashed throughout numerous stories about McCaw, to the point where it took on legendary status. "Craig McCaw, who once declared he wanted to be the Wizard of Oz . . ." ran a typical lead. But what had Craig really been trying to say? No one really knew for sure, until Robert Ratliffe, who had joined the McCaw team just before the infamous retreat, at last cleared up the mystery years later.

Soon after Ratliffe started at the company, Craig spoke in front of an all-employee meeting in a local auditorium. In his usual shy, self-deprecating way, Craig opened by saying, "I don't do this very well, it's just not my thing. I'm not very good at communicating," before getting to the substance of his remarks.

Ratliffe, a veteran of motivational seminars and a believer in the power of positive thinking, watched Craig stumble through the beginning of his speech with dismay. When Craig finished his talk and invited questions from the audience, Ratliffe raised his hand.

"When are you going to stop affirming that you're so bad at everything?" he demanded of his CEO. "If you keep saying how crappy you are at this stuff, you're always going to be bad at it." All around him, the auditorium was silent. His colleagues looked on in a kind of bemused horror.

"Everybody came up to me after the meeting and said, 'Wow. You're history. It was really nice knowing you,'" remembers Ratliffe. So when the offsite meeting was over and the employees were back at the office, Ratliffe made his way up to Craig's office to try and control the damage.

"Craig," he told his boss, "I hope you didn't think I was out of line, but tomorrow I'd like to show you a videotape. I want you just to think about it. My impression is that we all sort of brainwash ourselves, and if you say, 'I'm really good at something,' or 'I'm really bad at something,' then a man does as a man thinketh." Craig—who fortunately seemed unfazed by Ratliffe's temerity at the meeting—agreed to meet with him.

The next day, having been promised fifteen minutes of Craig's time, Ratliffe went back to the CEO's office. He popped a videocassette into the VCR, and the face of motivational speaker Lou Tice appeared. He was talking about the Wizard of Oz.

As Ratliffe describes the video, "He says, 'The Wizard of Oz, obviously, was just a regular guy standing behind a curtain, but what he was doing for people was one-time affirmations and rites of passage. . . the Wizard is just a regular guy, but because of the power vested in him, because he's Wizard—or the chairman—he says, "By the power vested in me, I declare you a great company. Or a great person."'" The wizard was only a wizard, in short, because he used ordinary powers to urge others on to extraordinary things.

Craig watched the video intently. When it finished, he turned to Ratliffe. "I like that," he said. "That's good."

The next weekend was the retreat, and Craig tried, in his own way, to express this new truth he'd learned. As Ratliffe recalls, "It was so typical of Craig, if you get to know him. He didn't finish telling the story! He didn't tell anybody what the hell he meant!" When the story was leaked, the damage was done: The "Wizard of Oz" declaration was "in every publication that came out for the next five years," as Ratliffe recalls.

The "Oz" story highlighted an enduring problem: Whenever Craig spoke for public consumption, his team was apoplectic with the fear that he'd say something off-the-wall. As Mark Callaghan recalls, "[CEO] Rufus [Lumry] was just scared to death of having Craig go someplace and talk to people who didn't know him, because he knew he couldn't control what he was going to say. There was always the possibility of people misinterpreting." Craig was, in the words of Callaghan, "not scriptable." Part of the reason for that was because his vision of technology was so, well, untechnological.

He was as concerned as any CEO about penetration rates, equipment, customer service and coverage, but Craig also spoke in surprisingly touchy-feely terms about cellular. In interviews, he was more likely to speak of "changing the way people live and work," or "our nature-state as nomads" than he was of stock prices. "We are not product-driven," he told *Telephony* magazine, "we are information-driven. . . The only thing to fear is an unwillingness to change. That's the only real threat to telecommunications today."

As his team feared, his stream-of-consciousness utterances occasionally veered into the realm of the bizarre. "If you mate a brontosaurus with a stegosaurus," he announced at a Digital Media conference, using a tortured metaphor for old-style companies, "you're not going to get a pterodactyl or a Tyrannosaurus Rex."

One of the most well-known oddities Craig uttered came during a speech at a CTIA conference in Reno, Nevada, in February 1990. Because Craig rarely made public appearances, his scheduled lunchtime speech elicited a kind of rock-star rippling of interest. "Everyone was amazed that they were actually going to hear and see Craig McCaw," remembers Larry Movshin. "It was kind of like he was the Howard Hughes of the cellular industry."

With hundreds of executives, engineers and marketers jammed into the cavernous conference hall, Craig launched into what initially seemed to be standard conference rhetoric. But then, he went on a tangent.

While talking about the seamless nationwide network, he segued into one of his favorite subjects: the future. Being able to reach anyone at any time and anywhere was good, he said, but the day was coming when something more fantastic would be commonplace. One day, he said, humans would have miniature wireless communicators implanted in their brains. Instead of having to dial a phone and talk to someone, everyone would simply be able to communicate brain-to-brain, by wireless telepathy. In fact, he would later tell *Fortune Magazine*, it would be a good idea for the FCC to set aside spectrum for this purpose.

Was he crazy? Or was he simply so far ahead of everyone else that it just seemed that way? There was no consensus in the hall that day; when the speech was done, attendees turned to each other and murmured, "Did he say what I think he said?"

The conventional wisdom at McCaw was that Craig saw over the horizon. As one anonymous McCaw executive told Seattle-based *Eastsideweek* magazine, "He's operating in the fourth dimension. He sees it four years down the road." This explained why McCaw went out on any available rickety limb to grow his company's wireless presence as opposed to sitting back, as Don Pels had done. A much bigger, much different future, he believed, lay just around the corner.

As the executive concluded, "The only thing he's trying to do right now is keep the baling wire and chewing gum around [McCaw] until it can become a new kind of phone company."

In fact, Craig McCaw began thinking concretely about how to make McCaw a "new kind of phone company" immediately after the LIN purchase. But not in the way most observers expected.

Just a few months after the LIN purchase, Craig placed a call that would lead to the most difficult business decision of his life: He called AT&T chairman Robert Allen. McCaw was, as usual, stretched nearly to the breaking point: Already burdened with debt, the company would now have to come up with money both to build out the nationwide network and to buy the remaining LIN shares. "We were in trouble," recalls Scott Anderson.

Time and time again over the past decade, McCaw had bought what it couldn't afford, letting its own bidding ratchet up the public perception of values and thereby increasing the amount McCaw could borrow on its mounting pile of spectrum assets. But this cycle couldn't expand indefinitely; LIN was almost certain to be the high-water mark in per-POP prices, and the only way to finance the massive buildout of McCaw's multiple markets was to justify values with operating cash flows. All of Craig's optimistic musings about how the common man would want to be freed from wired phones would now have to come true—and if it didn't come true fast enough, McCaw was going to run out of cash.

So once again, as it had done with Affiliated, Scripps Howard and British Telecom, McCaw sought another equity partner, a company with lots of cash and a strategic need to get in the wireless business. A number of companies were candidates: According to *Business Week*, McCaw's bankers considered Motorola, MCI and Sprint as well as AT&T. Motorola was a long shot, but the choice of any of the three long-distance companies carried with it an irrefutable logic. After all, a true nationwide footprint required not only dots of coverage in all the cities, but also a long-distance network to connect those dots into a seamless picture.

The most logical choice among long-distance companies—and the company with by far the fattest treasury—was AT&T.

A deal between AT&T and McCaw would bring instant benefits to both sides. For McCaw, it meant not only cash and access to the biggest long-distance fiber-optic backbone network, but also strong distribution and a strong marketing team (something McCaw had always lacked). For AT&T, it meant recapturing what had been lost in the antitrust suit: direct access from its backbone network to the consumer, without passing traffic (and revenues) through the hands of the RBOCs.

Quietly, Wayne Perry worked on negotiations with the long-distance giant. Though analysts noted that McCaw was a prime takeover target, there was no overt indication from Kirkland of what was brewing with AT&T. But in his own oblique way, McCaw left hints.

At a conference in May 1992, Craig spoke in characteristically new-agey terms about the relationship between traditional phone companies and wireless companies. "Landline companies need to take down their guard toward us," he said. "There isn't much threat to the telephone industry except fear. But there isn't that much to fear because we are you.

"The future isn't something that happens to you," he continued. "It's something you do. We'd very much like to do it with you."

Six months later, AT&T and McCaw announced a strategic partnership. AT&T would pay $3.73 billion for one-third of McCaw's shares, and McCaw would market its cellular service under the AT&T brand. AT&T would get three board seats, and BT would sell its 22-percent stake in McCaw to AT&T as part of the deal. Observers who were accustomed to the iconoclastic, emphatically independent ways of Craig McCaw were surprised: Wasn't this making a deal with the devil? But in a statement, Craig was unequivocal. This was "a logical and powerful alliance," he declared. "No deal ever made more sense to me."

Unfortunately, making sense of the deal's finer points soon proved elusive for the dealmakers. Though Craig and Robert Allen had agreed in principle to the arrangement, things got sticky when it came time to determine specifics. Who would take charge of producing and selling services? How did the split of wired and wireless revenues work? In the months following the announcement, it began to seem as though the mechanics of the deal would prove too complicated to sort out.

And these weren't the only worries. How would McCaw, with its free-wheeling, nonhierarchical, irreverent atmosphere, be able to work with buttoned-down AT&T? Even a cursory look at the two companies revealed huge differences in culture: McCaw had 7,000 employees, while AT&T had 300,000. The average age of a McCaw employee was thirty-three; at AT&T, it was forty-three. Craig McCaw worked in a relatively modest office (especially considering the fact that he was the highest-paid CEO in America in 1990); Bob Allen's AT&T suite was so large, *Time* magazine wrote, "that he has to get up and walk 50 yards if he wants to reach out and touch someone."

Like a gawky young suitor, Bob Allen gamely tried to ingratiate himself with the McCaw executives. At one corporate dinner, *Forbes* reported, Craig

McCaw had instigated a food fight—the kind of spontaneous, esprit-building goofery the company was known for. The next evening, when Allen addressed the same group in an attempt to soothe lingering worries about the partnership, he ended his speech by pulling a dinner roll out of his suit pocket and tossing it at Craig's head. *Forbes* noted, for the record, that Craig ducked.

Talks between the companies continued through the spring, with little progress made. Finally, in mid-August 1993, Allen reached what was beginning to seem like the inevitable conclusion: Partnering with McCaw was simply proving too complicated. So he made another proposal. He suggested AT&T buy McCaw outright.

Allen, who had just returned from a business trip to China on Friday, August 13, met with Craig McCaw in New York the next day to discuss a deal. And one day was all it took: At 7 P.M., in the hallway of the Waldorf-Astoria hotel, Craig McCaw made the decision many thought he would never make. He shook hands with Bob Allen and agreed to sell the only company he'd ever worked for.

In 1982, AT&T had given away its right to enter the cell phone industry, letting it fall instead to the Baby Bells. Now, a decade later, it had to buy its way in at a staggering price. For $12.6 billion ($17.5 billion if the figure included McCaw's debt), AT&T bought a piece of the industry it could once have had for free.

The $17.5 billion purchase price made the deal the second-largest takeover in U.S. history at the time, behind only Kohlberg, Kravis & Roberts Company's purchase of RJR Nabisco in 1989. Critics howled that the price was appallingly high: McCaw Cellular, after all, had only 2 million subscribers, had never made a profit and controlled only 30 percent of metropolitan America. But with AT&T's money behind it, the McCaw team could now rev up the acquisition machine once again, armed with the cash needed to continue piecing together the nationwide network.

To some, AT&T's decision to market its cellular service under the AT&T name seemed perverse. After all, "Cellular One"—that catch-all name coined so randomly by George Duncan ten years earlier—was used in nearly every market in the country. Licensed to the nonwirelines, and eventually used even by Southwestern Bell, Cellular One had hard-won name recognition. But AT&T was one of America's most powerful, familiar brands—and not only that, one 1993 survey showed it was the second most recognized brand in cellular service. Bizarrely, this was before AT&T was even in the cellular business.

Predictably, the RBOCs were livid about the merger. For more than ten years, they'd had the wireless industry to themselves, in competition only with smaller, cash-poor nonwirelines: In 1994, they controlled 75 percent of the cellular market. Now AT&T was crashing the party, and doing it with those upstarts from Kirkland. It was like having your mom show up at your senior prom—with the prom king on her arm. The RBOCs protested that the merger posed a monopoly threat, but their complaints were eventually swatted aside by the FCC and the D.C. Circuit Court.

The deal was done, and the industry landscape was forever changed. Craig McCaw described the merger within his usual philosophical framework: "While we recognize it's a very difficult [move] for both companies—probably more for us than for AT&T," he said in a statement, "we believe in the dream we've had about uplifting the human being by putting in their hands a more powerful communications tool."

To the *Los Angeles Times*, he declared, "We are at the beginning of global revolution in the way people work and communicate. This is a moment of fulfilling dreams more than just dreaming." Cynical observers could be forgiven for noting that, with Craig and his brothers personally realizing $2.5 billion on the sale, they certainly could afford to fulfill any dreams they might have.

A decade after the FCC began giving away cellular spectrum, the complete scrambling of license ownership they had created was coalescing into a few cellular powerhouses. The AT&T-McCaw juggernaut and the Baby Bells controlled some 270 million POPs, essentially covering the entire United States (including competing service in many markets), and this consolidation trend was destined to grow.

With only two systems in each market—and in some markets, the competing systems were owned by Bell brethren—prices didn't come down as quickly as they might have if more creative competitors (or simply more competitors) were battling for market share. Was the duopoly system, devised by the FCC to keep the phone companies from dominating this new industry, a flop? In the end, the phone companies controlled just about everything anyway—and it certainly didn't appear that the customers were any better off for it. Though usage numbers were growing quickly, some feared cellular technology would forever be viewed as an expensive complement to regular phone service.

Unless, that is, some other form of competition arose. In 1993, just as the duopoly was settling into its plodding domination, two other competitors suddenly appeared on the horizon. One was planned by the FCC, and the other seemed simply to come out of nowhere.

20

THE NEXT BIG THING

SINCE THE BEGINNING OF THE INDUSTRY, there had been only one way to run a cell phone system in America: You had to get your hands on one of the 1,468 licenses the FCC gave away throughout the 1980s. Whether a company won its license in a comparative hearing or lottery, agreed to share it in a settlement group or bought or swapped for it from someone else, that was the sole option for becoming a cell phone carrier.

Or so everyone thought.

One man, FCC lawyer Morgan O'Brien, thought he saw another way. There was, O'Brien knew, another block of spectrum being used—and used inefficiently—for another type of mobile communications. Could it, he wondered, be used to carry telephone calls? Even if it could, the regulatory and technological obstacles to such a scheme were tremendous—no one so far had proven bold or naive enough to believe it could work.

O'Brien was a lawyer, but he'd always wanted to make it in business. One of eight children, he'd grown up a fair-haired, bespectacled youth in an Irish family in Washington, D.C. He got his law degree at Northwestern University, then clerked for a federal appellate court judge who made the remark that would change his life. Frustrated with the poor quality of the government lawyers' work, the judge told O'Brien, "You ought to go over to the FCC and straighten those guys out." Gamely, O'Brien took the judge's advice, and following his clerkship he took a position with the FCC's Mobile Services Division.

Soon after starting at the FCC, O'Brien was handed Docket 18262, the document that set aside spectrum for both cellular and Specialized Mobile Radio, or SMR—the technology used by all manner of dispatch services, from taxicabs to courier services. Docket 18262 increased the amount of spectrum designated for mobile services by a factor of more than 1,000; the field of communications, O'Brien realized, was about to be revolutionized. Though he quit the FCC just eleven months after he started, he resolved that somehow he would take part in that revolution in the private sector.

As a communications attorney, O'Brien did work for dozens of clients in the SMR and cellular industries. Along the way, he authored articles, spoke at industry conventions and became a well-known expert in SMR. At the same time, eager to branch out from practicing law, he launched a handful of entrepreneurial ventures, none of which panned out; to the disappointed O'Brien, it looked as though he'd never get away from a career that was measured by billable hours. But the work he did for his clients provided him the singular insight needed to attempt his final foray into business.

By 1987, two things were becoming clear to O'Brien and other observers of the spectrum rush. First, cellular-spectrum licenses were phenomenally valuable, much more so than anyone had initially expected. Second, cell phones were becoming so popular with the public that the seemingly enormous amount of spectrum the FCC had set aside for cellular was fast proving inadequate. In September 1986, in fact, the FCC had been forced to allocate an additional 10 MHz of spectrum to cellular. (The commission simply handed it to the existing operators.) Even that wasn't enough to fix the capacity problems, and it wasn't at all clear where the FCC would find additional spectrum to throw at the problem.

O'Brien's experience allowed him to see something that everyone else missed: that it was possible to cobble together a third wireless phone system using SMR spectrum. SMR, which operated in the 800 MHz band of spectrum (very close to cellular), was the old-fashioned technology used by taxi dispatchers, courier services, cement truck fleets and others to communicate with large groups at once from a central location. Though most SMR radios worked on the old push-to-talk technology, in the 1970s a newer version had been developed: This version looked like a telephone, and it could be rigged to dial into the regular landline telephone network. Why not, O'Brien thought, simply reverse the focus? Why not market SMR radios as phones, rather than as dispatch units with a supplemental phone function?

O'Brien's plan, while theoretically workable, had one major problem: In order to create an effective "third system" in even one U.S. city, the multiple slices of SMR spectrum would have to be bought up, pieced together and reengineered to form one system. And SMR-spectrum licenses were even more scattered than cellular licenses were: There were literally dozens of them in each city, held by scores of small operators and family-owned dispatch businesses that had no plans to sell out and no plans to upgrade.

Convincing the multiple SMR operators to sell, and getting enough financing to buy, would be gargantuan tasks for the inexperienced O'Brien. But in snatching up dozens of disparate carriers, O'Brien would simply be following the model of some early cellular pioneers: John Kluge had bought up little paging carriers to get "local presence" for his cellular applications, and McCaw was at that time scrambling all over the country buying out dozens of random lottery winners. But Kluge and McCaw had one advantage over O'Brien: They had teams of negotiators doing the footwork. Morgan O'Brien had only himself and his newly incorporated company, dubbed Fleet Call. True, the naturally gregarious O'Brien was well suited for the hundreds of negotiations that lay ahead, but the enormity of the task was daunting—especially considering O'Brien also had a full-time day job as an attorney at the nation's largest law firm, Jones, Day, Reavis & Pogue.

It would be impossible, O'Brien knew, to implement his plan across the whole country. So he initially focused on six big markets where cellular demand was likely to outstrip supply and where FCC rules favored his plan: New York, Los Angeles, Chicago, San Francisco, Dallas and Houston. Uncertain of success, short of money and strapped for time, O'Brien began what appeared to be a hopelessly quixotic quest.

Between 1987 and 1989, O'Brien jetted all over the country, talking to mom-and-pop SMR operators while somehow managing to keep up his billable hours in his regular job. Beginning with a $25,000 seed investment from Mark Warner, O'Brien leapt from ice floe to ice floe in a frigid sea of financial uncertainty, always struggling to find the cash for his acquisitions. A Who's Who of Wall Street firms—Salomon Brothers, Goldman Sachs, J. P. Morgan—turned down Fleet Call's entreaties; then the frustrated O'Brien was introduced to financier Peter Reinheimer, head of his own New York–based boutique investment-banking operation, Reinheimer & Co.

Intrigued by Fleet Call but leery about O'Brien's total lack of experience, Reinheimer introduced him to Brian McAuley, a seasoned operations manager and accountant who promptly created the financial models needed to justify O'Brien's grand vision. With McAuley's expertise in the mix, Reinheimer now had sufficient confidence to raise the first of several rounds of venture financing.

On paper, O'Brien's plan was simple. First, Fleet Call would buy up a majority of the SMR spectrum licenses in America's six biggest cities. Then, in each market, Fleet Call would consolidate the spectrum slices from multiple operators into a single large block, allocating existing dispatch traffic more efficiently to just a couple of channels. This would leave potentially dozens of newly open channels, which could then be used to carry mobile-telephone traffic. The SMR phones wouldn't be as sophisticated as the newer cellular ones, but with cheap spectrum, Fleet Call could afford to sell lower-priced service. In a later interview with *Forbes*, Brian McAuley described Fleet Call's strategy: "[SMR] customers are paying $15 for seventy-five minutes of airtime on a frequency that is functionally equivalent to a cellular one," he explained, "where cellular is getting $100 for the same thing."

Though Fleet Call found itself constantly scrambling for financing, O'Brien and McAuley knew it was more important to present an image of wealth than it was to actually be wealthy. Anxious to convince potential sellers to trust their offers, the pair decided to throw a lavish party at the next industry convention, replete with elegant hors d'oeuvres, an open bar and engraved invitations. "We just hand-selected the people we invited," remembers O'Brien, "so it got to be like, if you weren't invited to Fleet Call's party, what was wrong with you? Because that's where the hot people in the industry are." With luck, O'Brien recalls thinking, the party would ensure that "people would be embarrassed to say, 'Prove to us that you have the $2 million to buy this property.'"

Like McCaw, Fleet Call attracted hordes of naysayers who thought the company was crazy to spend so much money for its spectrum. O'Brien remembers, "I had people call me during our acquisition binge and say, 'I've known you for years; I consider you a friend, and I can only hope that this is not your money, because you're going to go broke.'"

But to O'Brien, the prices he was paying were an obvious bargain. "Here people were paying millions of dollars for [cellular] RSAs in places that nobody had ever heard of," he recalls, "and over here, Los Angeles channels are available for a penny on the dollar." With Peter Reinheimer's help, the tiny Fleet Call team managed to talk enough telecom-hungry investors—including venture capitalists at Chase Manhattan and First Chicago—into backing their effort. Stealthily, the company continued to buy up SMR businesses in its six target cities.

Though O'Brien envisioned his Fleet Call system capturing some of the cellular carriers' traffic, his plans were actually relatively modest at first. Not only did he plan to compete in only six cities, he also knew that he wouldn't be able to take on very many customers. The FCC would require Fleet Call to continue providing dispatch service for existing SMR customers; thanks to the limits of SMR technology and the limited number of channels available, there were only so many mobile phone customers the company could accommodate. Because O'Brien's system couldn't really compete with the much greater customer capacity of cellular systems, the big carriers hardly noticed his spectrum quest.

That would soon change, after Morgan O'Brien had his second epiphany.

While on a flight to Houston in the late 1980s, O'Brien was using some rare downtime to catch up on his reading. Perusing an article about digital technology and the cell phone industry, he suddenly looked up from the magazine in his lap, startled by an audacious thought. Why not, he wondered, convert the SMR systems from analog to digital?

Though cellular systems still ran on analog in 1987, operators were exploring digital technology as a fix for one of the industry's biggest new problems. Analog technology, or the translation of voice vibrations into electrical modulations, was the same system Marconi had used at the turn of the century. It was more than adequate for simple voice communications, but when the popularity of cellular began to spiral upward, engineers were faced with a new, urgent task: to increase the capacity of the existing cellular spectrum.

Digital technology promised to do just that. Made possible by newly developed integrated circuits that were just coming into mass production in the late 1980s, digital worked by converting voice signals into microsecond pulses of binary code. The nature of digital allowed multiple conversations to be carried on one radio channel—effectively tripling or quadrupling capacity as well as the amount of revenue that could be gleaned from any given slice of radio spectrum.

In addition, digital technology would allow for the transmission of not only voice, but data—short text messages, numeric pages and the like. Cellular carriers, frustrated by customer complaints about busy signals, dropped calls and poor connections on their overcrowded analog systems, were anxious to employ digital technology as soon as possible.

If he switched Fleet Call's system to digital, O'Brien could conceivably pull off a coup of staggering proportions—assuming he could convince his old associates at the FCC to make a few key rule changes.

Fleet Call had bought its SMR licenses for a fraction of the cost of what cellular licenses were selling for, because no one had dreamed that SMR spectrum could be used to compete with cellular carriers on their own terms.

There was good reason for that expectation: Half a dozen or more FCC rules governing the use of SMR spectrum would have to be changed in order for Fleet Call to seriously compete. The single greatest constraint on SMR was its old-fashioned system architecture: The SMR licenses required that radio signals be broadcast at high power from a single site (high and loud), while cellular (low and soft) got to reuse its frequencies many times over in each city by using multiple cell sites. If O'Brien planned to subdivide once with digital, why not take it a step further and subdivide the subdivision by getting permission to use multiple towers in a cellular architecture?

This would require a series of FCC rule changes, but if the commission consented, Fleet Call could increase its spectrum capacity by 100 times or more—giving O'Brien a competitive third system for a fraction of the cost of cellular. If not, he would have little more than a fancy dispatch service and more phone revenue to show for his work.

There was one final hitch: Though digital cellular phones were ready to be shipped to stores, no one had yet invented a digital SMR phone. In addition to successfully lobbying the FCC, Fleet Call would need to find a technology partner who could build a new kind of phone. As Fleet Call launched its lobbying battle at the FCC, O'Brien knew it was time to share the secret of his backdoor attack on the cellular industry with a possible partner.

―――――――――

ON FEBRUARY 14, 1990, Morgan O'Brien and Brian McAuley paid a visit to Chicago, calling on George M. C. Fisher, the CEO of Motorola. The success or failure of Fleet Call, they knew, could well hinge on Fisher's reaction to their idea. With gallows humor, McAuley joked that they could be heading into another Valentine's Day Massacre.

Neither McAuley nor O'Brien knew Fisher, so a colleague had arranged the meeting. It was extremely unusual, they knew, to be granted a meeting with the powerful Motorola CEO without first going through lower channels. As the person who arranged the visit told them, "I can get you one of these [meetings] in your lifetime. Are you sure this is the one you want?"

O'Brien and McAuley walked into Fisher's office and immediately got down to business. "We want to tell you about an idea we have," O'Brien began, "and if you don't like the idea, if you are opposed to it, we would expect you to fight us and that's fine. We would just ask that you tell us that." The pair explained the idea behind Fleet Call, then told Fisher how much spectrum they had already amassed.

After a moment's thought, Fisher said, "We had no idea you had acquired so much spectrum." The next thing he said caught the entrepreneurs by surprise. "We have a technology we've been working on for years that would be perfect for this. You're a couple of years ahead of where we thought the industry was." As McAuley recalls it, the CEO then told them, "I think you guys are going to be very rich."

That same month, Motorola invested $260 million in Fleet Call while its engineers set about perfecting the SMR digital phone. Teams of lawyers and accountants began debating how much Fleet Call would pay for that new technology, and despite Motorola's capital investment, those negotiations dragged on for months. Through the spring of 1990, Fleet Call negotiated with both Motorola and, as a backup, E. F. Johnson. In the meantime, O'Brien continued his acquisition binge, buying every megahertz of spectrum he could find, while observers still assumed he was simply—and inexplicably—trying to become the king of taxicab dispatching. By the summer of 1990, Fleet Call had spent $250 million acquiring about 1,600 dispatch channels in its six target cities, and still O'Brien continued his manic scramble to find more money.

Paradoxically, the success of the cellular story on Wall Street in the late 1980s would prove the biggest hurdle for Fleet Call to overcome in trying to finance its alternative mobile-phone system. When he went to visit one group of investment bankers, O'Brien recalls, they flatly refused to believe that SMR channels and cellular channels could be used interchangeably. "You're lying," he recalls one banker declaring. "Cellular is a duopoly. What you're talking about is a complete hoax."

"They just didn't want to be told there were any chinks in the cellular story," says O'Brien, "because at that point the cellular story was so hot." If someone could indeed build a third network out of these spectrum dregs, then the soaring cellular values would be seriously undercut, potentially costing cellular investors hundreds of millions of dollars. Was O'Brien right? Most of Wall Street refused to believe he was.

Even as Fleet Call amassed its spectrum hoard, the company's lobbyists continued to seek FCC permission to switch to digital plus cellular architecture. The company's reasons for requesting the rule changes were, of course, financial: Fleet Call could accommodate and sell service to thousands more people. But the lobbyists' argument took a different angle.

Getting a third mobile telephone competitor on the air in already-overloaded big cities such as Los Angeles and New York, Fleet Call's lobbyists argued, would give customers more choice and cause prices to fall. Given that the FCC's stated mission was public service, there was no good reason why the commission shouldn't encourage more efficient use of the neglected SMR-spectrum bands. Why shouldn't the commission encourage competition? The answer, of course, was that it should.

Despite vigorous lobbying from cellular operators, who were aghast at the idea of a third competitor suddenly springing up out of nowhere, the FCC granted Fleet Call authority to build digital mobile systems in its six cities in February 1991. Not unexpectedly, the commission also decreed that the company would have to continue serving the existing dispatch customers: Fleet Call would have to keep offering central dispatch features on its phones, rather than being allowed to market simple mobile telephones. But overall, that was a small price to pay for a decision that could lead to a much bigger payoff than O'Brien had envisioned when he first scribbled his plan on a yellow pad four years earlier.

The cellular carriers were incensed by the FCC's decision. The industry had always been defined by the duopoly of license holders; why was O'Brien suddenly allowed to change the rules? He'd gotten his spectrum for a fraction of what they'd paid for theirs, and now his company was poised to steal their rightful customers away. But not everyone was dismayed by the ruling: As the cellular operators griped, Fleet Call copycats began organizing. Fleet Call had snatched up the top six markets, and a "son of Fleet Call" O'Brien had helped start, a company called Dispatch Communications (DisCom), was going after the next six, but new copycats began buying SMR licenses in the smaller cities Fleet Call and DisCom had ignored.

By the fall of 1991, Fleet Call's momentum was surging. In September, Motorola introduced the fruits of its labor: the world's first combination digital dispatch radio and cell phone, which they dubbed Enhanced SMR (ESMR). Fleet Call became the first customer for the new technology. By December, O'Brien's four years of tireless campaigning had brought Fleet Call some 61 million POPs, for which it had paid an estimated five dollars per POP. Riding high on expectations for its new systems, Fleet Call planned to go public: It would offer up to 11 million shares at eighteen to twenty dollars in an IPO scheduled for January 1992.

Unfortunately, that winter the U.S. economy was in the midst of a cold spell—particularly for wireless stocks—and when the Fleet Call offering was served up, investors proved reluctant to wager on something so speculative. Adding to investors' jitters was a *Wall Street Journal* story critical of Motorola's technology; the ESMR phones, the story predicted, would never be as good as cellular phones. With investor reaction lukewarm, Fleet Call had no choice but to scale back its aspirations for the IPO. In January, the company went public, selling 7.5 million shares at fifteen dollars—raising only half the $200 million O'Brien had hoped for. Still, O'Brien's five-year odyssey looked worth it so far; his Fleet Call shares gave him a paper net worth of more than $18 million.

Over the next year and a half, Fleet Call ate through the IPO proceeds and struggled to survive on the revenues of its older dispatch businesses, while McAuley and Motorola raced to get the company's first ESMR system on-line in Los Angeles by August 1993. Morgan O'Brien, now hopelessly addicted to the spectrum hunt, kept acquiring other SMR operators even as Fleet Call began marketing to its target customers in Los Angeles. By now, O'Brien's aspirations had spread well beyond the top six markets: With the roll-up of DisCom in 1993 and a host of new, more far-flung acquisitions, Fleet Call was developing an enviable footprint. As the Los Angeles launch approached, O'Brien—who had finally given up his law practice—looked at what the last six years of frenetic deal making had wrought.

Learning as he went, risking his comfortable career, borrowing millions of dollars and trusting in his ability to sway FCC bureaucrats, this former lawyer had somehow, improbably, built the framework of a wireless powerhouse. What had been a relatively primitive tool for specialized dispatch services—the SMR radio—was now a digital mobile phone. What had been neglected bands of spectrum were now the underpinnings of a new cellular company. And to the surprise of just about everyone, the latest blitz of acquisitions made Fleet Call by March 1993 the largest holder of wireless POPs in the country. Although the spectrum was skimpy and the new ESMR phones were unproven, Fleet Call now held more POPs than even McCaw—and better yet, it held 100-percent ownership of all the top markets. Suddenly, Fleet Call was in a position to beat Craig McCaw to completing a nationwide footprint.

Once a quaint idea for a niche product, Fleet Call was, O'Brien now believed, the vanguard of the next generation of telecommunications. He wanted his company's name to reflect that. On March 24, 1993, Fleet Call officially changed its name to Nextel. The last six years had been a phenomenal ride, but O'Brien had even bigger plans for the next three: He aimed to complete the nationwide network by the end of 1996.

EVERYTHING WAS GOING WONDERFULLY. Then the new phones got turned on.

When Nextel's L.A. system went on-line in August 1993, the reaction to the phones was searing. "Nextel's handsets are heavy, clumsy and expensive," Roger McNamee, a general partner at Integral Capital Partners, told the *Wall Street Journal*. "Why would anyone want one of these?" Cellular consultant Ronald Bennett complained about the coverage in the same article, charging that, "You get cut off and fade out." Though Nextel and Motorola insisted that the new ESMR technology was working well, similar complaints were legion in the early days of its hardware rebuild.

Even though its technology received less-than-rave reviews, Nextel enjoyed a remarkable run as one of the hottest telecom companies through the fall of 1993. Much of the hype was driven by Nextel's aggressive growth. Not only was the company engaged in an unending spectrum rush—in October, the company announced it would acquire PowerFone as well as the West Coast assets of Questar and Advanced MobileComm Inc.—but by this time, Nextel had more than 350 employees, and its annual revenues were in excess of $53 million. Nextel had also attracted some big-name equity investors, including Comcast and Nippon Telephone (NTT). And O'Brien's biggest deal was yet to come.

In November, Nextel announced it would buy a raft of SMR licenses from the company that owned more of them than anyone: Motorola. Though it owned more licenses than Nextel, many of Motorola's markets were smaller and scattered—not much use to the equipment behemoth, but valuable for Nextel in its quest to bill itself as a nationwide player. The Motorola deal called for a stock-for-spectrum swap worth about $1.8 billion; Motorola would get 20 percent of Nextel, and Nextel would get dispatch systems in twenty-one states.

"It's the mother lode of acquisitions!" O'Brien gushed at a news conference announcing the deal, which would give Nextel licenses covering an astonishing 180 million POPs. "Nextel is better positioned than any other," he continued, "to put together a nationwide network using one technology." Nextel was now assured entry into the big leagues: MCI predicted that this deal plus Motorola's digital technology would give Nextel "a two-year jump on existing cellular providers." "Everyone else," declared O'Brien, "will be playing catch-up."

Wall Street seemed to agree. In late 1993, Nextel's stock soared to fifty-five dollars—a 350-percent increase over the IPO price—giving the company a valuation of over $3 billion. And incredibly, an even bigger announcement—one that packed a delicious irony—was yet to come.

In February 1994, MCI announced plans to purchase 22 million shares—about 17 percent—of Nextel stock, at a price of $1.3 billion. Coming only eight months after AT&T's purchase of McCaw Cellular, the deal seemed to signal a trend: The big long-distance companies that had foolishly abandoned cellular in the early years were now paying dearly to get back in. The irony was that MCI's original cellular properties—the POPs it sold to McCaw in 1986 in the Airsignal transaction—had made up a significant chunk of what McCaw was now in the process of selling to AT&T. And now MCI had to look to Morgan O'Brien's taxicab licenses for its belated reentry into local wireless services.

Following the MCI announcement, things moved into hyperdrive for Morgan O'Brien and his company. In its push to cobble together enough POPs for a true nationwide network, Nextel began buying up its copycat competitors in earnest through the summer of 1994. In July, Nextel announced it would buy OneComm, its biggest SMR copycat. In August, Nextel announced a joint venture with Dial Page Inc., another major SMR aggregator.

The buying spree had a single goal: to erase Nextel's only well-known marketing disadvantage. The nation's cellular systems might have been owned by dozens of different competitors, but the phones, at least theoretically, worked anywhere. Sure you might have to pay roaming charges when using regular cell phones, but at least they worked—a Nextel phone only worked in those few big cities where common ESMR systems could be constructed. O'Brien wanted that coveted nationwide footprint so he could go head-to-head with his "it works anywhere" competition.

But behind the scenes, all was not well. Though Nextel had announced both the Motorola and MCI deals, neither one had yet been finalized. And while Motorola had close ties with Nextel thanks to their equipment deal, Motorola executives were very unhappy with the proposed MCI investment—because MCI was unhappy with Motorola's ESMR technology. Ill feelings were exacerbated by MCI's bullheaded insistence that their deal be announced before Motorola and Nextel could work out a solution to the technical issues.

Things hadn't changed at MCI; the company's hallmarks were still arrogance, pretentiousness and presumption. When Brian McAuley warned MCI executives that, in the event of an irresolvable power struggle, Nextel would jettison its MCI deal in favor of Motorola, they refused to believe him.

"It was almost like cold war politics," remembers O'Brien. "Each of them had their own vital interests, and to some degree their vital interests were at cross-purposes. And for us to be able to do this deal, we had to resolve them."

The issue was simple: Motorola's phones "stunk," in the words of one MCI executive. They didn't work because Nextel (and now MCI) wanted them to do too much.

There were two related problems. First, Nextel had been cobbled together from numerous old SMR licenses; the company owned different channels—and varying numbers of channels—in every market, which required the phones to search out sometimes scarce open channels. Second, the hardware was more expensive than cellular, for two reasons: ESMR phone technology was brand-new, and Nextel had only one supplier.

Nextel was caught between having unexpectedly large ESMR construction costs and a still limited amount of spectrum. It would take a lot of customers making a lot of phone calls to pay the bills, which had led Motorola to deploy a capacity-stretching hardware design: The ESMR phones used a high-capacity digital processor that forced six conversations into one channel, as opposed to the three or four conversations per channel the new digital cellular phones were using.

In the Motorola lab, the ESMR phones worked flawlessly. But once the system was installed on radio towers and rooftops in the hills and valleys around Los Angeles, the service proved to be surprisingly poor. Now came the sticky part. Motorola was a major Nextel stockholder, and the owner of an enormous amount of SMR spectrum that Nextel still hoped to buy. This produced a thorny conflict-of-interest problem between Nextel and MCI: Who would decide whether Motorola's product was acceptable? Who could force them to rip it out and start over? And who would pay for it?

As MCI saw it, the only solution to the quality problem was to cut the number of calls the systems would jam into a channel. Instead of six to a channel, three to a channel would restore quality sound. Unfortunately, this threw the arithmetic of the MCI deal completely out of whack. Cutting the channel capacity in half meant cutting in half the number of customers Nextel could eventually serve. But reducing the number of customers in MCI's financial models also meant cutting the revenue forecasts. And cutting the revenue meant cutting the price MCI thought it could pay. MCI had offered Nextel $21 per share in the deal; the way Richard Liebhaber, MCI's senior VP in charge of the Nextel negotiations figured it, the ripple effect of decreasing the digital channel capacity could devalue Nextel stock down to about $14 per share. And that's the price MCI offered in a renegotiated deal. O'Brien and the Nextel board balked.

"It blew up at the last minute," says O'Brien. Wall Street was quick to judge the collapse; Nextel's high-flying stock slid from $30.50 to $25.25 on the news.

The MCI deal's collapse was a stupefying blow to O'Brien. The grander his plan became, the more capital it required. With MCI's money, he would have been able to go head-to-head with AT&T and the RBOCs in building a nationwide system. But now he was back in the ranks of the amateurs, having been unable to close the last deal that stood between him and the big leagues. Now O'Brien would have to start over in his search for cash—if he had time before the money ran out.

By March 1995, Nextel announced that it needed financing totaling $700 million to build out all its acquisitions, including forays O'Brien had made into Canada and Mexico. Worse yet, Nextel's biggest stockholder was his troubled hardware supplier, and with MCI's exit, O'Brien had just lost his best negotiating leverage over Motorola. The higher the stakes, the harder the fall, and O'Brien could see his business lurching toward insolvency.

Not long after the MCI deal collapsed, O'Brien turned fifty—a particularly difficult milestone on which to reflect on a recent failure. "It was terrible, terrible times," he recalls. To combat his growing anxiety, O'Brien threw a huge party for himself, setting up a complex of heated tents in his backyard and inviting 250 people to celebrate. "This is how I [decided] to respond to the fact that life was trying to push me down," he said later. He even invited a contact from MCI, to show he had no hard feelings.

In the first eleven days of 1995, Nextel's shares dropped a sickening 25 percent, and the slide continued until shares were selling at less than ten dollars—down from fifty-five dollars a mere eighteen months earlier. Nextel's phones, with their newfangled technology, were continually slammed in the press by dissatisfied users, at least one of whom compared their sound to being "like you're underwater." Rumors began circulating that Motorola was planning to abandon Nextel as well.

Had Morgan O'Brien made an eight-year-long, billion-dollar mistake? Perhaps his dream of creating a viable third network was just that: a dream. There was probably a reason, after all, why none of the cellular geniuses had gone after that cheap SMR spectrum.

Nearly despondent, O'Brien went with his wife and four friends to the Caribbean getaway of St. Lucia, the same day his company's stock slumped to nine dollars. What would he do next? Looking ahead, he didn't see too many realistic options on the horizon. Was this the end of the line?

THE FIRST MORNING IN ST. LUCIA, the phone rang. It was a colleague of O'Brien's calling.

"Can you meet Craig McCaw this afternoon or tomorrow morning in Washington?" he asked.

"I can't think of anything else I'd rather do than meet Craig McCaw," replied O'Brien, "but please don't make it tomorrow." But Craig didn't want to wait. He wanted to talk to O'Brien as soon as he could. Why not, the intermediary suggested, talk to him on the phone, just as long as there was no one else around to overhear it? O'Brien agreed, and a time for the call was arranged.

Soon, O'Brien found himself on the phone with the now-legendary cell phone entrepreneur. "He's saying, 'I don't really have any fixed ideas about this,'" O'Brien recalls, "'but it just seems to me that maybe I could become a shareholder. Maybe because of my experience, I could add value to the company. I need to know whether that would be something you'd be willing to consider.'" To O'Brien's astonishment, Craig made no mention of the fact that Nextel was clearly in a desperate position. It would have been easy, O'Brien recalls, for him to have said, "you're over a barrel and you're damn lucky to get me." But Craig simply—and rather humbly, thought O'Brien— submitted that he might be able to help the company.

When O'Brien got off the phone, he called Nextel vice president Jack Markell. "I have proof of the existence of God," he said. "Guess who's interested in being an investor in Nextel."

Just like that, with one out-of-the-blue phone call, Nextel had found its savior. Craig McCaw was, of course, not your ordinary investor: In most investments, the money is the key benefit. But Craig, O'Brien knew, could offer not only money but a team of telecommunications' savviest executives. Besides that, there was tremendous value in the mere fact that Craig was showing interest in Nextel. Following the sale of McCaw to AT&T, Wall Street had revised its earlier, skeptical view of the inscrutable CEO: Now Craig McCaw's ideas were granted instant legitimacy and cachet. If Craig was interested in Nextel, went the conventional wisdom, then he must be seeing something everyone else was missing.

If Craig invested in Nextel, it would be a remarkable full-circle move for the cellular pioneer. When he sold McCaw Cellular to AT&T, he had more or less exited the industry he'd helped build. Buying into Nextel would put him right back in the action, as a competitor with his former company.

True to form, Craig McCaw was more interested in making a deal than in talking endlessly about it. About three months after his January phone call to O'Brien, the details of the McCaw investment were nearly finalized.

A phalanx of negotiators was involved in the final week of talks. A delighted O'Brien worked with Scot Jarvis (who'd declined work at AT&T in order to stay with Craig) and Dennis Weibling, and they joined teams of lawyers from both sides in a New York law firm to finalize things. Craig, meanwhile, stayed in a nearby hotel suite, keeping abreast of things while staying away from the meeting rooms.

Everything went remarkably smoothly, and on the evening of Tuesday, April 4, the documents were ready for signatures. A press conference had been scheduled for the next morning, at which Craig, O'Brien and Motorola chairman Chris Galvin would speak. Pleased with their efforts, the negotiating teams prepared to end their last meeting. Then the phone rang.

It was Craig. He had a short message for his team.

"I don't want to do this," he told them.

"Oh, Jesus," thought Jarvis as he glanced at Dennis Weibling. Craig couldn't be serious, could he? All this negotiation, everything nailed down, only the signatures left to fill in. And suddenly Craig wants to back out?

Tim Jensen, Craig's general counsel, took the phone. "Craig," he said gently to his billionaire boss, "I'm afraid that time has passed. You could back out if you want, but you're subjecting yourself to a big lawsuit for not negotiating in good faith."

Jarvis watched Jensen's face as he listened to the response. Grudgingly, Craig relented to the purchase, drawing relieved sighs from his team. The next morning, the press conference went on as scheduled; no one had any idea how close the deal had come to being derailed.

The deal called for Craig and his family to invest up to $1.1 billion in Nextel over the next seven years, taking up to 23.5 percent of the company in return. Though he would own less than a quarter of the company, Craig received unusually broad control in the deal. "Mixing one part Craig McCaw vision with one part Motorola technology gives us at Nextel a recipe for even more potent integrated wireless business solutions," O'Brien declared at the April 5 press conference announcing the deal. The market seemed to agree; Nextel's shares leapt from $13.25 to $16.625 that day.

The deal, wrote the *Washington Post*, made Craig McCaw the "Michael Jordan of the communications industry." After selling the dominant American cellular company for the equivalent of $275 per POP, he was now entering the wireless fray through another door—and paying less than $20 per POP for the privilege.

There was one other subplot to the purchase that the glowing press accounts missed. In his original call to Morgan O'Brien, Craig had really only been interested in buying Nextel's huge spectrum assets at "bargain-basement prices," as Jarvis recalls. It was only after negotiators struck the original deal that the issue of Motorola's failing ESMR technology came up.

Craig's impulse was to ditch the ESMR technology in favor of a simpler, less compressed (and thus potentially less valuable) analog technology. For the man seen as the visionary of the wireless industry, this was a puzzling decision: Digital was clearly the future of wireless; why go backwards toward analog, especially when Motorola had done so much work on its digital ESMR?

Scot Jarvis thought Craig's analog suggestion was folly. "Why don't we take a look at what we have here," he asked his boss, "and see if it's fixable?" After all, Jarvis argued, Nextel "had so much debt and so much invested in this technology." Once again, Craig consented. And once that decision was made, he made fixing the broken technology a primary goal. If O'Brien hadn't had the clout to get Motorola motivated to solve its technological troubles, the addition of Craig McCaw to the Nextel team solved that problem. At the insistence of Craig, Motorola redoubled its efforts to fix the ESMR phones.

For his part, Craig became enamored of the very feature of the ESMR phones that O'Brien had wanted to jettison. When the FCC had ordered Fleet Call to keep its dispatch features on its new digital phones, O'Brien had been disappointed. But Craig seized on the feature, touting it as a one-of-a-kind strength. At the press conference announcing his investment, he characterized the Nextel phones this way: "If cellular is Chevrolets and Hondas, this is a Jeep. It's a more flexible product. You can have, for instance, five or six people working in stream-of-consciousness mode. . . They would pick up the receiver and reach the whole group or just one person. They could never accomplish that on a switch-based telephone." The phones' dispatch ability, Craig believed, would prove a valuable feature for the business customers Nextel hoped to attract.

With Craig McCaw's money and influence, a retooled phone and a growing spectrum footprint, by 1995 Nextel was positioned to change the cellular industry. At the same time, a new form of competition was arriving on the scene, this one the product of a new FCC spectrum allocation. But this time, the FCC wouldn't be giving away its spectrum licenses.

21

GOING, GOING, GONE

TEN YEARS AFTER DISTRIBUTING THE FIRST CELLULAR LICENSES, the government finally put a stop to the great federal giveaway.

Throughout the '80s, the FCC had fiddled repeatedly with its spectrum-distribution rules. From comparative hearings to lotteries, then to the multiple-rule variations for the lotteries, the FCC had tried in vain to figure out how to bring some order to the distribution of these public resources. In 1986, then-FCC chairman Mark S. Fowler had articulated the views of many when he told the House telecommunications subcommittee that the FCC should stop handing out licenses like free school lunches. Instead, Fowler said, the FCC should auction off any new licenses to the highest bidder.

"The biggest surprise is not the size of the missed opportunity," he told the lawmakers, "but that we persist in missing it. It's time to end the free ride."

The Reagan and Bush administrations both favored auctioning off spectrum, but congressional Democrats stonewalled, believing auctions would unfairly benefit larger, more deep-pocketed companies. But through the late 1980s, as the lotteries rewarded totally random speculators who then turned around and sold their licenses for huge sums, embarrassed FCC officials grew increasingly convinced that auctions were the only answer.

There was, however, one big problem: The FCC had no authority at that time to hold auctions. It would take seven years following Fowler's testimony before Congress granted the FCC auction authority in August 1993.

Within months, the FCC announced it would auction off another slice of spectrum, for a brand-new kind of wireless phone.

Standing on the South Lawn of the White House on July 22, 1993, Wayne Schelle found himself again at ground zero of a new telephone technology. He'd helped launch Baltimore-Washington's experimental cell phone system in the late 1970s, and through the 1980s he'd been at the forefront of the industry. Now he was helping introduce a new kind of phone—but as he addressed the gathering on the historic expanse of green outside the White House portico, it didn't sound like he was talking about a phone at all.

"PCS technology," Schelle announced, "will enable the newspaper to become a living, changing document that will combine the immediacy of television with the depth, power and convenience of the written word."

PCS, or Personal Communications Systems technology, was touted as a system that would one day soon bring all manner of data—including news, weather and stock quotes—to people's wireless phones. Because PCS used new blocks of higher-frequency spectrum, the phones could transfer more data at higher speeds than ordinary cell phones, though not yet to the degree Schelle talked about on the White House lawn. The main draw of PCS in the mid-'90s was something else altogether, something that had little to do with futuristic technological features. PCS (which was already up and running in some European countries) was, in the words of *The Economist*, "the industry's master plan for bringing mobile telephones to the masses."

Even in its simple, "me-too" cellular incarnation, PCS promised a number of benefits over regular cellular service. First, it used the latest versions of digital compression, allowing carriers to squeeze from three to ten times the capacity of cellular out of the spectrum—an important distinction as user numbers began their steep climb in the '90s. Second, PCS promised better reception, thanks to the fact that towers were positioned closer together and the phones used static-free digital technology. Third, lower-powered, tightly clustered architecture meant that PCS phones were smaller, lighter and less power-hungry, which translated into longer battery life than that of cell phones.

PCS technology offered, in short, the promise of better sound quality, more services and greater convenience than cell phones. But most important, the mere presence of another competitor on the wireless scene promised to drive cellular airtime prices down. These new phones would, the analysts believed, draw in the fourth wave—the late majority—to what was becoming a wireless revolution.

On the South Lawn that day, newly elected President Clinton and Vice President Gore echoed Schelle's enthusiasm for the new technology, but for different reasons. An auction of PCS spectrum would create, President Clinton declared, an information age "gold mine" comparable to the 1849 gold rush. The president cited a Congressional Budget Office study that predicted that auctions could bring more than $7 billion to the Treasury. In addition, he announced, "These new technologies will add at least 300,000 jobs."

The South Lawn demonstration was, in the words of one observer, little more than a "feel-good event." But no matter how hyperbolic the sound-bite rhetoric might have been, the upcoming PCS industry was in fact poised to change the face of wireless communications.

When the Omnibus Budget Reconciliation Act of 1993 granted the FCC authority to auction off spectrum, newly installed FCC chairman Reed Hundt—who had represented cellular lottery winners as a Washington communications lawyer—took up the auctions cause with something approaching religious zeal. Auctions would, Hundt believed, cure the litany of disorders afflicting the FCC's spectrum distribution. Unfortunately, Hundt failed to foresee that one element of the new auction plan would end up creating as much havoc as the lotteries had.

In deference to Congressional Democrats' concern that auctions would unfairly squeeze out smaller competitors, the 1993 act contained language directing the FCC to "ensure that small businesses, rural telephone companies, and businesses owned by members of minority groups and women are given the opportunity to participate in the provision of spectrum-based services." Further, the act directed the FCC to "consider the use of tax certificates, bidding preferences, and other procedures" to make this happen. This directive ensured that the auctions—nominally a free-market exercise—would eventually be sidetracked by yet another government welfare-style giveaway.

The first job facing Hundt and his staff was to develop rules for the PCS spectrum auction. The FCC decided the spectrum should be divided into six blocks, labeled A through F (as opposed to cellular spectrum, which had been divided into just two blocks, for wireline and nonwireline).

A- and B-block licenses, for huge 30 MHz swaths of spectrum comparable in capacity to that of cellular, would be sold for each of fifty-one huge Major Trading Areas (MTAs). The auction rules allowed for unrestricted competition—the capitalist's ideal of wide-open bidding, with the spectrum simply going to the highest bidder. The RBOCs, AT&T and other large companies were expected to be major bidders for these two blocks. The remaining four blocks, C through F, were four new licenses in each of 492 smaller regions called Basic Trading Areas (BTAs), with the C- and F-blocks set aside for so-called "designated entities"—the small and minority-owned businesses mentioned in the act.

Like the A- and B-blocks of spectrum, the C-block was comprised of a larger slice of spectrum; it was expected to generate the most auction competition among the "little people" bidders. What the FCC didn't anticipate was that it would also generate the same kind of greed, gambling and gall that had infected the lotteries.

———

THE A- AND B- BLOCK AUCTIONS, WHICH BEGAN ON DECEMBER 4, 1994, were marked by an eerie quiet. Instead of the tens of thousands of applicants the lotteries had attracted, there were only thirty. And instead of herding lottery hopefuls into a public auditorium to watch an antiquated plastic drum full of Ping-Pong balls spin around, the FCC bureaucrats simply sat staring at a handful of computer screens. It was an odd scene: Neither the applicants nor their attorneys were anywhere to be seen—they were miles away from Washington, staring at computer monitors of their own. Though the scene appeared quiet, it was dramatic nonetheless, with tens of millions of dollars being pledged via instantaneous software messages.

Three major bidders stood out. First, there was the newly merged AT&T-McCaw powerhouse. Second, there was "PCS Primeco," a joint venture formed by four RBOCs: Bell Atlantic, Nynex, U.S. West and AirTouch. Third, there was Sprint Telecommunications Venture, an alliance of Sprint Corp. and three cable TV companies: Cox, Comcast and Tele-Communications Inc. (TCI).

These major bidders sought PCS spectrum as a critical competitive weapon. The two consortia pooled resources in hopes of assuring themselves a "nationwide footprint" with which to battle AT&T, while several dozen smaller bidders—companies such as Alltel, Century Telephone, Comcast and TDS—aimed to expand their own regional footprints.

The auctions, conducted in a series of multiple daily-bidding "rounds," stretched over a period of months. Through January and February 1995, bids spiraled upward as companies tested each other and vied for their desired turf. Four months after they had begun, the A- and B-block auctions quietly came to end, when no one was willing to bid higher. The results that thrilled observers on all sides: Bidders had pledged nearly $8 billion—more than fifteen dollars per POP—for these new PCS licenses.

Success! An elated Reed Hundt took center stage at a photo op in which he presented an oversize check for $7.7 billion to President Clinton and Vice President Gore. The auction represented a revolution in American telecommunications policy, and Hundt, a man of apparently limitless self-regard, was happy to tell anyone who would listen that he was the man at the center of it. The A- and B-block auctions brought in bids 300 percent greater than most analysts had projected. Everyone benefited: the taxpayers, the FCC—and even, it could be argued, the bidders, as they were able to simply bid directly to the FCC for licenses, rather than having to chase down random lottery winners across the country.

At last, the FCC seemed to have figured out a successful, sensible formula for spectrum distribution. Then, just as quickly, they sabotaged it.

Even as the commission's halls resonated with self-congratulation, the intensive lobbying and planning taking place in its offices began to bode ill for the upcoming C-block auction. Congress had directed the FCC to encourage participation by women-owned, minority-owned and small businesses. In an effort to comply, the commission now spent weeks, then months, puzzling over the best way of doing that. What the commission neglected to consider was that the delay—which eventually stretched into a full year of deliberation—allowed dozens of would-be bidders to find ways to exploit every possible loophole in its sloppily drafted rules. It also meant a longer head start for A- and B-block license holders, which in turn meant a decrease in the value of the C-block licenses, which would logically lead to lower bids for it.

On December 18, 1995, the C-block auction began. It was obvious from the outset that things in this auction would be different: Almost 400 would-be bidders filled out the short forms required for participation. Lawyers preparing the paperwork made great sport of the new rules, often claiming their clients' companies deserved special consideration as "small businesses" when the opposite was closer to reality. One New York–based company, NextWave, applied as a "small business" even though it was headed by executives associated with giant cellphone manufacturer Qualcomm and had enough capital to make the tens of millions in deposits needed to bid on every single market. A company our firm launched, Go! Communications, also applied to bid as a "designated entity," even though we'd raised some $100 million in equity capital and another $700 million in loan commitments from a blue-chip list of investors. "Small business," indeed.

The lure for all these "designated entities" was the C-block auction's ridiculously generous financial rules: The FCC required that winning bidders pay only 10 percent down, while the remainder could be paid in installments over ten years. With license purchases being financed by the U.S. taxpayers, it was practically irresistible to bid.

Less than an hour after the C-block auction began, it looked as though things were already getting out of hand: PCS 2000 LP, a newly minted startup, bid $10 per POP for several top markets—an amount five times more than what its competitors were bidding. In four months of bidding, the A- and B-block licenses had slowly risen to a final average price of only $15 per POP; from this opening round, it looked as if the C-block bidding might leapfrog that in a matter of days.

How much were PCS licenses really worth? Were the experts who had dropped out of the A and B auctions at ten or twelve dollars per POP that badly mistaken about values? Or were these C-block bidders wildly over-bidding? With cellular POPs selling in the triple digits in the mid-'90s, it seemed reasonable to assume that bids of fifteen or twenty dollars per POP for PCS licenses were bargains. Yet they weren't.

First, these prices were simply for licenses; there were no systems in place, no customers and no revenues. Second, the "microcellular" design of PCS required many more towers than cellular, making the systems expensive to construct. Third, the C-block PCS licenses would grant the winning bidders the right to be the fifth or sixth carrier online in a given market: In many markets, five carriers—two cellular companies, Nextel and two PCS companies (the A- and B-block winners)—would already be up and running. With so much competition already in place, the C-block winner would have to build out its whole system immediately in order to compete; this was a tremendous financial burden and risk, especially compared to that faced by early cellular carriers, who only needed a couple of towers to get started. And because the existing operators would already have raked in the easy customers, there was no guarantee a latecomer C-block winner could draw enough users to make money.

The final reason was perhaps the most vexing, and it was further confirmation of the bidders' naivete. Though many expected that post-licensing financing would, as it had in cellular, be easy to come by, the reality would prove very different. As analyst Jonathan D. Foxman told the *Washington Post* midway through the auction, "For some companies, the bidding is getting very out of hand. People have the notion that just having the license is the key to success, that it doesn't matter what they bid because they'll be able to raise the money afterward. But that's a real mistake."

Unconcerned with such trifles as where to get financing, auction participants continued to bid with abandon. And in one remarkable instance, a
company bid with considerably more abandon than it had intended.

PCS 2000, a startup founded by former GCC application-mill heads
Quentin Breen and Anthony Easton, was funded with some $80 million
raised from the pair's usual list of gullible investors. Breen and Easton—
whose main concern was raking off their percentage "fees" from the partnerships they sold—bid eagerly on C-block licenses across the board, wan-
tonly pledging millions of dollars with a few strokes at a computer keyboard.

On January 23, 1996, Anthony Easton committed what came to be
known in FCC lore as the "fat finger" mistake: Intending to bid $18 million
on the Norfolk, Virginia, license, Easton apparently typed in an extra zero
by mistake. The company's bid: $180 million.

No one at PCS 2000 caught the error until that auction round was closed,
and according to the FCC's rules, the bid—as absurd as it was—would stand.
In a single keystroke, Easton had overbid by $162 million—more than dou-
ble the total capital PCS 2000 had in the bank. This simple error would result in years of chaos, with an FCC investigation, claims of misrepresenta-
tion and a lawsuit eventually leading to a decision to allow withdrawal of
the bid. Easton had made a fantastically boneheaded mistake, but it really
only pointed up a larger mistake being made by the FCC in the auctions.

All the bidders had submitted extensive financial documentation to the
FCC, including information on how much capital they had raised. During
the auction, the commission could have required that companies bid only
as much as their capital reserves would cover. Instead, it allowed bidders to
bid as high as they liked. For Reed Hundt, the only measure of auction success was the bottom line: the bigger the oversize check in his photo op, the
better the publicity.

Soon, bidders were pledging tens of millions of dollars in excess of their
available capital. Some didn't even have the money to cover the 10-percent
down payment—much less the other 90 percent of the purchase price. They
would, according to the auction rules, have ten years to pay. Still, many
knowledgeable observers were alarmed that bidders would so blithely blow
past the limits of their available capital.

By April, the rumblings of concern intensified. The list of active bidders
was, as expected, shrinking. But a closer look at the dropouts was revealing.
One by one, the bidders best positioned to evaluate the true value of the licenses—companies like Personal Connect, backed by Craig McCaw; Go!,

headed by ex-MCI executive Steve Zecola; and U. S. Airwaves Holdings, Inc., headed by former US West cellular president John DeFeo—were dropping out in disgust. Their combination of experience in the business and expert financial projections convinced them that the bids had risen above rational levels. Soon, the only bidders left were the relative amateurs—and their bids kept going higher. "This whole thing is a big mess," analyst Taylor Simmons told *RCR Wireless News*. "Can any good possibly come out of all this, except for more PR for Reed Hundt? I see a 'lose-lose' situation here: The winners will be in debt and the losers will badger the winners with lawsuits."

At last, Hundt sensed trouble. The FCC, he declared, would take a hard line on any company that bid more than it could ultimately pay; it would "go after" any deadbeats and reauction their licenses. It was a good sound-bite, but the FCC's rules would end up making this an embarrassingly hollow threat.

The C-block auction came to an end five months after it started, on May 6, 1996. On the face of it, it was fabulously successful, apparently netting more than $10 billion—an average of some forty dollars per POP—for the U.S. Treasury.

Three months later, about the time when the FCC began auctioning the D-, E- and F-blocks, that myth began to unravel. Just when the commission hoped more bidders would step up to pay big prices for these newest blocks of spectrum, word spread that the C-block winners were having trouble coming up with their initial 10 percent down, which was due in a matter of days. As the new auctions began, bankers were spooked by the sudden glut of spectrum. The *Wall Street Journal* summed up the situation: "Major C-block license holders are urgently trying to raise equity in the private and public markets," the paper reported. "They are being rebuffed on two counts: Some simply paid too much. They are 90 percent debt-financed with very little or negative equity below it compared to their publicly traded PCS peers. . . . The second major turnoff is that workouts are near impossible.

"The only player in these deals who can take a haircut is the government," the story concluded. "And it can't or won't—yet." But soon enough, it would appear the government would have no choice.

Inevitably the time of reckoning arrived. Eight of the winning C-block bidders—including the top three of NextWave, General Wireless Inc. and Pocket Communications Corp.—defaulted on their bids. Despite their grand plans and promises to pay, they simply couldn't come up with the money. Then things turned truly ugly.

As an embarrassed Hundt and FCC general counsel (later chairman) William Kennard maneuvered to reclaim and reauction the defaulted licenses, they made an astonishing discovery: They couldn't legally get the spectrum back. No one at the FCC had done enough homework on creditors' rights and bankruptcy law. The winning bidders insisted—citing legal authority—that they now "owned" the public radio spectrum, even though they hadn't paid for it. It was as though someone had contracted to buy a car with a minimal deposit and the dealer, having forgotten to include a lien in the paperwork, allowed the new owner to drive it away for a few hundred bucks and then claim it as an asset in bankruptcy court. No self-respecting used-car dealer would ever make such a basic mistake. Yet that's what the FCC lawyers had done.

When the top bidders sought bankruptcy protection, the once-promising auction devolved into a complete fiasco. Of the $10.2 billion pledged for C-block spectrum, at least $7 billion vanished with the defaults, a scandalous result that led to a change in FCC policy: In future auctions, bidders would have to pay in full rather than in installments.

It would take four agonizing years, the work of dozens of lawyers and several court rulings before the FCC could regain control of the disputed C-block licenses. Even so, appeals against pro-FCC court rulings continue.

In December 2000, the commission at last began to reauction those licenses, under rules that highlighted the conflict between its competing goals of maximizing auction profits while encouraging small business and competition. Under heavy lobbying pressure, the FCC once again rewrote its rules, opening gaping new loopholes that allowed the massive telecom providers to own up to 85-percent stakes in ostensibly "small-business" bidders.

By the time the reauction ended after 101 rounds of bidding on January 26, 2001, nearly $16.9 billion had been pledged—but 90 percent of the licenses intended for small business had been claimed by affiliates of the world's largest wireless carriers. Predictably, legitimate small-business bidders threatened lawsuits, while even the federal Small Business Administration joined the critics, calling its sister agency's latest rule rewrite "illogical and contradictory." The *New York Times*, calling the results "the worst of both worlds," quoted an anonymous FCC official as admitting, "this certainly does make us look like a bunch of idiots."

———

IN NOVEMBER 1995, WAYNE SCHELLE'S American Personal Communications became the first commercial PCS system to go on-line. A joint venture between Schelle's company and the Washington Post Co., APC went up in the Washington, D.C., area under the brand-name Sprint Spectrum.

The mere presence of a new, third option in Washington's wireless phone market (Nextel was then still straightening out its hardware glitches) would have been enough to spur competition and price battles. But Schelle also proved himself exceptionally adept at figuring out ways to lure new customers. As a result, competition among Washington carriers heated up almost instantly.

Before Schelle's PCS company rewrote the rules, cell phone pricing was a complex jumble of often confusing plans. Two things were universally true: Cell phone systems typically required customers to lock into one-year contracts, and in return they offered customers lower prices for the phones themselves. There were countless service pricing plans, using variables like peak and off-peak minutes, larger free roaming areas, free weekend calls and any other variable carriers could dream up. But no one had yet offered one seemingly obvious variant: Service without a contract.

Schelle's company turned the standard formula upside-down. Instead of subsidizing the cost of the handset by requiring a long-term commitment, he charged the actual (higher) cost of the phone and then allowed the customer the freedom of starting and ending service as he or she pleased. In retrospect, it seems a simple enough option, but at the time, no one had tried it.

Another element Schelle's company pioneered was the "phone in a box." Ever since the first cell phone system had gone on-line, the standard way to get a phone was to go to a carrier's or agent's office, fill out lengthy forms and then wait—sometimes for hours—for your credit to be checked and your phone to be activated. Americans, Schelle realized, like to be able to touch and handle potential purchases, and to have them work immediately. For the first time, APC allowed wireless customers to walk into a store, buy a phone, turn it on and get it instantly activated.

The only real drawback to PCS phones was the lack of coverage. You could only use a PCS phone in a market where a PCS system was running, and in the mid-'90s, hardly any had been built out yet. Until more cities got on the air, PCS phones would be worthless when traveling.

The major PCS players raced to fix this flaw; by 1997, Sprint PCS had licenses covering 190 million POPs across the country, and it was busily building out its nationwide network. AT&T was simultaneously chasing the same goal; with more than 75 percent of the country covered by its analog and digital holdings, the company continued filling in spectrum holes with

PCS licenses and affiliate agreements with other carriers as it sped toward total nationwide service.

Many observers had expected PCS to overtake cellular as the wireless medium of choice. Over the next few years, however, they were surprised to see another trend: Customers didn't know—or didn't care—about the difference between analog cellular, digital cellular and PCS. As John Kane, CEO of Telseon, told *Telephony* magazine, "It's kind of like a postage stamp on a social security check. People want what's in the envelope. They don't care about the stamp." Already wireless was becoming just another commodity, and consumers were quickly learning that the only things that mattered were price and sound quality.

As a result, PCS carriers soon learned to stress their lower prices over their phones' data capabilities or special features. The price wars that PCS launched in the late 1990s brought the cost of wireless phones down to a new tipping point, and at last the fourth wave of customers began buying up phones.

In early 1998, AT&T launched its own smart bomb in the battle for subscribers, one that proved a devastating blow to its wireless competitors. AT&T's Digital One Rate was the first to allow customers to pay a flat rate for an allotted number of minutes. In addition, some versions of the plan promised no extra long-distance charges and free roaming wherever AT&T offered service (which was nearly the entire United States). No other company could match these last two offers, for two reasons: AT&T owned the long-distance wires, and it was the only wireless carrier with a nationwide license footprint big enough to allow it to offer free roaming. For prices ranging from $60 per month (for 300 minutes of monthly talk) to $150 per month (for 1,400 minutes of use), the Digital One Rate plan blew away the competition.

Hundreds of thousands of customers flocked to buy the plan, so many that even AT&T was surprised. "We underestimated the demand for simplicity," AT&T's Daniel Hesse told *Time* magazine, "We had no idea how successful it would be."

With prices falling, handsets shrinking, battery-life lengthening and sound quality improving, wireless phones finally, in the late 1990s, turned the corner from luxury items to must-have items. The wireless revolution was now a reality.

22

EVERYBODY'S GOT ONE

THOUGH IT WAS FIFTEEN YEARS IN THE MAKING, the cell phone revolution seemed to happen all at once. Suddenly, every other person strolling down a city sidewalk seemed to be chattering away on a phone. High-school students began carrying them to school, and soon their little brothers and sisters were carrying their own to the playground as well. When a phone rang in a coffeeshop, nobody peered in curiosity toward the source of the sound anymore; everyone instinctively reached toward his or her own pocket or bag.

Theaters began posting "Please turn off cell phones now" signs in their lobbies, and occasionally patrons were publicly rebuked from the stage when high-pitched rings interrupted a soliloquy. Plagued by substandard sound quality, many cell phone users were forced to raise their voices, even shout, to be heard on their portables, irritating countless fellow citizens within earshot—and drawing a reprimand from syndicated columnist Miss Manners in 1997, who decried all the shouting as an "etiquette violation."

In restaurants, clashes occurred between cell phone users and patrons who felt that noisy, one-sided conversations were an unacceptable form of noise pollution. One company seized on the growing discontent, marketing a $900 device that electronically (and illegally, under FCC rules) jams cell phone signals, creating a quiet zone wherever it's used. Some restaurateurs instituted "no cell phone" policies in their dining rooms, though the directives were usually couched as a gentle urging rather than an outright ban for fear of offending users. One Manhattan restaurant printed a warning on its menu: "The use of cellular phones in the restaurant interferes with the preparation of the risotto."

That warning was a tongue-in-cheek reference to one of the more controversial policies regarding cell phones: the banning of their use on commercial airlines. In 1988, the FCC proposed a ban on cell phones on planes in flight, warning that they "could disrupt all other communications using the same frequency within the market and in adjacent markets." Several years later, the FAA followed with a broader ban, forbidding the use of cell phones (as well as laptops, CD players and other electronic devices) at any time, in flight or on the tarmac. In practice, however, many flight attendants have given up enforcing the ban while on the ground, partly because so many people ignore it. From a technological standpoint, this is no problem, as there was really no compelling reason to enact such a ban in the first place. The only thing it accomplishes is saving irritated, weary passengers from having to listen to their seatmates yammer on their phones.

On many airlines, flight attendants cheerily announce pre-flight that cell phones may interfere with cockpit navigation systems. This is untrue, for two reasons. First, there are no instruments in the cockpits of commercial aircraft that operate in—or even close to—the 800 MHz cellular spectrum band. Second, the FCC's design specifications for all manner of radios specifically prohibit the manufacture of any device that would interfere with any other device at another frequency.

Then why is there still a strictly enforced ban on in-flight use of cell phones? The original FCC ban was enacted for another, somewhat less dramatic reason. When a cell phone user makes a call on the ground, the phone's wireless signals are naturally blocked by topographical and man-made obstructions—hills, buildings and the like. But when a user calls from high up in the air, where there are no obstructions, wireless waves travel for miles in every direction, to multiple cell towers—all of which may try to carry the call. If even a fraction of the millions of travelers jetting across the country every day used their cell phones while aloft, chaos would ensue on the ground.

The airlines are happy enough to enforce the bans, especially since they receive up to 15 percent of the revenue from the seat-mounted wireless phones installed for passengers' use. Because these phones use a different set of radio frequencies and a different system architecture than cellular, they don't interfere with each other the way cell phones might at 30,000 feet. At rates of a few dollars per minute, these in-flight phones bring in a nice chunk of found revenue for the airlines.

Still, why would the airlines perpetuate the myth of interference with cockpit instruments? Thanks to a few unexplained incidents in which navigational instruments malfunctioned while electronic devices were in use during flight, the airlines consider it justifiable to issue these stronger warnings. It is difficult enough to convince passengers to forgo making calls during flights; the suggestion that safety may be compromised is a compelling reason for passengers to comply. Even so, many flout the ban, either by sneaking calls in the airline toilet or by brazenly calling despite the flight attendants' admonishments. A few transgressors have been prosecuted, and at least one—a British oil worker who refused to turn off his phone on a British Airways flight from Spain—was sent to prison.

Talking while traveling is a hot-button issue not only on airplanes, but in cars as well. From the earliest days of the industry, consumer groups warned that drivers distracted while chatting on cell phones were a hazard on the nation's highways. Cell phone apologists argued that talking on a phone was no different than talking to a passenger, which no one would dream of outlawing. Though both sides agreed that using a hands-free headset reduced the risk of an accident, the gap between those who would ban cell phone chatting in cars and those who defend it has only widened with time.

A controversial 1985 study sponsored by AT&T, Bell Atlantic and the American Automobile Association concluded that "drivers with car phones spend twice the average time on the road, but are only half as likely to be involved in a traffic accident." Those figures would be disputed by later studies, which found significant increases in risk when drivers were on the phone.

In 1996, a Rochester Institute of Technology study found a "34 percent increase in risk of having an accident when using cell phones in cars." And in 1997, a University of Toronto study stated that "drivers face a fourfold increase in risk of having an injury-producing accident when using a cellular telephone." The numbers were sobering, but it was another statement in the Toronto study that created a public and media frenzy. The relative risk of driving while talking, the study declared, was "similar to the hazard associated with driving with a blood alcohol level at the legal limit, .10 percent."

That statement was like a rhetorical missile for the antiphone crusade. Media outlets pounced on the comparison, opening stories with shock-value leads and headlines. "Car Phones as Big a Menace as Drunken Driving," blared one headline. "Reach Out and Crash Into Someone," went another. And *Time* magazine gravely intoned, "Imagine if every time you took to the road, 35 million of your fellow drivers were legally drunk."

The studies, not surprisingly, raised as many questions as they professed to answer. There were simply too many variables: Was the cell phone-using accident victim talking hands-free, or was he trying to dial a handheld cell phone while smoking a cigarette in a snowstorm? Was he (or the driver of the other car) drinking? Were there other distractions in the car, such as children arguing in the back seat? The debate continued to simmer, with the occasional high-profile accident temporarily inflaming calls for a ban. When country music star George Jones crashed his sport utility vehicle while reaching for a cell phone in 1999 (the accident, in which his liver was pierced and a lung punctured, nearly killed Jones), the pro-ban lobby took advantage of the headlines to press its case. But when a AAA study released in 2001 showed that cell phones were a factor in only 1.5 percent of accidents between 1995–98, many felt the issue had been put to rest.

In the mid- to late-90s, a few towns and municipalities across the country began passing laws to curb talking and driving. In Brooklyn, Ohio—the Cleveland suburb generally recognized as the first to implement mandatory seat-belt laws—an ordinance was passed making it illegal to talk on a cell phone while driving unless both hands were on the steering wheel. Taxicab and limousine drivers in New York were banned from using phones while their vehicles were in motion. But while increasing numbers of lawmaking bodies passed such measures, most were afraid to consider the most draconian move: an outright ban on using cell phones in cars.

Some countries did enact total bans, notably Spain, Brazil and Israel. But in the United States, the power of the libertarian lobby was too great, even though one survey sponsored by the Colonial Penn Safe Driver Center indicated that nearly half of Americans would support such a ban. Not surprisingly, 85 percent of those respondents who supported a total ban did not own cell phones themselves. The study didn't ask how many were registered voters, but as U.S. cell phone usage approaches 40 percent, the odds of a total ban continue to shrink. Of the thirty-seven states that by December 2000 had considered such legislation, only three—California, Florida and Massachusetts—enacted restrictions, and none of those were outright bans.

———

As if the prospect of plunging airplanes and car wrecks wasn't enough to put people off cell phones, another scare emerged in the 1990s. This one had the potential to destroy the industry completely.

In 1992, Florida resident David Reynard filed a lawsuit against several industry names, including his cell phone carrier and manufacturer NEC, claiming that radiation from his wife's cell phone had caused her to develop a deadly brain tumor. In early 1993, Reynard appeared on CNN talk show *Larry King Live* to press his case, kicking up a national media whirlwind. The story had everything: controversy, death, danger, and at the center of it, a sexy, hip product. For months, the debate raged on television, in the newspapers and around the watercooler: Is your cell phone killing you?

Reynard's suit was tossed out, but the effect of his allegation was that of dropping poison in a well: Though his wife's death was an isolated case, and though there were hundreds of millions of healthy users worldwide, the suggestion that cell phones might cause cancer immediately tainted the entire industry. This was simply too serious—and too superficially believable—to ignore.

Cell phones put out electromagnetic radiation that is, the critics are quick to note, only a slightly different version of the stuff that bakes chickens in microwave ovens and causes birth defects at Chernobyl. What they're not so quick to note is that everyday things such as television sets, police radar guns, personal computers—even a sunny day at the beach—also expose us to electromagnetic radiation.

If cell phones could be proven to increase the risk of cancer, it would be a financial disaster for the industry. With billions of dollars and the health of millions of users at stake, universities, foundations, the industry and the government launched studies to examine the issue. And while the Cellular Telephone Industry Association's (CTIA) position suggested the uproar was about nothing, stating that "Electromagnetic radio signals, characteristic of those of wireless telephones, are not a cancer initiator or promoter," the multitude of studies suggested that it was, unclear what the risk, if any, might be.

The studies ran the gamut, from finding no risk at all to indications of probable risk. Dr. Mays L. Swicord, Motorola's director of biological research, was quoted in *Business Week* insisting there was no "repeatable or established" evidence of problems due to cell phone radiation. A study of Motorola employees undertaken over a twenty-year period, from 1976 to 1996, seemed to bear him out: There was no increased incidence of cancer among the study's sampling of nearly 2,000 employees (many of whom used cell phones from the very first days they were available). On the other hand, an American Health Foundation research team found, after studying nearly 500 brain-tumor patients, that in a subgroup of 35 patients "there was some correlation between cell phone use and a rare type of brain cancer." And in

May 2000, a British government report inflamed anxiety by recommending that children not be allowed to use cell phones.

Fears were greatly mollified in February 2001 when a study of 430,000 Danes—the biggest study yet undertaken—found no sign of increased rates of cancer among cell phone users. Still, the issue is not a simple one, partly because cell phones haven't been around very long in relative terms: The majority of customers have been using their phones for a decade or less. Also complicating matters are the different characteristics of the phones themselves. In Europe, for example, the frequencies deployed are different than those in the United States. In addition, the strength of emitted radiation varies widely among different types of phones, depending on both manufacturer and technology (PCS-GSM versus cellular TDMA, for example).

Given the uncertainty, the industry faced two main problems by the late 90s: First, that consumer fear could harm sales; and second, that lawyers might file large-scale lawsuits on behalf of consumers, in much the same way that suits had been filed against the tobacco industry. The lawsuit fear was intensified by the news that Peter Angelos, a phlegmatic, bullheaded plaintiffs' attorney (and owner of the Baltimore Orioles) who had successfully sued the U.S. tobacco industry, was considering filing such a suit. Faced with these problems, the industry took action.

First, though they still maintained that phones posed no risk, the biggest phone manufacturers—including Nokia, Motorola and Ericsson—agreed in the summer of 2000 to provide radiation data with all new phones sold. Though the move would do nothing to protect consumers, it would protect these companies from suits charging that they hadn't provided enough risk information. Second, the CTIA agreed to put $1 million toward research on cell phone customers' health issues. At the same time, the World Health Organization planned to undertake a massive ten-country study to determine potential links between cell phone use and head and neck cancer. Until these studies—or any other studies—indicate anything more conclusive, the debate is unlikely to fade.

"It's far too early in the game to say that cell phones are the harmless little objects the industry makes them out to be," remarked former physiology professor C. Ross Adey to the *New York Times*. Swedish neurosurgery professor Leif G. Salford was even more blunt. Cell phones, he told *Business Week*, constitute "the world's largest biological experiment ever."

As cell phones grew more popular, Americans argued not only over the phones themselves, but over the towers increasingly springing up in their neighborhoods, fields and hilltops. As emitters of radio waves, the towers were cited (without any supporting evidence) in the brain cancer scare as well. But it is the aesthetic injury they inflict that draws the most ire.

Cell towers can be ugly things, looming steel poles or gangly lattice girders of severely utilitarian design. At heights of up to 200 feet or more, they can poke out from their surroundings like industrial weeds. In the early days of the industry, when the limited number of subscribers allowed carriers to cover a city with a handful of widely scattered towers, no one much noticed or complained. But as the buildout intensified, more and more towers were needed, and when the "microcellular" PCS systems came on the scene, with potentially six new carriers in every market, towers suddenly seemed to sprout overnight.

By the summer of 2000, there were some 100,000 towers in place in the United States, and the number was growing geometrically. In September 2000, the *New York Times* reported that "as many as one million cell sites would be installed by the time technology companies reached their desired capacity for wireless data and voice transmission."

Angry homeowners reacted to towers like antibodies to a virus. "It's like having a trash dump at the end of your driveway," one complained to the *Wall Street Journal*, while another demanded to know "Why should I have to live with that monster across the street from my house—so some rich guy can make a call from his car?"

It wasn't only towers close to homes that drew the wrath of critics: In Manassas, Virginia, local citizens were outraged when authorities approved a 150-foot tower to be erected right next to a historic Civil War battleground. For history buffs and reenactors, the Manassas battleground had long been a hallowed spot, a place where one could stand in the cooling fog of a summer morning and take in a landscape essentially unchanged since the war. For them, the very idea of a cell phone tower piercing the mist and despoiling the view was a terrific insult. In Washington, D.C., citizen activists fought the placement of a tower in federally protected Rock Creek Park, arguing that not only was it an eyesore, but drug dealers would now be able to prowl the park at night doing business thanks to the improved cell phone reception in the thick woods.

The industry was for the most part unmoved by the complaints. Compared to the spiderwebs of telephone wires marring the view of the sky in every borough, hamlet and neighborhood in America, what were a few isolated towers in comparison? Bell Atlantic Nynex lawyer Priscilla Triolo summed up the industry's view succinctly in the *Wall Street Journal*: "Alexander Graham Bell didn't have to go before a zoning board and describe a telephone pole or put on the kind of show we're being forced to," she complained. "It's an incredible impediment—an incredibly unnecessary impediment."

Nevertheless, carriers realized they gained no social capital from angering possible customers. So in the mid-'90s, they began looking for ways to placate the critics. Encouraged by new zoning ordinances, competing carriers began colocating—agreeing to share space on a single tower. Today, such arrangements are increasingly common, with one large tower carrying as many as four or five arrays of cellular and PCS antennae.

Some companies began making cell towers disguised as other things: One company called Valmont Industries specializes in pine and palm trees, made by coating the towers with epoxy and pressing patterns in the "trunks." Another company specializes in molded-fiberglass Saguaro cactuses, complete with woodpecker burrows. The cost for these "stealth" towers is higher by tens of thousands of dollars per tower—but it's ultimately cheaper than battling outraged citizens' groups.

Another option for cutting down on the visual insult is to hide the transmitters in existing structures. One company, Stealth Network Technologies, stows transmitters in clock and bell towers, and the company pioneered the technique of installing them in large motel signs. In Canada, one carrier drew the wrath of citizens when a large cross it donated to a church was found to have transmitters inside. Another company cut an enterprising hidden-transmitter scheme with Domino's Pizza. Domino's agreed to have a $500,000 artistic "sculpture" designed and installed on its training campus in Ann Arbor, Michigan. The sculpture's primary purpose was not, of course, aesthetic: It was erected solely to hide a transmitter.

The uproar over towers was exacerbated by an unusual characteristic of the U.S. mobile-phone industry: Compared to many European countries, the United States required more towers. The reasons lay in the fundamental differences between how the European and U.S. industries evolved.

━━━━━━━━

BY THE YEAR 2000, THIRSTY FINNS could get a cool drink at a soda machine in Helsinki by communicating with the machine and charging the cost via their wireless phones. In Italy, users could verbally declare "I'm hungry" to their phones, and receive a text list of nearby pizzerias in response. Across the globe, Swedes, Japanese and Germans had begun using the next generation of data-enabled phones, while their American counterparts remained largely oblivious to what they were missing.

The reason for the Europeans' head start on these new technologies was simple: Most of their cellular systems were first launched by government-owned and -subsidized monopoly telephone companies. In most cases, a single governmental agency could dictate uniform technology standards, making it easier to adopt new innovations. Today, European Union cooperation provides for similar continent-wide uniformity.

In the United States, by comparison, technology standards were left to the marketplace to sort out. Hundreds of geographically distinct markets in America were licensed to hundreds of different operators, each of which might, by the late '90s, have chosen one of many types of incompatible technologies—CDMA, TDMA or GSM—to use. And the problems caused by this technology jumble were exacerbated by the huge geographic area U.S. carriers had to cover—a daunting prospect, especially compared to Europe's compact boundaries and greater population density.

As the *Wall Street Journal*'s Walter S. Mossberg put it, "It's harder to do anything wireless in the U.S. Three sets of transmission towers must typically be built. Any hardware innovator wishing to sell mobile wireless phones or other devices in the U.S. must make them in three varieties and court the slow-moving, bureaucratic cellular phone carriers, such as AT&T and Verizon, who have a chokehold on innovation." Other theorists counter that the U.S., with five or more competing carriers in each market and an open-market policy toward technology, will eventually surpass the more regulated economies not only in technological innovation, but with lower prices as well.

The American market-driven system has allowed American carriers to avoid some costly mistakes. Many of the digital features first touted by PCS manufacturers—as in Wayne Schelle's "newspaper of the future" speech on the White House lawn—have proven a hard sell at the glacially slow wireless data speeds available in the last years of the twentieth century. With superior wired-phone service available and abundant telephone-modem outlets in public places, Americans weren't eager to embrace these wireless gimmicks until they functioned more reliably and at higher speeds.

These higher speeds would come with the introduction of "2.5G" technology. In wireless parlance, analog cell phones were the first generation—or "1G"—of technology. These were the same phones developed by Bell Labs in the 1960s, and they could be used only for voice transmission. Digital cellular phones and early PCS phones were 2G technology, capable of transmitting bits of data such as short text messages.

The phones available in Europe and Japan at the beginning of the twenty-first century were 2.5G technology, more sophisticated phones capable of more quickly transmitting larger amounts of data. Japanese teenagers were able to send love letters via their phones, and Swedish businessmen could check their stock quotes. This was closer to what Schelle had been referring to, but the real revolution in phones will come with 3G technology, which promises the transmission of photos, Web pages and greater amounts of text, as well as connections to Palm Pilots and handheld computers. This new 3G technology, which should be available in the United States after 2004, will transform the way Americans look at their phones: They will become all-in-one communications devices rather than simply a portable alternative to wired phones.

But that's in the future, as a *Wall Street Journal* review of phones in 2000 made clear. "The gizmos are only going to get more elaborate as U.S. carriers struggle to keep up with Europe, where cell phones can already do practically everything but cook and clean," the review declared, before noting that Internet access through U.S. phones was a "completely unsatisfying experience on the phones we tested. . . For all the high-tech bells and whistles, we found ourselves falling time and again for the low-tech conveniences," like the "built-in walkie-talkie" on Nextel's i1000 phones.

"I don't need or want a microwave oven in my cell phone," writer Daniel Schneider told the paper, "I wish they'd simply just focus on making the calls work better so I'm not disconnected 45 times a day."

Schneider's complaint was a common one as the decade drew to a close. With the number of customers soaring, carriers struggled to find enough tower sites and install enough radios to accommodate them all. Dropped calls, poor connections and maxed-out systems continued to plague the industry. And still, unbridled competition amongst a half-dozen carriers led to more cut rates and new promotions to draw in even more customers.

The most popular plans offered customers something "free" for signing up. "In 20 percent of ads," noted *RCR Wireless News* in 1997, "cellular carriers offered free phones; 19 percent offered free activation; 17 percent promoted no contracts; and 10 percent contained some mention of free airtime." Not only did "free" offerings draw more customers, but AT&T's new Digital One Rate spawned similar offerings from competitors rushing to match AT&T's nationwide network and roaming coverage. If it seemed the carriers had been writing the rules for the first fifteen years of the industry, it was clear that now the users were in charge. The average monthly bill dropped from nearly $100 in 1988 to just more than $50 in 1995 to $40 in 1999. Usage rose as the average price per minute fell from 50 cents in 1994 to 20 cents by the first half of 2000. And the new plans kept coming.

Prepaid phones drew hordes of new users in 1997 and 1998, appealing especially to younger users, customers with bad credit, phone addicts and cash-based businesses (including drug dealers). For carriers, prepaid phones protected them from getting stuck with unpaid bills and brought them a whole new class of customers they might ordinarily shun as potential deadbeats—college students, for example. Ads for the service went unabashedly after this demographic. "Of the 452 messages your roommate will take for you this year," asked one Bell Atlantic ad, "how many of them will you actually get?" With no contracts, no unexpected bills and the ability to buy a phone on impulse, prepaid phones goosed user numbers even higher.

Once viewed as a high-tech purchase that required considerable deliberation and care, buying a cell phone eventually ended up having about as much cachet as buying batteries at the drugstore. One Airtouch promotion in 1997 offered customers a chocolate cell phone and a real cell phone for making a fragrance purchase worth fifty dollars or more. In 2000, Nextel offered two phones for the price of one. On eBay, phones were bought and sold like paperback novels. And at drugstores, 7-Elevens and gas stations, customers could pick up a cell phone with their pack of gum or magazine.

With the popularity of cell phones soaring, it's easy to argue now that the boom was inevitable. After all, who wouldn't want the convenience of talking on a phone whenever, wherever they wanted to? But even as late as 1995, no less a respected observer than *Forbes* magazine still didn't see it coming. "Cellular operators. . . say they can offer something completely different from and better than wired service, letting you make calls when you're away from home and the office. But there's something else that lets you do that too," the magazine sneered. "It's called a pay phone."

Despite *Forbes*'s shortsightedness, it's now clear that wireless phones are changing the nature of communications: Dialing a person rather than a place has become a reality. In the coming years, cell phones will continue to evolve, offering more and better wireless services, and new customers will continue to join the surge.

"This is the most popular product known to man," Chase Hambrecht & Quist analyst Ed Snyder told *Time* magazine last year. In 2000, according to Snyder, "more cell phones will be sold than all the computers, TVs, personal digital assistants and pagers combined." The boom led *Newsweek* to observe that "What was once a toy" has become "an indispensable appendage. . . It's starting to seem as though mobile phones are part of the human physique, as inescapable as our eyes and ears."

23

AFTER THE GOLD RUSH

OVER THE COURSE OF TWO DECADES, THE FCC GAVE AWAY or auctioned off nine separate blocks of radio spectrum now used for wireless phones: two for cellular, one for SMR and six for PCS. The thousands of licenses that comprised these blocks ended up in the hands of tens of thousands of owners. The result was a messy patchwork—an operational jumble that couldn't last.

Though it started slowly, the consolidation of the industry accelerated by the latter half of the '90s, and, incredibly, by the year 2000 the wireless phone industry had been basically distilled down to six mammoth carriers. In a quintessentially Darwinian evolution, small fish were gobbled up by big fish, who in turn were eaten by bigger fish until only the largest remained.

It began with the big cable companies. Lured by the promise of cellular's lucrative cash flows, they began snatching up systems in the late 1980s, following McCaw's lead. In February 1988, for example, Comcast bought AmCell for $230 million, and two months later, Century Cable bought the midwestern properties of Providence Journal Cellular. But though their pockets were deep and their acquisitions impressive, the cable companies weren't as well positioned as the RBOCs to capitalize on the cellular land rush. The RBOCs had three compelling reasons to join the spectrum rush. First, because they already had cellular systems running, they knew the business—and knew as well as anyone how profitable it could be. Second, they had literally billions in cash from their landline businesses. And third, cellular was one of the few ways they could grow their businesses within the strictures imposed by the consent decree that had broken up AT&T.

The seed of the RBOCs' eventual domination lay in the March 1986 court ruling that allowed PacTel to purchase half the San Francisco nonwireline system—the first time a wireline had encroached on nonwireline territory. The ruling was expected to propel the RBOCs into a buying spree, but like so many bloated, bureaucratic companies, they were slow to seize the momentum. It took nearly a year for another RBOC to move, when Southwestern Bell outbid PacTel for Metromedia's cellular properties. And six months after that, PacTel, led by Sam Ginn—who was perhaps the only RBOC head to fully grasp cellular's promise—purchased the Detroit regional nonwireline system. This made three deals in four years, hardly a trend especially considering what was going on among the smaller players.

As they had done since the days of the Grand Alliance and Big Monopoly trading session, the nonwirelines continued their frantic swapping and consolidating as the RBOCs slumbered. A few companies, such as CCI, Metro Mobile, Vanguard and TDS, grew steadily as they bought out lottery winners. When the RBOCs at last awakened, they began snapping up these companies' properties: BellSouth bought MCCA and the remnants of Graphic Scanning, Ginn's PacTel bought CCI, and Bell Atlantic bought out Metro Mobile. Eagerly, the RBOCs paid fat prices for licenses they could have bought earlier for much less—had they been paying attention.

Until 1992, most buying and swapping was driven merely by everyday competitive business instincts. But when McCaw announced its "alliance" with AT&T that year, everyone in the industry suddenly understood that the storied national footprint, Craig McCaw's much-ridiculed pipe dream, could now become a reality: McCaw had the licenses, and AT&T had the money, to make it happen. No longer could phone companies like BellSouth or Ameritech sit complacently in their marble headquarters and sell phones relying solely on the strength of their brands; now they had to compete with the McCaw-AT&T juggernaut on its own terms: by creating their own nationwide footprints. And the only way to do that was by merging with each other, the next step on the evolutionary chain.

The RBOCs began doing just that. Bell Atlantic and Nynex merged in 1996. Airtouch, the former cellular division of PacTel, bought US West's cellular division in 1997. Southwestern Bell, renamed SBC, bought PacTel in 1997 and Comcast in January 1999. The urge to merge accelerated in 1998 following AT&T's announcement of its Digital One Rate plan. With this single stroke, any carrier that didn't have a nationwide network couldn't hope to compete. Soon after the announcement, Bell Atlantic (which now included Nynex) announced it would merge with GTE. In the course of forty-eight months, the number of major phone companies in the United States had shrunk by more than half.

The increasing merger activity attracted attention from Europe, where several ambitious national carriers—including British Telecom, Deutsche Telekom and Telenor of Sweden—were eyeing the U.S. market. In January 1999, British mobile-phone giant Vodafone bought Airtouch—bringing an end to the career of Airtouch's Sam Ginn, the most acquisitive of the RBOC heads. Twenty-one months later, the new Vodafone-Airtouch powerhouse announced yet another merger, with Bell Atlantic—which was at that time still completing its merger with GTE.

When this gargantuan three-way merger was completed, a new wireless giant was born—one that encompassed the combined wireless operations of the old PacTel/Airtouch, US West, Bell Atlantic, Nynex and GTE operations. The new company, dubbed Verizon in April 2000, vaulted over AT&T Wireless to the rank of world's largest wireless phone company, with 26.3 million cellular and PCS subscribers in 96 of the top 100 U.S. markets. By comparison, AT&T had 12 million U.S. subscribers, Sprint PCS had 6.5 million and Nextel had 5 million. The giants were taking over the land.

By the spring of 2000, only one of the seven original RBOCs—Bell-South—remained. It, too, was soon swallowed in a mammoth merger: In April 2000, SBC (which had swallowed up Ameritech a year earlier) and Bell-South merged to create a wireless network covering forty-two of the nation's top-fifty markets. Like Verizon, the merged companies consolidated their multiple brands into a single new one: Cingular. After the remnants of US West were acquired by Qwest Communications in 2000, the original seven RBOCs and GTE had now effectively been reduced to two major players: Verizon and Cingular.

Based on public spectrum valuations of 2000, the nine systems of wireless phone licenses are now worth, in the aggregate, some $500 billion. The steward of the licenses, the federal government, distributed them all while receiving a paltry $37 billion or so (from the PCS auctions) in return. The wireless revolution has emerged from an archetypal capitalistic carnival of buying, selling and brokering, and thousands of the people who took part have managed to hold on to some of the billions that changed hands. Here's how some of them fared.

ALREADY ONE OF THE RICHEST MEN IN AMERICA, septuagenarian John Kluge could reasonably have been expected to slow down following his Metromedia-Southwestern Bell deal. Not surprisingly to those who know him, he did the opposite.

Throughout the late '80s and early '90s, Kluge, who was once described in *Fortune* magazine as being "convulsed by a new idea every ten seconds or so," embarked on a series of eclectic new investments. In 1988, he bought a majority stake in Orion Pictures, the independent studio responsible for such films as *Bull Durham*, *Mississippi Burning* and a dozen Woody Allen releases. With that purchase, Kluge reentered the world of entertainment he'd exited in the previous decade, when he sold his stable of television stations, the Ice Capades and the Globetrotters as part of Metromedia's mass liquidation. The Orion purchase was a rare mistake for Kluge; the company sank into bankruptcy in 1992, and although it managed to recover, it continued to struggle until it was bought by MGM in 1997.

In 1992, Kluge reentered cellular. He and longtime right-hand man Stuart Subotnick paired up with an unlikely new partner—ebullient, abrasive Dick Sherwin, fresh from presiding over the dissolution of Graphic Scanning. With Sherwin's encouragement, the pair founded Metromedia International to exploit new, farther-flung underdeveloped wireless markets in Eastern Europe and the former Soviet Union. But though Sherwin's drive and cellular knowledge were still formidable, he retained, as well, his reckless style; within a few years, the soft-spoken billionaire Kluge would terminate the relationship.

Kluge's foray into international wireless helped balloon his already considerable net worth, but it paled in comparison to his next telecom deal. In 1997, Kluge and Subotnick invested $33 million for a 26-percent stake in a new company, one that aimed to lay fiber-optic cables in the tunnels snaking beneath Manhattan. With that investment, the newly named Metromedia Fiber Network (MFN) launched Kluge into the competitive telecommunications business.

Once again, Kluge's timing couldn't have been better. Just as Internet usage and corporate data networks upshifted into hyper growth, MFN was there with a high-capacity-fiber network ready to carry the trillions of bits of traffic—and charging millions of dollars per day for the service. MFN is on track to lay 3.6 million miles of fiber strands beneath the streets of sixty-eight cities in North America and Europe by 2004—enough for *Forbes* to dub MFN a "challenger for the title of world's biggest layer of fiber." With 2001 revenues estimated to be $475 million, and a public market capitalization of $20 billion, by the fall of 2000 MFN had added nearly $3 billion to John Kluge's net worth, which had grown to $13 billion.

Now listed by *Forbes* as the fifteenth-richest man in America, Kluge—at age eighty-six—has finally begun cutting back on his day-to-day involvement in business. With his new wife, Tussi, he has built an apartment in Germany, the country he had fled so many years before. According to one art dealer, Kluge's new pied-à-terre is the largest and most elaborately decorated residence built in Munich since before the Second World War. It is one of six homes Kluge maintains, including a castle in Scotland; an estate in France; a New York apartment; a historic plantation home near Charlottesville, Virginia; and a compound in Palm Beach, Florida—where Kluge can still be found betting on card games with friends, just as he did as a student at Columbia University more than a half-century before.

Kluge has also proven a generous philanthropist. He has given substantial sums to both Columbia University and the University of Virginia, and in September 2000, the Library of Congress announced that Kluge had given the institution its largest single donation ever: $60 million. Though Kluge is semiretired, the Metromedia empire continues, now run by Stuart Subotnick.

———

OF ALL THE NONWIRELINE PLAYERS from the industry's early days, Metromedia fared as well or better than most (except, of course, McCaw). Many others who sold out too early were forced to watch from the sidelines through the 1990s, as the industry charged on without them.

Western Union, the once-proud leader of the American communications industry, misplayed its cellular hand spectacularly, and by the early 1990s the company was driven into bankruptcy. Ted Berner, the irascible Western Union board member who engineered a coup and seized control of the company just before the critical Big Monopoly game—died in 1990, the same year Western Union's stock plunged to an embarrassing low of twenty-five cents per share. Bob Flanagan, the CEO whom Berner ousted, has retired, as has Jim Ragan, the former marine who led Western Union's meteoric but brief cellular foray. From his comfortable home in Guilford, Connecticut, Ragan still laments the tragicomedy of errors that reduced Western Union to the skeletal money-wire business that's the company's last remnant.

Graphic Scanning's Barry Yampol, the mercurial CEO who single-handedly created, then destroyed, the most advantageous position in the new cellular industry, splits his time between homes in Long Island and Florida. He continues to drive racing powerboats and collect gems and minerals, and he owns mining operations in Brazil and California. His various ventures, including a substantial investment in the Brazilian telephone company Telebras, have left him with so much money that, in his words, he "can't even spend the interest."

Dick Sherwin, who had once run Graphic's cellular business, ended up with far less. Once he'd been let go from Metromedia International, he set up shop as a telecom consultant—a far cry from his early role as the steward of the largest pile of cellular spectrum anyone had yet assembled.

MCI chairman Bill McGowan, the man who "almost single-handedly brought about the end of the Bell System monopoly" (*USA Today*), dropped dead of a heart attack while exercising at Georgetown University Hospital on a Monday morning in 1992. A longtime smoker and workaholic, McGowan began an exercise regimen at the hospital following his first heart attack in 1986. He had turned over CEO duties to Bert Roberts, Jr., about six months prior to his death, but the loss of the flamboyant, excitable and now legendary McGowan was a huge blow to MCI—and to the entire telecom industry.

In a final irony, MCI—which had already had two bites at the wireless apple, in the early cellular days with Airsignal and in its failed 1994 Nextel investment—tried one more time to get into wireless. In 1999, the company entered serious takeover talks with Nextel again, but no deal could be reached. Having sold its cellular properties to Craig McCaw for a pittance back in 1986, MCI (now merged with WorldCom) tried and failed to get back in the business by buying Craig's company thirteen years later.

———————————

GEORGE LINDEMANN, WHO GAINED FAME in the industry as much for his baguette-sized cigars as for his considerable business skills, was one of the very few early players who sold at the height of the market.

In the industry's first few years, Metro Mobile amassed a portfolio covering 11.6 million POPs. Then, rather than chasing more-POPs-at-any-price McCaw, Lindemann simply built and ran the systems as prices rose. While all around him companies succumbed to the chill of fear and sold out, Lindemann held on until September 1991, when he finally conceded the inevitable, merging his company's cellular assets into Bell Atlantic for $2.45 billion (more than $200 per POP) worth of the RBOC's stock.

As it had been with his earlier businesses, Lindemann's timing was brilliant for a variety of reasons. Metro Mobile was at that time facing hundreds of millions of dollars in capital needs to expand its networks and add digital technology. In 1991, money was tight in the banking community and on Wall Street—and Bell Atlantic's stock was correspondingly cheap. In the twenty-four months after the sale, Bell Atlantic stock rose 50 percent while Lindemann sat on the sidelines watching his tax-deferred fortune grow and letting the RBOC worry about borrowing money.

Like Kluge, Lindemann didn't simply sit back after his cellular success. In 1989, he purchased Southern Union Co., a natural gas distribution business based in Austin, Texas. For society-page habitué and longtime technology investor Lindemann, propane distribution seemed a ridiculously mundane choice for a new business—but in a decade under Lindemann's guidance, Southern Union's revenues grew from $200 million to $670 million. During that time, the company's stock outpaced the S&P 500, rising from $3.71 to $21.50 per share.

All told, Lindemann's investments—propelled in large measure by his cellular success—have placed him at number 236 on the Forbes 400 list for 2000. At his sprawling homes in Long Island and Palm Beach, Lindemann enjoys the fruits of a family net worth estimated at $1.2 billion.

———

DESPITE THE FCC'S EFFORTS TO SHUT DOWN the application mills and sanction the hustlers, nearly all the schemers emerged from the cellular giveaway as wealthy men.

Even Nick Wilson, whose inattention to detail and compulsion to immediately spend any money he got cost him millions, is today comfortably wealthy thanks to his many spectrum schemes, from the bogus tax-write-offs to the 1-percent loophole to the "risk-sharing" plan. It is this last scam that outraged industry observers most—though not because of what Wilson did, but because of how the FCC responded.

The risk-sharing plan came to light after attorneys David Kaufman and Rick Brown saw Greg Neely's document in the late-night meeting at the Westfields Conference. The attorneys convinced Neely to report it to the FCC, which then launched an investigation. A morass of litigation followed, and to the commission's embarrassment, the fate of the two dozen licenses won by Wilson and Neely's clients—licenses destined to be worth hundreds of millions of dollars—hung in limbo for the next eight years.

It was clear to all involved that Wilson and his customers had flouted the rules: By employing a semantic tweak, Wilson had allowed a group of applicants to share in each other's chances of winning even though the FCC's lottery rules specifically prohibited it. Even Wilson knew he'd overstepped; before the investigation even got going, he handed over nominal title to the company to Greg Neely, cleaned out the bank accounts and took off for California.

In 1992, in a scathing sixty-five-page court decision, FCC judge Walter Miller ruled that Wilson's clients were guilty of dozens of rules violations, including submitting false or incomplete data, abusing the FCC's rules, concealing facts and "basic deception." Wilson and his clients were guilty, the judge wrote indignantly, of "multiple and flagrant violations that cannot and should not pass unnoticed," violations that "eat at the very heart of our system of government due process, fair play and open proceedings." When Wilson's clients appealed Judge Miller's decision to the full commission, nearly everyone expected that the FCC would reject the appeal out of hand, leading to a relottery of the disputed licenses (there were no second-through tenth-place finishers designated in the RSA lotteries).

But the logic of that decision was overridden by an uglier logic exercised by FCC chairman Reed Hundt. Appointed in November 1993, Hundt was keenly aware of how spectacularly the FCC's spectrum lottery had failed. He had gone out on a political limb, declaring that on his watch the FCC would never again lottery off spectrum. The FCC would, Hundt was determined, become that rare entity: a federal agency that actually showed a profit.

The risk-sharing appeal brought Hundt's grandstanding politics head-to-head against principle. If the guilty were punished with revocation of their license ownership, FCC rules required a relottery—just what Hundt had pledged to avoid. For eight years, the FCC sat mute, gridlocked by this conundrum. Finally, when it appeared that most everyone had forgotten about the controversy, Hundt quietly reopened the case.

The FCC then announced a decision that shocked even the most jaded industry observers: Under Hundt's guidance, the commission simply held its nose and handed a half-billion dollars' worth of licenses to the risk-sharing partnerships. Despite Judge Miller's strongly worded denunciation and the demoralizing impact on the FCC staff, the commission washed its hands of the matter, showing no regard for the years of painstaking investigations, millions of dollars in legal fees spent, and the mountains of evidence compiled against the license winners. The decision was, in the words of former Mobile Services Division chief Kevin Kelley, "outrageous." It was the most egregious example yet of one of the commission's most serious failings: the apparent inability to police its own rules

The ruling brought with it one last bit of irony. Greg Neely, Nick Wilson's long-suffering, stubbornly loyal lieutenant, emerged as one of the risk-sharing scheme's biggest winners. Neely had put together a last-minute, slapdash partnership to apply; joined the risk-sharing cabal; and been declared the nominal winner of the Alabama-1 RSA license, which covered 340,000 POPs between Birmingham and Huntsville. When the FCC issued its ruling on the risk-sharing affair eight years after the lottery, Neely found that, thanks to soaring cellular values, his little partnership's license was now worth at least $75 million. In the end, Neely—long dismissed by Wilson as a naive flunky—trumped his former boss a dozen fold in net worth. The FCC's decision to award his partnership the license was, he exulted, a "gift from God."

Wilson made and spent millions of dollars in the spectrum rush, but it pales in comparison to what he might have made if he'd paid more attention to the making instead of the spending. When his wife, Nancy, won an Illinois RSA in 1989, Wilson hurriedly mortgaged the $40 million license for some quick spending money and was then pressured into selling it to Leroy Carlson's TDS for a fraction of its value. When he and Nancy separated, according to former associates, Wilson took most of the proceeds and disappeared back to California with his latest girlfriend, leaving Nancy with the tax bill for the capital gains. He settled in a hilltop home in Marina Del Ray, where he could sip vodka while peering through a telescope at his latest motor-yacht, docked on the waterfront about a mile from his house.

PETER LEWIS, WHOSE BOYHOOD FASCINATION with a new set of walkie-talkies led to a mercurial career in wireless, ended up one of the more tragic figures in the cellular industry.

As one of the few purely entrepreneurial applicants in the first three rounds of the giveaway, Lewis helped launch the industry. As an African American, he personified the power of new technology to create color-blind fortunes for energetic entrepreneurs. With his partners, Bernie Cravath and Bill Welch, he entered 1984 with a huge portfolio of 9 million cellular POPs.

But it all went downhill from there. Out of capital and unable to raise any in a world that had yet to appreciate the value of spectrum, Lewis and his partners were forced to liquidate their portfolio before the first commercial cellular system was built. Lewis and his partners realized only a tiny fraction of what their POPs were worth.

Undaunted, Lewis reinvented himself, creating a full-time applications-preparation service. But though this second business was initially successful, Lewis was unable to adapt to the changing world of application mills, mass marketing and cheap pricing. So once again, he reinvented himself, hatching the scheme that would lead to his humiliating downfall.

The ultimate embarrassment for this proud entrepreneur came while he gave a deposition in front of a pack of powerful and antagonistic lawyers in the midst of an FCC hearing about his tainted-applications scandal. Having long denied the existence of any application-sharing deals between him and the legions of know-nothings for whom he filed lottery applications, Lewis was at last brought up short. When an attorney handed him a rule-breaking agreement bearing his signature, he continued, now under oath, to deny any knowledge of it. Eventually, under pressure from his own lawyer, Lewis was forced to recant his testimony.

Lewis walked out of his deposition in disgrace, leaving his clients' hopes for tens of millions in cellular licenses in tatters. To this day he believes he was unfairly accused, targeted by a federal cabal because of his race. In his mind, the FCC went after him not because he schemed to circumvent their lottery rules for profit, but because so many of his clients who won licenses were black.

Though Lewis made, according to some accounts, several million dollars in his many cellular incarnations, he ultimately made far less than he could have. But not surprisingly to those who know him, Lewis hasn't given up. As the new millennium dawned, he was running a small wireless data communications company called MobyTel; he still hasn't stopped chasing the telecom fortune that seems perpetually, tantalizingly out of reach.

━━━━━━━━

ALREADY A MULTIMILLIONAIRE AND PERSONA NON GRATA at the FCC, Mack Johnson could simply have retired following the lottery-stuffing scandal of the mid-1980s. But not only did he continue his manic quest for more riches, he again did it brazenly in the commission's halls.

In 1985, the year he hatched his cellular applications scheme, Mack Johnson quietly strolled into the FCC's public record room in Washington, D.C., and photocopied seventy-two pages out of a set of documents. These pages, the engineering section of a complex application for a new mobile satellite telephone service, would form the basis of Johnson's most audacious scheme yet. With millions of dollars worth of photocopied engineer-

ing in his hands, Johnson then filled out his own, nearly identical application for the same new mobile satellite communications licenses.

Johnson had no intention of launching a billion-dollar galaxy of satellites from his one-man home office in Crossville, of course—he had neither
the means nor the expertise even to dream of it. What he did have was an
unparalleled understanding of how to make money off the system. With
hundreds of millions of dollars' worth of spectrum at stake and powerful
companies vying for it, Johnson figured he'd be able to parlay a seat at the
table into some kind of windfall.

Once again, Johnson's instincts were right on. After years of legal challenges, corporate maneuvering and confusion at the FCC (during which
Johnson, acting as his own lawyer, calmly and shamelessly insisted on his
right to take part in the giveaway), he got what he wanted. Realizing that
battling even a bogus competitor would be expensive and time-consuming,
executives for the ultimate aspirant for the licenses, American Mobile Satellite Corp. (a consortium of industrial corporations that included General
Motors and McCaw) offered to pay Johnson to dismiss his application.

So it was that Mack Johnson—a man who knew nothing about satellites,
and who had invested less in his application than most people spend on a
weekend in Las Vegas—received $2.5 million from American Mobile Satel-
lite Corp. It was an impressive reward for plagiarism.

In 1989, when the RSA cellular applications began pouring into the FCC,
longtime observers of the spectrum rush were surprised to see that none of
them bore the telltale zip code of Crossville, Tennessee. Where was Mack
Johnson? Had the FCC finally rid itself of this persistent country hustler?
But the dreaded zip code did eventually appear, in another class of documents: Petitions to Deny. One by one, RSA winners were being hit by legal
claims that their applications were defective.

It wasn't Johnson filing the petitions, however—it was an attorney no
one at the FCC had heard of, a woman named Vivian Warner. When the big
consolidating operators like McCaw, TDS and the RBOCs began offering the
RSA lottery winners millions in cash for their licenses, the winners, unable
to sell—thanks to the petitions filed against them—were faced with an uncomfortable choice. On one hand, they could fight the spurious claims of
this Vivian Warner—but the ensuing legal battle could last months or years,
and it could cost hundreds of thousands of dollars in lost interest income
on sales they might otherwise close immediately. On the other hand, the
winners and their buyers could, like American Mobile Satellite Corporation

had done with Johnson, offer Warner cash to dismiss her claims, a move that would save time and money. The only drawback to this option was that honest winners were being forced to pay real money for patently specious claims.

More often than not, expediency trumped principles: Most winners elected simply to pay off Warner. A decade after she launched her scheme, no one knows how much money she cleared, though one attorney involved in several of the proceedings estimates that it may have totaled as much as a million dollars. None of Warner's petitions, this attorney believes, would have warranted an FCC hearing, much less a license dismissal. Yet Warner proved remarkably adept at repeatedly extracting the maximum payoff, adroitly conceding at precisely the right point in each negotiation and showing a surprising understanding of spectrum values for someone apparently new to the game. It was, perhaps, no great surprise when the disgruntled winners learned the name of Warner's boyfriend: Mack Johnson.

A millionaire many times over, Mack Johnson still lives in Crossville, in a comfortable lakeside home. His new business is speculating in used business jets; for the moment, at least, he appears to be finished with outwitting FCC bureaucrats. "The FCC," he mused recently, "will always screw it up. That's the one thing you can count on."

━━━━━━━━━

THOUGH THERE WERE MANY WHO MADE THEIR CELLULAR MILLIONS in bizarre, inventive and sometimes unscrupulous ways, there were many more legitimate businessmen who played by the book and came away with well-earned fortunes in the spectrum rush. Some of them, as even the FCC's critics had to grudgingly admit, brought exactly the sort of enterprising, competitive innovation to the new cellular industry that the commission had intended way back when it decided to set aside a nonwireline spectrum block.

At CCI, George Blumenthal and Bill Ginsberg teamed up with former FCC chairman Charles Ferris and wunderkind Barclay Knapp to build a small empire around cellular licenses in the rust belt cities of Ohio—markets that the likes of John Kluge and Donald Pels had spurned as marginal. Leveraging a small nest egg of $2 million in venture capital, Blumenthal and Ginsberg eventually sold CCI to Airtouch in a $2.5 billion transaction. But they also were too young and too enthralled by the promise of telecommunications to quit then. They parlayed a stake in some old CCI microwave licenses into a second telecommunications empire that includes NTL, Inc., a huge British and Irish cable-television operator, and in the process they are building fortunes that may, before long, place them too on the *Forbes* list.

Similarly, Leroy Carlson took his small conglomerate of largely rural telephone companies at Telephone and Data Systems, Inc. (TDS) and built it into a family empire. Beginning with a handful of mostly fractional interests in metropolitan licenses, he then spread out all over the country, snapping up licenses with a fervor matched only by McCaw. Eureka, California; Humboldt, Iowa—Carlson considered no place too small or rural to be worthwhile.

When the FCC auctioned off PCS licenses, Carlson—already in his seventies and a very wealthy man—used TDS to launch a new company called Aerial Wireless. By 2000, TDS, with its basic telephone service companies buoyed by its 80 percent of U.S. Cellular and its 81.5 percent of Aerial Wireless, had a market value of some $6.5 billion—of which Carlson's family controlled a stake of nearly 11 percent. Like John Kluge, industry legend Carlson greeted the new millennium with the entrepreneurial zest of a man half his age.

———

LEROY CARLSON HAD ENTERED THE SPECTRUM RUSH with an eight-figure net worth and a lifetime of dealmaking; it was perhaps not surprising he did so well in the spectrum rush. For a team of amateurs from North Carolina, however, their success over the same fifteen-year period was cause for wonder.

Steve Leeolou and Rich Preyer, the former TV newscaster and sometime tennis pro, had begun their quest for riches by flogging cellular applications from Preyer's old Subaru back in 1983. Together they'd traveled across the South, selling application services to friends and family in the mistaken belief that the FCC would continue giving away licenses through comparative hearings. When the FCC switched to lotteries, the pair's business partner— amoral attorney Lee Lovett—had figured a way to finagle around the new rules by flooding the commission with applications, thus giving their customers their money's worth.

The scheme kept the duo in business, despite the outraged attempts of competing applicants to get them kicked out of the running. They then hired former oil distributor Haynes Griffin as CEO, and the fledgling company, now named Vanguard Cellular, embarked on a fifteen-year odyssey that was every bit as seat-of-your-pants as that initial applications scheme.

But over the years, in fits and starts, the Vanguard team transformed the company from a handful of fractional interests in some Round III and IV applications into a sizable cellular company. By the late 1990s, Vanguard was a publicly traded company with a market capitalization of $1.3 billion, cellular systems in thirty-seven markets covering 6.9 million POPs, and nearly 700,000 subscribers.

One of the last of the independent operators, Vanguard continued to operate on its own, often blindly ignoring both risks and opportunities, until October 1998, when the forces of consolidation finally swept them into the arms of AT&T for $1.5 billion, or some $205 per POP. The three "amateurs" ended up clearing more than $50 million apiece.

———

AFTER THE GRAND ALLIANCE TRIGGERED A CIRCUS of swapping, buying and selling, it didn't take long before a new breed of entrepreneur appeared: the cellular broker. When Mark Warner held the world's first cellular-spectrum auction in 1986, selling off CellTelCo's Round IV markets to McCaw and Wayne Schelle, he launched a brand-new specialty business. It was a business that would make him very rich.

Soon after the CellTelCo auction, Warner teamed up with Robert Blow to form a Washington, D.C.–based brokerage firm called Capital Cellular. In addition to brokerage deals, Warner and Blow lit upon a second arbitrage opportunity—the thousands of 1-percent license pieces that were the cellular equivalent of untradeable shares of penny stocks. With loans from McCaw, Capital Cellular set up a mini stock exchange, buying up these tiny fractions, aggregating them into meaningful shares of licenses and reselling them to McCaw and other operators—while keeping millions in markups for themselves.

Through the late '80s and early '90s, I worked with a handful of partners to take advantage of this Wild West atmosphere of spectrum dealmaking. Warner, Blow, Schelle and I formed a new firm and negotiated the settlement of the contested Lewis and Johnson lottery-stuffing scams, clearing millions for ourselves after two years of complex dealmaking. Warner, Blow and I then teamed up with former Providence Journal Cellular president David Mixer to form Columbia Cellular Corporation; we soon added a fifth partner, Mark Kington. In the first decade of the spectrum rush, Columbia brokered more than $4 billion in transactions, representing both the major cellular carriers (such as McCaw and TDS) as well as dozens of lottery winners, and for a short time we even sold a few applications. We spent five years matching buyers and sellers, helping to consolidate the industry and disentangling the scrambled ownership created by the FCC's lottery process.

Following the spectrum rush, Columbia slowly evolved from a mergers-and-acquisitions business into Columbia Capital, a venture-capital business specializing in telecom investing that today manages more than $1.5 billion in assets. Mark Warner, the bold young lawyer who began his career sleeping in the back of his Buick, is now a centimillionaire currently running for governor of Virginia (following a failed U.S. Senate seat bid in 1996). Mixer, Blow, Kington and I have given up our day-to-day involvement in Columbia and manage private venture investments of our own—including, when we can find them, new wireless technologies and services.

AND WHAT OF THE COMPANY THAT TRANSFORMED the industry? When McCaw's epic ride ended with the company's sale to AT&T in 1993, the executive team went on to a variety of sometimes surprising pursuits.

For Craig McCaw, the sale of McCaw Cellular marked the beginning of a whole range of new wireless ventures, starting with his investment in Nextel. Within five years of Craig's investment, Nextel had grown into the country's fifth-largest wireless carrier, with more than 6.6 million subscribers, service in 96 of the top 100 markets, $5 billion in annual revenue and a market capitalization in the fall of 2000 of $45 billion—$36 billion more than when Craig took over in April 1995. (That figure shrank along with everyone else's telecom fortunes in the market slide of 2001.) Along the way, Craig's stake, which had cost him $1.1 billion, and only a fraction of it in cash, had by late 2000 grown in value to some $7 billion.

And Nextel wasn't the only "next big thing" Craig invested in. Around the same time he invested in Nextel, he launched yet another new company in a new industry. Like Kluge's MFN, Craig's Nextlink took him into the world of wires: fiber-optic cables. Nextlink was launched as a small local broadband service provider, beginning with the construction of urban fiber-optic telephone and data networks in cities like Spokane, Phoenix and Albuquerque. Ex-McCaw executives Wayne Perry and Scot Jarvis managed the company's startup, and by the end of the '90s, Nextlink had grown from a small local fiber-optic company into a large publicly traded competitive local exchange carrier ("CLEC").

Then, in 1999, Craig merged Nextlink with another in his stable of "nexts": Nextband, a local wireless broadband service provider. Like he'd done with his cellular company, Craig used this new company to engineer the pursuit of spectrum at all costs, purchasing microwave spectrum licenses for point-to-point wireless technology at an FCC auction in spring 1998. In less than a year, Nextband merged with the largest buyer at that auction, WNP Communications—a company founded by my firm, Columbia Capital. Nextband paid WNP's investors $695 million to secure licenses covering virtually the whole United States, and it's now poised to launch wireless fiber-like connections using microwave radios—a new technology that connects urban buildings without trenching up the streets and sidewalks to lay cable.

Once merged, Nextlink and Nextband were renamed XO Communications. By late 2000, the company was the largest private owner of radio spectrum bandwidth in the world, holding licenses covering 95 percent of the top thirty markets in the United States. XO Communications offers service in a total of forty-nine markets, connected by 430,000 miles of metropolitan fiber-optic backbone (enough fiber capacity to handle all the traffic currently carried by AT&T), with 384,000 miles more under construction. The company also owns some 160,000 miles of fiber in Europe, serving London, Frankfurt, Brussels, Amsterdam, Paris and sixteen other cities.

In early 2000, XO acquired Concentric Network Corporation, the nation's third-largest independent Internet-service provider, in a $2.54 billion merger. By 2002, XO plans to be using its microwave spectrum to carry data and Internet traffic to its fiber-optic network in sixty of the biggest cities in the United States and Canada. XO Communications has rocketed in size and value; combined, the merged companies closed the year 2000 with more than 6,000 employees in fifty-one markets and projected revenues of more than $475 million. Even after a major downturn in CLEC stocks, XO Communications had, in late 2000, a market capitalization of some $10 billion, and Craig McCaw owned 29 percent of the stock and a 50-percent (effectively controlling) voting interest.

But all the insight and luck that made Craig wealthy couldn't protect him from a few disappointments. One project, a spectacularly ambitious venture cofinanced by Bill Gates, aimed to construct a wireless Internet access service to be run from a complicated network of 840 satellites (since reduced to 288) called Teledesic. Intended to make wireless data available anywhere in the world, Craig trademarked it as the "Internet in the Sky." But in the ten years since the $10 billion project was announced in 1990, not a single Teledesic satellite has been launched.

Dubbed by the *New York Times* as "the most ambitious commercial project in space," Teledesic may never get off the ground. An even larger competitor, Motorola's Iridium Satellite Network, went bankrupt in March 2000, having failed to attract enough customers after spending $5 billion worth of investment capital. It remains to be seen whether Teledesic, which is currently scheduled to begin service in 2004, will meet the same fate.

Regardless of whether Teledesic succeeds or fails, Craig McCaw has established himself over the past two decades as a daring and unpredictable entrepreneur. His eccentricities seem, if anything, to have become more pronounced as he gets older. Though he still sporadically reports to work in Kirkland, he has apparently reconfigured the office space, reserving almost an entire floor for himself so that he can interact with as few people as possible.

Now fifty-one, Craig is a fabulously wealthy man, worth nearly $8 billion by late 2000, according to *Forbes*. So vast is his wealth, in fact, that when he divorced his first wife, the former Wendy Petrak, in 1997, her share in the settlement—much of it in Nextel and Nextlink stock—eventually vaulted her onto the Forbes 400 list. And perhaps more important to Craig, his national footprint idea has been validated as one of the most insightful ideas in the industry's history: In a fall 2000 survey, two-thirds of all respondents rated regional or national coverage as the single most important factor in choosing a wireless carrier. The second most important factor, price, was listed by only 20 percent of respondents.

Along with his wealth and success, Craig appears to have achieved a measure of relative happiness in his life. In 1998, he donated more than $4 million to free Keiko the killer whale, the five-ton star of the film *Free Willy*. When he was allowed to swim with the whale in its tank, the man a PBS documentary called Keiko's "guardian angel" declared it was the "greatest experience of my life."

That same year, Craig married again, taking Bay Area investment banker Susan Leigh Rasinski as his second wife in a ceremony with entertainment by Johnny Mathis and saxophonist Kenny G. The couple now has two children—a first for the restless billionaire. Now building a 300-foot boat, Craig pilots an ever-growing collection of boats, planes and helicopters. "Things won't make you happy," he has reportedly told friends, "but once in a while, you have to test that idea."

———

BRUCE, KEITH AND JOHN MCCAW, CRAIG'S BROTHERS, profited handsomely from their association with their more famous brother. Thanks to their early joint inheritance of that tiny cable-TV system, in Centralia, Washington, all four brothers shared nearly equally in the massive sale of McCaw Cellular to AT&T; each holds a fortune now estimated at $1.6 billion. In May 2000, the brothers donated $20 million toward the renovation of the Seattle Opera House, which will be renamed the Marion Oliver McCaw Hall in honor of their mother, a longtime opera enthusiast and arts supporter.

Though they all exhibited relative degrees of talent in their fields, and though John and Keith both worked for McCaw Cellular at various times, there is no doubt that Craig's three brothers won their billions simply by latching on to their brother's ascending star. In the words of Craig's erstwhile cellular competitor, George Crowley, the three McCaw brothers are "ultimate members of the lucky sperm club."

WAYNE PERRY, ONE OF THE KEY BEHIND-THE-SCENES ARCHITECTS of McCaw Cellular's astonishing ascent, went back to work with Craig soon after the company was sold. Following a brief stint at AT&T Wireless, Perry helped build Nextel, Nextlink and Nextband, working all the while from a position at Craig's investment management firm, Eagle River Investments LLC. In 1999, he at last ended his long professional association with Craig; he left Seattle for the sunnier enclave of Bend, Oregon, where he founded his own rural wireless company, NewCom Wireless, and a second firm, Edge Wireless, that sells AT&T-branded service in rural markets. Perry flies his own high-speed, propeller-driven plane and has established himself as a generous philanthropist.

Another of McCaw's dream team also settled in Oregon: Ed Hopper, the mastermind behind so many of McCaw's daring high-wire financial deals, retired in the late 1980s; he owns and operates Resort at the Mountain, a complex of Scottish-style buildings located in the shadows of Mt. Hood. And Scott Anderson and Scot Jarvis, the duo responsible for McCaw's buying blitz through Middle America, continue to work together at Cedar Grove Investments, an early-stage venture-capital firm based in Kirkland, Washington. Their office, located on the waterfront a short walk from the old McCaw headquarters, is in the same building as that of Craig McCaw's current office. Though both work hard at their new firm, the days of frantic, round-the-clock dealmaking and manic travel are over. Blessed with young children, impressive net worths and active life styles, both Anderson and Jarvis are enjoying the fruits of the fantastic cellular boom.

In varying degrees, all the members of the McCaw team moved on to new accomplishments. But not surprisingly, it's former wonder boy John

Stanton who has achieved the most remarkable success—success that rivals even that of his old boss, Craig McCaw.

———

AFTER JOHN STANTON AND CRAIG MCCAW had their epic explosion at a staff meeting in 1987, Stanton took a six-month sabbatical. He spent most of that time in Breckenridge, Colorado, skiing and spending time with his wife, former McCaw executive Theresa Gillespie. In the coming few years, he would work with McCaw on a few projects, but that shouting match effectively marked the end of his full-time work at the company.

At the time of his departure, Stanton held McCaw stock and options estimated to be worth $50 million. He'd helped build McCaw Cellular from scratch, and, in corralling the members of the Counter Alliance and Le Grand Deal, he'd helped shape the industry. But now that he was off on his own, few expected to hear much more about him.

Stanton's first moves seemed to reinforce that expectation: In the early 1990s, he began buying up a handful of America's most remote and seemingly worthless rural cellular licenses through his two small startups, Stanton Communications and Pacific Northwest Cellular. One of the first markets he bought, Colorado-7, was nothing more than a mass of granite wilderness in the Rocky Mountains some 200 miles north of Santa Fe. Absolutely nothing was attractive about the market except the price: $4 per POP.

As his little startups grew, Stanton bought up assets from other companies: In April 1992, he bought half the assets of floundering CIS, the company Richard Treibick was running into the ground. Later that year he bought licenses in slightly bigger markets, places like Grand Forks, North Dakota, for anywhere from $4 to $15 per POP. At the time, the rest of the industry was focused on AT&T's $270+ per POP purchase of McCaw—a deal that put Stanton's former boss on the front pages of every business section in America.

By 1994, Stanton was looking abroad for deals. After merging his cellular portfolio into the remnants of General Cellular Corporation (Quentin Breen and Terry Easton's failed roll-up of applicants from their application mill), he began buying licenses in faraway, low-budget markets such as Ghana and the former Soviet republics of Latvia and Georgia.

To those who had watched Stanton in action during his '80s glory years, these odd little ventures seemed a quirky, sad denouement to a great cellular career. Even his former boss dismissed him; Craig McCaw "pooh-poohed him for years," says Scot Jarvis. "Dennis [Weibling, the president of Craig's Eagle River Corp.] and Wayne [Perry] and everybody said, 'God, what is he doing? He is crazy. He is crazy.'"

But Stanton kept adding licenses, and by 1996, he had a big enough portfolio to put together a modest IPO. The market valued his grab bag of cellular operations, now named Western Wireless, at $200 million.

That same year, Stanton showed up at the FCC's auctions for PCS licenses. He bid aggressively in the smaller D- and E-block auctions, purchasing licenses covering 61 million POPs. With an ever-growing portfolio, soaring user numbers, and the industry's dawning realization that even systems in the most remote, scrub-covered counties of America could make money, Stanton was now positioned to make his move into the big time.

With his former boss stealing the limelight as the true genius behind McCaw Cellular and his mid-'80s luster as a cellular wunderkind long faded, Stanton proceeded to demonstrate that his daring and insightful dealmaking while at McCaw had been no fluke. In October 1998, he divided Western Wireless into two public companies, spinning off the new digital PCS operation into a company called VoiceStream Wireless Corporation. This left Stanton controlling a pure PCS company that would be unencumbered by investors' doubts about his rural cellular operations—an ideal marriage partner for other PCS operators.

With the spin-off, observers now saw what Stanton had in mind: VoiceStream represented the seeds of a national PCS company, one that could be expanded to cover a new nationwide footprint. The *Wall Street Journal* noted that some of VoiceStream's new stockholders saw the company's potential as "a big player on the national cellular scene." In another story, the *Journal* noted that "those who know [Stanton] say he has the expertise and ambition to piece together a national GSM network."

Stanton, now forty-one years old, was betting his whole VoiceStream operation on GSM technology—a decision that drew derisive hoots from many of his competitors. GSM, the now-mature European digital cellular standard, had two drawbacks: limited spectrum capacity and a paucity of snazzy new data capabilities. But Stanton saw two clear advantages in choosing GSM. First, 220 million mobile-phone customers in 133 countries worldwide used GSM technology: Among American users who traveled, only VoiceStream GSM customers would be able to use their phones abroad. Second, because they were already spewing off the assembly lines by the millions annually, GSM handsets were cheaper than those that used new and yet unproven CDMA and TDMA technology. Still, Stanton's choice was viewed as unorthodox, and it was vigorously criticized by observers. "They thought he was just nuts to be buying this stuff and then to pick GSM," remembers Jarvis. "Why would anyone pick GSM?"

One month after the spin-off, Stanton saw himself on the front pages of the business press for the first time since he'd left McCaw. He announced VoiceStream's acquisition of OmniPoint Communications in a $2.04 billion merger. The deal was a blockbuster, akin to McCaw's acquisition of LIN: It brought Stanton licenses in seventeen of the nation's top twenty-five markets—cities like New York, Philadelphia, Miami, Boston and Detroit.

With the OmniPoint purchase, Stanton now had GSM-based operations on both the East and West Coasts. "We've created an opportunity of national scale almost overnight," Stanton boasted about the deal; and that wasn't the only good news. The acquisition also attracted fresh capital; Hong Kong–based telecom provider Hutchison-Whampoa Ltd. invested $957 million, and an Alaskan Indian tribe, Cook Inlet Region, Ltd., invested an added $400 million to its existing multimillion dollar stake in VoiceStream.

Just three months later, in September 1999, Stanton announced a second major coup: the merger of VoiceStream with TDS subsidiary Aerial Communications. The deal, valued at $3.3 billion, brought in GSM licenses covering the central United States, including Minneapolis, Houston, Tampa, Pittsburgh and Orlando. Now VoiceStream had coverage in twenty-two of the nation's twenty-five largest markets and 500,000 current customers. It also added a powerful new financial partner: Finland's Sonera Ltd., the national telecom firm, which agreed to invest $500 million in VoiceStream as part of the merger.

Analysts hailed the move as brilliant. "VoiceStream will have an awesome-looking spectrum position, and enough critical mass to generate as much as one could hope for," a Lehman Brothers analyst told the *Wall Street Journal*. Another observed that "A VoiceStream-Aerial combination also illustrates the growing importance of providing nationwide and even global cellular coverage."

Within thirty days, Stanton was on the move again, announcing that merger partner OmniPoint would spend another $120 million to acquire licenses in L.A., additional coverage in Washington, D.C., and a few western markets, giving VoiceStream coverage in twenty-three of the top twenty-five markets. By now, VoiceStream had some 260 million POPs and a customer base of more than 3 million. Analyst Thomas Lee of Salomon Smith Barney remarked to the *Wall Street Journal* that "investors are realizing that this is one of the best managed companies out there."

But the hype generated by the Aerial merger brought with it a brand-new problem: Suddenly, the hunter risked becoming the hunted. Stanton's success in assembling spectrum assets where others had seen only hopeless confusion now made VoiceStream a prime takeover target. Ignoring the takeover talk, Stanton forged ahead, consolidating his three big acquisitions and, in February 2000, lining up a staggering new $3.25 billion line of credit to fund his buildout efforts.

The stock market loved it. In the nine months between the May 1999 spin-off and February 2000, VoiceStream stock shot from $22 to an astonishing $159.38—a seven-fold increase. Just like that, John Stanton found himself CEO and chairman of the newest wireless megasystem: VoiceStream was now one of the half-dozen big wireless companies, and it covered a nationwide footprint.

Stanton wrote the final scene of this phenomenal drama in the summer of 2000, when he engineered a bidding war for VoiceStream between Japanese wireless provider NTT DoCoMo and Germany's Deutsche Telekom. On July 21, Deutsche Telekom won the bidding, claiming VoiceStream with an offer valued at $51.5 billion—some $265 per POP, or nearly $200 per share. The deal called for Stanton to stay on at the company.

As 2000 drew to a close, the VoiceStream acquisition was not a done deal. Protectionists in Congress challenged the merger, and Democratic Senator Ernest F. Hollings of South Carolina introduced legislation to block it. Despite Hollings's dyspeptic carping that the merger was "unthinkable," it looked likely the deal would go through.

The Deutsche Telekom purchase marked the highest price ever garnered by a purely wireless company, and it brought a hugely profitable payday to the investors who had dared to bet on Stanton. The deal was a "10-bagger," in the words of T. Rowe Price Associates' Robert Gensler. When the various federal transfer applications were filed in fall 2000, Hutchison-Whampoa stood to turn its $1.2 billion investment into $11 billion. Goldman Sachs stood to garner over $2 billion from an $80 million investment. Even Jamie Lee Curtis, the actress hired by VoiceStream to star in the company's commercials, made a small fortune on the stock options she accepted as part of her fee.

━━━━━━━━━

NEARLY TWO DECADES AGO, A TALL YOUNG MAN walked up to the door of an office in Bellevue, Washington. His ambition that day was simply to be hired as a consultant. He was prepared to fail, and he would have walked away had Ed Hopper not decided suddenly to take him on.

John Stanton's visit to McCaw that misty spring day in 1982 arguably changed the wireless world forever. Three of America's six major wireless companies at century's end—AT&T-McCaw, Nextel and VoiceStream—trace their mammoth success directly to the tiny team of dreamers in that office.

Today, Stanton—just forty-five years old—still reports to work in Issaquah, Washington, though he sits on a small fortune left over from his work at McCaw, a larger fortune from his original 10-percent stake in Western Wireless, and a Forbes 400–size fortune of $1.1 billion (as of fall 2000) from VoiceStream.

But there's something more important to Stanton than the money. By steering his little startup from the fringes of wireless to the industry's pinnacle, he has achieved the one thing consistently denied him at McCaw: public recognition of his skills. Even before the VoiceStream sale, Stanton had plenty of money; now he has the distinction of being called by the *Wall Street Journal* "the consummate deal maker." At last secure in his legacy, Stanton lives in Washington state with his wife, Theresa (who is an executive vice president at Western Wireless), their two children, an impressive cache of vintage wine and a growing collection of 1980s cell phones.

EPILOGUE

The growth of cellular in the United States surprised nearly everyone. In July 2000, the number of U.S. cellular subscribers topped 100 million—more than 100 times the number AT&T had projected back in 1980, and 2.5 times more than Donaldson, Lufkin, Jenrette predicted in 1990. By the end of 2000, 109 million Americans, nearly 40 percent, had cell phones, and with penetration rates climbing about 1 percent per month, fully 70 percent of the U.S. population is expected to have cell phones by 2007.

And U.S. usage is only the tip of the iceberg, representing less than 10 percent of the estimated 1 billion users worldwide by the end of 2000. The true "digital Valhalla" (as the *New York Times* called it) is Scandinavia, where penetration rates are up to twice that of the United States: In Norway, 81 percent; in Finland, 73 percent; and in Sweden, 76 percent, for example. In Europe as a whole, penetration rates are growing at 1.5 percent per month, and Bear Stearns projects up to 90 percent penetration in Germany, Italy, the Netherlands, Sweden and the United Kingdom by 2002.

The popularity of cell phones, already soaring, is expected to increase in the coming years, due mainly to two factors. First, many customers—particularly young people—have begun using their wireless phones as a replacement for their landline phones. (As one young Swedish entrepreneur commented to the *New York Times*, "Why would you be glued to the wall to talk to someone? What a terrible stinking idea.") In the United States, only 0.3 percent of users fell into this replacement group in 1999, but that number grew to 3 percent in 2000. With wireless accounting for only 5 percent

313

of all U.S. telephone traffic in 2000, the potential for future growth is huge. By fall 2000, more than 1 million U.K. residents had ditched their telephone service for cellular, while in Japan and Korea, the number of wireless subscribers has already surpassed the number using traditional wired phones.

The second factor is the increase in wireless phones' capabilities. Next-generation networks are capable of delivering data—now in the form of short e-mail-type messages, and someday in video form. In Europe and Japan, where this data technology was launched ahead of the United States, text messaging has already become a hugely popular communications medium. Nokia estimates that in Finland (where a recent report showed that virtually everyone between the ages of fifteen and thirty-nine owns a cell phone), each teenage user sends an average of more than 100 messages per month. And in Japan, NTT DoCoMo's "i-mode" ("i" for information) service, a short-message wireless e-mail service, has become a pop craze. Since i-mode's 1999 introduction, 1 million Japanese have been signing up *per month*. As Wit SoundView financial analyst Tim O'Neil observes, "Culturally, one of the most embarrassing moments for a Japanese teenager is when all of their friends get a wireless alert, but they don't."

Data transfer over handheld portables is no longer a futuristic dream: By late 2000, more than 40 million people worldwide had wireless Internet access, and analysts project that by 2003, one-third of the world's cell phones will be data-connected. They also project that by 2004, more Americans will access the Internet through wireless phones than through personal computers. In Asia, that crossover is expected as early as 2001. The mobile Internet is, in the words of Morgan Stanley Dean Witter wireless analyst Gregory Lundberg, "the most radical development since Marconi invented wireless telegraphic radio in 1894."

Though wireless penetration has been remarkable in the industrialized world, there's an even larger untapped market in lesser-developed nations. In such countries as China, India and the African nations, comparatively few people have phones of any kind—wired or wireless. Given the plummeting cost in wireless technology and the daunting cost of wiring underdeveloped areas, it's very likely that those populations now without wired service will never own a tethered telephone—they'll leap straight to wireless instead.

―――――――――

ALL THE TRENDS SEEM TO POINT TO continued explosive growth in wireless. BUT there are a few looming problems that threaten the industry as the new millennium dawns.

First, there are lingering issues of health and safety. Despite increasing statistical evidence to the contrary, shrill warnings about cell phones and brain cancer could threaten industry growth, especially if U.S. trial lawyers decide to pursue the issue.

Another problem, at least in the United States, is the need for more tower sites. In Europe, telecommunication policy is government-controlled; by dictating the use of a single technological standard—GSM—and by imposing national standards for tower-siting, the European nations have saved themselves from the confusion of multiple technologies and paralyzing construction delays. In the United States, tens of thousands of separate local zoning ordinances and the existence of a half-dozen different carriers have resulted in a costly, cumbersome tower-siting process. The nearly 100,000 towers spread across the United States today are only a fraction of what's needed: Some estimates suggest we'll need some 200,000 more tower sites just in the first five years of the new century. More sobering still are estimates that the new 3G networks will require four to sixteen times as many towers to get the same coverage as PCS. This will require untold hours of brokering compromises among carriers, environmental activists, disgruntled customers and local governments in an effort to simultaneously protect signal quality and neighborhood aesthetics.

The plethora of technological standards creates other problems as well. The *Wall Street Journal* described the U.S. situation as "a Tower of Babel–like syndrome. . . a hodgepodge of competing standards that [makes] it difficult to achieve a seamless world-wide wireless experience." The United States lags behind Europe and parts of Asia in employing new common technologies. But there does appear to be some hope for resolving the situation.

Market demand for international interoperability is driving the European and Asian carriers toward a common new third-generation (3G) digital technology standard. Meanwhile, in advance of 3G, Japan's NTT DoCoMo has been buying global converts to its intermediate "i-mode" data standard. "I-mode" looks likely to take root in the United States, thanks to NTT DoCoMo's $10 billion purchase of a 20 percent stake in AT&T Wireless, announced in December 2000. NTT DoCoMo has also purchased similar stakes in European, United Kingdom and Taiwanese carriers.

Still, three different standards are reportedly competing for the 3G business of U.S. carriers, and the service isn't expected to be available here before 2004 at the earliest. Following the example set by John Stanton and VoiceStream, at least one of the major U.S. license winners will likely adopt the new European 3G standard, which would be another step toward increasing global uniformity. It may be a decade or more before everyone's telephone can easily jump from network to network, but slowly, step-by-step, some standardization is coming.

A larger, more immediate problem facing the industry is the cost of new radio spectrum. Creating new wireless data networks requires more spectrum, and, in many nations, carriers will be purchasing the new licenses for these wireless data networks at auctions in 2001. In 2000, 3G-spectrum auctions cost carriers $75 billion in Germany and Great Britain alone. According to analysts' estimates, European carriers will spend from $136 to $150 billion on new spectrum—a tremendous number that could have been even higher if it weren't for a few national quirks. In socialist-leaning economies such as Finland and France, for example, the governments plan to give away some of the spectrum through "beauty contests" that are likely to favor incumbent national carriers. And in Asia, the governments of South Korea and Japan have given away the new licenses to national firms free of charge.

In the United States, carriers are scrambling to line up capital to bid for spectrum in new auctions, which are, after three delays, scheduled to start in Fall 2001. The amount of money to be spent promises to be huge. Nextel, for example, is estimated to have only about half the spectrum that it needs (thanks to its taxi-dispatch spectrum history); it alone could spend as much as $12 billion or more on spectrum acquisitions. And spectrum purchases are just the start—according to some estimates, worldwide carriers will spend another quarter of a trillion dollars building their next generation of networks.

Complicating this spending spree is the enormous risk factor involved. Simply put, there is little solid verification that these new 3G services will attract enough customers or produce enough revenue to justify their cost. Though text-messaging services in Finland and Japan allow nothing more than short e-mails, they are wildly popular partly because they are interactive in nature; accessing larger blocks of data, on the other hand, is a largely passive activity for the subscriber, and it is unclear whether there will be much demand for it. Increasing the risk factor, ironically, are rising European penetration rates: As mobile usage saturates the population base, carriers are more likely to sacrifice profits in the competition for scarcer customers, further threatening their balance sheets. So high are the risks, and so substantial the costs, that *The Economist* dubbed the 3G-spectrum buying spree "the biggest gamble in business history. . . a leap in the dark of titanic proportions."

Given the risks, where will the money come from? Building 3G networks could, according to equipment manufacturer Nortel, require spending some

$250 billion in just the next three years. By late 2001, operators such as British Telecom, France Telecom, Deutsche Telekom and Verizon had all suffered credit-rating downgrades and share price declines as the markets braced for these big new credit risks. The financial markets had so weakened by the end of 2000 that a number of countries—Italy, Austria, Switzerland, Brazil and France among them—had delayed their spectrum auctions in deference to cash-strapped would-be bidders. The big consolidated carriers— such as Deutsche Telekom, Vodafone-Verizon and Cingular—will likely rely upon the revenue base of their old-fashioned wired voice networks, and, perhaps, cost-sharing with competitors to leverage the new wireless infrastructure. But any long-running downturn in the global capital markets could seriously slow wireless growth.

THERE IS ONE FINAL, DAUNTING PROBLEM threatening future wireless growth, particularly in the United States. It is the phenomenon former FCC Chairman William Kennard called the "spectrum desert."

Spectrum is valuable partly because there is a finite amount of it. The most useful spectrum in the United States is allocated to one of three categories of users: the military, public safety (fire, police and emergency services) and the broadcast industry (television, radio and the like). The amount of spectrum licensed for mobile communications in America is comparatively small: As of late 2000, the United States had made just 189 MHz of radio spectrum available for commercial mobile applications, compared with 300 MHz in Japan, 364 MHZ in the United Kingdom and 395 MHz in France.

That 189 MHz is already proving inadequate, and the problem is destined to get much worse: By some estimates, the burgeoning demand for wireless communications will ultimately require three times as much radio spectrum as is currently licensed for mobile communications. In October 2000, even President Clinton took notice, declaring, "if the United States does not move quickly to allocate [3G data] spectrum, there is danger that the U.S. could lose market share in the industries of the 21st century." But virtually all available spectrum is currently allocated; getting a big, useful block for mobile communications means taking it away from someone else.

Who can give up some? The spectrum allocations of two of the three largest users—the military and public safety—are virtually untouchable thanks to their public importance. That leaves the broadcast industry.

Broadcasting, and particularly television broadcasting, is the place from which the government must take spectrum to meet the exploding demand for mobile communications. Put simply, television broadcasting is a spectrum hog. The industry utilizes 1940s-era "high and loud" technology, whereby network affiliate stations and local UHF channels spew tidal waves of electromagnetic radiation across the urban landscape, while only a tiny fraction of it is being used at any given moment. Meanwhile, more than 93 percent of U.S. households have access to scores of channels—including the same ones that are wasting all that radio spectrum—via the far more efficient cable-television system. Taking into account both cable and satellite television broadcasters, the number of American homes that don't need broadcast signals to get television programs is approaching 100 percent.

The case for reallocating spectrum from broadcast television seems clear. But in 1997, the U.S. Congress did the opposite: it passed legislation granting even more spectrum—1,600 new licenses—to the broadcast industry, which promised to use them for High Definition Television (HDTV). The networks pledged to implement the service by 2006, yet nearly four years after this unconscionable grab for spectrum, the broadcasters have almost no incentive to broadcast in high definition because neither consumers nor advertisers have any incentive to pay for it. As technology writer Chris O'Malley wrote in *Popular Science*, "the FCC hasn't admitted it yet, but it hardly takes a soothsayer to know that the 2006 date is dead."

If HDTV is a failure, and if cable, satellites and fiber are video's future, why did Congress take such a huge step backward, reserving scarce spectrum interstate highways for broadcasters' horses and buggies? The answer is clout. In the U.S. political system, where reelection is dependent largely on television exposure, no one commands more fear and attention from members of Congress than their local TV stations.

With the technological innovations of each passing year, the broadcasters' stranglehold on large swaths of spectrum grows increasingly anachronistic. U.S. telecommunications firms are now racing to build a host of massive fiber-optic networks that will enable "video on demand," or the capability of transporting any video file, anywhere at anytime. The bandwidth needed to carry voice, data and video signals to every corner of America is growing so rapidly that its cost is plummeting to what some predict will be near zero. This optical interlacing of America is another telecommunications phenomenon, comparable to the cellular phenomenon of the 1990s; if scientific logic ultimately prevails over politics, it should lead to the end of the broadcasters' control of wastefully underutilized spectrum.

IN 1965, ENGINEER GORDON MOORE, who would go on to cofound Intel, made an observation. Every year since the integrated circuit was invented, he said, the number of transistors per square inch had doubled—effectively doubling computing power for essentially the same price. And computing power would, he predicted, continue to increase at that rate.

Thirty-five years later, the statement now known as Moore's Law stands correct, though the incremental time frames are more like eighteen months than one year. The increases in computing power have been phenomenal: In 1981, at the dawn of the cellular era, IBM's revolutionary "Personal Computer" contained 29,000 transistors; in June 2000, Intel unveiled a new processor with 150 million transistors on a single chip. Moore later observed that if cars had improved at the same rate as computers, we'd now be driving automobiles that got 150,000 miles to the gallon.

These increases in computing power have accounted for many of the advances in mobile communications—brick-sized analog phones shrinking to palm-sized 3G mobile Internet terminals, for example. And in the long term, they could account for many more. Transmeta Corporation's "Crusoe" chip, for example, promises to deliver the next generation of mobile computing power using only a fraction of the battery life demanded by current cell phones. Increased computer power is expected to lead to cheaper, lighter, longer-talking cell phones with Internet access and video images. And Moore's Law could understate the performance of revolutionary new forms of computing—technologies undreamt of in Moore's world of silicon. Futurists now envision whole new forms of even faster, unimaginably compact clumps of organic materials doing molecular-scale computing, or even quantum computers operating at subatomic scale where silicon circuits serve today. Such dramatic changes in computing power and scale would lead to drastic changes in communication.

The longer-term solution to the "spectrum desert" lies not in incremental political bartering over slices of broadcast spectrum, but in developing new computer-processing of radio signals that will allow us to use radio spectrum more efficiently. Extremely powerful computers in each handheld phone, for example, could easily pluck out of the airwaves coded bits of radio energy intended for each one-in-a-million device—making today's methods of subdividing the airwaves seem about as logical as trying to subdivide the water in the ocean. New ultra-wide band software-defined radios will be able to spread their signals like so much background noise across huge swaths of radio spectrum, permitting simultaneous use of the airwaves by everyone.

Improvements in computing power may also be harnessed to further subdivide radio signals based on their electrical and magnetic polarization. In
January 2001, scientists at Bell Labs and Harvard announced research that
promised as much as a sixfold increase in spectrum capacity by applying
new polarization technology that would, in turn, require more phone-based
computing power.

But people are impatient. They don't want to wait for these long-term,
futuristic solutions. They want to talk and exchange information now, and
they need more spectrum to do it with. As this book has shown, the methods employed by the U.S. government to allocate radio spectrum in the last
twenty years have been fraught with misguided public policy, political
cronyism and occasional stupidity. How do we fix the problems?

One short-term fix is to develop rules allowing spectrum license holders
to rent underutilized spectrum to others who have greater demand for it—
a system the FCC is now implementing on a trial basis in hopes of creating
what Chairman Kennard called a "fluid market in spectrum." Properly implemented, this would require the lifting of outmoded regulations limiting
the purposes for which certain spectrum bands can be used. This would
allow spectrum to be bought and sold as a commodity—like soybeans or
pork bellies—and used in any noninterfering way the buyer chooses. But
though it would be a sensible incremental step, the creation of such a secondary spectrum market will hardly be adequate to fill the need for huge
new blocks of spectrum for new generations of digital services. Here greater
near-term reforms are needed.

Government spectrum auctions have brought money into the public
treasury, but it has been at the ultimate cost of the cell phone users. Whatever the carriers spend at auction is repaid by their users in their monthly
bills. In the United Kingdom, one analyst has estimated that 25 percent of
the total cost of the next 3G networks will go toward the $32 billion the car-
riers spent at the spectrum auctions. You can bet that every penny of it—including interest on the debt that financed it—will appear on the monthly
phone bills of the British using 3G phones.

Are these kinds of auctions—essentially nothing more than a method of
taxing users—the most efficient public policy? The answer is no. If we are
to reap the full promise of wireless, we need to implement three broad
changes in public policy.

First, the nature of auctions must be changed. Because they require carriers to pay huge sums up front—years in advance of any return on their
investment—current auctions strain the capital markets unnecessarily. This

results in auction prices discounted for capital risk, lower revenues for the public treasury and unnecessarily high service costs for the users. It's time for the FCC and the rest of the world's spectrum policy makers to make a simple, fundamental change: to rent spectrum instead of selling it outright.

Instead of having bidders offer all cash up front for a license, bids should be in fractions of the bidder's future annual gross revenues. Each spectrum-license winner would obligate itself to pay the government a smaller lump sum at the time of license grant (a kind of down payment), followed by the high bidder's designated fraction of all the revenues derived from that spectrum as long as the license is held.

In this way, scarce capital could be deployed to build networks quickly, and to bring innovative and presumably profitable new services to the public. It would also encourage smaller, more entrepreneurial bidders. Ultimately, such a system should, as the wireless systems grow and evolve, bring far more revenue into the treasury than an up-front payment system. The financial models, the security laws and even the legal forms for this type of "percentage of the gross" leasing are commonplace—they can be found in any shopping mall's real estate lease.

Second, the licensees should be free to use their spectrum for whatever changing services the market demands. Not only would such a policy spur innovation, but the public treasury would benefit as licensees squeeze new sources of revenue out of licenses with new technology developments.

Third, the U.S. Congress and the FCC should bring an end to the wasteful misuse of the broadcast spectrum, including the HDTV spectrum. Although the ownership of these public airways has already been given away, there is no legal impediment to the government's using its constitutional power of eminent domain to condemn the spectrum in order to get it back in the hands of the public. Following is a plan for doing that.

The FCC should reconsider its "must-carry" rules to assure that the content presently broadcast over the most badly needed of the underutilized TV channels, including HDTV signals, is carried by the cable and satellite systems. This would minimize the "loss" to current license-holders when their licenses are "taken" back from them.

Next, independent financial appraisers should evaluate the residual value of this spectrum, taking into consideration current license limitations that restrict its use to video broadcasting. These experts could then place a value on the use of the same spectrum assuming the FCC were to allow its use for mobile wireless. Comparing the two appraisals would yield a ratio: The value of a given license if used for broadcasting might be, say, 30 percent of what it would be worth if used for mobile data services.

The next step would be for the FCC to put the spectrum up for sale in a "three-sided" (two sellers and one buyer) auction, in which bidders would be required to bid an aggregate lump sum amount for each license. Using the ratio determined by the independent appraisers, the winning bidder would then be responsible for paying the incumbent broadcasters their fraction of the winning amount—due in cash at the close of the auction. The balance due to the federal treasury could then be paid part down, with the remainder incorporated into a lease as outlined above. In this way, needed spectrum will be freed up quickly, with the original owners—the broadcasters—being fairly compensated.

These changes in auction policy could help the United States regain the technology lead it held when the scientists at Bell Labs first invented cellular. But to hold that lead long-term, the government must fashion even more enlightened public policy, and it must show greater resistance to the lobbying of entrenched spectrum owners.

As the power of computing and the sophistication of software-defined radio accelerates over the next decade, Congress and the FCC must make one more politically difficult decision: They should allow ultra-wide-band spread-spectrum radios that will make use of minuscule, indiscernible bits of everyone's radio spectrum. Though the government and spectrum owners have been historically averse to allowing the sharing of spectrum usage, their resistance grows increasingly anachronistic as the power of computing accelerates. Only through ultra-wide-band spread spectrum technology can we enable every person to communicate using the public radio spectrum—at last allowing everyone to share the natural resource of spectrum in the same way we share other natural resources, such as air and water.

———

TECHNOLOGICAL DEVELOPMENTS LIKE THESE ARE COMING, and for those of us in the business, the great fun will be in picking the commercial winners. If there is one thing we can learn from the spectrum rush, it is who *won't* win these next races. AT&T Wireless, Vodafone-Verizon, Deutsche Telekom and the like are great companies, but they bear more than a passing resemblance to the Western Unions, IBMs and ITTs of 1982. It's unlikely these big companies will lead the charge.

Somewhere out there is another John Stanton, another underfunded, risk-taking entrepreneur who will make billions from 4G data networks or ultra-wide-band spread-spectrum technology or other mobile wonders we can't yet imagine—perhaps even from the kind of telepathic wireless brain implants Craig McCaw predicted. As much as has happened in the last two decades, the wireless race and the fun of betting on it have just begun.

AFTERWORD TO
THE PAPERBACK EDITION

When I finished writing *Wireless Nation* in December of 2000, the wireless phone business was at its financial pinnacle. Along with the rest of the telecommunications industry, cellular companies had grown virtually unchecked for 19 straight years—a period when telecom created more value, more rapidly, than any other industry in history.

Yet as the seventeenth-century French moralist La Bruyere once observed, all success can be attributed to either "one's own industry or the weakness of others." In the case of cellular valuations, it now appears that 2000's astronomical values were due in large measure to the gullibility of the investing public. January 2001 marked the start of a dramatic reversal of fortune in the telecom industry—one that would destroy wireless wealth far more rapidly than it had been created. What happened to the wireless industry over the past 18 months? Could we have seen it coming? And what lies ahead now?

The seeds of the downturn in wireless values were planted in January of 1995 when the FCC began auctioning off PCS spectrum. Over the next three years, telecom firms gambled billions to buy up spectrum, then began operating systems in markets already served by three carriers—wireline, nonwireline and Nextel. With so many carriers in each market, price wars erupted, and between 1998 and early 2002, wireless service rates have dropped an average of 25% a year—down to a current average of 14 cents a minute. Despite the fact that minutes of use per customer have continued to grow 38% annually, in 2001 the average monthly cellular bill dropped again, another 8%.

Two other factors have compounded the problem for the big carriers. First was the new class of customers who were now joining the wireless revolution: the fourth wave, or "late majority." These were teenagers, blue-collar factory workers, and the less credit-worthy purchasers of pre-paid service plans, whose usage patterns were lower and accounts less profitable than those of the early adopters. Second was the emergence of a new class of carriers, such as Leap Wireless and MetroPCS, which offered budget PCS service—with unlimited minutes but a very limited calling area—for as little as $32 per month. All told, the industry's average phone bill has fallen 72% since 1994.

Between 1996 and 2001, the carriers eagerly snapped up $1.3 trillion in debt and equity in order to build out their systems—cash that was provided by Wall Street's junk bond pushers and investors eager for a get-rich-quick piece of the wireless action. But sixteen months later, the telecom industry is a smoking crater in the financial landscape: By Wall Street Journal estimates, the telecom industry as a whole has lost some $2 trillion in market value between 2000 and 2002. The three largest independent wireless phone companies, AT&T Wireless, Sprint PCS, and Nextel saw their collective market value fall 80 percent: from over $182 billion in July 2000 to $38 billion in May 2002.

Other problems have further fueled public investors' disillusionment with wireless stocks. Ever since the first systems went on line in 1984, the gross number of new U.S. cellular users has increased progressively each year through 2000, when 23.4 million new users signed up. But those increases couldn't continue forever: As the industry topped 108 million users—40% of the U.S. population—it became increasingly difficult to find more than 23 million unserved customers the next year. Predictably, growth is slowing: in 2001 some 21 million new customers signed up for service (the first ever decrease in new subscriber totals), bringing the national total to some 130 million. Also, for the first time, analysts have begun projecting further declines in rates of growth—down to 17 million new customers projected for 2005.

As the new PCS systems came on line, the cutthroat competition created an additional problem that exacerbated the pain of falling revenues: "churn," or the turnover of customers from one carrier to another. *Forbes* predicts that in 2002 alone, 20 million customers will ditch their cell phone carrier for a new one. Churn is now costing carriers 30% of their customers each year—up from 25% five years earlier. This trend is doubly troubling to investors who see not only lost revenue, but increased marketing costs, to follow: It costs an average of $360 to gain each new customer—in many cases equaling the total annual revenue that new customer can produce. According to *Forbes,* the industry could spend $8.5 billion in 2002 just replacing lost customers.

Customer dissatisfaction with cell phone performance has further dulled the industry's luster. "Fast busy signals and dead zones where you can't get a signal are still facts of the wireless life," observes the *Wall Street Journal,* while *Forbes* notes that the wireless industry has become "infamous for shoddy service, poor coverage, and outright hostility towards its customers." Nationwide, any ten-minute cell phone call currently stands a 10% chance of being dropped, and a recent *Consumer Reports* survey showed that only half of the industry's customers were satisfied with their service.

"The wireless industry has a collection of hopping mad customers," wrote *Forbes* in September 2001. "They snatch prospects with lowball pricing plans, and then chisel them to death with roaming fees, surprise surcharges and termination fees. No wonder the industry is losing money." Which leads to the biggest investor red flag of all: after 17 years of operations, most cellular carriers are still losing money. Morgan Stanley projects that, despite service revenue of nearly $80 billion, the U.S. wireless industry will burn through $10 billion in fresh cash in 2002.

Little wonder then, that amidst the turmoil in the general telecom financial markets, cellular stocks were down an additional 45% during the first four months of 2002—evaporating another $45 billion in shareholder value. And the carriers are not the only losers: As the bad news rippled through the world economy, stocks such as that of cell phone equipment suppliers Ericsson and Lucent (both down 90% from their highs) were also devastated. "People are petrified, they've lost so much money so quickly," commented one CSFB senior trader to the *Wall Street Journal.*

In retrospect, we should have seen it coming—after all, average monthly bills had been dropping and customer demographics eroding throughout the late 1990s. So, why the surprise? The answer, in Alan Greenspan's words, was the "irrational exuberance" of the markets—an exuberance inflamed by a raft of Wall Street analysts.

Wall Street firms, many flush with fat advisory fees from the same companies they were "analyzing," kept touting wireless stocks as "buys" while their price-to-earnings ratios, their price-to-sales ratios and their debt-to-equity ratios ballooned to stratospheric numbers. As late as January 2001, Merrill Lynch and Lehman Brothers were trumpeting $23 Sprint PCS shares—with Lehman Brothers even reiterating its "buy" rating with a "target price" of $55 per share before the stock subsequently slipped to $7.22. Similarly, Morgan Stanley Dean Witter and UBS Warburg touted AT&T Wireless shares, and in January 2001 UBS and Deutsche Bank Alex Brown both rated Nextel a "buy" with price targets of $82 to $83—while the stock was beginning its thirteen-month precipitous slide from $37 to just $3.35. Everyone wanted to believe—and in the end, everyone fooled each other.

Public investors weren't the only losers in the bloodbath; some big names—the heroes of the spectrum rush—have suffered as well.

―――――

John Kluge ended the year 2000 ranked by *Forbes* as the fifteenth richest man in America. With a fortune estimated at $13 billion, he looked invincible. But despite his widely diversified investments—in everything from coin laundries to Russian broadcasting—Kluge traced much of his wealth to telecommunications, and few telecom ventures suffered worse than Kluge's did in the 2001 meltdown.

In less than 18 months, the entire market value of Metromedia Fiber Networks (MFN) was virtually destroyed. Starting in late 2000, the company's wholesale fiber customers began going bankrupt in droves, leaving MFN with billions of fiber optic network assets lying dark, and billions more of construction work in progress and painfully expensive to halt. By April 2002, the company had technically defaulted on billions of dollars in debt and its chief executive, Mark Spagnolo, had resigned. Shares in MFN dropped from a high of nearly $50 in early 2000 to a low of $0.05 in 2002. Verizon was forced to write off $1.7 billion of its investment in MFN.

Kluge's other investments also suffered in the 2001 recession. His flagship Metromedia Corp. saw its stock plummet from a 2000 high of $10 per share to less than a dollar amid stockholder complaints of mismanagement. In March 2002 Kluge, now 87 years old, resigned as chairman of the board of the company he'd spent half a century building.

And yet, despite the carnage 2001 wrought on his holdings, Kluge can still claim prescience in some areas. Two of the industries hardest hit in the recession, cellular and long distance, are businesses Kluge exited well in advance of the bust; his billions in holdings (which today would have been desiccated shares of Cingular and MCI WorldCom) have long since been converted to cash or alternative investments. Though Kluge's spot near the top of the Forbes 400 is bound to have eroded by the time the list is next compiled, the setbacks haven't discouraged his generosity; in August 2001 he donated 7,378 acres of Virginia farmland and estates to the University of Virginia.

Craig McCaw, too, has seen his personal fortune—estimated by Forbes at $8 billion in 2000—shrink precipitously. And his reputation for foresight and financial legerdemain has eroded as well.

Two of Craig's biggest holdings—XO Communications Inc. and Nextel—took a thrashing between 2000 and 2002. His stake in XO, once valued at nearly $5 billion, has been pulverized, and by March 2002 the *Washington Post* and *Business Week* were both predicting a bankruptcy filing for the company. In December 2001 with the capital markets tightly shuttered, XO stopped making payments on some $7 billion in liabilities. By May, two legendary investors—Theodore J. Forstmann and Carl Icahn—were locked in a death struggle over the bones of XO while Craig McCaw sat silent on the sidelines. Though Craig had managed to unload $117 million in XO shares in 2000, he (and XO's legion of common shareholders) lost billions as the value of XO shares plummeted from a high of $66 in March of 2000 to less than $0.07 two years later.

Nextel has fared better than XO, but not much. Despite frequent rumors that Nextel may be a consolidation target for a larger carrier, the company's stock has been pummeled by closure of the capital markets, public disillusionment over the scanty profits in cellular generally, and continued concern over Nextel's paucity of radio spectrum. By the spring of 2002, Nextel's stock price had dipped below $5, down from a high of $79.81, crushing the value of Craig's holdings from $7 billion in 2000 to less than $500 million.

By the fall of 2001, estimates *Forbes*, Craig McCaw had lost 65% of his net worth. That year, the *Washington Post* reported that Craig sold his "football-field-length yacht" to Paul Allen for $200 million, sold two houses for $27 million more, sold "a few jet airplanes" and offered for sale his private Canadian island and his 10,000-acre ranch. And then—in the most telling downsizing move of them all—Craig announced that he would stop supporting the re-acclimatization project for "Keiko" the killer whale.

Yet, as Craig told Forbes, "Losing money isn't the thing I mind as much as giving up on companies. It's a game to see how much you can do." And still, there's one company Craig refuses to give up on, despite the decade-long chorus of doubters assailing it: Teledesic, his risky "Internet in the Sky" venture. In February 2002, Teledesic announced a contract with Italian satellite builder Alenia Spazio to begin construction of its first satellites. It remains to be seen whether Craig McCaw can resurrect his old magic and engineer another astonishing ascent in the world of new communications technologies.

John Stanton, Craig's alter ego from his heyday at McCaw Cellular, has come through the telecom recession bruised, but looking as nimble as ever. By 2002 his rural cellular firm, Western Wireless, is one of the few carriers left that was still occasionally blessed with a favorable word from Wall Street analysts, who continued to tout it for its stable rural customer base—as well as its potential as an acquisition target. Meanwhile, the 46-year-old Stanton's biggest gamble, VoiceStream, is serving only to enhance his reputation as a deal maker. Though Stanton and his shareholders have seen their stock price, like those of most cellular carriers, cut by more than half, his whirlwind creation of the firm by aggregating a host of PCS licenses—and his subsequent sale of it all to Deutsche Telekom (DT)—now looks divinely inspired.

Precariously assembled atop a mountain of debt, VoiceStream faced enormous additional capital needs in 1999, as it attempted to build out its network and to market in the face of fierce competition from a half-dozen competitors in every market. The company would almost certainly have suffered the fate of Kluge's MFN or McCaw's XO had it entered 2001 burdened with billions of debt as the capital markets imploded. Instead, Stanton had adroitly merged the firm with DT, a huge European public telephone company that was flush with cash flow from its older telephone businesses—cash flow that should see VoiceStream emerge from the recession as a survivor. While Stanton's DT stockholdings have lost a lot of value, the damage is a far cry from the decimation a less clever executive would have suffered.

Although Stanton's net worth had slipped considerably by late 2001 (he'd fallen from #260 to #341 on the Forbes 400 list), he showed no loss of his vaunted enthusiasm for wireless. In early 2002 Stanton went into the stock market and gambled over $12 million of his personal wealth, scooping up one million shares of his own Western Wireless stock, as the price was skidding from double digits to a May low of $3.08.

Those who fared best during the telecom recession were the punters who were smart or lucky enough to exit the wireless business early. Some of the hundreds of lottery winners sold out immediately for cash, but others had exchanged their spectrum licenses for stock in firms like TDS, U.S. Cellular, Vanguard and the Bell companies. When they foolishly held their shares, reluctant to pay capital gains taxes, they watched their investments shrink as values plummeted by 50% and more. Still others had long since liquidated their cellular holdings, diversified their newfound wealth over a broader spectrum of investments, and gone on to other happier pursuits. One fine example of the latter is my business partner—the country's original cellular license broker, Mark R. Warner. Warner liquidated big stakes in Nextel and U. S. Cellular long before the crash, and then, buoyed by a sizeable private war chest, he ran a successful campaign to be elected governor of Virginia in November 2001.

But the best example of a savvy trader who sold at the top of the market and escaped the post–2000 telecom mayhem is surely George Lindemann, the founder of cellular powerhouse Metro Mobile, Corp. In 1991, Linde-mann swapped his stake in Metro Mobile for stock in Bell Atlantic—and then, in an improbable move, he purchased control of a natural gas com-pany called Southern Union Co. Over the past decade, the company's an-nual revenues have grown from $200 million to $1.9 billion, and Linde-mann's wealth has grown apace. By the fall of 2001, Forbes pegged it at $1.4 billion—ranking the acerbic hustler ahead of most of his cellular executive brethren who'd stayed in telecom businesses. While his former rivals strug-gled to right their sinking fortunes, Lindemann could be found aboard his 185-foot, two-masted Cuban mahogany schooner "Adela," serving guests smoked reindeer for lunch. Retired from active management at Southern Union, he still serves as chairman and calls the office for 45 minutes daily while cruising the Mediterranean or relaxing in his Palm Beach mansion.

During the frenzied days of the spectrum rush in the 1980s, our little firm, Columbia Capital, managed many mergers and acquisitions between lucky lottery winners and big operating companies. Our best negotiator on many of those deals was Robert Blow, who had a knack for convincing re-luctant lottery winners to sell out while prices were high. "No tree grows to the sky," Bob would often intone, as he pushed a contract across the table. It's an observation that some of the industry's moguls would have done well to heed.

―――――――

So, where do we go from here? Perhaps surprisingly, the future of wireless is not as bleak as it seems. Despite the fact that the recession of 2001 wreaked havoc with wireless stock prices, it had little impact on the un-derlying business: The industry added nearly 20 million new subscribers during the year, recording almost 19% growth. True, the industry suffered a slowdown in construction, system expansion and the rollout of new services. And more worrisome was the fact that investors—badly spooked by horrendous equity losses—shunned all forms of telecom equity and debt, leaving the industry starved for new capital. But still the new cus-tomers kept coming.

By 2002, the wireless industry posed a financial conundrum for investors. Customer numbers were still growing at nearly 20% annually, and usage per customer was up. But per-minute pricing was down, and service was lousy—so most of the carriers were still losing money. Where does this lead us?

The wireless industry is undergoing a classic example of economic evolution, defined by renowned conservative economist Joseph A. Schumpeter as the inevitable "creative destruction" wrought by capitalism. As the raging competition claims its victims, some bankruptcies are inevitable. But because the business is fundamentally sound, the future will see the strong continue to devour the weak as the industry continues to consolidate.

This consolidation is receiving a boost from recent FCC rule changes, including a plan to eliminate by January 2003 the "spectrum cap" that limits the number of licenses a single competitor can own in one market. Once the cap is abolished, the Darwinian process will play itself out, and the country will eventually be left with just three or four major carriers—as well as a handful of smaller niche carriers providing specialized services such as local-only or mobile data-only calling.

Yet the efficiencies we can expect from consolidation will not solve the larger, long-term problem of spectrum shortages. In the midst of a crisis in which customer complaints rise as the industry struggles to force rapidly increasing traffic through a paucity of congested airwaves, nearly one-quarter of PCS spectrum—spectrum which the FCC specifically intended to help mitigate the shortage—remains tied up in court in the Nextwave litigation. Bankruptcies, lawsuits and FCC re-auctions tracing back to the 1996 auctions (in which Nextwave overbid, then defaulted) have left a badly confused set of labyrinthine claims to the spectrum that may not be resolved until 2004 or later.

Back in late 2000, the industry was looking hungrily at two separate sources of poorly utilized spectrum: TV broadcasters and the military. The events of September 11, 2001 and the growing military reliance on increasingly sophisticated communications systems have combined to take one of those sources—military spectrum—off the table. As Secretary of Defense Donald Rumsfeld has pointed out, "In Kosovo, we had one-tenth the number of people we had in the Gulf War, and we used 100 times the bandwidth [for battlefield communication]." With figures like that, it is inconceivable that Congress or the FCC will grant any military spectrum to the commercial communications industry.

It appears that the only possible near-time solution to the "spectrum drought" is the much-delayed auction of UHF TV channels 52–69. Unfortunately, this auction poses as many problems as it does solutions. UHF TV broadcasters—led by Lowell "Bud" Paxson, Chairman of Paxson Communications Corp—stand to make millions by "greenmailing" wireless carriers, blatantly capitalizing on confusion created by the federal rules governing the stations. Instead of simply reclaiming the underutilized spectrum these stations are sitting on, the government plans to allow the UHF broadcasters to request payment from the bidders—in addition to the bid price they must pay to the government to win it at the auction—for surrendering their title to the channels ahead of schedule. In this scenario—fraught with inevitable delay—the taxpayers, wireless carriers, and wireless users all suffer, while only the broadcasters and their stockholders profit. So it is that few observers see the UHF spectrum licenses providing any near term answers to the wireless industry's woes.

The investment picture is cloudy, and the spectrum-starved and under-capitalized carriers are struggling to provide quality service. So, whatever happened to the new technology solutions that were supposed to solve these problems?

While "smart antennae" and other new compression technologies promise some incremental improvements, most analysts still point to wireless data—2.5G and 3G networks—as the next big source of profits for the wireless industry. Research firm Frost and Sullivan expects the wireless data market to jump from $1.2 billion in 2001 revenue to $20 billion by 2005, a year in which RCR predicts over 72 million Americans will be using SMS ("short message service") e-mail conversant mobile phones.

Optimists point to the tripling of the number of these 2.5G enabled phones (up to some 13.4 million by 2002) and the tripling of SMS traffic on those phones (up from 20 billion messages per month in 2000 to an estimated 60 billion per month in 2002). But they cite as even more promising the experience of other nations where 2.5G networks arrived earlier. By early 2002, for example, 30 million users had signed up (all since early 1999 and most of them in Japan) for NTT DoCoMo's i-mode service. By the fall of 2001, SMS traffic in the Philippines had reached 100 million messages per day. As *Forbes* reported, text messaging is so widespread there that "one message that claimed the International Exchange Bank was going to fold triggered a bank run."

As of the spring of 2002, two major U.S. carriers had rolled out 2.5G service: AT&T and VoiceStream; with Sprint PCS's launch planned for the summer. But other carriers may be slower to follow than originally anticipated, and the much-ballyhooed 3G mobile video service may be several years behind schedule. The primary cause of the slowdown is the state of the capital markets: the fresh cash needed to build the new networks is scarce. The Yankee Group has projected that the U.S. industry will need $16 billion to buy licenses (presumably including the cost of buying off the UHF-TV broadcasters), plus another $26 to $30 billion to upgrade their networks. In Europe, where carriers spent $35 billion buying 3G spectrum licenses, the carriers are suffering from what *Wired* magazine dubbed "the winner's curse": The Europeans' balance sheets are now so burdened with auction debt that they're having an especially difficult time finding the capital they need to build the newfangled data networks.

And another problem has deferred the 3G rollout: technology. The manufacturers have been slow to perfect the complex hardware and customer handsets needed to deliver the Internet to your belt. In addition to the technical bugs delaying the new hardware, there's also the chicken-or-egg issue, in which manufacturers are unwilling to build what their customers can't yet afford.

In the meantime, an entirely unexpected phenomenon has arisen—one that simultaneously proves the potential popularity of mobile data, while threatening the future profits of 3G carriers. During 2001 and 2002, an entire technological subculture was spawned around a new wireless technology known as "WI-FI" or 802.11 (called "eight-o-two-dot-eleven," and named after the electrical engineer's standard that governs the use of this small slice of short-range, unlicensed radio spectrum). Dubbed "the next big thing" by *Fortune*, WI-FI employs inexpensive short-range radio hubs—located in places like Starbucks coffee shops, university dormitories and on the housetops of netheads—to enable laptop computer users to connect to the Internet without using wires.

Like the original, non-commercial Internet and Linux software, the WI-FI movement has grown organically, driven by a neo-communistic subculture preaching share-and-share-alike. The good news is that manufacturers can barely keep up with the growing demand for radio cards that plug into laptops, but the bad news for the 3G planners is the cost of most WI-FI service: free. With consumer price expectations set so low, who will pay fat monthly fees for similar 3G service to a smaller (albeit mobile) device—one that lacks a full keyboard for input? For the big carriers, a partial answer to the WI-FI threat lies in its technical and potential bandwidth shortcomings, but the new fad still troubles many bidders contemplating the need to pay billions for 3G spectrum.

Not all the mobile carriers have missed the WI-FI message. One of the earliest attempts to commercialize WI-FI involved a company known as Mobile-Star—the firm that originally supplied a chain of Starbucks coffee shops with WI-FI "hotspots." When Mobile-Star went belly-up in the 2001 recession, a surprising bidder showed up in October to buy its residual assets: John Stanton and VoiceStream wireless. Meanwhile, Sprint PCS has backed another commercial WI-FI startup, Boingo Wireless.

———

All told, the future of wireless is not nearly as grim as 2001's short-sellers would have us believe. The number of users continues to grow, while the number of SMS data users is growing at an even more rapid pace, and consolidation promises to mitigate some of the worst coverage, service and price erosion problems. In addition, the industry has begun to shift its focus away from subscriber-growth-at-all-costs to improving cash flow. This, in particular, is a sign of newfound maturity that promises value ahead for investors.

Ironically enough considering the history of the wireless industry so far, the best hope for the industry's long-term health may lie in the most unexpected source of all: the FCC. New FCC chairman Michael K. Powell, appointed by George W. Bush and the son of Secretary of State Colin Powell, has begun his term with some bold initiatives, promising to deregulate everywhere he can and to promote open market competition. Powell has also led the fight to lift the spectrum cap and encourage the economies of consolidation.

Perhaps most significantly, it is Powell who has begun pushing for the use of ultra-wide-band spread-spectrum technologies, which will use software-defined radios to enable the sharing of huge swaths of spectrum. Many observers believe that this spread-spectrum technology will ultimately solve both the problems of spectrum shortages and the current inefficient use of the public's airwaves. If it happens, it will mean that the FCC, once the root of so many problems related to spectrum use, will have, in the end, led the charge for solving them.

May 15, 2002

ACKNOWLEDGEMENTS

First, I would like to acknowledge the invaluable contribution Lisa Dickey made to this book. She brought to life what could have been a dry narrative; the book's readability and style are a testament to her tireless efforts. Though our work together was at times as combative as it was collaborative, ultimately we forged a union of strengths—mine in business, technical and legal details, and hers in the art of writing.

In addition to Lisa's help, I had great research assistance from Courtney Miller Santo, and earlier from April Scee. In the process of researching this industry, both have become business experts—April so much so that she's abandoned her literary aspirations for an MBA and a career on Wall Street. Perseus editor Jacqueline Murphy offered invaluable suggestions and assistance, and my agent Deborah Grosvenor provided early and enthusiastic support.

I also owe thanks to my business associates, Dave Mixer, Bob Blow, Mark Warner, Mark Kington, Phil Herget and Jim Fleming (to name only those who were most affected), who tolerated my years of partial absences while I worked on this project. Special thanks is also due Peggy Clarity and Donna Rogers, who helped me juggle a full-time business career in the process.

This book should also be credited to the more than five dozen industry executives and lawyers who contributed their valuable time to talk with me. Much of the book consists of information and anecdotes unavailable anywhere else, as most of the companies involved were privately held during the most exciting periods of the spectrum rush. I owe a debt of gratitude to everyone who spoke with me, but a few especially noteworthy contributors must be singled out.

Tom Gutierrez, FCC lawyer and client advocate *par excellence,* and his assistant, Jennifer McCord, spent countless hours helping me. Tom provided valuable insight from his days as an FCC staffer and some great anecdotes from his legal work, and Jennifer dug up copies of FCC rules, court decisions and other hard-to-find documents.

Two lawyers, venture capitalist and ex-McCaw executive Scott Anderson and former head of the FCC's Mobile Services Division Michael Sullivan, were especially helpful. In addition, Scott Anderson's venture partner and ex-McCaw executive Scot Jarvis was unusually candid; I'm proud to call both Scot and Scott good friends.

Former McCaw executive Wayne Perry is not only a great raconteur and the source of many terrific quotes and stories, he's one of the finest business executives I've ever met. Metromedia's Stuart Subotnick, a key architect of John Kluge's phenomenal business success, was also very helpful and cooperative. Washington communications attorney Jonathan Blake, who easily ranks as one of the finest lawyers in America, discussed his insights at length with me. And the list could easily go on.

My only regret is that space constraints required me to leave some great stories untold. With literally thousands of licenses changing hands and hundreds of companies involved, the stories could easily have filled three books. To the many friends, acquaintances and business associates who shared anecdotes that didn't make the cut, I apologize. But even in the cutting, everyone's insights contributed collectively to this book—just as they did earlier to the spectrum rush. I thank you all.

Finally, words cannot express my love and gratitude to my wife, Bruce, who has tolerated innumerable evenings and weekends of neglect to support the completion of this work. Hers has been a lifetime of collaboration, for which I am grateful daily.